Sociocultural Dimensions of Language Use

LANGUAGE, THOUGHT, AND CULTURE: *Advances in the*
Study of Cognition

Under the Editorship of: E. A. HAMMEL

DEPARTMENT OF ANTHROPOLOGY
UNIVERSITY OF CALIFORNIA
BERKELEY

Michael Agar, Ripping and Running: A Formal Ethnography of Urban Heroin Addicts

Brent Berlin, Dennis E. Breedlove, and Peter H. Raven, Principles of Tzeltal Plant Classification: An Introduction to the Botanical Ethnography of a Mayan-Speaking People of Highland Chiapas

Mary Sanches and Ben Blount, Sociocultural Dimensions of Language Use

Daniel G. Bobrow and Allan Collins, Representation and Understanding: Studies in Cognitive Science

Sociocultural Dimensions of Language Use

Edited by

MARY SANCHES

BEN G. BLOUNT

Department of Anthropology
University of Texas
Austin, Texas

With a Foreword by John J. Gumperz

ACADEMIC PRESS   *New York San Francisco London*

A Subsidiary of Harcourt Brace Jovanovich, Publishers

ACADEMIC PRESS, INC.
111 Fifth Avenue, New York, New York 10003

United Kingdom Edition published by
ACADEMIC PRESS, INC. (LONDON) LTD.
24/28 Oval Road, London NW1

Library of Congress Cataloging in Publication Data
Main entry under title:

Sociocultural dimensions of language use.

    (Language, thought, and culture)
    Bibliography: p.
    Includes index.
    1.   Sociolinguistics–Addresses, essays, lectures.
2.   Language and culture–Addresses, essays, lectures.
I.   Sanches, Mary.   II.   Blount, Ben G., (date)
P40.S55   301.2'1   74–17974
ISBN 0–12–617850–X

Contents

An Ethnoscience View of Schizophrenic Speech   349

Oswald Werner
Gladys Levis-Matichek
With Martha Evens and Bonnie Litowitz

Subject Index   381

List of Contributors

Numbers in parentheses indicate the pages on which the authors' contributions begin.

Michael Agar (41), Division of Research and Program Planning and Evaluation, New York State Drug Abuse Control Commission, New York, New York

Ben G. Blount (1,117), Department of Anthropology, University of Texas, Austin, Texas

Jan Brukman (235), Department of Anthropology, University of Illinois at Urbana-Champaign, Urbana, Illinois

Jenny Cook-Gumperz (137), Institute of Human Learning, University of California at Berkeley, Berkeley, California

Martha Evens (349), Department of Anthropology, Northwestern University, Evanston, Illinois

Dale K. Fitzgerald (205), Department of Anthropology, Lehman College, City University of New York, Bronx, New York

Charles O. Frake (25), Department of Anthropology, Stanford University, Stanford, California

John J. Gumperz (81), Department of Anthropology, University of California at Berkeley, Berkeley, California

Eleanor Herasimchuk (81), Department of Anthropology, University of California at Berkeley, Berkeley, California

Claudia Mitchell-Kernan (307), Department of Anthropology, University of California at Los Angeles, Los Angeles, California

Keith T. Kernan (307), Neuropsychiatric Institute, Mental Retardation Center, University of California at Los Angeles, Los Angeles, California

Bonnie Litowitz (349), Department of Linguistics, Northwestern University, Evanston, Illinois

Gladys Levis-Matichek (349), Department of Computer Science, Northwestern University, Evanston, Illinois

Michelle Zimbalist Rosaldo (177), Department of Anthropology, Stanford University, Stanford, California

Harvey Sacks (57), School of Social Sciences, University of California at Irvine, Irvine, California

Mary Sanches (163,269), Department of Anthropology, University of Texas, Austin, Texas

Henry A. Selby (11), Department of Anthropology, Temple University, Philadelphia, Pennsylvania

Brian Stross (317), Department of Anthropology, University of Texas, Austin, Texas

Oswald Werner (349), Department of Anthropology, Northwestern University, Evanston, Illinois

Foreword

JOHN J. GUMPERZ

The development of communicative technology in recent decades, improvements in means of travel, and the explosive growth in factual knowledge about the variety of human beliefs and behavior patterns are forcing a major reorientation in social science. There is increasingly less justification for the classic ethnographic approach to human populations as isolated, self-contained, and culturally uniform units. Traditional disciplinary boundaries are shifting. Anthropologists can no longer be regarded exclusively as specialists in and interpreters of the customs of geographically remote, informally organized peoples, differing in kind from peoples living in politically and economically complex societies. As we gain information about the quality of interaction in previously little-known groups, the old dichotomies between primitive and civilized cultures, developed and underdeveloped societies, are losing their meaning. Yet, when we apply some of the insights gained from the study of exotic groups to the societies we know, we find that underneath the taken-for-granted facts of everyday life there is much that is problematic about the effect of culture and social relations on our own behavior. There are many deeper issues we tend to gloss over that require new forms of investigation.

Anthropologists, accordingly, are moving more and more into the study of well-known urbanized societies and are beginning to apply the principles developed in the analysis of lesser-known cultures to deal with specialized subjects quite similar to those ordinarily covered by other social science disciplines. Topics such as social mobility in urban society, interethnic and interclass relations, urban politics, population migration, enterpreneurship, the development of modern religions, and class and ethnic differences in language or dialect have now become common topics of anthropological research. Research techniques of related disciplines are being adopted, and new interdisciplinary fields are developing.

Yet if there is one characteristic that distinguishes the anthropological approach to these common topics from that of other disciplines, it is the focus on ritual and sociocultural constraints on behavior. No matter what seemingly reasonable, utilitarian justification members might give for their practices, the anthropologist tends to see behavior as having both rational, or goal-oriented, as well as conventionalized, arbitrary, and culture-bound components. It is the clarification of the role of ritualized, routinized, unconscious, and often glossed-over aspects of behavior, of the way they enter into everyday instructional tasks, that best characterizes the anthropologist's contribution to our understanding of human society and the role of language in it.

Still, while the term *ritual* has survived the shift in research focus from little-known to well-known societies, the definition of the concept, the specification of what aspects of behavior can be seen as ritual, and our notion of the place of ritual practices in human life have changed radically. The early nineteenth-century anthropologists were mainly explorers, missionaries, and colonial administrators, intent on comparing what they saw abroad with what they had learned as part of their own backgrounds. They tended to see human society primarily in an evolutionary perspective and were interested in locating the customs of unknown groups in reference to their own society's scale of development. In their descriptions, they naturally focused on the types of activities that were most different from what they knew, assuming that what seemed familiar required no special explanation. Among the striking phenomena they noted were the prevalence of seemingly purposeless types of activities, which appeared unrelated to what they regarded the main tasks of productive endeavor to be. The term *ritual* was, in these early descriptions, largely a cover term to catalog practices that the anthropologist could not understand in other terms.

Turn-of-the-century Durkheimian social theory marks a major paradigmatic shift away from the study of primitive societies within a Western frame of reference towards the systematic analysis of social groups in their own terms. The basis of Durkheim's sociology is the analytical distinction drawn between the social and the individual, and between the sacred and the profane (Aron, 1970). Social systems are seen as independent structures, different from, and to some extent independent of, the sum of individual group members' behavior. These structures are made up of functionally related social elements or components and sustained by a system of cultural values or beliefs. The term *sacred* refers to the institutions and values that function to sustain and reaffirm the cohesiveness and separation of the group. *Profane* refers to the aspects of society that function to fulfill practical, everyday goals. Ritual activity is the part of human activity that relates the individual to the social and cultural, that demonstrates how the social and cultural intermesh in human behavior. *Ritual,* here, serves as an abstract explanatory concept; it does not refer to a particular type of concrete act. What early anthropologists saw as strange practices, relics of man's past, attributable to superstition or strange forms of religious beliefs, now become the key to what is social in human groups and to the maintenance of their functional integrity.

With the breakdown of social boundaries in all parts of the globe, it can no longer be maintained that social acts are dependent on the existence of some territorially bounded population aggregate. Yet it is, nevertheless, true that human activity, to the extent that it communicates, is always constrained by shared norms. There has been a shift in emphasis, therefore, from the notion of group as the ultimate referent of social activity to more detailed study of social relations of various types, and of the shared values and unspoken assumptions they reflect. Similarly, the dichotomy between sacred and profane can no longer be taken as absolute. Few aspects of society are usually sacred or wholly profane, few activities wholly ritual. Edmond Leach (1954), in fact, defines ritual activity as the component of human acts that cannot be seen to contribute to some rationally defined goal. Mary Douglas (1966) points to the pervasiveness of ritual components in everyday human practices, such as those surrounding bodily functions, dietary habits, cleanliness conventions, and the like. She shows that these are historically relatable to similar customs in earlier civilization and equivalent to many found in modern tribal societies. Douglas' view of ritual is reminiscent of that of many psychoanalysts, who argue that the ritualized, repetitive actions of an individual's everyday routine serve to sustain personality. She sees ritual aspects of daily activities as functioning to maintain social boundaries and preserve the separation between spheres of activities and different types of cultural values. What ritual does, then, is to create a common kind of reality for those who, by virtue of their background, follow similar practices. It leads actors to define phenomena in similar ways and to reinforce social ties with those who act as they do.

The disappearance of the old polar distinctions between sacred and profane, ritual and everyday acts, along with the expansion in geographical scope of anthropological research, gives rise to serious empirical problems. If ritual is an integral aspect of most human acts, how do we explain the working of ritual processes, how do we identify the ritual components of behavior in our own as well as in other societies? Recent work in symbolic anthropology is, in large part, concerned with these questions. Much of the impetus for this work derives from Levi-Strauss' studies of cultural symbolism in myth and folk narratives. Levi-Strauss deals with symbolism as a kind of language, analyzable in terms of its own abstract logic and grammarlike rules (Rossi, 1974). Like linguistic phenomena of other kinds, symbols can be studied at two levels: the level of abstract underlying features and the level of surface realization in context. Underlying structures consist of relatively simple, largely universal logical primitives, that is, features that can be found to be common to human acts everywhere. Surface realizations are complex and culturally specific. As Chomsky has shown for grammar, the contrast between the two levels of structure enables us to account both for pan-human and for particular aspects of symbolism, and to suggest an explanation for creativity in communication by showing how new forms can be created through recombinations and transformations of underlying features.

While Levi-Strauss' analysis deals mainly with the logic of symbolic systems, others, notably Turner (1969) and Geertz (1966), are more directly concerned with the problem posed by Durkheim: the question of how acts function to relate the individual to the social and the cultural. Ritual processes are here analyzed in terms of the metaphorical ties that connect particular acts to their other kinds of experiences. Culture is seen as a system of metaphorical associations that link together different kinds of reality. Through ritual the individual affirms his ties with that system.

A great deal has been done in recent years to explain the structuring of cultural symbols and to clarify the nature of ritual practices. Yet the actual signaling process that gives rise to the association between context-bound acts and abstract symbols has hardly begun to be examined. It is by no means clear, for example, to what extent symbolic processes are grammar-like. Where symbolic analysis deals only with myth or with narrative themes expressed in words, as in Levi-Strauss' work, and where analysis focuses on abstract logical structure, the parallel to language is not hard to justify. But cultural symbols and ritual acts are in large part nonverbal. Although it is, perhaps, true that shared meaning and shared perceptions are ultimately communicated through language, a single iconic symbol can stand for a variety of linguistic realizations. There is no one way to relate such an icon, by any one grammatical algorithm, to any one set of words that might be employed to describe its effect.

Consider, moreover, the case of magical formulas or ritual texts that are verbal. These are, of course, readily analyzed grammatically and semantically. Yet their meaning—if we define meaning as the effect of a message on those to whom it is addressed—is quite distinct—in fact, often directly opposed to the overt literal sense of constituent sentences. Until quite recently, modern linguistics dealt only with the literal sense of isolated sentences, and our theories of grammar, especially those of Chomsky and of most other theoretical linguists, reflect this limitation. The questions of speaker's interpretation of context-bound messages and of the role of grammatical rules in this interpretation are still, in large part, unresolved. There is considerable controversy among linguists as to whether grammatical theory is capable of dealing with this issue. Until we learn more about speaking practices in a variety of settings, there is little hope of resolving the conflict.

In an effort to remedy the almost complete lack of attention to the facts of language usage, ethnographers of communication have launched a detailed set of studies dealing with speaking in culturally specific settings (Hymes, 1972). Because of the almost complete lack of data in this area, most work has concentrated on the discovery and description of speech events in a range of literate and preliterate societies throughout the world. As more descriptions become available, it can be shown that in all societies there exist speech events that are marked off from everyday verbal behavior by special rules of speaking. The differences in question are not simply matters of choice of words and topics, but involve a complex set of interrelated factors, including selection of pronunciation and grammatical alternates, intonation and speech rhythm, discourse structures, as well as constraints on social roles enacted by speakers and listeners, and constraints on setting. Constraints on performance structure in speech events are both paradigmatic, where they apply to selection among alternates, and syntagmatic, where they apply to the sequential order in which passages occur. In this sense, rules of speaking seem akin to the grammatical rules applying to the production of sentences. We have reason to suppose, therefore, that there exists a level of structure that operates in the realm of discourse and is analytically separate from the grammar of individual sentences. Communicative competence, that is, the ability to speak appropriately, implies a knowledge both of grammar and of rules of language usage. What Chomsky sees as human creativity—the speaker's freedom to create new sentences by innovative use of grammatical rules—is not simply a matter of free choice limited only by instrumental considerations of what the speaker wants to accomplish; it is also subject to social and ritual constraints. Potentially, therefore, the study of rules of speaking in communicative events could shed important new light on the relation of instrumental and noninstrumental factors in behavior.

Yet a number of problems remain. Most of our data so far apply to formal speech situations such as ceremonial gatherings, public performances, verbal games, and similar events, generally seen as separate from everyday interaction. The goal in collecting the data was to construct grammars of such formal events, to develop systems of sociolinguistic rules that would predict the incidence of linguistic forms from a knowledge of social norms and grammatical constraints. Less attention has been paid to the semantic implications of the concept of speech event. In their concern with structure, investigators sometimes tend to overemphasize the constraints that cultural norms play on language usage. They assume that the relevant social norms are known, or at least subject to study by conventional ethnographic methods. Thus, they fail to deal with the issues that have led others, including the less linguistically inclined symbolic anthropologists, to question the a priori nature of social categories and to stress the role of ritual in generating shared perceptions of reality and in both reshaping and reaffirming existing social bonds. While ethnography of communication has shown that the study of what Blount calls the realities of speech behavior can lead to some important insights into the role of social factors in the communication process, there is still a major gap between sociolinguistic description and symbolic analysis of social phenomena. A great deal of work remains to be done in the way of examining existing approaches to verbal data and questioning basic concepts if we are to develop empirical analyses of speaking capable of dealing with social symbolism in everyday communication.

The studies in this volume can be seen as a step in this direction. Following the tradition established in the ethnography of communication, analysis concentrates on verbal behavior in an actual context. Data consist of detailed ethnographic observations or tape recordings. But the basic approach to analysis leans heavily on ethnographic semantics. The focus is on the perceptual cues that speakers utilize in the categorization of speech context and on the semantic structures these reflect, rather than on attempts to relate the incidence of linguistic forms to social norms.

Ethnographic semantic analysis of terminological systems during the 1960s has shown that categorization of environmental cues into words is culturally specific (Tyler, 1969). Given any set of environmental cues, a speaker's cultural background will lead him to focus on certain features as significant, leaving others unnamed. For example, the continuous color spectrum may be split into a finite number of discrete categories, or the infinite gradations of plant and animal species in the environment may be grouped in terms of a limited few categories. Once terminological systems are established, they then affect the ease with which environmental features can be talked about. Thus, if a culture has certain color terms such as *red* and *yellow* but not others, it is these colors that are most quickly identified. Other intermediate hues, such as orange, can be noticed and, if necessary, identified by compound phrases. Unless, however, specificity is required, speakers are likely to talk about orange as a kind of yellow or a kind of red. In that sense, although they will not affect what a person sees or hears, terminological systems shape the communication of a shared perception. Verbal categories become conventionalized ways of communicating environmental cues, but they are only imperfect representations of reality. They tend to maintain themselves because of the need for communication with others, unless new circumstances arise to force recategorizations.

Most discussion in the area of ethnographic semantics has so far centered on such areas as kinship terminologies, botanical classification, zoology, etc., in which facts are easily obtainable. But some scholars, notably Frake (1964, 1972) and his students, have begun to apply similar techniques to the study of terms for speaking. The analysis here focuses on the isolation of verbal categories for differing kinds of speaking, examining local meanings of terms like *discussion, argument, chat,* and the like. The goal, as Frake puts it, is "to formulate the conditions under which it is congruous, neither humorous nor deceitful, to state that one is engaged in the speech activity in question. These conditions constitute the semantic characteristics of the activity [1972]."

Yet, unlike names for objects and animals that are identified and categorized by features subject to physical measurement, speakers' identification of named speech activities is based, in large part, on speech itself. Although, as pointed out earlier, such activities are constrained by setting and by socially imposed limitations on participants' roles, these are rarely the only determining factors. To distinguish between a discussion, an argument, and a chat, for example, we listen primarily to what is being said and how it is said. Apart from message content, voice qualities, rhythm and speed of articulation, and choice among lexical and phonological and other stylistic options also play an important role. Language communicates at two levels of meaning. As Bateson (1972) puts it, "It simultaneously communicates content and about content."

The use of language to communicate about content is one of the main themes of this volume. Frake's work isolates the lexical categories that segment the living space in and around a Yakan residence. He shows how these are related to social conventions governing entry into another's house, as well as the conventions governing courtship ritual. The same lexical categories when used in a description of a young man's entrance into his prospective bride's house become a metalanguage metaphorically depicting the stages of the courtship ritual and the characteristics of the individual's acting in it. Sanches uses a similar approach in her study of Japanese narrative performances. In this study, the narrator creates a context of symbolic association by his use of words, dialect variants, rhetorical strategies, and linguistic ettiquette, which sustains his performance. The study by Gumperz and Herasimchuk of a series of elementary school classroom teaching sessions shows how speakers signal basic activities, or "communicative tasks," such as "instructing," "conversing," "playing," and so on through speech. They point out that different individuals use different linguistic devices for signaling similar activities. Children, for example, tend to rely on stress, rhythm, and intonation, while adults use lexicalized phrases to signal what they are doing.

Rosaldo's study of the verbal form of hunting spells takes up a theme very close to that of traditional symbolic anthropology. From the point of view of their referential content, such spells take the form of random evocations of plant and animal names. Yet they are linked by virtue of the human qualities the culture associates with them. When they are listed together and spoken with the rhythmic and stylistic features of magical spells, the effect is to create metaphoric associations among different realms of experience and, thus, to create the context for the successful carrying out of the activity covered by the spell.

Terms for kinds of speaking, when seen in these terms, are members' semantic classifications of context that serve to segment the stream of human interaction into a limited, discrete, and culturally specific number of categories. Identification of stretches of speech as belonging to one or another of these categories is always a matter of matching form with content. It is not enough to simply refer to certain activities. The message must be couched in the proper form and must utilize conventionalized metalinguistic cues. It is the culturally specific association between form and content that generates the relevant symbolic associations.

The verbal categorization of context functions much like the verbal categorization of physical objects in channeling communication and guiding perception of reality. Once an activity is labeled, this labeling plays a significant role in the interpretation process. Agar explains a significant aspect of this phenomenon in his reconstruction of the cognitive world of drug addicts. Through enactment of typical drug scenes, he shows that the drug process involves several stages. These stages are sequentially linked so that enactment of any one stage implies expectations of what must have preceded and what is to follow.

The study by Sacks illustrates the conventional nature of communicated truth as opposed to absolute "truth values." He discusses a simple saying, "Everyone has to lie," reminiscent of sentences like "The king of France is bald," which were made famous through philosophical discussion of truth value. The use of the term *lie* in the context "has to" suggests that truth is a socially defined concept that must be interpreted relevant to certain norms of speaking or choices of what can be said. Without such social constraints on the meaning and use of words, conversation would not be possible at all. The very cooperative nature of interaction processes, therefore, requires some limitation on perception of reality.

Writing in a similar vein, Cook-Gumperz reexamines data on language socialization to suggest that the child's recognition of the need to cooperate, interact with, and influence others is prior to the acquisition of linguistic skills. Before the child begins to speak in sentences, he must learn certain basic principles of interaction. The development of other, more sophisticated metalinguistic uses of languages is, similarly, a function of the development of interactional rules. Kernan and Mitchell-Kernan deal with the developmental aspects of one kind of act: insulting. Insulting requires both cultural knowledge of the kinds of descriptions that count as insults and linguistic knowledge of proper verbal forms of insulting. Acquisition of both types of knowledge is subject to developmental constraints.

Note that the notion of "social factors in speech" that emerges from these studies is quite different from the conventional notion. Social factors and contextual factors are seen as underlying constraints on the interpretation of messages. They affect the way an individual interprets messages. This suggests that by studying the meanings speakers assign to sentences in context and by comparing different interpretations of similar events, we can study the effect of social constraints on verbal behavior in somewhat the same way that the linguist can show the effect of grammatical constraints. Particular interpretations of messages can then be seen as a result of both semantic phenomena and unverbalized social presuppositions applied to the interpretation of sentences. Selby's criticism of psychological attribution theory is an instance of this type of analysis. Selby shows that incidents, statements, and decisions that are seen in our culture as reflecting personality characteristics are explained in quite different terms by Zapotec Indians in Mexico. This difference in the way we interpret an incident is a matter of social norms. Given the fact that Zapotec Indians and American psychologists have different unverbalized social assumptions, they will also be led to give different interpretations of similar verbal events.

Treatment of social and contextual factors in communication in semantic forms also accounts for speakers' creative use of these factors to accomplish communicative ends. There are two aspects to this type of creativity: the use of language to create a context for the interpretation of what is said, as discussed earlier, or the metaphoric extension of constraints on performance to channel messages or convey information about participants in speech activity. This latter metaphoric use of social and contextual constraints is an important theme in several studies. Blount discusses the interplay of factual elements and social strategies in the construction of genealogies among the Luo of Eastern Africa. Genealogies are indisputable only up to a certain minimal depth. Beyond that point, when facts are in doubt, their construction becomes a matter of group negotiation; they are a way of ranking the individual within the social system, and factionalism and individual prestige play an important role in the outcome. Brukman shows the individual history in devising appropriate joking strategies. He then goes on to demonstrate that once the question and response pattern characteristic of joking is established, it can be used to trick a joking partner that leads to a compromising response. Stross applies the distinction between form and content to the analysis of creativity in song performance.

A final question, the problem of the formal aspects of symbolic communication, is touched on by Werner et al. in their analysis of schizophrenic speech. The authors draw a distinction between two semantic processes: syllogistic reasoning, in which meaning is a conclusion derived from a series of propositions by a process of logical entailment, and metaphor, in which categories are associated by virtue of the fact that they are seen to have shared qualities. Traditional grammatical semantic analysis has dealt with language only in terms of the former process, although what is deviant about schizophrenic speech is the aberrant use of metaphor. Werner's distinction suggests a partial answer to the question of the parallels between grammatical rules and symbolic processes. Symbolic processes are grammarlike to the extent that they are automatic and take place below the level of conscious awareness. Yet they differ from grammatical rules in that they rely on both syllogistic reasoning and metaphoric association for the creation of meaning.

The studies in this volume do not constitute a theory of ritual and social communication; given the present state of our knowledge, such a theory would be, perhaps, premature. They do, however, present important implications for empirical research on ritual and social elements in speech. A number of the phenomena discussed, particularly issues of content and the role of speech functions as "instructing," "joking," and the like have been treated elsewhere in the linguistic and psycholinguistic literature. What is different about the present approach is the suggestion that these phenomena are treated as communicated semantic categories, that the signs by which they are signaled are culturally variable, and that their identification by speakers is subject to the same laws of perception and categorization that govern the assignment of lexical labels to features of the environment and of phonemic categories to sound. If we assume that ritual communication achieves its effect through the creation of contexts for the interpretation of signs, that interpretation takes the form of metaphoric associations of sentences to activities, and that these associations are mediated through metalinguistic signs, then the systematic analysis of these signs, and of their role in speakers' communicative strategies, could throw new light on the effect of social rules on behavior and clarify a number of problems of cross-cultural communication.

References

Aron, Raymond
 1970 *Main currents in sociological thought.* New York: Anchor Books.

Bateson, Gregory
 1972 *Steps to an ecology of mind.* New York: Ballantine Books.

Douglas, Mary
 1966 *Purity and danger.* London: Routledge and Kegan Paul.

Frake, Charles
 1964 How to ask for a drink in sutanim, *American Anthropologist* 66, pt. II, 127–132.
 1972 Struck by speech: The Yakan concept of litigation. In *Directions in sociolinguistics,* edited by John J. Gumperz and Dell Hymes. New York: Holt.

Geertz, C.
 1966 Religion as a cultural system. In *Anthropological approaches to the study of religion,* edited by M. Bantom. London: Tavistock.

Hymes, D.
 1974 *Foundations in sociolinguistics.* Philadelphia: Univ. of Pennsylvania Press.

Leach, Edmond
 1954 *Political systems of highland Burma.* Cambridge: Cambridge Univ. Press.

Rossi, I.
 1973 *The unconscious in culture: The structuralism of Levi-Strauss in perspective.* New York: E. P. Dutton.

Turner, V. I.
 1969 *The ritual process: Structure and anti structure.* Chicago: Aldine.

Tyler, S.
 1969 *Cognitive anthropology.* New York: Holt.

Sociocultural Dimensions of Language Use

I. THE CONSTRUCTION
   OF SOCIAL REALITY

Introduction

BEN G. BLOUNT

Innovations during the decade of the 1960s brought about impressive changes in linguistics and linguistic anthropology. The most revolutionary of those changes stemmed from the introduction of Chomskyan transformational grammar, which came to be the dominant force in linguistics on an international scale (cf. Lyons, 1970 for an overview). Although the work of Chomsky and his associates altered the scope and direction of linguistic theory, their impact on linguistic anthropology has been far more indirect and diffuse. Anthropological reaction to transformational grammar has tended to stress (1) that it is irrelevant to anthropological concerns except as a model of rigorous analysis (e.g., Burling, 1969) and (2) that even if the theory adequately accounts for meaning at the sentence level, which few would be willing to grant, it does not account for the interesting questions of the social dimensions of language use and change. The competence of speakers to assign grammaticality judgments correctly to sentences is undoubtedly an interesting linguistic phenomenon, but that competence does not enable a speaker of any language to communicate effectively, and it is this larger issue that has been a concern of linguistic anthropology (cf. Hymes, 1973).

One finds it difficult, however, to dispute the historical importance of Chomskyan linguistics for linguistic anthropology. Anthropologists interested in the study of language could not remain immune from the revolutionary impact of transformational grammar on the entire field of linguistics. One aspect of grammatical theory that was important in the development of linguistic anthropology in the 1960s was the insistence on an underlying reality as a base from which abstract linguistic structure is generated. Of course, the idea of an underlying, abstract base as an organizational component for language and behavior was present in anthropology long before the 1960s. For example, as early as 1911 Franz Boas argued that since linguistic structure was unconscious and generally unavailable to speakers of a language, the structure, once discerned, could be a valuable tool for ethnologists (Boas, 1911). Edward Sapir extended by analogy the abstractness of language patterning to society, suggesting that explanations of behavior should be sought in unconscious patterning of social phenomena (Sapir, 1927); and in 1951 Claude Levi-Strauss called to anthropologists' attention the far-reaching implications of the work in cybernetics and information theory, stressing the power of models that involved abstract bases and transformational rules that convert aspects of those bases into surface reality (Levi-Strauss, 1951). Still, the demonstrably overwhelming success of trans-formational grammar in linguistics had an impact on anthropology, in-tensifying the interests in underlying, organizational components of language and culture that already had a history in anthropology and were emerging in new developments in linguistic anthropology during the early years of the 1960s (cf. Frake, 1964; Gumperz, 1967; Hymes, 1967).

A second feature of Chomskyan linguistics that has been basic to linguistics, and has had considerable influence in allied fields such as lan-guage acquisition and psycholinguistics, is the emphasis on the creative aspect of language. Even though the term *creative* is used in a technical sense by linguists, some confusion as to its meaning continues to cause difficulties. It may be instructive to review here how Chomsky views creativity in linguistics. Building from a Cartesian view, Chomsky takes the creative aspect of language to be that which is "innovative, free from stimulus control, and also appropriate and coherent [1972:13]." Lan-guage creativity, according to the Cartesian position, was a reflection of what is essential in human intelligence but not reducible to any sort of psychical explanation. Chomsky views the Cartesians as correct in their rejection of physicalistic accounts. He writes, "It seems to me that the most hopeful approach today is to describe the phenomena of language and of mental activity as accurately as possible, to try to develop an ab-stract theoretical apparatus that will as far as possible account for these phenomena and reveal the principles of their organization and func-tioning without attempting, for the present, to relate the postulated mental structures and processes to any physiological mechanisms or to interpret mental function in terms of 'physical causes' [ibid., p. 14]." The immediate significance of this view is that mental structure is postulated as a theoretical apparatus that is relatable in formulated, i.e., rule-governed, ways to the phenomena of language. We might add paren-thetically that a similar apparatus is applicable to the study of culture. As a mental system, culture can be interpreted in terms of creativity, as, indeed, it has been treated in linguistic anthropology.

Language creativity can be viewed in another light, but one that Chomsky takes pains to distinguish from Cartesian creativity (cf. 1972:viii). Generative grammar has recursive projections, meaning, simply stated, that rules can, under specifiable conditions, be continually reapplied. Thus, there can be a finite set of base components and rules, but these can generate a potentially infinite set of sentences. Any ideal speaker of a natural language has the ability to generate (and understand) a potentially infinite number of sentences; equipped with underlying structure and a set of rules, a speaker can create novel utterances. This is merely a recapitulation of standard "infinite" syntax, but the significant point is that this potential for creativity must underlie human communication. It is a fundamental fact that must be accounted for by any theory of human communication. In one sense, speakers create communicative acts; these may or may not be novel either in some absolute sense or for any given addressor and addressee, but in any case there is a potential for creativity that is part and parcel of the human condition.

The "reality" on which speech is generated is spoken of as underlying and abstract. The surface manifestations are taken as epiphenomenal, i.e., as the end product of the generation of an utterance, or, conversely, the data from which the process of decoding is initiated. Stated otherwise, what is available for direct observation, for perception, is important as signs or signals, as, for example, the writing in a written message, but the reality of the message resides in the underlying components. However, from another perspective reality consists of what is immediately given, perceptible, what "one cannot will away." Reality can be defined as "that which has objective existence, and is not merely an idea" (mental construct) and, also, as "that which is absolute or self-existent, as opposed to what is derivative or dependent." Reality in the sense of "that which has objective existence" is probably a more accurate characterization of the social world than "that which is underlying, abstract, or derivative." That is, in the course of daily life a member of the social world goes about the business of making observable his actions and the actions of his fellow members such that common, reciprocal meanings are established, at least partially. The features on which these members base their efforts and actions are in the first instances observable, accountable phenomena (cf. Berger and Luckman, 1967; Schutz, 1967; Garfinkel, 1964). A theory of communication must account for the social processes of making observable and available for interpretation activities of societal members. Activities made observable have a reality that is relatable to an underlying reality and in relation to which creativity is possible, permissible, and assessible.

During the past decade several developments in linguistic anthropology began to make available the foundations on which a theory of communication could be based. Among the first of these developments was the emergence of the field of inquiry variously labeled "new eth-nography," "ethnoscience," and "ethnosemantics" (cf. Frake, 1964 and Sturtevant, 1964 for early and comprehensive accounts; Berlin and Kay, 1970 and Werner, 1972 for more recent assessments). The general goal of ethnosemantics as originally formulated was the discovery of folk taxonomies, utilizing rigorous methods and techniques in the research design and procedure. Among the particular merits of ethnosemantic research were the following:

1.   Systematic research design and procedure was an advance over conventional ethnography, since a record of the data collection and anal-ysis was a principal object of the research. Verification and replication of the studies were, thus, easier.

2.   Folk "knowledge" supplied the substance of data on which an ethnographic report was based, and, thus, a more accurate assessment could be made of what role the ethnographer's theories and hypotheses played in the analysis.

3.   The results of the research were theoretically more consistent with the goal of ethnography that an ethnographic account should give information that allows one to know what is necessary in order to as-sume roles in the society and to fill them appropriately (cf. Goodenough, 1957).

Ethnoscience dealt with lexical semantics, specifically with the se-mantic features on which lexical domains were based and organized. A closely allied development focused on the issue of the psychological reality of information processing, building on the results of lexical se-mantic analyses. Questions about the psychological reality of semantic features derived from the fact that competing semantic analyses of the same basic data were possible. If different features and rules could be used to generate the same data, what criteria should be involved as grounds for selecting one solution over another? This question led to the larger issue of the functioning of the mind in processing information relating to lexical domain. This field of inquiry, cognitive anthropology, has incorporated a considerable portion of the ethnosemantic approach, such that a firm distinction between the two areas is difficult (cf. Romney and d'Andrade, 1964 for an early account; Tyler, 1969 for a more recent one).

The major development during the 1960s for linguistic anthropology was the creation of sociolinguistics as a field of study. Of the various new developments, sociolinguistics was the most broadly defined and has been the most productive in quantity of research. It has also incor-porated into its scope several historical traditions of social research, representing traditional disciplines such an anthropology, folklore, linguistics, social psychology, and sociology. The central tradition in the early development of sociolinguistics derives from language and culture studies in anthropology, specifically from the work of Dell Hymes, John Gumperz, and Charles Frake in the ethnography of communication (Frake, 1964; Hymes, 1962; Gumperz and Hymes, 1964, 1972). The ethnography of communication aims at the description of the communicative resources of a speech community and of the organization of these resources on a sociocultural basis. The method of research is ethnography, the focus is primarily on the organized use of speech as a communicative means, and a fundamental working hypothesis is relativity in the resources and organization of communication across cultures (cf. Hymes, 1966).

Two additional traditions of social thought have made seminal contributions to sociolinguistics. Since sociolinguistics is concerned with the coding of social information linguistically and the communication of that information within social frameworks, a theory of sociolinguistics must include formal components for social contexts. The importance of context as situation and for definition and allocation of social roles in communication has been stressed mainly in sociology and principally by Erving Goffman (1964; 1971). In addition, Goffman's insights into the underlying motivations for use of situation, role, personal space, and strategy such as maintaining and saving face and ritually affirming and preserving social rights have strongly influenced the development of sociolinguistics.

A second contribution to sociolinguistics from sociology has come from the ethnomethodologists. As indicated by the name, this subfield of inquiry focuses on methodology, stressing the necessity for the researcher to keep accountable his involvement in the social analysis. This involves not merely a statement of purpose, bias, and/or theoretical orientation but also the realization that social information is obtained by the researcher as a participating member in interaction, doing work to make observable and accessible the meaning of the interaction in ways that are similar to and often coincide with the ways anyone else in society does the work. Research problems and methodology are, thus, essentially one and the same, and they reveal the surface features of reality to which societal members attend in their work of making sense of the reality (cf. Cicourel, 1964; Garfinkel, 1964; and Sacks, 1972 for overviews).

The contributions of ethnomethodologists afford a systematic beginning for relating surface reality to underlying generative forms. Developments in sociolinguistics provide supportive contextual analysis and elaborate the importance of communicative acts as units of analysis, and cognitive anthropology investigates the reality of underlying components and organization. Creativity resides in the potentiality within the framework of the bipolarity of the two levels of reality. The communication chain consists of an underlying reality or, more precisely, realities — universal human features, language specific features, and mental organization such as part–whole relations, taxonomy and hierarchy, and others — and the generation from those bases of surface communicative phenomena that have a reality for social interaction. The generation of communication is a psychological and sociological phenomenon, operating within a cultural field and contextual constraints. No theory of communication as yet begins to encompass these features, but it is clear that any adequate theory cannot overlook them. At present, research in linguistics and language use draws from the various subfields of linguistics and anthropology, and a synthesis of these approaches should facilitate work toward the outlines of a satisfactory theory. By this, I do not mean theory construction through induction and more "parts" and "pieces," but that the bipolarity of communicative reality, if that term be allowed, is taken account of as researchers converge and coarticulate the areas of ethnosemantics, cognitive anthropology, sociolinguistics, and linguistics. Syntheses of this sort are likely to be major contributions to our understanding of language, communication, and the construction of social reality during the 1970s. The studies presented in Part I are testimony to such a synthetic approach.

In "Semantics and Causality in the Study of Deviance," Selby examines the crosscultural validity of attribution theory. The problem to which attribution theory is addressed is closely related to and perhaps a corollary of a central question in ethnomethodology, namely, how societal members go about the business of making sense of the behavior of others. Attribution theory holds that members of society attribute to one another intentionality based on decisions reached about the internal characteristics of others and on stereotypes consistent with those characteristics. In short, personality traits are assigned to a status of reality or truth. Selby argues that the reality derives from a shared semantic (or cultural) code in Western (or American) society, but that the Zapotecs of Mexico do not necessarily attribute reality to internal states as causes of social behavior. Zapotec solutions to the problem of making sense of others' behavior do not rely on a folk taxonomy in which individual personality traits are a motive force. Instead, they insist on sociological explanations, as Selby illustrates, using an ethnosemantic approach to the Zapotec ethnographic data.

The creation of social reality by participants in a cultural code is well documented by Frake in "How to Enter a Yakan House." The daily, commonplace activity of entering a member's house involves cultural knowledge that includes shared semantic features concerning the spatial configuration of a Yakan house, the importance of the position within the configuration of the owner/occupant during the exchange of information between visitor and host, and the meanings of verbal and nonverbal acts relative to the spatial and positional arrangements. The Yakan share a cultural code, an abstract reality, against which actual behavior can be judged and marked according to the congruity or lack thereof with the code. Sense is made out of a visitor–host encounter through reference to (aspects of) the code from the surface reality of behavior, which may thereby be construed as polite, impolite, hostile, obsequious, or whatever.

In "Cognition and Events," Agar reports on research conducted at the National Institute of Mental Health Research Center in Lexington, Kentucky, where he studied the subculture of addiction. Learning the argot of narcotic addicts was not sufficient for understanding the conversations of the various types of addicts. To be a competent participant in conversations about narcotic events, it was necessary to share the cognitive structure of narcotic event sequences, a structure against which behavioral units or episodes could be marked and attributes such as *burn, bust,* and *ripoff* could be assigned. The semantics of the lexicon and cognitive structure of events are both necessary in the work of communicating and understanding, but it is the inexact and flexible relationship among them that both makes necessary and provides the means for members to make sense of the behavior of others. The significance of a unit, cognitive and/or performative, must be demonstrated and not merely assumed. Aspects of the performance cannot reliably predict what the outcome of event sequences will always be. The information provided in a performance must be assessed against the cognitive background and in relation to what a probable outcome may be.

In "Everyone Has to Lie," Sacks formulates the problem of what kind of analysis is required to establish that what a member says about the social world may be falsified. Further, the analysis produces social organization in the sense that the criteria that are constructed to provide an account of how features of the social world may be true also make available to members arrangements to ascertain the truth of a statement. Sacks demonstrates that the analysis contains members' knowledge as to how a population is formulated (specifically, the population "everyone"), knowledge of the applicability to an assertion of a contrast class true–false (i.e., not all assertions may be judged by a true–false contrast), and knowledge of what constitutes a "minimal proper conversation," as, e.g., an exchange of greetings. In each of these cases members rely on semantic information, sociological considerations as to what is obligatory and proper socially, and how a proper structuring and sequencing of these must be carried out by members so that information is mutually available to them.

Gumperz and Herasimchuk analyzed taped conversations of children and teachers in a Berkeley, California, elementary school and concluded that communication could best be understood in relation to two semantic processes, namely, coding and marking processes (after Geoghegan, 1973). Code rules encode ideas into grammatical sentences, and marking rules interpret or reinterpret message elements in relation to other cooccurring elements, presuppositions, and other contextual and background information. If code rules are generalized to include interpretable rule-governed acts as well as grammatical sentences, and, if marking rules contain a reflexivity principle, this sociolinguistic approach is a specialized version of the interactional model as described in this Introduction. The particular merits of the Gumperz and Herasimchuk analysis are (1) the insistence that linguistic analysis must be extended beyond grammatical, phonological, and lexical analyses and (2) the demonstration of variables, such as prosodic aspects of speech, that constitute optional strategies in communication in the speech of the first- and second-grade children in their study.

In "Agreeing to Agree on Genealogy: A Luo Sociology of Knowledge," I present ethnographic background illustrating how the Luo structure discussions about genealogical histories. The structure has external components, prescribing under what contexts the discussions can occur and who is eligible to participate in them, and within those speech events the participants have recourse to strategies for shaping aspects of the genealogies for their own advantage. These strategies are based on assessments of speaking competence, knowledge of Luo folklore and social positions—the latter determined by the dimensions of seniority according to absolute age and kinship organization. A speaker has access to the background information, especially folklore and social organization, from which he can generate particular acts and against which other members can judge his behavior and reach decisions about that behavior and how they may choose to relate and react to it. The product of a genealogical discussion is a jointly produced activity, creating a genealogical charter that supports lineage organization, and, thus, the Luo can be said to construe reality in the way they talk about it.

The final paper in this section of the collection—"The Child as Practical Reasoner," by Cook-Gumperz—presents a background for a central issue in socialization of children, namely, how children acquire and put into practice the knowledge that the social world is a given but nevertheless jointly produced existence. For a child to learn to communicate, he must acquire the knowledge that participants in communication must work to make available practical information. Once this knowledge is mastered, its role in communication may take on more of a taken-for-granted quality, but realization of the social world is at first especially problematic and must have an ontogenetic development. Confronted with the task of communicating, children rely on a variety of possible channels and symbols, but language is a central one. However, as Cook-Gumperz demonstrates, effective language use by a child entails symbolic manipulation of social and contextual information. Language acquisition and socialization proceed as a child becomes more effective as a practical reasoner, as he can relate and integrate social, contextual, and linguistic information so as to produce for societal members an account that relies on the existence of the social world as given.

References

Berger, Peter and T. Luckman
    1967   *The social construction of reality: A treatise in the sociology of knowledge.* New York: Doubleday.
Berlin, Brent and Paul Kay
    1970   Some theoretical implications of ethnographic semantics. In Current directions in anthropology, edited by A. Fischer. *American Anthropological Bulletin* 3(2).
Boas, Franz
    1911   Introduction. In *Handbook of American Indian languages.* BAE-B 40 (Part 1), Washington, D.C.: Smithsonian Institution.
Burling, Robbins
    1969   Linguistics and ethnographic description, *American Anthropologist* 71, 817–827.
Chomsky, Noam
    1972   *Language and mind* (enlarged edition). New York: Harcourt.
Cicourel, Aaron
    1964   *Method and measurement in sociology.* Glencoe, Illinois: Free Press.
Frake, Charles O.
    1964   Notes and queries in anthropology, *American Anthropologist* 66(2), 132–145.
Garfinkel, Harold
    1964   Studies of the routine grounds of everyday activities, *Social Problems* 11(3).
Goffman, Erving
    1964   The neglected situation. In The ethnography of communication, edited by J. Gumperz and D. Hymes. *American Anthropologist* 66(2).
    1971   *Behavior in public.* New York: Basic Books.
Goodenough, Ward
    1957   Cultural anthropology and linguistics. In *report of the seventh annual round table meeting on linguistics and language study,* edited by P. Garvin. Washington, D.C.: Georgetown Univ.

Gumperz, John
   1967   On the linguistic markers of bilingual communication. In Problems of bilingualism, edited by J. MacNamara. *Journal of Social Issues* **23**(2).
Gumperz, John and Dell Hymes (editors)
   1964   The ethnography of communication, *American Anthropologist* **66**(2).
   1972   *New directions in sociolinguistics: The Ethnography of Communication.* New York: Holt.
Hymes, Dell H.
   1962   The ethnography of speaking. In *Anthropology and human behavior,* edited by T. Gladwin and W. Sturtevant. Washington, D.C.: Anthropological Society of Washington.
   1966   Two types of linguistic relativity. In *Sociolinguistics,* edited by W. Bright. The Hague: Mouton.
   1967   Models of interaction of language and social setting. In *Problems of bilingualism,* edited by J. MacNamara. *Journal of Social Issues* **23**(2).
   1973   "The Scope of Sociolinguistics" in R. W. Shuy, ed. *Sociolinguistics: Current Trends & Prospects.* Report of the 23rd Annual Round Table Meeting on Linguistics and Language Studies, Number 25. Washington, D.C.: Georgetown University.
Levi-Strauss, Claude
   1951   Language and the analysis of social laws, *American Anthropologist* **66**(2).
Lyons, John
   1970   *Noam Chomsky.* New York: Viking Press.
Romney, A. K. and Roy D'Andrade (editors)
   1964   Transcultural studies in cognition, *American Anthropologist* **66**(2).
Sacks, Harvey
   1972   An initial investigation of the usability of conversational data for doing sociology. In *Studies in social interaction,* edited by D. Sudnow. New York: Free Press.
Sapir, Edward
   1927   The unconscious patterning of behavior in society. In *The unconscious: A symposium,* edited by E. Drummer. New York: Knopf.
Schutz, Alfred
   1967   *The phenomenology of the social world.* Evanston, Illinois: Northwestern Univ. Press (originally, 1932, *Der sinnhafte Aufbau der Sozialen Welt.* Vienna: Springer).
Sturtevant, William
   1964   Studies in ethnoscience, *American Anthropologist* **66**(2), 99–131.
Tyler, Steven A.
   1969   *Cognitive anthropology.* New York: Holt.
Werner, Oswald
   1972   Ethnoscience 1972. In *Annual review of anthropology,* edited by B. Siegel. Palo Alto: Annual Reviews.

Semantics and Causality in the
Study of Deviance

HENRY A. SELBY

Anthropologists have realized for a long time that their informants and subjects are astute philosophers and social theorists. True, they may lack advanced degrees in social science, but they own a more impressive credential—they have lived in a comparatively small-scale, stable situation that they have had to study and understand in order to survive. As a result, they have developed elaborate (if sometimes implicit) theories about how they and their societies tick. In the past the anthropologists have tended to concentrate on the philosophy, jurisprudence, and cosmology of non-Western peoples, but more recently some have shifted their interest to the field of psychology, with cognition and cognitive process being more widely studied, along with theories of the person and local theories of personality development. It seems likely that more and more input to the development of a cross-cultural psychology can be expected in the coming years. These developments are examples of an interest on the part of social scientists in thinking about the influence of sociocultural factors in individual performance, but, strangely enough, the one area of social science that I almost defined in the last sentence—social psychology—seems to be least affected by and to be least affecting the transcultural studies carried out by anthropologists, despite the fact that there is a good deal of anecdotal data and interest on topics such as conformity, motivation, cognitive dissonance, social learning, and the like. This may be because it is so difficult to replicate experimental settings in anthropological field situations, but I think it also arises from a lack of communication between the two styles of social science research. I would like to contribute to a potential dialog by examining the cross-cultural validity of an important and growing area of social psychology—attribution theory. I want to bring ethnographic data from my study of Zapotec to bear on the question of whether attribution theory is cross-culturally valid. By the end of the discussion, I will have stated my opinion that (1) it is not universally valid, but (2) it is important in Western (or American) culture because it implies the reality or truth of personality descriptions, which are themselves (3) not "true" in any external sense but derived from a shared semantic (or cultural) code.

Attribution Theory

Since the publication of Heider's (1958) book on the psychology of interpersonal relations, studies of how we explain other people's behavior have increased rapidly, at times rivaling the theory of cognitive dissonance in both explanatory and hypothesis-generating power. Jones and Nisbett (1971) have recently written a summary of the research that most concerns this study. They point out that one of the most stable results in the study of how we explain the "problematic" behavior of others is by the attribution of character traits to him or her. An example concerns the teacher and the student who are in a familiar situation — they have both failed to meet the deadline for an article or paper. From the professor's point of view, the reasons for missing the deadline lie in family responsibilities, teaching duties, and committee assignments, which have all conspired to keep him or her away from the work table. By contrast, the reason the student has failed to meet the deadline is laziness. The student reverses the emphasis, but the process is the same. We *attribute* our own problematic behavior to circumstances beyond our control, or to situational constraints, whereas we *attribute* the behavior of others to internal characteristics (thereby, attribution theory). The effect was noted by Heider (1958) and has been examined in the work of Jones and Davis (1965), Kelley (1967), and Rotter (1966), who has translated the idea into psychological terms and made much use of the distinction between people who see themselves as movers and controllers (internals) and people who see themselves as situationally controlled (externals). Tagiuri sums up this general finding:

> The inclination to attribute *intentionality* to others even when such an attribution is objectively unwarranted, to see others as *origins* of actions, thus forcibly integrating the person and the situation shows again the effort made by the organism to *make sense* of the other person's behavior. Whether the cause of a person's action is believed to be internal or external to him is a very strong determinant of how he is understood and, in particular, whether he is seen as *responsible* for the action [1969:422].

Similarly, Aronson talks about the attribution process in his remarks on prejudice:

> If Mr. Bigot passes Mr. Anglo's house and notices that a trash can is overturned and some garbage is strewn about, he is apt to conclude that a stray dog has been

searching for food. If he passes Mr. Garcia's house and notices the same thing, he is inclined to become annoyed, and assert that "those people live like pigs." Not only does prejudice influence his conclusions, his erroneous conclusions justify and intensify his negative feelings. Thus negative stereotypes do not simply lie there in a dormant state; rather, they form part of a person's *attribution process.* When we see a person doing an entirely reasonable thing, we will attribute motives and causes to his behavior that are consistent with his stereotypes [1972:174–175].

In a broad sense, then, attribution of causes to other people's behavior involves making decisions about how to explain people's behavior in the absence of perfect information.

Kelley (1967) has examined the likelihood that we will make internal attributions, and Kanouse (1971) summarizes the theory succinctly: "Other things being equal, a person (or internal) attribution is more likely to be made if the relation is *unique to the person,* or *general across objects,* while an object (or external) attribution is more likely to be made if the relation is *unique to the object,* or *general across persons.*" He gives the example of a friend's recommendation of a film. If only my friend liked the film (unique to the person), or if my friend likes all films (general across objects), then I am likely to think that his recommendation should be taken with a grain of salt, since it arises out of his personal dispositions, i.e., personality, which is another way of saying that I will make an internal attribution. But if my friend were John Simon, who detests practically all films and liked this one (unique to the object), or if a lot of people liked it (general across persons), then I could conclude with some confidence that it was a good film (object or external attribution). Two further results of research in attribution theory bear directly on the Zapotec materials I will discuss. It appears that there is a relationship between the amount of good information we have about the person and the probability that we will make an internal attribution. If I intepret Lazarus (1966) and Aderman and Berkowitz (1970) correctly, we are more likely to attribute causality to personality if we do not know the actors well. Second, the greater the gravity, or magnitude of the effect of, a person's problematic behavior, the greater our need to make an attribution of some kind, if I can generalize from Walster's (1966) study of people's greater tendency to require or make attributions in the case of a serious accident than in the case of a milder one. "The worse the consequences of an accidental event, the greater the tendency to assign responsibility to the person possibly responsible for it [Kelley, 1967:223]."

I will summarize for the purposes of this discussion:

1. People are accustomed to respond to problematic behavior by explaining it as an internal characteristic of the person (ceteris paribus).

2.   There is explanatory value in a folk theory that locates causation in the individual and permits generalization from acts to dispositions.

3.   Personality traits are "real" in the sense that they provide accurate predictions about people's behavior across settings and over time.

In the rest of this chapter, I would like to cast doubt on these propositions. I will bring transcultural (i.e., non-Western) data to bear and hope to convince the reader that there is an alternative set of formulations that equally well explain behavior and deny that psychological variables, e.g., personality traits, have explanatory value.

Psychological Traits as Explanatory Mechanisms

The vigor and longevity of trait psychology attest to the persuasiveness of the folk model of explanation but do not necessarily lend validity to it, as some researchers have documented. As early as 1928, Hartshorne and May adduced evidence to show that the psychological traits are very bad predictors over time and over behavior settings. In their well-known study of deceit (Hartshorne and May, 1928), they showed that dishonesty in one setting did not predict dishonesty in another; that, in effect, the identification of a purportedly stable personality trait as a predictor of behavior was not very effective. It was true that children who cheated by consulting the answer key on a pencil-and-paper test were likely to cheat by consulting the answer key in another. However, the attribution that the child was thereby dishonest, and would cheat generally, was a bad prediction. Mischel (1968), who has examined data on the predictive power of hypotheses based on personality attributions, has concluded that there is a "personality coefficient" of about .30 between settings. That is, one can explain slightly less than 10% of the variance in observed behavior by recourse to a personality description, and this correlation can equally be generated by taking traits at random.

The reason trait-based explanations of problematic behavior have enjoyed such a vigorous life is that they are common sense to us. It seems that we carry about in our heads theories of personality in the form of trait intercorrelation matrices, and we use them to keep the world under cognitive control.

Two kinds of evidence attest to this proposition: (1) data from the study of personality assessment and (2) data drawn from the study of the relationship between semantics and personality theory. In reference to the first, Passini and Norman (1966) found that the amount of knowledge about and familiarity with a person did not alter one's account of their personality. Factor structures were the same for trait descriptions of total strangers as for familiar friends. Our theory about why people do things does not seem to be altered by incremented knowledge about them, at least so long as we explain them by using personality.

D'Andrade (1966, 1972) has worked on the relationship between semantics and personality, and his work shows where those trait inter-correlation matrices come from. The correlations are based on the semantic relations of similarity and dissimilarity and not on the observations of behavior at all. We know that a person is aggressive if he is energetic because of the semantic relations of similarity between the two categories, not because energetic people are "in fact" aggressive or because you have repeatedly observed that this particular person is both.

In his earlier (1966) work, D'Andrade compared the trait intercorrelations derived from personality assessments with the intercorrelations derived from similarities in meaning of the descriptive categories and found a suspiciously high (.86) correlation between them. It was apparent from this work that it was difficult to tell whether one was talking about semantic relationships or relationships between personality traits external to the system of meaning. He has since clarified this problem by looking at three kinds of data: behavior observations, reports about the same behavior made at the end of the observational period, and semantic relations between the descriptive categories used in the earlier two tasks. His work was based on the earlier work of Borgatta, Cottrell, and Mann (1958), and that of Mann (1959), who had noted that behavior observations and behavior reports were yielding quite different results when the Bales (1969) descriptive categories were used. D'Andrade added results derived from the similarities in meaning between the descriptive categories and found very high correlations between meaning and behavior reports, and low correlations (near zero) between either of these and the descriptions obtained from actual observations. He concludes that

> [It] is not just that there is memory drift when people make ratings or rankings of other people's behavior, but that this "drift" is systematic nonrandom, moving in the direction of "what is like what." More abstractly stated, it is hypothesized here that given a series of attributes (such as behavior traits) which can apply to a class of objects (such as people), . . . there will be a systematic shift in the individual's recall of which attributes are possessed by which objects, such that the more similar the individual's conception of any pair of attributes, the more likely it will be that the individual recalls both attributes as belonging to the same objects. As a result of this type of memory shift, any attempt to discover how human behavior is organized into multibehavior units, such as dimensions or clusters, which is based on data consisting of judgements based on long term memory will result in conclusions which reflect the cognitive structure of the subjects [1972:35].

It seems likely that attribution theory "generates" trait psychology, and what we have is a social science version of a folk explanatory model, rather than an explanatory theory of human behavior.

Deviance, Attribution, and Semantics

I believe that data that I have collected on the sociology of deviance in a traditional Mesoamerican community also throws some light on the problem. I have developed the argument in detail elsewhere (Selby, 1974), but I will outline briefly here what I have discussed more fully there. The Zapotecs seem to agree with the idea that the validity, or explanatory value, of personality trait descriptions is questionable. In critical instances they separate the semantic issue from the psychological issue, and where we would be most likely to insist on an internal attribution they desist and focus their attention on the sociological properties of the situation. Their epistemology is entirely Durkheimian in its insistence on sociological explanations of social facts, with the result that they agree entirely with the interactionists in sociology in locating explanations of deviance in the process by which people come to be assigned to deviant categories.

Attribution and Witchcraft

One of the problematic things people do in small-scale, traditional communities is to practice witchcraft. It is a serious form of delict because witchcraft can kill, maim or sicken one's family, animals, and self, and cause one's crops to fail and fortunes to perish. It is interesting to examine the way the Zapotec account for witchcraft, since it is serious and, in general, performed by people whom they do not know very well, both conditions that promote internal attributions. My persistent questions about causal attribution in witchcraft cases produced repeated conversations like the following circular exchange:

SELBY: *But, why did so-and-so bewitch you?*

INFORMANT: *Because he is a witch!*

SELBY: *What do you mean? What kind of person is he?*

INFORMANT: *During the day he is a warm and friendly person, always willing to do you a favor. But he has the familiar spirit of a supernatural cat, and that makes him a witch.*

SELBY:　　　　*How do you know he has the familiar spirit of a super-natural cat?*

INFORMANT:　*Because he is a witch!*

SELBY:　　　　*How do you know he is a witch?*

INFORMANT:　*Because he has an evil way about him.*

It seems to me that these conversations are in line with D'Andrade's discussion about the reason for the correlation between personality traits and meaning. If one examines the domain of deviance by doing a structural semantic analysis, one finds that the head term, or superclass term, for the domain of deviants is the expression *having an evil way*. All deviants have evil ways, and the term is equivalent to *is deviant*. So when my persistent attempts to elicit an attribution yielded the insight that the person in question so acted because he had an evil way, in fact I was eliciting no more than the previous information that *he does witch-craft because he is a witch*, where *witch* equals *a person who has an evil way*, **and** *who has the familiar spirit of a supernatural cat*. Even drastically bad interviewing with leading questions failed to elicit psychological attributions from the informants. They remain adamant in their implicit insistence that one cannot go outside the taxonomic realm of kinds of persons to the realm of kinds of personality traits for explanations. For the Zapotec the attribution of causality for a very serious form of deviance was a problem in meaning and not in trait psychology. Interviewing about every form of deviance yielded similar results; when asked why someone performed some deviant act, the closest the informants came to a psychological explanation was: "That's the way they are, they're deviants."

Eliminating the Individual as the Locus of Explanation

A consequence, or correlate, of the "inability" to attribute problematic behavior to internal causation involves the Zapotec cultural axiom that the individual is not a proper explanatory category. This is so foreign to our way of thinking—though very common in small-scale, traditional communities—that an example of how they define "psychologically disturbed" or "abnormal" behavior is in order. An examination of the case materials on the problem of "abnormality" reveals that it is defined not in a psychological theory but, rather, in a sociological theory. A good case is Alejandro, whose problematic behavior is described as follows:

He doesn't allow kids to go into his patio. In fact he comes all the way over here to take a shit. He used to fight with his children a good deal. He used to tell his oldest boy that he didn't belong to them, but rather was a bastard by some lover of his mother's. He had another kid, a boy, who moved away when he got married because he couldn't stick it with his father. Alejandro has an evil way about him. Sometimes his children would go to work with him in the fields and if they didn't do something, then Alejandro would grab a stick and scream: "You stupid fucking animal . . . !" and would beat them as if they were burros shouting at them: "Go home to your goddam mother!"
He would go home and dinner wouldn't be ready and he would say "You lazy fucking woman, what have you been doing? Why isn't dinner ready?" Then he'd grab something and beat her like an animal.

In interpreting these data one must be careful to purge oneself of the commonsense notion that data about an individual compel interpretation and explanation in terms of the individual. What the informant is saying is that the locus of Alejandro's abnormality lies in his interpersonal relations. The statements about Alejandro are a litany of symptoms of social disorganization. The fact that children are not allowed in Alejandro's patio means that Alejandro cannot participate in the local neighborhood group, because children (see Hotchkiss, 1969) are the intelligence operatives of the society. Children collect and disseminate the information about adults that alone permits appropriate behavior within the inside network of kinsmen and neighbors. The defecation routine is abnormal, not because a normal Zapotec is enamored of human waste (quite the contrary) but because animal waste symbolizes the symbiotic relationship between man and animals on which the economy (the *social* relations of production, etc.) is based. In derogating his eldest child and impugning his genealogy, Alejandro stresses a distinction between "legitimate" and "illegitimate" children that is not salient in this society, and is denying the bond between himself and his son. By beating his wife and publicly proclaiming her infidelity, he is not attacking his own sexual attractiveness; rather, he is stating that the central symbol that legitimizes the kinship network—sexual intercourse—does not orient him to his kinsmen but is in disarray. We should not feel that his wife is abnormal in having extramarital relations, for this is a most frequent and common circumstance. The problematic aspect of Alejandro's conduct lies in the fact that he publicly proclaims the irrelevance of the central symbol for his social relations. He thereby denies himself the possibility of access to the symbols of kinship. A man who is enmeshed in a system that lacks two most important component links (spouse and son) is in a very peculiar situation.

The case of Alejandro defines in brief the conditions for abnormality in Zapotec. The reason the informant adduces this behavior to explain abnormality lies in the publicity that Alejandro gives to his own condition of social limbo. Sexual intercourse is defined in Zapotec as being properly confined to husband and wife, and this definition, along with the incest regulations, provides a symbolic reference point for the most important symbols of kinship. And Alejandro cannot participate in this symbol any more than he can in the symbol of "parent" because he treats his child the way he does. His social universe includes two spoiled, negated symbols, and, clearly, anyone who is enmeshed in this kind of social network is impaired. Alejandro is abnormal, but we should note carefully that he needs a transactional therapist, not a "psychotherapist." Therein lies the difference between his society and ours in the way abnormality is defined.

The Consequences of Absent Attribution

Though it is not my intention to make the argument that trait psychology, or the folk model as represented in attribution theory, has pernicious consequences per se, I can point out that the Zapotec explanatory model of deviance is very close to the interactionist model in sociology. I am referring to the emphasis developed by Becker (1963, 1964, 1971), Douglas (1970), Goffman (1960), Lemert (1951, 1967), Scheff (1966), and Szasz (1961), among many, which is summarized in Rubington and Weinberg (1968). Though the interactionists underline that their perspective on deviance is an emphasis rather than a theory, in Zapotec hands it takes on theoretical status, and it is interesting to see the results. Like the interactionists, the Zapotecs imply by their perspective that deviance is

> . . . *not* a quality of the act a person commits, but rather a consequence of the application by others of rules and sanctions to an "offender." The deviant is one to whom that label has successfully been applied; deviant behavior is behavior people so label [Becker, 1963:9].

Clearly, the Zapotecs go one step further than Becker and deny that any particular behavior can be classified as accurately predictive of deviant status, and label deviants in accordance with the rules of the social structure. Witches are a good example. For the Zapotec the "witch" is a very serious deviant. But there is practically no consensus on who the witches are, nor any stable list of traits or behaviors that would enable an observer to classify someone as a witch. Every subject has his own witch list, which he shares only with his immediate family and, at that, not completely. Subjects start off by classifying people who are outsiders as witches — people in the next village, people in their own village who are not related to them — and that relieves them of the burden of proof or explanation for witchlike behavior. Of course witches (and outsiders) maim your children, destroy your animals, and attack you with sickness, "that's the way they are." They have no interest in you and are not affected by your impaired status in any case. They are beyond the boundaries of kinship and, therefore, are a "natural" source of malignancy. The interactive processes that buttress your classification of an individual as a witch follow the boundaries and communication networks of the social structure precisely; therefore, the same activities that give rise to good (coded as kinlike) relations also give rise to bad (coded as witch–victim) relations. The labeling of the witch (and the associated problem of the provenance of evil) is a social structural problem and does not involve the imputation of detailed motives, nor the observation of behavior.

Zapotec Personality Theory

But one should not conclude that the Zapotec have no theory of personality. In fact, they have quite an elaborate theory that, at times, misleads and confuses them almost as much as ours confuses us. Their theory of personality is based on genealogical considerations — personality traits are believed to be stable over generations — and explained in a very rich ideological scheme that involves the association of animal or spirit familiars with each individual. (Recall the "supernatural cat" of the witches.) If one, for example, has the familiar spirit of a lion, then one is brave and carnivorous, lithe and quick-witted, and shares in the anthropomorphized characteristics of pards and felines. If one has the familiar spirit of a snake, on the other hand, one has the power to summon the rain, is shrewd in commercial transactions, something of a hoarder, and very affiliative in social groups, and tends to be a leader in a quiet way. In their theory of homeopathic medicine, the Zapotec believe that the successful curer has the same spirit familiar as the patient, since only a fellow spirit recognizes the variability in illness symptomatology and is able to control for idiosyncratic, i.e., personality, interpretations.

Likewise, it would be unfair to conclude that the Zapotec are unaware of their own internal, emotional states. They have a rich descriptive lexicon of emotion, and they believe that it, too, has explanatory value for the understanding of illnesses, particularly the class of illnesses that we classify as "folk illnesses." Fitzsimmons (1972) has shown that they track the course of illnesses by monitoring emotional states, and he has been able to map the monitoring process by utilizing the Helmreich (1971) Mood Adjective Check List and the Taylor (1953) Manifest Anxiety Scale. But it is equally clear that however much they admit their theory of psychology to the study of their own internal states, they do not have a companion theory, such as we do, that internal states have explanatory power for understanding social relations.

Generality of the Result

I cannot claim to have researched the literature fully, but I have the hunch that this result is quite general for small-scale, traditional societies, where face-to-face interaction is the dominant mode of social intercourse, and I can adduce some corroborating evidence. A remark by Oscar Lewis strikes me as being very relevant; he points out that the villagers of Tepotztlan (which is an ancient town like the community I have studied) do not "know each other" very well, despite the fact that they are relatives and have been living cheek by jowl for centuries. This squares with my intuitions, and the explanation lies not in deficient powers of observation or lack of empathetic concern for neighbors and kinsmen but in the fact that it does not matter whether you rationalize the causes for other people's behavior in terms of their motives, traits, and cognitive sets — one's relations with them are coded and decoded in sociological terms. The townsmen of Tepoztlan, like the Zapotec, do not have to know each other very well to get along; rather, they have to be good sociologists and epistemologists, know their social theory well, and know how to construct an adequate world view by utilizing sociological, rather than psychological, concepts. Gearing, in an offbeat and sensitive study of the Fox Indians of North America, has recently commented in a similar way:

Our contemporary Western life draws into sharpest focus the birth and continuing flow of experience and the resulting personal qualities of mind of individual human organisms; when we meet another we want to know where he has been, what he has done, what kind of man he has become, and where he seems to be going. As for that other definition of reality, enduring organization, we of course must continually act in its terms and are therefore aware of it at some level of mental activity. We think often, for example, of those aspects of organization that affect and express ranked status. But it seems that we rarely think about enduring organization with clarity and direction and completeness, except under special circumstances (as when we are required to describe the table of organization of a factory). To appear to think consistently in everyday life about one's social positions and the positions of one's fellow seems, to us, a little indecent.

For the Fox, the emphasis appears to be reversed. The primary reality habitually considered with full awareness by a Fox, somewhat systematically and with clarity and direction, is enduring organization. A Fox, I think in retrospect, sees another most correctly and precisely when he views him as an incumbent in a social slot, sees him moving into the slot, occupying it at the moment and acting appropriately or not, and moving out. Primary Fox reality is, I believe, such a system of social relations that endure.

I think of my friend: "Joe (who is a father . . .)." A Fox thinks of his friend: "This father (who is Joe . . .)" [1970:137f].

The Zapotec would agree and, in agreeing, would deny the validity of explanations of social behavior based on the individual and see psychological (trait-based) explanation as another perverse foolishness of Western man, who unwittingly has taken a folk model based on his propensity for internal attributions as a scientific model, thereby failing to make the critical domain distinctions not only between meaning and behavior but also between rationalization and theory.

References

Aderman, David and Leonard Berkowitz
    1970   Observational set, empathy, and helping, *Journal of Personality and Social Psychology* **14,** 141–148.
Aronson, Elliot
    1972   *The social animal.* San Francisco: Freeman.
Bales, R. F.
    1969   *Personality and interpersonal behavior.* New York: Holt.
Becker, H.
    1963   *Outsiders: Studies in the sociology of deviance.* New York: Free Press.
    1964   *The other side: Perspective on deviance.* New York: Free Press.
    1971   Labeling theory revisited. Paper delivered at the British Sociological Association Meetings, March 1971.
Borgatta, E. F., L. S. Cottrell, and J. H. Mann.
    1958   The spectrum of individual interaction characteristics: An interdimensional analysis, *Psychological Reports* **4,** 279–319.
D'Andrade, Roy
    1965   Trait psychology and componential analysis. In *Formal semantic analysis,* edited by E. A. Hammel. Menasha, Wisconsin: American Anthropological Association.
    1972   Symbols, memory and behavior. Unpublished manuscript. Univ. of California, San Diego.
Douglas, Jack (editor)
    1970   *Deviance and respectability.* New York: Basic Books.
Fitzsimmons, Charles
    1972   A case study of *Susto* in the Zapotec Pueblo of Teotitlan del Valle, Oaxaca, Mexico. Unpublished manuscript. Univ. of Texas, Austin.
Gearing, Frederick
    1970   *The face of the fox.* Chicago: Aldine.
Goffman, Erving
    1960   *Asylums.* New York: Doubleday.

Hartshorne, H. and M. A. May
  1928 *Studies in the nature of character,* vol. 1: *Studies in deceit.* New York: Wiley.
Heider, Fritz
  1958 *The psychology of interpersonal relations.* New York: Wiley.
Helmreich, Robert
  1971 The Tektite 2 human behavior program. *Office of Naval Research Technical Report No. 14.*
Hotchkiss, John
  1969 Children and conduct in a Ladino community of Chiapas, Mexico, *American Anthropologist* **69,** 711–718.
Jones, E. E. and K. E. Davis
  1965 From acts to dispositions. In *Advances in experimental social psychology,* vol. 2., edited by L. Berkowitz. New York: Academic Press.
Jones, Edward E. and Richard E. Nisbett
  1971 *The actor and the observer: Divergent perceptions of the causes of behavior.* Morristown, New Jersey: General Learning Press.
Kanouse, David
  1971 *Labeling, language and attribution.* Morristown, New Jersey: General Learning Press.
Kelley, Harold H.
  1967 Attribution theory in social psychology. In *Nebraska symposium on motivation,* edited by D. Levine. Lincoln: Univ. of Nebraska Press.
Lazarus, Richard S.
  1966 *Psychological stress and the coping process.* New York: McGraw-Hill.
Lemert, Edwin
  1951 *Social pathology.* New York: McGraw-Hill.
  1967 *Human deviance, social problems and social control.* Englewood Cliffs, New Jersey: Prentice-Hall.
Mann, R. D.
  1959 The relation between personality characteristics and individual performance in small groups. Ph.D. dissertation. Univ. of Michigan.
Mischel, Walter
  1968 *Personality and assessment.* New York: Wiley.
Passini, Frank T. and Warren T. Norman
  1966 A universal perception of personality structure? *Journal of Personality and Social Psychology* **4,** 44–49.
Rotter, J. B.
  1966 Generalized expectancies for internal versus external control of reinforcement, *Psychological Monographs* **80,** 1.
Rubington, Earl and Martin S. Weinberg (editors)
  1968 *Deviance: The interactionist perspective.* New York: Macmillan.
Scheff, Thomas
  1966 *Becoming mentally ill.* Chicago: Aldine.
Selby, H. A.
  1974 *Zapotec deviance: The convergence of folk and modern sociology.* Austin: Univ. of Texas Press.
Szasz, T.
  1961 *The myth of mental illness.* New York: Harper & Row.
Tagiuri, Renato
  1969 Person perception. In *Handbook of social psychology,* vol. 3, edited by G.

Lindzey and E. Aronson. Pp. 395–449. Reading, Massachusetts: Addison-Wesley.

Taylor, J. A.
  1953 A personality scale of manifest anxiety, *Journal of Abnormal and Social Psychology* **48**, 285–290.

Walster, Elaine
  1966 Assignment of responsibility for an accident, *Journal of Personality and Social Psychology* **3**, 73–79.

How to Enter a Yakan House

CHARLES O. FRAKE

Even if Poor-Boy was asked to come up to the porch, he wouldn't come up. Finally he came up to the top of the ladder. For two days the Sultan's daughter kept telling him to come inside. Even her parents told him. For two days Poor-Boy was there at the top of the ladder. Finally he ventured onto the porch. After three more days he approached as far as the floor beam at the doorway. For three days he was there. Even when he was given clothes he wouldn't wear them. Even when he was given money he wouldn't take it. After four days he finally went inside from the doorway floor beam. Then, because he was already there inside, he and the Sultan's daughter were able to get married. But after they had been married a long time, he still hadn't slept with his wife. He had not yet entered the room of the Sultan's daughter.

— excerpt from a Yakan story

The Yakan construe Poor-Boy's plight as humorous because he is acting out a parody of cultural expectations governing the occupancy of a physical setting for a social encounter. These expectations derive from a cultural code that defines distinctive settings in and around a house, the sequence whereby one moves through settings, and the signals for initiating and terminating moves. To one who knows the code, variations in performances signal something about the social occasion at hand. A record of actual performances, matched with informants' interpretations of performances as appropriate, awkward, gracious, hostile, self-conscious, ridiculous, insincere, etc., provides evidence for the existence and character of the code. Our purpose is neither to describe what has happened nor to predict what will happen, but to set forth what one needs to know in order to make sense of what does happen. To the extent that we succeed, our statement is a description of that portion of Yakan culture of which these behaviors are an artifact.

The domain of behavior being considered is special in several ways. One way in which it is special for the anthropologist is that it is not at all special for the people being studied. Entering a house is commonplace, everyday activity. It is high-frequency behavior, and it is also incidental behavior. It is not planned and performed for its own sake but occurs as

25

an incident within some encompassing event. When a Yakan is queried about his plans for tomorrow, he is not likely to reply: "Well, the first thing I'm going to do is go out and enter a house." Another special feature of this behavior is that its domain is defined by the spatial boundaries within which it occurs. We are concerned with the various behaviors that occur in a given setting, rather than taking a given kind of behavior and considering, as one of its attributes, the various settings in which it occurs. Finally, the performances involved are largely verbal.[1] The topic, then, is an example of high-frequency, incidental speech behavior entailed in the occupancy of a behavior setting.

The Yakan are Philippine Moslems inhabiting the island of Basilan, which lies just off the southwestern point of Mindanao at the northeastern end of the Sulu Archipelago.[2] They are strictly land-oriented agriculturists, in contrast to the sea-oriented Moslems, the Samal, who inhabit coastal villages around the island. The northern portion of Basilan is occupied by Filipino Christians. The Yakan live in dispersed neighborhoods of nuclear family dwellings organized into small, local political units based on Mosque affiliation. Warfare among these political units, as well as against Christians and other Moslem groups (notably the Taw Sug), is endemic. The weaponry includes not only locally made spears, swords, and shotguns but also the latest in U.S. military small arms — a fact not without relevance to the construction of a Yakan house.

The Yakan house (*lumaq*) is a rectangular, ridge-roofed, single-room dwelling raised on piles some two to three meters off the ground. A cooking shed of similar structure but smaller dimensions is attached by a platform to either end of the house. Floor space varies from about 30 to 100 m². Floors and walls are thickly planked. The floor has a hole or two drilled in it for betel expectoration, and the end wall opposite the cooking shed has a window opening, either very small or securely sealable. The steeply pitched, concave-sided roof is thatched. The main

---

[1] That is to say, my observations have been restricted largely to the verbal aspects of house-entering performances. A large amount of nonverbal signaling, which has escaped my attention, undoubtedly takes place. The present account suffers accordingly. For a study of nonverbal greeting performances in American society, see Kendon and Ferber (1973).

[2] Field work among the Yakan was conducted in 1962, 1963–1964, and 1965–1966 under a grant from the National Institute of Mental Health. Subsequent brief visits were made through 1972. During the course of this work, I was a member of two Yakan households in different areas of Basilan. I have performed as both an insider and an outsider in house-entering events. Yakan critiques of my performances, often awkward or unintentionally humorous, have made me painfully aware of the problematic nature of everyday behavior.

room has two doorways, one connecting to the platform leading to the cooking shed, the other, located midway along one side, leading to a roofed porch running the length of the house. Ladders or notched poles connect both porch and cooking shed platform to the ground. Individual houses are dispersed in fields and groves and are never attached to other structures. There is no physically demarcated house yard. Houses vary in construction details: A few have bamboo rather than planked walls; a regrettably increasing number substitute a hotter, less aesthetically pleasing, more expensive, but more prestigeful galvanized-iron roof for the traditional thatch; and an occasional house lacks a porch — the only variation relevant to the present discussion.[3] (Sultans' daughters may have private rooms, but there are no sultans to be found in the Yakan habitat.[4]) In spite of these variations, any Yakan dwelling is easily distinguishable from the homes of other ethnic groups, either Christian or Moslem, on Basilan.

Yakan dwellings are also easily distinguishable from other structures built by the Yakan: field huts, graves, and mosques. Field huts are simply temporary work shelters built in fields that are some distance from the owner's residence. Graves are ditched mounds topped with a carved and painted boatlike structure and clustered with other graves in groves of ritual trees. Mosques are similar in size and structure to dwellings, except that the porch is at one end, which is unwalled. At the other end is a projecting semicircular apse. Houses, mosques, and graves all differ in orientation. The long walls of a house are aligned along the east–west axis, with the wall opposite the doorway — known as the 'head wall' (*kokan lumaq*) — facing 'up-slope' (*padiataq*).[5] "Up-slope" is a conventional directional axis at right angles to the east–west axis but oriented northward in southern Basilan and southward in northern Basilan. Mosques are oriented with their long walls aligned with the Meccan axis (*kiblat*) so that the apse faces Mecca. In Basilan the Meccan axis points WNW. Graves are oriented along the 'Meccan axis of the dead' (*kiblat mamateyin*), at right angles to the Meccan axis proper, so that a body lying on its right side is facing Mecca (Figure 1).

Field huts, graves, and mosques all have specialized social functions,

---

[3] The porch of some houses lacks a roof, which extends the domain of the "inclement weather unless clause" (to be discussed) and thereby restricts the range of events likely to be held on the porch.

[4] Since the time of field work, the titular 'chief' (*datuq*) of the Yakan (who is of Christian descent) has proclaimed himself a sultan (*sūtan*). He lives in a largely Christian market town in a Western-style house that, to be sure, has private rooms.

[5] An acceptable alternative arrangement, occasionally employed, is to have the head wall facing west.

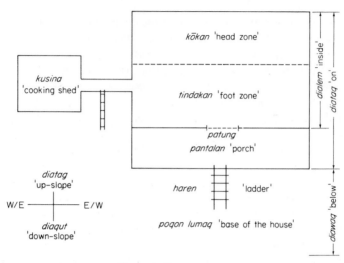

Figure 1. *House settings.*

whereas the limited variety of physical locales afforded by a Yakan house must serve as settings for a wide variety of social events. The Yakan conceptually organize the space within and around a house into an arrangement of discrete settings (Figure 1).[6] These settings are labeled hierarchically (Table 1). In locating people, objects, and events

TABLE 1
Terminology of House Settings

1.	*si bihing lumaq*	'in the vicinity of the house'
2.	*si lumaq*	'at the house'
2.1.	*diawaq*	'below'
2.1.1.	*si poqon lumaq*	'at the base of the house' (foot of the ladder)
2.2.	*diataq*	'on'
2.2.1.	*si bukut, si pantalan*	'outside' (= "in back"), 'on the porch'
2.2.2.	*dialem*	'inside'
2.2.2.1.	*si tindakan*	'at the foot zone'
2.2.2.2.	*si kōkan*	'at the head zone'
2.2.3.	*si kusina*	'in the cooking shed'
2.3.	*silung*	'underneath'

[6] There are two alternative locations of the ladder. The one shown in Figure 1 was selected for diagramatic convenience. It is actually somewhat more common to locate the ladder at the end of the porch away from the cooking shed. This positioning of the ladder allows more space between the entrance to "on" and the entrance to "inside," a more comfortable arrangement for large parties of outsiders, since they can fill space on the porch niche without moving away from the access point to "inside."

with respect to a house, one can select a level of contrast according to the degree of specificity required. Saying that someone or something is 'at a house' (*si lumaq*) can denote any setting closer than 'in the vicinity of a house' (*si bihing lumaq*). Using 'on' (*diataq*) a house denotes any setting above 'below' (*diawaq*). There is no physical demarcation of the outer limits of "in the vicinity," nor of the boundary between "vicinity" and "below." "Vicinity" is any position within sight and calling range of a house. "Below" is any position on the ground below (but not "underneath") the house within normal conversation range with someone "on" the house. The boundary between "below" and "on" is marked by the kitchen and porch ladders. Since the kitchen is a private "back room" reserved for household members, its ladder is not a normal access to the house for outsiders. The area of "below" directly in front of the bottom of the porch ladder is known as the 'base of the house' (*poqon lumaq*). The boundary between "outside" (on the porch) and "inside" (the main room) is marked by a 'floor beam' (*patung*) that runs along the base of the wall fronting the porch and appears at the doorway slightly raised above the floor. Poor-Boy exemplifies a common use of the *patung* as a sitting place neither clearly inside nor outside. The top of the ladder provides a similar niche neither clearly below nor on. At night, or when no householders are at home, these access points are removed. Ladders are raised and doorways barred shut. 'Inside' (*dialem*) is further divided into 'head zone' (*kōkan*) and 'foot zone' (*tindakan*, literally 'kicking zone'), the "head zone" being the portion of floor space adjacent to the head wall opposite the doorway. The head zone is the sleeping area for household members. During the day, when sleeping mats are rolled up, it is simply bare floor, physically undistinguishable, but conceptually quite distinct, from the adjoining "foot zone" floor space. The head wall, not the entrance wall, defines the "front" of the house facing "up-slope." From the perspective of a person inside the house, someone on the porch is 'in back' (*si bukut*). This means that one enters a Yakan house through what is conceptually the back door, there being no entrance in front.

The physical arrangement of household settings, together with the hierarchical structure of their terminology, reflect the sequence of positions through which an outsider must pass in gaining entrance to a house. One can characterize a social encounter between householder and outsider by the degree of penetration of household settings achieved by the outsider, penetration being measured by the number of moves across setting boundaries required to reach a given position. Thus, to achieve maximal penetration to the head zone requires the following moves:

1. from "vicinity" to "at"
2. from "below" to "on"
3. from "on" to "inside"
4. from "foot zone" to "head zone"

The accomplishment of these moves requires displays of proper etiquette (*addat*) by both the householder and the outsider. (Terms for describing these routines, together with some examples of specific formulas, are listed in the Appendix). Proper etiquette requires the householder to 'render attention' (*asip*) to the outsider; the outsider, in turn, should 'display respect' (*moqo mātabat*). The householder issues 'invitations' (*pellun*) to advance to the next setting—each move has its unique invitation—and proffers provisions requisite to social engagements in each setting: tobacco or betel quids on the porch, snacks or a meal inside. The outsider's display of respect requires that he never withdraw from a setting without asking 'permission to leave' (*baqid*) and receiving this permission from the householder, usually in the form of a drawled *aweq* 'OK', an expression that is a hallmark of the Yakan.

Grammatically, invitations appear as active imperatives, requiring the use of a second-person pronoun optionally accompanied by a term of address. The use of a term of address, selected on the basis of age, sex, kinship, and title, enables marking of status relationships and expression of special affect, but, since this use is optional and pronoun selection is indifferent to status, invitations can be issued in a status-unmarked form.[7] It is not the form of the invitation so much as the context of its issuance that carries social meaning.

Gross categories of household entrance events can be sorted out according to the number of verbal engagements that occur in occupying their ultimate setting. First, by manner of entrance, we can easily distinguish two classes of people: class one, those who can legally enter a house, penetrating to any setting without pause and without saying a word; and class two, those who cannot proceed beyond the setting "below" without a verbal invitation from a member of class one. Class one consists of all the residents of the household; class two consists of all other persons. This contrast between interaction among those who have legal free access to a setting and interaction and those who do not pertains to all behavior settings. Any Yakan behavior setting—house, mosque, field, water hole, trail—is public to the social group whose

---

[7] Yakan address term usage is similar to that of their close linguistic kin, the Balangingi Samal, as described by Geoghegan (1969).

members have legal free-access rights, and private to all others.[8] An outsider cannot enter a setting private to him without an invitation from an insider. A violation of this rule will be interpreted not simply as humorous, discourteous, or stupid but as downright illegal. The offender has violated a proprietory relationship and is subject to legal penalties, if not to on-the-spot elimination. The concern of this study is with how an outsider enters a private setting; the patterns of informal interaction among householders will be ignored.

The second major cut we can make sorts not people but kinds of occasions. There are events that enable outsiders, after receipt of a distinctive greeting reserved for such occasions, to immediately approach the house, climb the stairs, and enter without pauses or further verbal exchanges along the way. These events all share the property of having been scheduled in advance. We will set them aside for later consideration.

In order to uncover the meaning of household entrance, we focus initially on cases involving the unscheduled arrival of one or more outsiders, situations of uncertainty in which the acts of householder and outsider become informative signals of the other party's intentions as well as strategic devices to further one's own intentions. This uncertainty, together with the fact that neither party can uniquely determine the outcome, gives household entrance a gamelike character. There are two players: householder and outsider. The game goes through a fixed sequence of plays corresponding to the sequence of household settings. At each stage of play except the last, one of three outcomes is possible: terminate, hold, or advance. In the last stage advance is not a possible outcome. The outcome of a play is the product of the respective moves by each player.

The initiation of play is up to the outsider; it is he who has the option of appearing on the scene or not. As he comes to the "vicinity" of the house, he can adopt one of two strategies: 'making a pass' (*palabey*) or 'approaching' (*pasōng*). In making a pass, the outsider simply walks on by a regular trail. The rule in this situation is that if any householder is visible, then permission to pass must be called out. If no householder is visible, no interaction will take place. A householder, upon receiving a call for permission to pass, has the option of immediately granting it by

---

[8] Frake (1969) describes a relationship of 'legitimate interest' (*dapuq*) that can pertain between an individual and an object or another individual. "Legal free acess" is the *dapuq* relation applied to a behavior setting. The *dapuq lumaq* 'householders' are those with legal free acess to a house.

yelling back *aweq* 'OK', thereby terminating interaction, or he can pose a "customary question" (see Appendix). A "customary question," in this context, is subject to interpretation performatively either as a 'greeting' (*sagina*) or as a real question inviting further interaction. An exchange of greetings, whereby interaction is initiated by a customary question (e.g., *Where are you headed for?*) and terminated by a customary response (e.g., *Over there yonder someplace*), is an interaction sequence appropriate to encounters taking place in a setting, such as in town or on a trail, to which both parties have legal free access. In a hosted encounter, where one participant is an outsider, such an exchange is not appropriate. The outsider is accountable for justifying his presence on the scene. Provided that the trail is a public setting for the passer-by, a construal by both participants of the question–response exchange as a simple greeting exchange terminating further interaction is possible. Of course, further interaction after a greeting can occur. The desire for continuance is signaled by the nature and elaborateness of questions and responses, in effect, the mutual construing of grammatical interrogatives as performative questions. Further signals for continuance include requests for betel and tobacco and, I am sure, nonverbal gestures and posturings that have escaped my observation. Unlike a trail encounter, however, the passing-by scene is conducted not at normal conversation range but at calling range. Furthermore, one participant is in a setting private to him. For continued interaction to take place, the outsider must approach the house (which at this point, having adopted the "making a pass" strategy, he can do only upon invitation), or the householder must go out to the trail (in most circumstances a rather rude signal that no invitation to enter the house will be forthcoming). In either case the householder has control over the continuance of interaction. If the outsider accepts an invitation to come to the house, he approaches to "below" and house-entrance play begins.

If the outsider initially elects the option of approaching, he can enter "below" as far as the base of the ladder (*poqon lumaq*) and stand there. This move is functionally equivalent to a knock on the front door in our society. It is a "summons" (cf. Schegloff, 1968), albeit an inaudible one. It is incumbent on the householder to 'notice' (*batik*) the outsider standing there. He must answer the summons. Failure to notice is a serious breach of etiquette as well as an unusual lapse of security. The householder reveals that he has noticed by posing a "customary question," but in this case not as a greeting. A summons presupposes that the summoner has a topic of conversation to pose. A response to a summons, in the form of a question, is an invitation to the summoner to present something to talk about, something to justify his presence in a private setting. Change, or lack of change, in the householder's physical position is an important element of this summons–response sequence. The householder has the option of changing his position to one closer to that of the outsider. If he is inside, he may move to the porch. If he is on the porch, he may join the outsider below. The most unmarked position for the householder to assume initially is on the porch. This spot allows comfortable conversation with the outsider below while not ruling out the possibility of either early termination or prompt advance of the outsider to share the porch. For the householder to join the outsider below signals rather strongly that he wishes the engagement to advance no further. For the householder to remain inside, where conversation with someone below is somewhat difficult, is, depending on whether or not an invitation is forthcoming, a strong signal of either desired advance or desired termination. The householder cannot, in any case, withdraw to a setting further removed from the outsider before the encounter terminates.

Once play has been engaged, the interplay of moves by householder and outsider determines further progress through the sequence. Although the inventory of verbal routines seems rich, in fact there is a severe restriction on the kinds of moves available to each party. A householder can only invite; he cannot ask a guest to leave. An outsider can only ask permission to leave; he cannot invite himself further into the setting. These rules, though they sound familiar to us, are not so obvious as they seem. In Yakan social encounters where neither party has exclusive rights of free access to the setting, the rules are quite different. For example, if two people meet and engage in conversation on a public trail, it is perfectly polite for one party to terminate the interaction by saying: *You go now.* Similarly, in public settings one party can freely request tobacco or betel from the other, behavior that would be a violation of etiquette by an outsider in a private setting. The rules for making moves in house entrance give the householder explicit control over who can come into each of the settings under his control, and give the outsider control over termination of the event. The householder can prevent advance by not signaling invitation; the outsider can prevent termination by not signaling permission to leave. Once a signal has been sent, the other party can accede to it, or he can make a countermove returning play to its original state. These possibilities can be represented by a gamelike matrix (Figure 2).

If both parties do the same thing, either both move or both not move, play holds in the same setting. If householder moves and outsider does not, play advances to the next setting. If outsider moves and householder does not, play terminates.

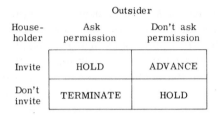

Figure 2. *Matrix of invitation–permission outcomes.*

The gamelike performances I have been describing occur when the rules of house entrance are applied in encounters whose course and outcome are initially uncertain. Household entrance loses its gamelike character when guests arrive for a scheduled event. In such cases a 'prior invitation' (*pasan*) has been issued. The issuance of an 'invitation' (*pellun*) to advance upon arrival is predictable and uninformative. Householders greet approaching guests with a call of 'approach' (*pasōng*), a blanket invitation to move up to the setting appropriate to the occasion. "Conferences," "negotiations," and "litigation" are generally held on the porch (Frake, 1969). The householder is providing a setting but is not really a host. Religious rites, shamanistic seances, life cycle celebrations, and weddings are held inside.[9] The householder is a host and must provide food for his guests. Rituals are held at the "head zone," with functionaries entitled to a position there throughout the duration of the gathering. The unscheduled arrival of a very high-status person heralds a special event calling for immediate blanket invitation and procuring of the provisions to make a formal scene. At the opposite extreme of formality are the daily routines of householders themselves, who may freely pass through settings without ritual. Thus, the etiquette of household entrance is simplest at the two extremes of the formality scale of events, precisely the cases in which there is minimal ambiguity about what is going on. It is in the ambiguous cases, in which house entrance etiquette becomes a way of defining the formality of the occasion, and not simply a reflection of predetermined formality, that moves become complex and their outcomes informative.

There is one occasion, however, when the Yakan make fun of their code of house entrance, staging an elaborate parody of the whole procedure. The occasion is the event of "fetching the bride," which takes

[9] At very large gatherings guests may be fed outside and many participants may remain outside most or all the time. All, however, have been officially invited in and may enter the house freely.

place on the first night of the three-day wedding ceremony. The bride must be taken by the groom's party from a house where she is secluded to the house where the wedding ceremony will be performed. At the approach of the groom's party, the bride's party is jammed onto the porch, forming a tight barricade at the top of the ladder. The groom's party is interrogated at length in a parody of the routine of "customary questions." They are required to put on singing, dancing, and oratorical performances before finally being allowed up to the porch. There, mock accusations are hurled at the groom's party. Trials are held and fines extracted before the groom's party is allowed inside, where snacks are served while mock arguments continue over the bride price (an issue settled, in fact, long before), the qualifications of witnesses, the whereabouts of allegedly key representatives of the groom, and so on. Finally, as dawn approaches, members of the groom's party are allowed to go to the "head zone" and fetch the bride from under a canopy. Permission to leave each setting is not granted until token fees are paid to the bride's party. The bride, despite being tightly veiled, hangs onto doorway and porch posts until the groom's party pays up. Poor-Boy's performance, then, was only an exaggeration of what every groom goes through—a parody of a parody.

House entrance rules have restrictions in scope: They are not for kids and they are not for sex. Children do not have authority to invite outsiders in, but as outsiders they can enter freely without formality—a fact that makes them useful as message and gossip carriers (cf. Hotchkiss, 1967). If householder and outsider are of opposite sex, sexually mature, and without other companions on the scene, household entrance is a new game with a new set of rules, including legal rules that proscribe, but by no means prevent, the issuance of an invitation to enter.

One other special contingency deserves mention. Some houses lack porches, thereby eliminating a behavior setting from the sequence. Such houses, generally small and bamboo walled, are restricted to a few relatively poor people, often widowed or divorced women heading partial-family households. Lack of a porch condemns one to a somewhat marginal position socially, since there are a wide variety of informal events that one cannot host. When a visitor arrives, he must be invited in right away if a sustained social encounter is to take place. The only house that did not have a porch in the community where I spent most of my time belonged to a young divorcee who did not participate much in social affairs but was allegedly very hospitable to male visitors.

Any set of rules for social behavior also has its "unless" clauses that may be invoked at times of unpredicted crises. The inclement weather unless clause permits a traveler caught in the rain to seek shelter (*pa-*

saindung) underneath a house, calling up an announcement of his presence. He can generally expect to be invited up. This is the only situation in which 'underneath' (*silung*) a house becomes a setting for outsider–householder interaction. The refugee unless clause covers eloping couples, people fleeing from enemies, and people forced to evacuate their homes because of hostilities or some natural disaster such as fire. It also covers a large class of people, called in Yakan *wantid,* sought by Philippine authorities. In emergencies all such people can expect entrance into houses of friends, kin, and allies without worrying about the niceties of etiquette. Sometimes, when rules have been broken on the grounds of emergency, there is room for argument over whether the emergency was serious enough to justify the violation. A divorce case arose when a woman, caught out at night in a sudden rainstorm, took shelter in the house of her husband's brother who was alone at the time. The husband claimed that his brother should have broken the rule of granting shelter in times of inclement weather rather than breaking the rule of not spending the night with someone else's wife.

The everyday behavior of Yakan house-entering routines bears on at least three general problems in the understanding of social encounters: the analysis of speech acts in actual performative contexts; the use of these verbal performances to situate events both physically in space and conceptually along a dimension of formality; and the relation between actual performances and the "rules" for their interpretation.

Yakan invitation–permission routines represent a genre of speech act sequences concerned with the progress and termination of social encounters. Summons–response sequences and greeting exchanges are other genres concerned with the initiation of encounters and the mutual recognition of participants. The illocutionary force (Searle, 1969) of a given utterance is a product of the outcome of a sequence of utterances and nonverbal signals exchanged between two parties. It cannot be determined from an analysis, no matter how deeply pursued, of the structure of an isolated utterance. It cannot be matched with the grammatical form of an utterance. What is grammatically an interrogative may be used performatively as a summons response, a greeting, a request, or, on occasion, to ask a question (Hymes, 1971). Similar kinds of speech acts seem to appear everywhere, but their diversity and complexity are such that a complete inventory and description of performative genres can be achieved only by careful ethnographic description of speech behavior. The research method of current theoretical linguistics — conjuring up examples from inside the theoretician's head — is not sufficient. The anthropologist's distinction between "terms of reference" and "terms of address" represents a naive and incorrect typology of speech acts. What is "address"? A greeting? A summons? A tag? The use of a proper noun in any speech act?

Rather than removing events from their temporal and spatial context and grouping them under functional rubrics such as economic, religious, or legal, we have here been experimenting with a sorting of events by the setting they occupy, in this case a house. Unlike our own culture, in which we have special settings for many kinds of events — classrooms for classes, churches for religious rites, law courts for litigation, concert halls for music — among the Yakan a single structure, the house, provides a setting for a great variety of social occasions. But a house, even a one-roomed Yakan house, is not just space. It is a structured sequence of settings where social events are differentiated not only by the position in which they occur but also by the positions the actors have moved through to get there and the manner in which they have made those moves. There is first of all a contrast between "insiders," those who have legal free access to the setting, and "outsiders." Social events involving only insiders proceed differently from those in which some participants are outsiders. For one thing, an outsider cannot enter a setting without an invitation from an insider. Any interaction in which all participants are outsiders is thereby illegal. These rules apply to all Yakan behavior settings: mosques, cemeteries, fields, etc., as well as houses.

A second, and independent, dimension of social events displayed by house-entering behavior is that of "formality." We can say, for example, that Yakan litigation, which takes place on a porch, thereby requiring only one move to reach and involving no feasting, is a less formal activity than a ceremony of graduation from Koranic school, which takes place inside and involves rites at the "head zone" and provision of festive food by the host. Formality is a cultural marking of social events as special, a phenomenon akin to what is called marking in linguistic theory (see Greenberg, 1966). A marked category is signaled by adding something to an unmarked category. In language it may be voicing, nasalization, an affix, or a component of meaning. Social events are marked in our society by things like neckties, refined speech, fancy food, and explicit rules of etiquette. Social events in a Yakan house are marked by, among other things, the degree of penetration required for an outsider to reach their setting. Marked social events, like marked linguistic forms, occur less frequently than corresponding unmarked categories. In language, marking often neutralizes contrasts appearing within the unmarked category: fewer nasal vowels than oral vowels, fewer case distinctions in the plural than in the singular, etc. Similarly marked social occasions often allow abeyance of social distinctions relevant elsewhere.

Formality is a dimension of social events in all cultures, but there are differences not only in the number of differentiations of degree of formality but also in the way different kinds of events are positioned on this scale. Among the Yakan, house-entering behavior reveals three degrees of formality, corresponding to porch, "foot zone," and "head zone" of the house.[10] Litigation falls into the least formal category. Among the Subanun, a Philippine pagan group, the formality scale is binary; events either are formal, requiring festive food and drink, or they are not. Subanun litigation is a formal event. Subanun houses, it is interesting to note, lack porches. One is either inside or below (Frake, 1964, 1969).

This study purports to describe a code for interpreting the speech acts (including nonverbal moves) involved in occupying the behavior settings of a house. The code can be considered as the "competence" a person must have to play the game of entering a Yakan house. Actual performances, however, are not automatically "generated" by this competence. Participants make use of it to send and read messages whereby they construct — give an interpretable structure to — a particular social encounter. The shared expectations of participants derived from this competence provides a background against which special meanings — hostility, affection, humor — can be marked. The expression of humor, especially, is highly valued and ever present among the Yakan. Even their rites, as we have seen, often portray, not symbolic representations of underlying metaphysical oppositions, but jokes on themselves. The Yakan play with, bend, and break their codes for fun. House entrance etiquette is no exception. Teen-age girls will approach a friend's house and yell out, *Hey, start cooking; we're here!* a gross violation of the "rules" that, in another context, could cause deep trouble. The problem is that a rule violation signaling humor in one situation may signal hostility in another. One must bend the rules with care, for expression of hostility, ridicule, or scorn can be very dangerous. Violence, as well as humor, is a fact of Yakan life. One must be constantly on guard. Not even the most formal scheduled event can be depended on to unfold according to the rules. One party of guests, upon approaching the site of a major celebration, was greeted with a shower of spears causing several deaths, an incident in a long, bloody feud. The rules of house-entering etiquette presented here will not enable you to predict when you might be greeted with a spear instead of a speech act, but they will tell you that if you are, you, like the victims in the incident just described, have a right to be surprised.

---

[10] A complete analysis of formality contrasts among Yakan events would, of course, require consideration of events held in other settings. In mosques, for example, formal events are held whose participants all have legal free access to the setting.

Appendix
Yakan Terminology and Formulas
of House-Entering Etiquette

addat custom, appropriate behavior; habitual or typical behavior

pagaddatan behaving appropriately toward someone; showing respect

mātabat respect

moqo mātabat display respect

asip attending to a guest, rendering a guest his due according to *addat*

batik noticing, verbally responding to a summons, the obligation of a householder to verbally acknowledge the approach to "below" (a summons) of an outsider. A typical formula is *kaqu hep yuq* 'So it's you there!' (an assertion that is invariably correct), followed by a greeting.

sagina a verbal greeting (a nonverbal greeting is *salam*). Yakan greetings are, grammatically, always questions. The proper use of greetings and greeting responses is *addat magtilewin* 'questioning custom.' Typical greeting formulas, grammatical questions to which terms of address may be added, are the following:

> *amban kew* 'Where are you coming from?'
>
> *tungan kew* 'Where are you going?' (not appropriately asked of someone who has approached to "below")
>
> *sine saweqnun* 'Who's your companion?' (most appropriately posed as a greeting to someone who is alone)
>
> *ine binoqonu lu* 'What are you carrying there?' (most appropriately asked of someone who is carrying something the identity of which is obvious, a string of fish, for example – otherwise the utterance would be subject to construal performatively as a real question.)

pellun on-the-spot invitation to advance in a household setting. An invitation issued beforehand to come to some later event is *pasan*. Typical invitation (*pellun*) formulas, grammatical active imperatives to which terms of address can be added, are the following:

> *pesōng be kaqam* 'Approach you-all!' (a blanket invitation to immediately proceed to the appropriate setting for a scheduled event. Used only when a *pasan* has been issued beforehand.)
>
> *pitu be kew* 'come' (to below)
>
> *manaqik be kew* 'climb up' (to the porch)
>
> *parialem be kew* 'enter' (to inside)

segeq to persist in a *pellun* in spite of outsider's requests for permission to leave

ohatan to hold a guest, dissuade him from leaving by persistent invitations to advance, to eat, to confer, etc.

baqid asking permission to leave or pass through a setting with respect to which the speaker is an outsider. Typical formulas, grammatically active declarative sentences, are the following:

> *moleq ne ku* 'I'm leaving now'
>
> *hap lumaq ne ku* 'I'm going home now'

palanjal ne kami 'We're continuing on' (said when the encounter has not proceeded beyond "below")

pitu du kami 'We'll be on our way' (said when the encounter has not proceeded beyond "vicinity")

tiaq kami palabey ēq 'We'll just pass by, huh' (permission to pass by)

ngaweq the granting of permission. Typical formulas are the following:

aweq 'OK'
anduquq 'a pity' (formal or jocular)
gaq kaqam legga 'You weren't treated badly?' (jocular)

References

Frake, Charles O.
  1964   How to ask for a drink in Subanun, *American Anthropologist* **66,** 127–32.
  1969   Struck by speech: The Yakan concept of litigation. In *Law in culture and society,* edited by L. Nader. Pp. 147–167. Chicago: Aldine.
Geoghegan, William
  1969   The use of marking rules in semantic systems, Working Paper no. 26. Berkeley, California: Language-Behavior Research Laboratory.
Greenberg, Joseph
  1966   Language universals. In *Current trends in linguistics,* vol. III: *Theoretical foundations,* edited by T. A. Sebeok. Pp. 61–112. The Hague: Mouton.
Hotchkiss, John
  1967   Children and conduct in a Ladino community of Chiapas, Mexico, *American Anthropologist* **69,** 711–718.
Hymes, Dell
  1971   Sociolinguistics and the ethnography of speaking. In *Social anthropology and language,* edited by E. Ardener. ASA Monograph no. 10. New York: Tavistock.
Kendon, Adam and Andrew Ferber
  1973   A description of some human greetings. In *Comparative ecology and behavior of primates,* edited by R. P. Michael and J. H. Crook. London: Academic Press.
Schegloff, Emanuel A.
  1968   Sequencing in conversation openings, *American Anthropologist* **70,** 1075–1095.
Searle, John R.
  1969   *Speech acts: An essay in the philosophy of language.* New York: Cambridge Univ. Press.

Cognition and Events[1]

Michael Agar

When an anthropologist enters an alien cultural setting, he is confronted with a number of humans who move around and make noises. His goal is to understand what the noises and movements mean to members of the group. At first, he probably recognizes some aspects of this behavior. For example, certain universal paralinguistic and kinesic indices of an affective state may be correctly interpreted (Ekman, Sorenson and Friesen, 1969). On the whole, though, most observed behavior will be confusing.

To begin to understand, the anthropologist must first impose some kind of basic order on this ongoing confusion. This first step usually consists of two basic analytical maneuvers — segmentation and decomposition. In segmentation, he places boundaries around some chunk of the ongoing confusion. In decomposition, he pulls various cooccurring pieces of this behavior apart. In the first case, he makes sequential divisions; in the second, simultaneous divisions.

These two processes can be illustrated by examining the behavior of a hypothetical linguist. First, he might decompose the ongoing behavior into verbal and nonverbal behavior. He would do this automatically by using a tape recorder, which would capture only the verbal material. Then he might segment the data into sentences. The two basic processes would result in the kind of data that linguists like, and he could then move into an analysis of phonology, syntax, and perhaps even semantics.

Even if he could render a thorough interpretation of any given sentence in the language, and the results were judged correct by native speakers, could he return to the ongoing behavior and understand the verbal material in the wider context of the ongoing interaction? He probably would not claim that he could. In fact, such an empirical problem

[1] An earlier version of this study was presented at the AAA meetings in Toronto, November 1972. The analysis of events, as applied to natural conversational data, appears in more elaborate form in Agar (1973). Tables 1, 2, and 3, taken from that volume, are used courtesy of Seminar Press.

motivated this paper. In my work with heroin addicts, I found that an understanding of addict argot was insufficient. After learning about 300 argot terms, I could render acceptable paraphrases of almost any given sentence that an addict might utter in interaction with other addicts. Yet even with this understanding I remained confused about the overall meaning of larger segments of ongoing interaction. My understanding was acceptable for sentences in isolation, but not for sentences in use. Other information is necessary.

There are at least two ways to approach this problem. In the first, one stays within the theoretical bounds of the linguistic description of sentences. Other information is pulled into the theory to interact with the particular sentence. There are many examples of this approach. McCawley (1968), for example, uses the notion of "discourse feature" to account for "politeness" morphemes in Japanese. Weinreich (1966) posits a "semantic calculator" that allows situational inputs to determine a variable range of grammatical deviance, e.g., more for a poetry reading, less for a business lecture.

Alternately, one can define the linguistic description of sentences as one component of something larger. There are numerous traditions illustrating this strategy, ranging from linguistics (Pike, 1967), anthropology (Gumperz and Hymes, 1972), and psychiatry (Scheflen, 1972) to sociology (Goffman, 1959) and psychology (Miller, Galanter, and Pribram, 1960). One then looks for other components that might be present in addition to the speaker's ability to produce single sentences. Possible examples of such other components include things like settings, participants, goals, etc. All components might interact with each other, with the output being the verbal (and nonverbal) behavior of the actor.

Of course, these approaches are not mutually exclusive but, rather, are different perspectives on the same problem. It is clear that we need to learn more about other components of communicative behavior, and it is equally clear that we need to specify how these interact in the production of a given sentence. For now, though, I want to emphasize the second approach. Let us surrender the segmented and decomposed sentences back into the ongoing stream of motion and noises, and look for an initial segmentation at a more inclusive level.

How should one begin? Rather than focusing on the way social scientists segment behavior, perhaps the actors themselves have a working knowledge whereby they segment the ongoing interaction. To the extent that they learned to do so, it must have been communicated to them as they learned the culture — culture in Goodenough's (1957) sense. Man's most flexible, efficient vehicle of communication is his language. Thus, we might expect that the events that are culturally important are frequently discussed and efficiently encoded as lexemes of the language. Naturally, this will not solve all our problems, but as Frake (1962) points out, it is certainly a good place to begin.

Events and Event Structure

I have mentioned the specific problem of addict behavior. For two years I worked as a cultural anthropologist at the National Institute of Mental Health Clinical Research Center in Lexington, Kentucky.[2] While there, I became interested in the notion of a "subculture of addiction." Most of the Lexington patients represented a type of narcotic addict labeled *righteous dope fiend, stone dope fiend,* or *street junkie.* Attributes of this type included use of heroin, obtaining of money or drugs through illegal means, and residence in urban areas. Black or white, young or old, New York or Chicago, *street junkies* who had previously not known each other seemed able to communicate over a wide range of topics in a manner not understandable to an outsider. Such a fact is a manifestation of a shared culture.

The first step in my study was the collection of addict argot. After collecting 300 items, I was able to understand almost any sentence. Although I could now understand observed or reported interaction much better, I remained confused about the overall meaning, partly because I did not understand the larger "unit" of which the sentence was a part. To give one example, consider this brief exchange:

SPEAKER A: *Say man, you got your works with you?*

SPEAKER B: *Yeah, they're right here in my pocket.*

After learning the argot, one can paraphrase *works* as "implements used to inject heroin" and correctly interpret the sentences.

Yet more than literal meaning is conveyed to a *street junkie* by the utterance of those sentences. They also signal that some event is being initiated by the communicative behavior of the actors. My initial attempt to relate the sentences to broader events was only partially correct; I assumed that the speakers were about to use heroin and, consequently, were concerned that a set of *works* was available.

Later I learned that the sentences also indicated concern with avoiding arrest. Possession of *works* is illegal in most states. Con-

[2] Research with heroin addicts was conducted while the author was a commissioned officer in the U.S. Public Health Service. Support by the Center, particularly the Social Science Section, is gratefully acknowledged.

sequently, the speakers in the example must be certain that the *works* can be easily disposed of if the police approach. To understand what is happening, then, a lexicon explaining the meaning of *works* is inadequate. Also needed is a broader knowledge of the events of which the sentences are a partial realization. In the example just mentioned, the nonjunkie must learn about using heroin, being arrested, and the relationships between the two before he can understand how the sentences relate to the *junkie's* notions of the events in his day-to-day life.

To begin an ethnography of events, I examined the argot and listened to addict speech in a search for lexically encoded examples. Three lexemes occurred with particularly high frequency. Logically enough, the three encoded highly significant, central events in the life of the *street junkie.* They were *hustle, cop,* and *get off.* First of all, I elicited some straightforward folk definitions of the lexemes. Meaning was almost always specified in terms of the purpose or desired outcome of the encoded event. An addict *hustles* to get *bread* ('money'); he *cops* to obtain *stuff* ('heroin'); and he *gets off* to get *straight* ('not sick').[3] Here are three event categories, defined by outcomes that might provide clues about more inclusive units of behavior.

Events, together with their outcomes, are not isolated units. Rather, events may be interrelated in a number of ways. By adding the notion of prerequisite, one type of event relationship becomes apparent. In order to perform an event whose outcome is desired, certain prerequisites are necessary. The linkage is defined when we consider the possibility that the outcome of one event may provide a prerequisite for another.

This prerequisite outcome linkage suggests a logical ordering and interdependence among events. Recall that the outcome of a *hustle* is *bread;* this is also a prerequisite for *copping.* The outcome of *copping* is *stuff,* which is a prerequisite for *getting off.* One outcome of *getting off* is to be *straight,* which is a prerequisite for *hustling.*

Of course, these prerequisite linkages are not the only possible ones. *Bread* could be obtained in any number of ways. A legitimate job could provide money, although the amount of money necessary to support most habits is usually not obtainable from ordinary jobs. A parent could give the addict money, although the same constraints operate here. Besides, skillful *hustling* is an attribute of high status in the *junkie* subculture (Agar, 1971). A similar situation holds true for *stuff.* A *junkie*

---

[3] Getting *straight* is only one outcome of *getting off.* The *rush* ('sensation as heroin enters the body'), the *high* ('feeling of well-being'), and the *nod* ('semiconscious drowsy state') are three other possibilities. Discussion here is restricted to the *straight* outcome, since it is the link to the *hustle* event. For a more detailed discussion of other outcomes, see Agar (1973).

might find some heroin or he might steal some, but little is lost by another *junkie,* and stealing is a risky business, since the *junkie* from whom one steals is likely to retaliate, and perhaps kill. In short, the linked events are not the only possible series, but they represent a series of usual or high-frequency, or "unmarked" (Geoghegan, 1973), event interrelationships.

This preliminary framework served as the starting point for a detailed analysis of conversational material that appears elsewhere (Agar, 1973). For the present, it is sufficient to note that the analysis, restricted to *copping* and *getting off,* indicated that other prerequisites were necessary before events could be performed. In order to *cop,* for example, an addict needs not only *bread* but also a *dealer.* To *get off,* he needs not only *stuff* but also a place and some *works* ('implements to inject the heroin').

It also became clear that some events with undesirable outcomes were implicit in event performances. As the addict acquired prerequisites for the events whose outcomes he wanted to produce, he was also acquiring prerequisites for events he wanted to prevent because of their negative outcome. When he has *bread* and a *dealer,* the prerequisites for *copping,* the addict may be *burned* ('receive less *stuff* than he pays for'). When he has *bread* or *stuff,* another *junkie* may *rip him off* ('physically confront him and take his goods'). If he has *stuff* or a set of *works* or both, there is legal evidence that can result in his arrest and conviction if someone is there to do the arresting (*the man*). When the appropriate prerequisites exist, then, one may anticipate the possible occurrence of an undesired event.

Further questions could, of course, be asked. For example, *hustle* is a cover term that includes many more specific named events. *Getting off* can be decomposed into several named stage–process categories. The cognitive structure presented here is at a quite inclusive level, and some of the gaps remaining to be filled in will be mentioned in more detail later. Other questions could be asked related to decision making. How do *junkies* select if there is more than one possible prerequisite for an event? How do they estimate the likelihood of an undesired event, given the necessary prerequisite conditions? Some of the many decisions made by a *junkie* in the performance of events were studied in detail elsewhere, both on a group (Agar, 1973) and an individual (Agar, 1974) level. For now, this question is ignored in favor of further discussion of the study of events.

In summary, several assertions have been made. First, the ability to correctly paraphrase individual sentences is not sufficient for an outsider to answer the general question "What's going on here?" in a manner acceptable to a group member. This problem, recently noted in several disciplines, has generated some of the most recent research in linguistics and its relatives. Second, using approaches developed in cognitive anthropology we learn that an answer to the question will be the name of an event, perhaps monolexemic, perhaps not. From this it is concluded that one way to begin to understand ethnographically "what's going on" is to investigate the group members' knowledge of events.

While learning event names begins to teach the outsider which motions and noises are perceived as related by group members, two additional notions explicate event relationships. First, an event has one or more perceived outcomes; in this study outcomes were specified as the definition of the event. Second, before the event can be created by human actors certain prerequisites are essential; they are necessary conditions for an event performance.

Notions of prerequisite and outcome enable us to understand relationships that link one event with another. Recall the example utterances cited earlier in this paper. We now understand that the *junkies* are concerned about *works* because they are prerequisite to *getting off,* an event that the *junkies* want to create. Further, since *works* are prerequisite to being *busted,* the *junkies* also worry about their rapid disposal. Should someone appear who may be *the man,* all prerequisites for a *bust* will be present and that event becomes possible. If *the man* appears and the *works* are disposed of, the *bust* (at least a legal bust) is again impossible.

So one way prerequisites link events is that a prerequisite for an event that a person is attempting to create may also be a prerequisite for an event that would be undesirable should it occur. A second kind of link occurs because the outcome of one event may be a prerequisite for the next. In this link, two events are related in that the performance of one creates the conditions for another to occur.

All of this information is summarized in Figure 1. The events that the *junkie* wants to create, *copping* and *getting off,* are listed on the right

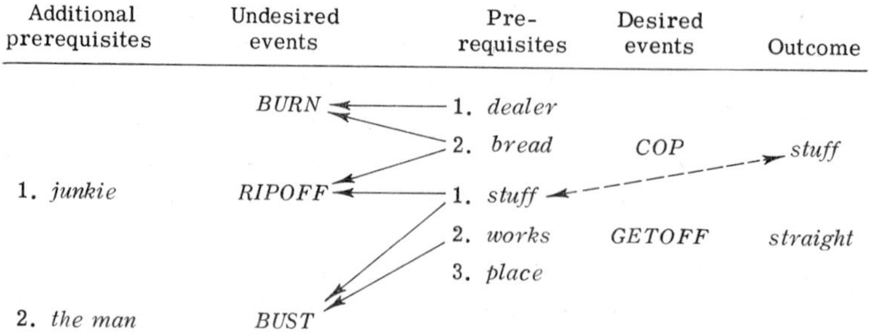

Figure 1. *Events, with their outcomes and prerequisites.*

side. The prerequisite–outcome link is indicated by a dotted line. The events he wants to prevent, the *burn, bust,* and *rip off,* are listed on the left. The link with prerequisites for the desired events is shown by a solid line.

Clearly, this is only an initial effort to systematize the ethnography of events. Among the ignored difficulties are the problems of multiple outcomes, as in the case of *getting off,* as well as the differentiation of ethnographically interesting prerequisites (e.g., the *dealer*) from the trivial (e.g., the *junkie* must be alive). But this framework can serve as a useful starting point.

The Study of Events in Cognitive Anthropology

Anyone who has read previous studies in the cognitive study of events (Frake, 1964, 1969; Metzger and Williams, 1963) will recognize the debt of this study to them. Although concerned with specific cases of ethnographic description, they abound with suggestions and implications, only some of which have been harnessed here. The event outcome-prerequisite distinction is implicit in the Metzger and Williams paper, and Frake hints at such things as interevent links and prevention of undesirable events as organizing principles. In a few respects, though, the addict study reveals a couple of areas of slight confusion, and it might be worthwhile to point them out.

First of all, in this study we have been talking about a cognitive structure. The structure is not necessarily identical to the actual occurrence of events over time in any specific empirical instances, although it does constrain the logical possibilities. In fact, interviews with addicts showed many variations in actual performances of the events. For example, an addict may occasionally receive money from parents. When he does, he does not need to *hustle,* since he already has the prerequisite for *copping.* Another addict might execute a particularly lucrative *hustle* – perhaps robbing a wealthy person's apartment – and not *hustle* for several days. Similarly, an addict might *cop* twice in a row and, if he *copped* a large amount, *get off* several times in a row over a few days without leaving his place.

On the other hand, other addicts described street experiences that followed the structure's outline fairly regularly. For example, one addict would *crack shorts* ('break and enter cars') and usually obtain just enough stolen goods to buy *stuff* and *get off* just before getting sick. Then he would immediately begin *hustling* again. Finally, all prerequisites are not necessarily realized as overt topics of conversation. If an event begins with the shared knowledge that a *dealer* has already been selected, then, naturally, there is no discussion of which *dealer* to *cop* from.

In addition to variations in sequence, there are variations in performance by individual actors. The event structure does not specify the particular realization taken by a segment of conversation. Although it helps to understand why a particular topic, for example, the *dealer,* might be the focus of verbal activity, it does not predict which of a possible set of linguistic and nonlinguistic alternates are selected to communicate that topic.

In suggesting a *dealer,* for example, nothing in the event structure prescribes exactly how the suggestion should be made. Verbal content may range from a short utterance of the *dealer's* name to an articulate speech listing his merits as a *dealer.* Paralinguistic signals might vary tremendously with the type of perceived social relationship and the affective state of the speaker. Physical posture can vary with the amount of time since the last *fix.* Clearly, there is much room for individual variation in the performance of events.

The point of all this is simply that event concepts and event performances are not the same thing. If these data are any example, the divergence is greater at this level of cognitive organization than at the level of the sentence. Recent work with the sentence shows that the form generated by the grammar and its actual performance are very similar, with most deviations describable by fairly straightforward rules (Kay, n.d.). In the case of event categories, this is less so. Certainly, one rule is that prerequisites must exist before the event outcome can be produced, but beyond this there is apparently room for many empirical variations.

Sometimes the earlier studies seem unclear on this important distinction. They refer to event frames, or the importance of relating an event to those that precede and follow it. Sometimes the distribution seems to be one of logical cognitive links, sometimes that of actual empirical occurrence. For example, one study discusses the probability of occurrence of a given event in a given slot. Predicting actual occurrence is an important question, but it is different from the question of cognitive structure. At least in this study, discrepancies between the two are possible.

A second problem relates to possible a priori components of an event. A number are suggested, such as "paraphernalia," "setting," etc. The addict study cautions that the existence of a particular component as a significant unit for a particular culture must be demonstrated, not assumed. The importance of this warning is reflected here. Take the case of *copping,* for example. A concern with "setting" (in the physical sense) is almost irrelevant to an addict engaging in the event.

Some *dealers* operate in the streets, while others work out of private dwellings. In no cases, though, was the location of the *dealer* a concern of the addict who wanted to *cop*. Attributes like quality of stuff and relationship with the dealer were the significant ones for the addict. A concern with "setting" here would have missed the point. Of course, if one is a *dealer* (where the same event is now labeled *dealing*), a concern with the setting does indeed become important. For the addict, though, the *dealer,* not the setting, is the primary consideration.

An etic notion of setting can always be applied to an observed instance of social interaction, since there is always some physical surrounding. An emic study of *copping,* though, shows that setting is not significant in the performance of the event from the point of view of the *junkie.* Future emic studies can revise and sharpen our event metalanguage.

A third problem that I want to mention here, one that I am also guilty of, is the prior decomposition of data into verbal and nonverbal. Some aspects of the cognitive structure can be alternately realized verbally or nonverbally, or in some combination. The event outcome of *copping,* for example, might be an addict walking up to a *dealer,* nodding, holding up two fingers, holding out a $10 bill, and taking two bags of heroin. At this level the ethnographer cannot restrict his data to the verbal; sooner or later he is going to have to come to terms with the nonverbal. Recent innovations in video recording and in kinesics suggest that this goal may not remain unattainable.

Psychological Reality of Event Concepts

A fourth problem, one that I want to spend some time on, is traditionally called "psychological reality" in the literature of cognitive anthropology. This issue, simply put, questions the relationship between the cognitive structure described by the ethnographer and the cognitive structure supposedly held by the members of the group. While such discussions sometimes have deteriorated into scholastic shouting matches, other, more empirically oriented approaches contribute substantially to the ethnographic task of understanding others (see, for example, Berlin et al., 1968).

In my study, an inclusive conceptual structure has been presented claiming to cover many of the day-to-day activities of the *street junkie.* To check the structure, let us examine another, independently obtained source of data. Perhaps we can test whether or not the cognitive structure depicted in Figure 1 has any relationship to knowledge drawn on in the course of other verbal segments. To see how this is done, refer to Table 1.

TABLE 1

Frame Elicitation Results for Desired Events

a.	*Hey Joe, what's happening, man?*		$U = .78,\ U_c = .84$
b.	*Like, you know, I'm just going to* _____.		

.95	I.	1. *cop* (12)
.98		2. *score*
		3. *cop, baby, you know*
.96	II.	1. *get off* (3)
1.00		2. *shoot*
		3. *shoot up*
		4. *tie up*
		5. *get high*
.93	III.	1. *try and get some cop money*
1.00		2. *hustle*
		3. *sell my goods*
		4. *make my hustle*
		5. *rip something off*
		6. *the hock shop*
		7. *make some money*
		8. *rip off something*
.67	IV.	1. *find my partner*
.73		2. *meet somebody*

NOTE: Numbers in parentheses represent the frequency of that response. Proportions in the left margin are values for A and, if appropriate, A_c. For explanations of these values, as well as the U and U_c values, see text.

The utterances at the top of Table 1 were taken from a taped conversation. In its original form, the second line read, *Like, you know, I'm just going to cop.* By deleting *cop*, a hybridization of a linguistic frame and a psychological sentence completion test is created. Now the frame can be administered to a number of addicts, who are asked to fill in the blank with as many different utterances as they want, as long as the utterances represent something that they might say in the streets. The frames used here were administered to a sample of 14 addicts, divided evenly along white–black racial lines and representing a variety of large Eastern cities and age groups.

The list of utterances obtained is then given to sorters, who are instructed to place utterances in the same pile if they are "saying the same thing." For these frames, three sorters were independently engaged in the sorting task. The numbers in the table represent simple proportional measures of the degree of "fit" of the utterances into the categories of the three sorters, both for the entire frame (U) and for each category (A).

TABLE 2
Frame Elicitation Results for Undesired Events

a.	*You can always go somewhere else and get*	$U = .83,\ U_c = .94$
	better stuff, too.	
b.	*But look at the changes. Taking a chance of* _____.	

.83	I.	1. *being taken off*
1.00		2. *getting ripped off somewhere else*
		3. *getting robbed*
		4. *getting ripped off* (3)
		5. *getting taken off*
.67	II.	1. *getting bad stuff*
.93		2. *getting garbage*
		3. *getting some bad stuff*
.62	III.	1. *getting burned* (3)
.92		2. *getting beat* (5)
.90	IV.	1. *getting busted* (9)
1.00		2. *getting busted by the man in a place you don't know*
		3. *getting cracked*
1.00	V.	1. *OD'ing*
		2. *maybe OD'ing*

The U_c and A_c values are U and A corrected for ambiguous utterances. (A full discussion of this procedure is contained in Agar, 1973.) Notice that the good fit of the utterances into the categories of three other addicts, as indicated by high U and A values, is a strong argument for a widespread "culture of addiction," in a cognitive sense.

Returning to Table 1, notice that the end result of the frame-eliciting task almost perfectly matches the three major categories of events that the addict wanted to produce. Category I represents *copping;* II, *getting off;* and III, *hustling.* In the next series of responses (see Table 2), the frame elicits the *changes* ('difficulties, hassles'). Again examining the responses, notice that Category I represents being *taken off;* II and III are indications of the *burn;* and IV is the *bust.* Once again, most of the responses to the frame are identical with the events — in this case the undesired events.

In Table 3, another frame is shown that presents the frequent argument over who gets to use the heroin first. Once again, there is a clear relationship between the responses and the earlier cognitive structures. The responses here are related primarily to the event prerequisites. Category I is the *works;* II, the *stuff,* and VII, the place prerequisite for *getting off.* Category V is the *bread;* and VI, the *dealer* prerequisite for

TABLE 3

Frame Elicitation Results for Prerequisites

a. *First.*	$U = .97$
b. *Second.*	
c. *Whoa, whoa, wait a minute.*	
a. *No good, man, no good. I called first. I don't want to hear it.*	
c. *No, man, I'm getting off first. I _____.*	

$A = 1.00$ I.   1. *. . . . it's my works*
                               2. *got the works*
                               3. *got the spike*
                               4. *. . . . it's my works. It's my gimmicks*
                               5. *. . . . it's my outfit*
                               6. *. . . . like, the works are mine, so you don't have no choice*
                               7. *got the works, man*

$A = 1.00$ II.   1. *brought the shit*
                               2. *bought the dope*
                               3. *copped*
                               4. *brought the stuff. I paid for it, dig?*
                               5. *. . . . it's my shit*
                               6. *am the one that copped*

$A = 1.00$ III.   1. *am bigger than you*
                               2. *. . . . that's all there is to it. Fuck the rest of you*
                               3. *. . . . like, much more lip and you won't use them at all*

$A = 1.00$ IV.   1. *. . . . we agreed upon it*
                               2. *said it before you*
                               3. *got off last last time*

$A = 1.00$ V.   1. *put in most of the money in this deal*
                               2. *had the most money*

$A = .90$ VI.   1. *. . . . it's my connection* (2)

$A = 1.00$ VII.   1. *brought you down to my place*
                               2. *. . . . it's my house*

$A = .86$ VIII.   1. *think I'm a little sicker than most of you*
                               2. *am sick* (2)

copping. Most of the responses, then, are prerequisites for events; a prerequisite is used as justification for the right of *getting off* first.

The frame elicitation data can be accounted for by the same cognitive structure. This ability of a posited structure to aid our understanding across a range of situations increases confidence that we are close to something the members of the group also use. The frame elicitation tasks add support to our belief in the cognitive salience of Figure 1.

Some Concluding Comments

This work only outlines a framework for the cognitive study of events. Numerous interesting questions remain unanswered. Let me mention at least a few. First, even though we rejected the a priori scheme of prerequisite classification, there might be other alternatives to consider. One is suggested by the nature of the event labels. Not surprisingly, they are all, in this case at least, verbs, while the prerequisites for the events are all nouns. Perhaps the structure of the sentences used to describe the event bears some interesting relationship to the event itself. Burke (Hymes, 1962) had this idea in mind, I think, when he spoke of "entitlement" — i.e., looking at a sentence as a title or summing up of some situation.

For now, let me mention at least one possible interpretation. Just as I am arguing that the event is central in the organization of behavior, so recent linguistic theory suggests that the verb is central in the organization of a sentence. Each verb carries a "case frame" (Fillmore, 1968) or "role structure" (Langendoen, 1970) specifying noun relationships that may be obligatory or optional. If we look at the kind of noun cases that have been proposed and then look at the prerequisites, the possible use of case notions to classify prerequisites suggests itself. For example, to *get off,* the addict needs *works* (instrument), a place (location), and *stuff* (patient). Further work along these lines may increase our ability to understand more about behavior from the way people talk about that behavior.

A second question has to do with the relation of the cognitive structure to actual instances of behavior. Two rules have already been mentioned. One is that prerequisites had to exist before the event could be produced. This rule helped explain that if a *dealer,* for example, was tacitly agreed upon, then there would be no discussion of which *dealer* to *cop* from in the tape. A second rule is that prerequisites and outcomes can be realized as topics of conversation. This rule is central in the understanding of segments of verbal behavior. Undoubtedly, there are other rules relating structure to behavior, and these have just begun to be explored.

Let me give a few quick possibilities. Recall that the elicited folk definitions of the events were purposive in nature. Actual interaction in process resembles a systems model with feedback. Perhaps, then, there is some kind of interaction routine with parameters, one of which gets filled in with the purpose of the event that the individual is about to engage in. The purpose becomes a goal-state to be monitored, using feedback processes. As another example, consider decision rules. Arguments among addicts are often phrased in terms of information important in decision making. Perhaps there are some rules that relate items of information in decision rules to group discussions about members of the set of things to which the rule applies. Loosely stated, if for some reason you want to select item *i* from set *S*, and you have to convince a group of others that item *i* is the most preferred member of *S*, then adopt an interaction strategy whereby as many positive attributes of decision rule *R* as possible are attributed to *i*.

As for our final question, note that this study was conducted in an urban American group that is highly focused in its activities. The life of an addict is strongly centered around the acquisition of heroin, and, thus, we might expect it to be more tightly organized and easily studied than the variety of events in a village in India, for example. I hope future work can address this problem. For now, though, a couple of suggestions might be appropriate. First of all, recall the focus on the unmarked sequence of the *hustle–cop–get off* events. Thinking back on ethnographies in general, it is apparent that unmarked "event sequences" are probably quite common in cognitive structure. Thus, for any group of people there are unmarked sequences of events that have to do with marriage, with agriculture, with religious ritual, and so on. In fact, the notion of "event sequence" probably only formalizes what has long been intuitively described by ethnographers.

Further, though the event sequence is tied together by prerequisite outcome links, where do the other prerequisites come from? Perhaps these other links are related to another long-held ethnographic intuition. Most ethnographers explicitly recognize that somehow they must partition the world into discrete areas for discussion — hence the traditional ethnographic chapter headings ("economics," "social organization," "religion," and so on). At the same time, they also note that this partition is to some extent artificial, since to talk about economics you must talk about social organization, etc.

Perhaps unmarked event sequences in a particular culture are the things that tend to fall into the usual discrete chapters of ethnographies, while prerequisites that are not links in the sequence are the things that tend to link a particular sequence with other kinds of sequences. To give one quick example from the Frake (1964) article, a certain kind of religious event is linked to the agricultural cycle, since a prerequisite of the event is the food provided by a successful harvest. Again, this framework may formalize well-established intuitions about the nature of culture.

At any rate, the cognitive study of events did help answer the original question. As a result of this study, I could understand longer sequences of verbal interaction much better. Further, it appears that the framework will be compatible with different ideas in linguistics, cognitive anthropology, and ethnography. Certainly, much more work will be necessary before its utility can be fully assessed.

References

Agar, Michael H.
  1971 Folklore of the heroin addict: Two examples, *Journal of American Folklore,* 332.
  1974 Selecting a dealer, *American Ethnologist* 2(1).
  1973 *Ripping and running: A formal ethnography of heroin addicts.* New York: Seminar Press.
Berlin, Brent, Dennis Breedlove, and Peter Raven
  1968 Covert categories and folk taxonomies, *American Anthropologist* **70,** 290–299.
Ekman, Paul, E. R. Sorenson, and W. V. Friesen
  1969 Pan-cultural elements in facial displays of emotion. *Science* **164,** 86–88.
Fillmore, Charles J.
  1968 The case for case. In *Universals in linguistic theory,* edited by E. Bach and R. T. Harms. New York: Holt.
Frake, Charles O.
  1962 The ethnographic study of cognitive systems. In *Anthropology and human behavior,* edited by T. Gladwin and W. Sturtevant. Washington, D.C.: Anthropological Society of Washington.
  1964 A structural description of Subanun religious behavior. In *Explorations in cultural anthropology,* edited by W. Goodenough. New York: McGraw-Hill.
  1969 Struck by speech. In *Directions in sociolinguistics,* edited by J. Gumperz and D. Hymes. New York: Holt.
Geoghegan, William
  1973 A theory of marking rules. In *Cognitive organization and psychological processes,* edited by K. Wexler and A. K. Romney. Washington: National Academy of Sciences.
Goffman, Erving
  1959 *The presentation of self in everyday life.* New York: Doubleday.
Goodenough, Ward H.
  1957 Cultural anthropology and linguistics. In *Language in Culture and Society,* edited by Dell Hymes. New York: Harper & Row.
Gumperz, John J. and Dell Hymes
  1972 *Directions in sociolinguistics.* New York: Holt.
Hymes, Dell
  1962 The ethnography of speaking. In *Anthropology and human behavior,* edited by T. Gladwin and W. Sturtevant. Washington, D.C.: Anthropological Society of Washington.
Kay, Paul
       Speech editing. Unpublished paper, University of California, Berkeley, Language–Behavior Research Laboratory.
Langendoen, D. Terrence
  1970 *Essentials of English grammar.* New York: Harcourt.

McCawley, James D.
   1968   The role of semantics in a grammar. In *Universals in linguistic theory,* edited by
          E. Bach and R. T. Harms. New York: Holt.
Metzger, Duane and Gerald E. Williams
   1963   A formal ethnographic analysis of Tenejapa Ladino weddings, *American Anthro-
          pologist* **65,** 1076–1101.
Miller, George, Eugene Galanter, and Karl Pribram
   1960   *Plans and the structure of behavior.* New York: Holt.
Pike, Kenneth
   1967   *Language in relation to a unified theory of the structure of human behavior.* The
          Hague: Mouton.
Scheflen, Albert
   1972   *Body language and the social order.* Englewood Cliffs, New Jersey: Prentice-
          Hall.
Weinreich, Uriel
   1966   Explorations in semantic theory. In *Current trends in linguistics,* edited by
          T. Sebeok. Vol. III. The Hague: Mouton.

Everyone Has to Lie[1]

HARVEY SACKS

This chapter reports an attempt to develop an experience for the problem: What should an analysis look like that has as its aim proposing that something that a member says about the social world is true? I will proceed by seeking to show that a particular commonplace statement that members make, *Everyone has to lie,* is true.

In its character, this discussion might be considered an "exercise."[2] By calling the discussion an exercise, I intend to point up the following features. When the study was undertaken, what a solution to its problem should have consisted of was not known. Instead, the investigation was undertaken so as to see, by producing a possible case of such a solution, what "solutions" might look like. On constructing what seems to be a satisfactory solution, that solution could be examined so as to find, e.g., what features such a solution should have *or* to determine how the given solution might be inadequate. We would hope to come up with something that could be investigated itself to see whether it was what we would like to have a theory be, and criteria for a theory could be constructed by reference to what it seemed to contain or lack. In that sense, then, it is an "exercise."

[1] This is essentially a transcription of a lecture, last delivered in 1968 in one of my courses on the analysis of conversation. Parts that served to integrate it into that course have been deleted. It represents a last point at which two strands of my research, on identification selection and on the sequential organization of conversation, were both current. More recently, the latter strand has been exclusively pursued. An extensive revision of the parts that deal with greetings and the *How are you?* sequence is now in progress as part of a general treatment of the openings of conversation that Emanuel Schegloff and I are preparing. The decision to publish it unrevised is based on the following considerations. First, the study has widely circulated in manuscript form for some years. Second, the revision will concern only certain parts of it, and, though we believe we have rather more powerful ways of dealing with those sequences, they are not inconsistent with the presentation here. Third, I am out of touch with its other parts but would not presume to say that, not now working on such matters, I know better than I once thought. The lecture has been befriended by various readers and is an old friend of mine, too—a distant friend but not an enemy or an embarrassment.

[2] I owe the observation that discussions like these should be called "exercises" to Erving Goffman.

Let us proceed to a preliminary consideration of what sociological interest there is in determining the truth of—being able to warrant as "true"—some statement that members make about the social world. First, in a sentence: An investigation directed to determining—that is, to constructing a sociologist's warrant for—the truth of some member's statement about the social world is one way of producing studies of social organization. That is to say, in seeking to find how it is that a possibly true statement that members make about the social world *is* true—can be said by sociologists to be true—what we are led to do is to examine the social arrangements whose organization can be said to constitute a "production procedure" that could provide for the truth of the statement in question. Now, so far there is no basis to differentiate a sociologist's statement about the social world and a member's statement about the social world, and, as such, no particular gains with regard to the study of social organization are made by virtue of the statement's having been a member's statement about the social world. Let us, then, turn to those gains. What is distinctive—for studies of social organization—about the fact that a member made such a statement, is this: We are led, in our construction or characterization of the arrangements of the social world that provides the "truth" of some statement, to possibly find *such arrangements as are available to members.* That is to say, one possibility is that if some statement is true, then if members make that statement they may know it is true. And if members know it is true, then they may know *how* it is true. So in constructing how it is true, we may be constructing that which—if not thereby proved to be available to members—is possibly known by them. We will have selected some phenomenon whose "known-ness" to them can then be investigated.

We note that, of course, the fact that members make a statement and that statement is true does not mean they know it is true. Furthermore, that they know it is true does not mean necessarily that they have available how it is true. Those matters need to be investigated separately.

That we can perhaps come up with or focus on features whose organization is available may be a relatively distinct gain. That is, studies of the truth of some statement that members make may have that gain. This is, then, one sort of interest in possibly true statements that members make. Again, the interest is that we are led to make controlled inquiries—controlled by the statements we deal with—into social organization. And the statements we select isolate for us states whose availability to members is directly of interest.[3] Also, a more academic interest is that, at least in ancient times, there was a rather deep relationship

---

[3] Such considerations as have just been presented heavily underlie the sort of inquiries presented in Sacks (1971).

between logic and sociology. The ancient relation between logic and sociology turned, in part, on the fact that, in its early days at least, logic was specifically, overtly interested in actual processes of argument and was specifically concerned to formalize actual processes of argument. Currently, such an interest seems again to be emerging on the part of logicians.

It would appear that sociology might have some part in such an interest in actual processes of argument and "various other logical issues" such as, of course, issues with regard to truth. Under that circumstance, then, the question *What would a demonstration of the truth of some member's statement look like?* is directly interesting. Further, in passing, insofar as the usual sociological and anthropological methodologies involve the use of members' statements about the social world, we may ask, *What would it take to warrant the strong use of such assertions?* e.g., the making of inferences from them. (I only mention this issue, but the reader might want to think about it.)

Let us turn, then, to consideration of the selection of the materials we will be examining, i.e., to the virtues of the statement *Everyone has to lie* for such an inquiry. First of all, that it is a commonplace, proverbial expression suggests the possibility that its reference might be something quite general, that the experiences it reflects are, and are perceived by their user to be, common and thereby, for a sociologist, possibly organizationally based.

Also, the research I have done on the topic "selection of identifications" has led me to believe that, probably in contrast to what we would intuitively think, a statement with "everyone" as its subject may be more amenable to a determination of its truth than a "more limited subject statement," such a one as would include, e.g., *doctors, wives, Protestants, Germans,* etc., as the subject term. I would guess that one would figure that the truth of a more "limited" statement, i.e., what we would figure is a more limited statement, would be more amenable to demonstration than the truth of a statement whose subject is *everyone.* For the detailed reasoning underlying my suspicion that our intuition on this is wrong, reference to the work on identification selection is necessary. However, let me sketch some of the reasons that recommend a statement with "everyone" for selection for determining truth.

First of all, as we shall see, it is not at all obvious that a statement with the subject term *everyone* names a larger population than a statement with, e.g., the subject term *doctors* or *men,* etc. Second, what may be crucial for a statement's truth is *how it is that a population is formulated,* i.e., what identificatory term is used. In saying this, what I want to notice is that, given a same-population in the sense of some bunch of people of whom something is to be predicated, the accept-

ability as correct of a statement saying something about them may turn
on which of some set of correct identifications are used in the statement.
For example, if *males* is used and is correct, then the statement may be
accepted as correct, whereas if *children* or *Protestants* is used with "the
same" predicate and the same set of people being referred to, the statement may be taken as incorrect or bizarre. In that regard, then, the
formulation of the population or the choice of a subject term may have
some important bearing on the acceptability of a statement by reference
to considerations other than that the term chosen designates some set of
people. It also ought to be noted in this regard that it may well be the
case that the selection by a party of an identificatory term may in part be
directed to such a selection as will involve, for what is predicated of the
identified people, that it be acceptable as true, or be heard as absurd or
beside the point. Consider in this regard possible variations in selec-
tional criteria for "The babies cried," "The males cried," "The Protestants cried" [Sacks, 1972].

Third, one basic trouble with regard to determining the truth of statements that have such terms as *lawyers, males, women,* etc., as their subject terms is that it is not obvious what constitute tests of the incorrectness of such propositions. In particular, it is not obvious that
showing that a person who could be so characterized, i.e., could be characterized as "a male," but doesn't behave as the statement proposes
constitutes a counterexample to the assertion. Instead, statements in
that circumstance may be treated as "programatically relevant" [Sacks,
1971] such that a discovered case that might stand in contravention of
the proposition has as its consequence, not asserting the error of the
proposition, but leading such a person as is not correctly characterized
by the proposition to change his ways so as to bring himself under its
auspices. Also, if a person seems not to be correctly characterized by
the proposition, then again, it may turn out that not the proposition but
his status as a proper member of that class is questioned. Let me present
an instance of this possibility: A woman asks, *What man would want a
forty-year-old, divorced, childless, neurotic woman? No man.* That apparently does not mean for her that no one approaches her, but that
those who do approach her are not "men," i.e., not socially males, not
properly motivated to pick a woman as one they might marry, etc. That
is, "He's not really a man," or not really what a proper man is. All I
want to note here is that one should not rush to employ the obvious test
of a proposition having, e.g., *men* as its subject term, i.e., to find a case it
does not characterize and thereby show its falsity—; for that technique
may be found to be inappropriate and not used for actual statements in
conversation, and is then not a suitable instrument for evaluating truth
or falsity in that domain. A search for the possible truth of a statement in

conversation can have as an alternative procedure and outcome a search for the procedures for evaluating truth or falsity in that domain, used in it, appropriate for it.

There is yet another problem: At least some – perhaps many – of the statements that have these "more limited" identificatory terms as their subjects seem to have the occasion of their use being just the occasion of their correct characterization of some circumstance. The consequence of this is that although one might treat such a statement as a thing one could monitor the world with, it does not turn out to be so used. And therefore, on occasions when it might appear to be usable to find that it is incorrect, such occasions might be characterized by another term than its subject term. So, e.g., the statement *women are fickle* might be used only on some occasion when someone who happens to be a woman was fickle. On some occasion when someone who could be so characterized was faithful, she might be otherwise characterized, as, for example, by saying *Older people are faithful.* It is not – at least for the re-searcher – obvious what is involved in selecting an identification that is used on some occasion. In short, the burden of my remarks so far has been, under this first issue with respect to the selection of a statement with *everyone* as its subject term, that selections – and in particular the selection of such identificatory categories as I have mentioned so far – seems troublesome with respect to determining what it is that would stand as an occurrence that faults them, how such an occurrence should be located with the assurance that the identificatory term in ques-tion would be used there.

A virtue of the statement *Everyone has to lie,* for having its truth de-termined, is, again in a sentence, this: For that statement it appears that you can state some ways that the contrast class true–false is relevant on that statement's occurrence. Having some way of showing that the con-trast class true–false matters for some statement is necessary because it is no longer seriously assertable that that contrast class is relevant for any statement. Large groups of statements have been exempted from such a supposition of the relevance of this particular contrast class to their assertion.

Consider, for example, the following possibility: Let us suppose that a first contrast class relevant upon the occurrence of a statement is whether it is intended to be serious or a joke. Then it may be that the relevance of true–false is conditional on the determination that it is in-tended to be serious, whereas if it is intended to be a joke the contrast class true–false is not relevant in dealing with it.

Since I wanted to reserve the application of the contrast class true–false to such a statement as seemed clearly to make that contrast class relevant, one ground for the selection of *Everyone has to lie,* is that there are means for establishing the relevance of true–false for it. This has at least the interest that establishing the relevance of true–false for *Everyone has to lie* will constitute a finding.

The line I am going to take is as follows. One way of fixing on "relevance" is in terms of "sequential relevance." Sequential relevance can involve sorts of actions that utterances can accomplish. In the case of actions like *complaining* or *offering an excuse,* one recurring type of utterance that goes directly after the action is an utterance that proposes either its truth or its falsity. Also, such utterances seem to implicate the effectiveness of the proffered complaint or excuse. Given a complaint or an excuse, a sequentially relevant next utterance can be concerned with acceptance or rejection of the excuse or complaint, and one way acceptance or rejection of a complaint or an excuse can be done is by reference to assertions of the truth or falsity of the *complaint* or the *excuse.* That is to say, at least with respect to certain ways in which *complaining* or *excusing* is done, acceptance of a complaint or excuse can be made via *That's true.* Rejections of a complaint or excuse can be made via *I don't believe it, It's not so,* or *It's false.* Then, as acceptance or rejection is relevant on the making of the complaint, the contrast class true–false is thereby relevant, that is, sequentially relevant.

Given the foregoing, we need now only note that the statement *Everyone has to lie* **can** be made either as a complaint or as an excuse — of course, other things also. When it is either of these, assertions about truth or falsity would thereby be sequentially relevant; and thereby, then, for some occasions of the utterance *Everyone has to lie,* its truth or falsity would be sequentially relevant.

We may also note in this regard that one way we have of determining that some statement is intended to be true is that it is used in the making of a complaint. That it is used in the making of a complaint or an excuse stands as one basis for seeing that at least the member who used that statement takes it that it is true. For such a statement it is not incidental that it is true — not incidental to its user. And for such a statement it is not merely that it is uttered and that we found it to be true that is relevant but, also, that the fact that it was uttered turned in part on its intended truth. In short, I suggest that one procedure for locating a corpus of statements intended to be true involves locating the set of statements used in the making of complaints or excuses.

For the actual case in which the utterance was used, it appears that *Everyone has to lie* was offered as a complaint, that is, as "Everyone has to lie and isn't that terrible," "Everyone has to lie and I can't do it," "Everyone has to lie and I hate to do it." What we may then be heard to have said is that the fact that members assert a statement in the doing of some activity can be informative for us of the status of that item in their corpus of knowledge. That they take it that the statement is true is evidenced by its use for doing some class of actions such as, for example, complaining. And the way it is dealt with can then be further evidence with regard to others' understanding that it is true. This, of course, is a matter that must be dealt with cautiously. For how it is that an utterance is dealt with — its acceptance or rejection — turns also on other things than whether, e.g., its recipients figure it is true or false, and whether they are then and there ready to acquiesce to the complaint. But, anatomically speaking, in any event, such sequences as *complaining and accepting, complaining and rejecting,* using a proposition for a complaint and making an acceptance of the complaint by acquiescing to its truth, are recurrent, actualized possibilities.

At this point I want to insert some further remarks about "everyone." I want to mention two ways in which "everyone" might be construed. The first I call "summatively." That is, for that usage "everyone" involves some list of people such that if the statement were true for "everyone" it would be true for the set of eaches. And it could be false for everyone were it not true for some one of those eaches. It is clear that some terms that refer to people seem to have such a usage. If I said *We went to the movies* and you took it that "we" was intended to include myself and my wife, then if you asked her and she said she did not, you might take it that the assertion "We went to the movies" was false, though, perhaps, "I went to the movies" was true.

I have noted that some of the categorical identificatory terms do not appear to be regularly used in the sense that, for them to be correct, each person they could characterize needs to have what is predicated of them true of them. And perhaps *everyone* is a sort of categorical term. If so, what sort might it be? "Everyone" is used for various category collections. For example, I have seen an advertisement that goes: *Something for everyone: An X for Dad, a Y for Mom, a Z for Brother, a T for Sister.* Here, *everyone* refers to the category collection "family." Now, what that suggests is that the size of the population being referred to by "everyone" can be quite small. That is to say, "everyone" could, intentionally, understandably, refer to "all the members of some family" or "all the persons playing some bridge game." If, now, "everyone" were used for reference to some family's members, while it may have a summative intention — be intended to hold for each — it would nonetheless be holding for what might be a rather small group. And then, too, if it held for a category, it might not have a summative intention to it.

In short, when "everyone" is used summatively it might not have a very large set-population intended; and when it is used where it might have a rather large population intended, it might not be used in such a way as to have *each* of that population intended. Consider such uses as

Everyone's going, can I go? This is not—though it might be so construed—a paradox. "Everyone" here is apparently being used in a programatically relevant fashion.

The upshot of this last discussion is: It may be the case that a determination of what "everyone" refers to turns on the utterance and the
occasion of its use. Some readings were suggested—such as that "everyone" can be used programatically, can be used for a rather small set-
population, can be used for categories. By use of these, an approach that
seeks, as ours does, to find how the statement might be possibly true
seems not necessarily burdened with what might appear to be a more at-
tractive approach—that is, to find that it could not be true (i.e., to
formulate such a sense of "everyone" as permits the ready location of
falsifying evidence). Such an approach might simply not be terribly informative about the *uses* of *everyone,* or about its social organizational
aspects.

With these considerations in hand, let us turn to another body of material, the use of which will set up our detailed analysis.

Several years ago I was working on a study of "greetings"—things
like *Hi–Hi, Hello–Hello,* etc. I had acquired various small points, and
finding them not overly interesting, sought—as a way of increasing their
interest—to see if some of those results could be incorporated into a
more extended investigation that would involve, by its turning on them,
a way of developing some of their interest. That rather independent
study of greetings turned out to have use for the consideration of the
truth of the statement *Everyone has to lie,* which I was also studying.

We will proceed with some points about greetings. First, two small
points: (1) greetings are ahistorically relevant, and (2) when they occur
they properly occur at the beginning of a conversation. To say that
greetings are ahistorically relevant as compared to, say, "introductions"
(which, having been gone through once or perhaps twice, or erroneously
three times or five times, are no longer appropriate) intends that in the
case of greetings as between any two people, without regard to how long
they have been acquainted, there is no rule that says "On some $N + K$
conversation, no longer begin conversations with greetings." Instead,
every conversation those two people have—they could have been married 30 years—can begin with some greetings. Not only that; their first
conversation can also begin with greetings. This is not to say that every
conversation must begin with greetings, but that there is no exclusion
rule for greetings.

With respect to the placing of greetings, there is a technical relevance
to the fact that greetings properly occur at the beginning of conversations. This relevance concerns the technical issues of an analyst's being

in the position to say that something did not happen, that it was absent. Now, saying that something was absent and thereby making some point is not, obviously, a simple task. For to say simply that any event T was absent, that T did not occur, potentially allows indefinitely extending the list of things that did not occur, and insofar as T is thereby a member of an indefinitely large class, the point that some particular T did not occur is made trivial. It is not discriminable from the rest of the things that also can be said to have not occurred.

However, insofar as there is a rule that says "If greetings do occur, they ought to occur at the beginning of a conversation," and insofar as there is a further rule that says "Greetings may occur at the beginning of any conversation," i.e., there is no exclusion rule for greetings, then there is a place to look to see where greetings should be found, such that if they are not there, they can be said to be absent in a way that other things cannot be said to be absent. For the relevance of occurrence of other things cannot be so established — or, in any event, unless their relevance of occurrence could be established, their absence is differently assertable than is the absence of greetings there. In that regard it may be noted that talk of absences, i.e., members' talk of absences of occurrence, is not apparently randomly done. That is to say, not anything is asserted to have been absent. Furthermore, of the things asserted to be absent, they are not asserted to be absent just anywhere.

Greetings are, however, asserted to be absent, and they are asserted to be absent when they do not occur at the beginning of a conversation.

OPERATOR: *Mister Savage is gonna pick up an' talk to* ⌐*yuh.*

LERHOFF: ⌐*All right*

              (Approx. 50 seconds intervening)

OPERATOR: *Did Mr. Savage ever pick up?*

LERHOFF: *If he did, he didn't say "Hello."*

OPERATOR: *Oh, all right* ⌐*sma(hh)rty, just hold on.*

LERHOFF: ⌐*heh heh heh heh heh*

OPERATOR: *heh!*

In this regard, note that for something like greetings to be asserted to be absent it is not necessary that nothing have happened. Greetings can be asserted to be absent when something, indeed, occurred. Here is a quotation from *The New York Times,* Tuesday, January 11, 1966, under the heading "Film Producer Lists Trials in Egypt" (about the movie producer Julian Blaustein):

Mr. Blaustein, in town briefly from his temporary London headquarters recalled how, on a location-hunting trip to Egypt he had come upon the craggy Mr. Huston sitting desolately on a rock in the eastern desert while technicians were setting up a scene for Mr. Huston's 'The Bible'. "John looked up. He didn't say 'hello' or 'how are you', all he said was, 'You're here as a tourist. You can't be thinking of making a film here. You must be mad.'"

In this regard, then, the fact that greetings have a place is of some technical interest. And we may be said to have shown one more extended interest of the otherwise no-news point that greetings occur at the beginning of conversation.

With these two facts in hand — greetings are ahistorically relevant and greetings properly occur at the beginning of a conversation — we proceed to construct some classes of conversationalists. We will establish a class of "proper conversationalists" and construct subclasses of that class. Let us call the first subclass Subclass A. We will say about Subclass A that what is definitive of it is that its comembers may engage in something we will call a "minimal proper conversation" and no more.

There is, of course, at least one other subclass, subclass B, about which we will say, for now, that what is definitive of it is that its co-members can properly mutually engage in a minimal proper conversation and more, or more than a minimal proper conversation without use of that set of objects that constitutes the objects of the minimal proper conversation *or* (what is crucial here) on any given occasion a minimal proper conversation and no more. The point is this: were the doing of a minimal proper conversation to reveal its performers as member of a subclass who could do only minimal proper conversations, that subclass might be vulnerable to exclusion from the class "proper conversationalists," and "minimal proper conversation" might become other than a sub-class of "proper conversation." If those who could do more on occasion do no more than a minimal conversation, then the integrity of the classes "proper conversation" and "proper conversationalists" is preserved. Let me emphasize at this point, though, that I do not intend that that line be some achievement of ours, i.e., something we choose to assert, but that it indeed characterizes conversationalists' real circumstances. We are trying not to arrange things conveniently but to find out how they are arranged.

The New York Times, July 20, 1967, reports a procedure used by an "influence peddler" which uses the inferences that are made by virtue of greeting exchanges for its effect. Here is a quotation from the story:

"Julius Klein is a top operator with unlimited guts and all," says a Republican politician who has known him for thirty years. "He rushes up to say hello to Senators, who of course, say hello to anybody, so as to give the impression he is on close terms with them."

The effectiveness of Klein's procedure turns not on having people see that he can engage in an exchange of greetings with a senator, but on their not being able to know from that, that he might be in a position to do *only* that (even if they were not "open people," or even if he knew them). What is, of course, of some technical interest is not merely that such an occurrence as the Klein procedure can be accounted for by the analysis we have been developing but also that Klein seems to have had the kinds of inferences that might or might not be made from an exchange of greetings available to him as a program that he could use so as to produce the inferences that he wanted. Again, that such a trick as Klein's could work stands for us as at least indirect data on the possibility that rather intimate people may merely exchange greetings on some occasions. It follows that the exchange of greetings only is not restricted to, e.g., Subclass A.

If we can say that a "minimal proper conversation" can consist of an exchange of greetings, then in the first instance we know—or at least have so far asserted—that Subclass A can do that. Comembers may be able to do no more, properly, than exchange greetings, but they can do that.

It is worth noting in this regard that there are people who do engage in conversations who are not comembers of a subclass of proper conversationalists but are, instead, "improper conversationalists." That they do engage in conversation is not itself evidence of the incorrectness of the claim that there is a class of proper conversationalists and a class of improper conversationalists, for it may be seen that when people who are not proper conversationalists engage in conversation, they do so, or begin to do so at least, often in special ways. Thus, for example, if a person seeking to engage another in conversation, and not being a proper conversationalist for that other person, is to bring off a conversation with that other person, then one sort of thing he may do—and does—is to begin not with greetings but by using an utterance, which we call a "ticket," that indicates the reason he is starting to talk with that other person. He may, for example, say *Excuse me, I'm lost.* That is to say, he uses such an utterance to locate how he comes to talk to that other person. This means that we are not merely saying that the class of improper conversationalists is coextensive with people who do not converse with each other—though there are many, and that fact is, of course, relevant—but also that it may be seen that when "improper conversationalists" converse, such conversations begin in distinct, i.e., characterizable ways and also, in particular, without greetings. And when they do not so begin, that matters. Regularly, if a greeting is offered by one it is *not* returned by the other (see page 74).

If the various subclasses other than Subclass A are somehow ranked by reference to intimacy, status relations, and the like, it nonetheless appears that even the most intimate of such people can on some occasion make only an exchange of greetings, without one party of such a pair feeling wronged. A couple married 30 years may, in passing on the dance floor, at a party, or elsewhere, just exchange greetings. And neither feels that the other has, by not otherwise talking, done an improper act.

Let me note that in talking of an exchange of greetings as a minimal proper conversation, I have not thereby intended to fit the notion "minimal proper conversation" to what Subclass A can properly do. Instead, the notion "minimal proper conversation" arises in the following way. First, it seems that the only satisfactory definition of conversation involves reference to the operation of the sequencing rules of conversation to characterize some body of talk (Sacks *et al.,* 1974). The sequencing rules of conversation do characterize an exchange of greetings; sequencing rules such as "a conversation may begin with an exchange of greetings" and "given a first greeting for proper conversationalists, a second ought to follow," do operate.

There are two issues for our consideration. The first — the placing of greetings — has been discussed. The second matter — that on a first greeting a second should follow — is evidenced not only by the fact that that does happen but also by the fact that when it does not happen it is notable. So, for example, a child may be told, *Didn't you hear A say* **hi** *to you?* which is itself an interesting way to inform the child that he or she should also have said **hi.** Also, when a first greeting is offered and not returned, a repetition may occur (Schegloff, 1968).

Since the exchange of greetings proceeds according to the sequencing rules of conversation, the exchange of greetings is at least part of a conversation. Insofar as the exchange of greetings is not required to be followed by more talk, the exchange of greetings is, thus, a minimal proper conversation.

I want now to introduce something I call a "greeting substitute." The particular sort of greeting substitute we shall be most interested in is such a thing as *How are you?* Let me state some features of the class. First, a greeting substitute may be used as a greeting. Instead of using *Hi,* one may use *How are you?.* You might ask, since *how are you?* can go where greetings can go, why not call it a greeting? Why call it a greeting substitute? A first reason for differentiating *How are you?* from greetings is that one property of greetings seems to be — and this property will then exclude *How are you?* from that class — that greetings are not repeatably used. That is, greetings should not be combined with greetings sequentially. That is, a pair of people should not, after saying

Hi–Hi, say *Hi–Hi* again. There is an exception to this: In the case of telephone calls, in which *Hello* is the appropriate utterance of the first speaker, i.e., the one who answers the phone, the answerer regularly does not know who it is he is saying *Hello* to; and while *Hello* is then returnable when on an exchange of *Hellos* the initial speaker discovers from the second *Hello,* by recognition of the voice, to whom he is speaking, he may then say *Hi,* and the other may then also return *Hi.* In the case of telephone calls, then, one does get *Hello–Hello, Hi–Hi.* But that is a special situation (see, for this sort of thing, Schegloff, 1967).

I have said that greetings are not repeatably used; i.e., a sequence of them does not occur directly upon completion of a prior sequence of them. But greeting substitutes can be used in combination with greetings. That is to say, one can have:

A: *Hi.*

B: *Hi.*

A: *How are you?*

B: *Fine, how are you?*

Furthermore, if greetings and greeting substitutes are combined, and both occur, they occur in a fixed order. Greetings precede greeting substitutes. But — and this is the point we want to retain — speakers can choose to use greeting substitutes when they do not use greetings, and a greeting will not be absent. In that regard, then, what I have said about greetings holds for greeting substitutes; that is, an exchange of greeting substitutes can constitute a minimal proper conversation. In other words, whoever may do greetings may do greeting substitutes, and perhaps no more; or, people who may do greetings may also do greetings *and* greeting substitutes.

With our new resource in hand, let us proceed further. Two more classes are needed. One of them I call "personal states," which consist of things like *mood, appetite, sleep,* etc.; the other I call "value states," which consist of terms like *good, lousy, great, rotten, wonderful,* etc. The latter terms are organized into three subsets, which I will denote by the symbols $[-]$, $[0]$, $[+]$. We will label personal states "describables" and value states "descriptors." Any of the value states can describe some personal state for some person at some time. *How's your appetite? Great!* (or *Rotten!*). Prototypical terms: for $[-]$, *lousy,* for $[0]$, *ok,* for $[+]$, *great.* The organization of the terms into subsets involves mutual exclusion as between subsets. If a term belongs to one, it does not properly belong to another.

Now, *How are you?* has its proper answers among the value state descriptors. So if you ask somebody *How are you?*, he or she should pick a term from among those.

Let me make a remark about a sufficiency that obtains for the use of the descriptors. We may get at this sufficiency by imagining that in order for the import, the use, the effectiveness of the value state descriptors to occur, it would be required that a recipient be in a position to determine, for the person who is to offer an answer, how that person goes about determining that he is *ok* or *lousy* or *great*. At least with regard to sequential relevance, such is not the case. (I will shortly state some of the sequential relevancies of alternative answers.) Here I mean only to point out that it is the business of an answerer to produce an answer in such a fashion that the sequential relevancies that turn on the occurrence of that answer turn on the occurrence of his particular answer. Access to possible private uses of each term, or to the measurement systems employed by each user, to determine the appropriateness of "lousy" as compared to "normal," is not required for one who would deal with a received answer. Instead, subclass membership is what the recipient may use; that an answer is a member of the [−], [0], or [+] subset.

To say that subset membership is mutually exclusive involves noticing such a thing as the fact that when correction takes place, by self or others, it occurs across subsets. If a person, upon being asked *How are you?*, answered *Lousy!* and corrected himself, the correction would be, e.g., "Actually, I'm ok" and not, e.g., "Actually, I'm rotten." If a person answered *Wonderful!* and another corrected him by virtue of, e.g., other information he may have, or the person's appearance, etc., he would not say, "You're not either. You're in the pink!" However, he might say, "You're not either. You're feeling lousy, aren't you?"

The sequential relevance of the answer proves to hold for any of the personal state questions. Given the occurrence of an answer from subset [0], e.g., *ok, fine,* etc., no further inquiries are appropriate. Given the occurrence of an answer from the [−] subset, a sequence is appropriately launched, directly, to determining "what's the matter." For example, that question or *Why?* should be used when, e.g., the answer to *How are you?* has been *Lousy!* (In the case of the [+] subset, some "comment" like *Great!* may follow the answer *Wonderful!* or an inquiry might also be launched via things like, e.g., *What happened?*) The sequence launched on the occurrence of an answer from the [−] subset, e.g., *Lousy!* to the question *How are you?* (launched, e.g., by the question *Why?* or *What's the matter?* I call a "diagnostic sequence," and it has at one point in it the offering of such an account as explains how it is that the answerer is in the [−] subset. It may be noted, also, that what will stand as an account is something that also regularly need not be a "private" matter—i.e., not private as to its understandability as an explanation: *I have to have an operation, I have an exam, My kid got arrested,* etc.

The occurrence of an answer from the $[-]$ subset is a sufficient condition for engaging in the diagnostic procedure. The relevance of *Why?* is established by the occurrence of an answer from the $[-]$ subset, i.e., to the question *How are you?, Lousy!* And recall that the question *How are you?* usable as a greeting substitute, is usable between *any* proper conversationalists.

Now, let us consider the information that may stand as the "diagnostic information." In particular, let us consider the *regulation* of its exchange as between any two parties. It seems, in the first instance (grossly), that it may be said that for any two parties not any item of such information may be offered to any given other. Stated otherwise, exchange of information serving as an answer to a diagnostic inquiry is independently regulated—independently, that is, of the regulations that provide for the relevance of the occurrence of diagnostic answers. In this regard it is, of course, also the case that such information need not, for its offering, turn on the occurrence of the *How are you?* question. One may call someone up and announce *I have to have an operation* instead of, e.g., standing in front of the other's house until he or she comes out and says *Hi. How are you?*

We need not deal in detail here with the particulars of that regulation of information exchange with regard to, e.g., "troubles." That is, we need not specify for any item who it is that can be told. We need only, in the first instance, establish that there *are* regulations on that score.[4] For such information as constitutes an answer to the question *Why?*, given the answer *Lousy!* to the question *How are you?*, regulations that exist concern such matters as what it is that should be held within the family, what should be told only to your doctor or a priest, and the like.[5] Fur-

---

[4] See, for example, Sacks (1971) and, with respect to the sequencing of the telling of such news (Sudnow, 1967).

[5] Such a situation of information regulation is, of course, a rather widely found phenomenon. To quote only one instance of its presence in other societies, we refer to Ethel Albert's (1964) observations with regard to the Burundi:

> In lesser matters than life and property and position, discretion still has its place. One may discuss with close friends and neighbors the problems created by a spouse who is a bit slow-witted, but not broadcast the fact far and wide. If one suspects that a neighbor is a witch, one refrains from mentioning it in his presence . . . There are then some truths not to be spoken aloud to anyone; some to a faithful spouse but nobody else; some to close relatives and neighbors. Only rarely is any statement so innocent that it is not necessary to consider the possibility that it will bring trouble [p. 47].

thermore, such regulations not only hold to exclude some people from hearing some items of information, but even for those who may hear such information there are appropriate sequences whereby they should be told, such that some people should not hear before others. Information varies as to whom it may be given to. Some matters may be told to a neighbor, others not; some to a best friend, others, while they may be told to a best friend, may only be told to a best friend after another has been told, e.g., a spouse.

Those two sets of facts with regard to (1) relative exclusion of people and (2) relative sequencing for those who can be told, turn out to be very important. We shall pick up their importance after we pause to formulate a notion of "lying" with respect to the question "How are you?."

We may say that the presentation of an answer to the question *How are you?* proceeds in two steps. A first step I call "monitoring" and a second step "selecting a term." The first step involves selecting a subset. The second step, given the selection of a subset, involves selecting a term from that subset. There are ways in which it would appear that the notion "monitoring" is artificial. Let me attempt to indicate what I intend by the use of that term. I intend to notice a difference between the way two different sorts of statements are dealt with. For the first, if, e.g., a little girl comes home and says to her mother, *Mama, I'm pretty* or *Mama, I'm smart,* the mother could say "Who told you that?." For the second, if someone says *I'm tired* or *I feel lousy,* etc., no such thing is asked. One is responsible for knowing some things on one's own behalf, in contrast to the situation in which one is treated as likely to be repeating what another has told him about himself. We have data to that effect: *You keep saying you're insane. Has somebody been telling you that recently?.* The notion, then, of "monitoring" attempts to come to terms with the difference between things that are heard as things you know on your own behalf and things that are heard as things you know by virtue of another's having told you. The answers to *How are you?* are things you know on your own behalf.

We will proceed, then, to the notion "lying." Lying, we will say, consists of announcing in your answer a term that is excluded by the monitoring operation. So if the monitoring operation comes up with [+], then one uses a term from [0]; if the monitoring operation comes up with [−], then one uses a term from [+] or [0], etc. With that in hand we can return to the regulation of information on "troubles" and to the question, How is it that, given the regulation of information about troubles, conformity to the rules that regulate that information is achieved? We will turn, also, to a newer question: Given the formulation of lying, why should anyone lie?

How, then, are the regulations about information transmission enforced? Let us note that the relevance of such regulations can be occasioned by the occurrence of the question "How are you?", since the answer *Lousy!* occasions reference to such troubles in the diagnostic sequence occasioned by that answer. And, as we have noted, the question *How are you?* is offerable by any proper conversationalist, including those who may exchange only greetings with one another. Thus, the problem of the operation of those regulations is of very extensive relevance. The regulations may be operative for any conversation – given, that is, that any conversation may begin with greetings or greeting substitutes and *How are you?* is a greeting substitute.

It is certainly imaginable that regulation of information (about, e.g., troubles) transmission is achieved by having a potential elicitor of such information, one who might ask *How are you?* and thereby potentially engender a diagnostic sequence, be constrained from asking that question if he is not in a position to receive the sort of information he might receive. If, for example, a possible asker of *How are you?* were not one – and knew that he were not one – who could receive certain information from the other person, e.g., a runaway child, a wife in an accident, or a parent who just died, then *How are you?* should not be asked, since if *How are you?* were answered *Lousy!* then *Why* should be forthcoming, and such a piece of information might be the answer to *Why.*

Such a system of regulations does not seem to be workable. In any event, it is not used. It does not seem to be workable by virtue of the fact that, even though a great deal of the information that *Lousy!* might occasion the offering of could be given to any person by another, some information might not be giveable, or, even if that information were giveable to a person, it might not be giveable *now,* i.e., until someone else had been given it. If such a set of regulations were operative, *How are you?* would be an almost unaskable question, but *How are you?* is not an unaskable question. It is, instead, the most askable of questions. The system of regulations involves not a potential asker's determination of whether he could handle any information but, instead, an answerer's determination of whether a given asker can receive the particular information or handle it now. That is, it is the business of one who is asked *How are you?* to determine whether the asker can handle that information, and to control his answer by reference to that determination. If such information as is not giveable to the asker obtains, and occasions that the monitoring product is [−], then the procedure for not getting into the diagnostic sequence is: Do not offer such an answer as generates the diagnostic sequence. Answer, e.g., *Ok* or *Fine.*

Let me note here that having the burden of enforcing some regulation on respondents is not unique to the *How are you?* situation. Campbell,

(1964), in his study of a Greek mountain village, reported that there are rules providing that "un-married, opposite sex persons should not converse." He notes, further, that "when an un-married male encounters an un-married female he may offer a greeting. It's the business of the female to not offer one back [p. 275]." In the classic ethnography *Deep South,* (Davis, Gardner, and Gardner, 1941) the rule against infidelity of a married person is discussed, and it is reported that "a male may make advances on another man's wife; it's her business to keep him off [pp. 100–101]."

What we have arrived at is that any person feeling lousy and having some trouble as the explanation of feeling lousy, if asked how he is feeling by someone who ought not to hear that trouble or hear it now, may control that one's access to that information by avoiding the diagnostic sequence, and the diagnostic sequence is avoided by choosing a term from a subset other than the subset the monitoring operation comes up with; that is, he may lie.

Now for a brief remark on the term *has to.* It might be said that while somebody in that situation might lie, we really should not say *He has to lie.* On the contrary, however, it is the case that such a situation is properly characterized by the term *has to,* for conforming to a violable rule is something one can say one *has to do.* People say, for example, *Everyone has to pay their taxes.* You do not have to pay your taxes, you can take your chances on going to jail. "Has to" apparently can properly be used where there is some rule that says "you ought to" and that rule has sanctions.

The foregoing seems to leave us in a situation in which we can say that it is at least conceivable that anyone might be in a position in which such "need" to lie would be present. This does not say that anyone *will* be in such a position. A generalization of the notion "lying" may be of assistance.

Before providing that, however, a remark about the possible "knowableness" of such a possibly true statement is in point. It happens to be the case that the particular occurrence of *Everyone has to lie* that occasioned the research I am here reporting on was asserted complainingly by one who had as part of her troubles that not only did she feel seriously lousy but also that others were routinely asking her *How are you?* while sometimes being quite uninterested in being recipients of a report of troubles and sometimes being distinctly improper recipients. Then, it is not unreasonable to suppose that she could see how the arrangement of conversation was a source of her troubles, or the part of them that focused on their being raised as potentially tellable to be then rejected for actually being told, and that such troubles were not at all hers in particular.

What we have seen about what we have called "lying" with respect to the *How are you?* situation is that lying involves the selection of a known incorrect answer to the question, Which of the value states is correct for you?, where what the possible answers are is known. We have, then, a situation in which the selection of a known-to-be-false answer can occur by virtue of its offerer's orientation to the sequential implications of alternative answers. This notion of "lying" is directly generalizable and, as generalized, seems to capture a correct sense of lying.

In circumstances in which alternative answers to a question are known, and the alternative answers have alternative consequences for that conversation or for other events, then one way in which people are known to attempt to control those alternative consequences is to select answers by reference to their intended selection of a consequence. If children are asked some question, one of whose alternative answers may occasion a rebuke and another not, then apparently they learn, and apparently it is learned that they have learned, to produce answers that are directed to avoiding the rebuke, which answer production can involve them in lying. Further, consider a seduction situation involving two college students:[6]

BILL: *Well, why not?*

ANN: *I won't; that's because that's the way I am.*

BILL: *Are you a virgin?*

ANN: *No.*

BILL: *Then, why not?*

ANN: *I mean I'm not gonna lie about it.*

BILL: *Oh // All right eh eh*

ANN: *I mean—that's // ridiculous. I never have lied about it.*

BILL: *Ehhhehh no doubt about that . . .*

BILL: *Oh well, that's good but there's no doubt about that, I w'uh so why are y'uh so what's the deal? I mean if you're not a virgin, hh //(   ).*

ANN: *"What difference does it make?" It makes a lotta difference // because when I give my love I give it because I love somebody.*

BILL: *hhhh!*

---

[6] The transcriptional conventions are Gail Jefferson's: // means overlap, and is placed where the overlap starts; (   ) means the segment of the recording cannot be heard.

In this regard, then, the situation of occasions of lying is much more general than the special case we have been considering, and indeed, many other cases may be much better as evidence than the case we have considered. For not only can it be argued that it isn't a "lie" to say *Fine!* when one is feeling lousy, but, e.g., etiquette books will advise you to say *Fine!* and propose that it is proper, not wrong, not really a lie. For example, Emily Post (1955), in a section entitled "The Answer to 'How are You?," writes:

> The trait of character which more than any other produces good manners is tact. To one who is a chronic invalid, or is in great sorrow or anxiety, a gay-toned greeting, "Hello Mrs. Jones, how are you! You look fine!", while kindly meant is really tactless, since to answer truthfully would make the situation emotional. In such a case she can only reply, "All right, thank you." She may be feeling that everything is all wrong, but to 'let go' and tell the truth would open the floodgates disastrously. "All right, thank you" is an impersonal and therefore strong bulwark against further comment or explanation. As a matter of fact, "All right, thank you" is always the correct and conventional answer to "How are you" unless there is reason to believe that the person asking really wants to know the state of one's health. [pp. 16–17]

Amy Vanderbilt (1963) writes:

> In greeting people we say "How do you do." We do not really expect an answer, but it is all right to reply "Very well, thank you," even if it is a blue Monday and you feel far from well. No one wants a clinical discussion in response to this purely rhetorical question. In fact you may answer Socratically with "How do *you* do?", expecting and getting no answer. [p . 212]

It may be noted that in both cases the notion of "truth" is used and that *Lousy!* will occasion a diagnostic question is assumed.

Note both that the effort to argue that saying *Fine!* when one is feeling *Lousy!* is not really a lie is, of course, evidence that an attempt at change is involved, that this sort of lying needs special extrication from its supposed status, and that with the generalization that has been offered, "having to lie" has been so extended that the possible exclusion of some instances for *How are You?* is inconsequential.

Some final remarks about "everyone" will suggest some further extensions of these phenomena. In returning to "everyone" we may proceed by considering the following conversation:

A: *Why do you want to kill yourself?*

B: *For the same reason everyone does.*

A: *What's that?*

B: *You just want to know if anyone cares.*

Now, in this excerpt there is a rather characteristic use of "everyone." It seems to be something we might put as "for the same reason as anyone in such a situation." If "everyone" can mean "anyone in such a situation as I" or "anyone in such a situation where what that situation is is characterizable," then a rather important shift may be made with respect to the issue of what people "everyone" characterizes. At least for some uses, "everyone" characterizes no people at all. This is not to say that it characterizes nothing. Instead, however, of "everyone" being another way of referring to, e.g., a designated person or to a category or a collection of categories, or to the incumbents of a collection of categories, "everyone" may also refer to what Garfinkel (personal communication) has characterized as "the sociologist's person, ideally," that is to say, a "course of action" person. Let me elucidate this concept.

There are uses of "everyone" that seem to be noting that the people so identified are sufficiently identified if the situation they are in is stated. That is, for whomever is in that situation, the specification of that situation constitutes a sufficient account of what they may be expected to do, how they may be expected to feel, or how they may be expected to behave.

Let it be noted that such uses of "everyone" are not at all infrequent.[7] And, among other things, it appears that what such uses of "everyone" accomplish is that having specified a situation — and again, this is so only, apparently, for some situations and members — no addition of iden-

---

[7] a. "Hardy might bawl the hell outta somebody but he can't do anything about something that everybody does — especially when it's already done [from Dalton, 1959: 32]."

   b. A: *Do you have a gun at home?*
        B: *A forty-five.*
        A: *You do have a forty-five?*
        B: *Uh huh. Loaded.*
        A: *What's it doing there, whose is it?*
        B: *It's sitting there.*
        A: *Is it yours?*
        B: *It's Dave's.*
        A: *It's your husband's huh?*
        B: *I know how to shoot it.*
        A: *He isn't a police officer?*
        B: *No. We just have one. Everybody does, don't they?*
        A: *It's a forty-five and it's loaded?*
        B: *Uh huh.*
        A: *And I suppose maybe everyone in Glasgow Park has one?*
        B: *I don't know. No, but I mean a lot of people have guns, it's not unusual.*
        A: *Oh, sure, I see.*

tificatory references gives, for example, motivational gains or explanatory gains with respect to formulating an account of what it is that that one did or will do, or why, or how. Such a use of "everyone" has as its specific import (not merely making irrelevant any numerical identifier or categorial identifier) that it is *productively* usable. By "productively" I mean the following. What is relevant for things that are known in such a way that "everyone" — properly used in the sense I have stated — is appropriate is not whether in the course of his life each person in fact finds himself in such a circumstance, or is found in such a circumstance, but that "anyone might." These matters, formulated situationally for such situations, seem not to be the specific troubles of "men, women, or children," "professional people," "members of various sects," and the like. Instead, they are known as matters that can happen to whomsoever and are, in any event, not excludable by some history one has had that may be formulated in terms of, e.g., one's categorical memberships.

Given the foregoing extension of "everyone," it now becomes unnecessary to find that some situation can be found for each categorizable population or each nameable person in which the organization of conversation, the rules of information regulation, and their personal circumstances converge to lead them to feel that they "have to lie." What is instead involved is that the statement is true if the organization of conversation is such that any next conversation can formally produce the problem of having to deal with some such sequentially implicative question as *How are you?* where the question is asked by one with whom the respondent, by reference to other rules, e.g., of information transmissal, is placed in a situation that he sees involves either getting into a sequence in this conversation that he should not get into or lying so as to avoid that sequence. The organization of conversation being such, the statement is *true*.

References

Albert, Ethel
  1964   Logic, rhetoric, and poetics among the Burundi, *American Anthropologist* **66**(6), 47.
Campbell, J.
  1964   *Honor, family, and patronage.* New York: Oxford Univ. Press.
Dalton, M.
  1959   *Men who manage.* New York: Wiley.
Davis, Allison, Burleigh B. Gardner, and Mary R. Gardner
  1941   *Deep South.* Chicago: Univ. of Chicago Press.
Post, Emily
  1955   *Etiquette: The blue book of social usage;* 9th ed. New York: Funk & Wagnalls.

Sacks, Harvey
  1971   An initial investigation of the conversational materials for doing sociology. In
         Studies in social interaction, edited by D. Sudnow. New York: Free Press.
  1972   On the analyzability of children's stories. In *Directions in sociolinguistics,* edited
         by J. J. Gumperz and D. Hymes. New York: Holt.
Sacks, H., Schegloff, E., and Jefferson, G.
  1974   A simplest systematics for the organization of turn-taking in conversation, *Lan-
         guage,* **50**(No. 4), 696–735.
Schegloff, E.
  1967   *The first five seconds.* The social organization of conversational openings, Ph.D.
         dissertation, Univ. Calif., Berkeley.
Schegloff, E.
  1968   Sequencing in conversational openings, *American Anthropologist,* **70**,
         1075–1095.
Sudnow, D.
  1967   *Passing on.* Englewood Cliffs, New Jersey: Prentice-Hall.
Vanderbilt, Amy
  1963   *Amy Vanderbilt's new complete book of etiquette.* Garden City, New York:
         Doubleday.

The Conversational Analysis of Social Meaning: A Study of Classroom Interaction[1]

JOHN J. GUMPERZ
ELEANOR HERASIMCHUK

The aim of this study is to work out an empirical method of conversational analysis capable of recovering the social assumptions that underlie the verbal communication process by focusing on actors' use of speech to interact, i.e., to create and maintain a particular definition of a social situation. The basic theoretical position that sets this work apart from other work in sociolinguistics is that, in the analysis of face-to-face encounters, the sorts of things that social anthropologists and sociologists refer to by such terms as *role, status, social identities,* and *social relationships* will be treated as communicative symbols. They are signaled in the act of speaking and have a function in the communication process akin to that of syntax in the communication of referential meaning. Just as grammatical knowledge enables the speaker to distinguish potentially meaningful sentences from nonsentences, knowledge of the social values associated with the activities, social categories, and social relationships implied in the message is necessary in order to understand the situated meaning of a message, i.e., its interpretation in a particular context.

Let us illustrate with a simple example. The utterances:

1. *They are holding a meeting to discuss the issue.*
2. *They are getting together to talk it over.*
3. *They're sittin' down to rap about it.*

[1] This study is based on data collected by Louisa Lewis under a grant from the University of California Urban Crisis Project, and it draws on her ethnographic observations (Lewis, 1971). We also consulted Ms Lewis on the interpretation of our transcriptions. Analysis of materials were assisted by grants from the National Science Foundation (GS30546) and the National Institute of Mental Health (5R01-MH18188).

We are grateful to Claire Lefebvre for her invaluable contribution to the transcription and analysis of the data, and to Clive Criper, William Geoghegan, Paul Kay and John Trim, who commented on parts of the analysis. Our special gratitude goes to Jenny Cook-Gumperz who has commented on all stages of the work and to whom we owe important theoretical insights.

Reprinted with permission from Georgetown University Round Table 1972, *Sociolinguistics: Current trends and prospects,* edited by Roger W. Shuy, pp. 99–134. Georgetown University Press, Washington, D.C.

can be used to describe the same event and are, thus, in a sense referentially equivalent, although their social implications are quite different.

Item one implies at least some overtly recognized division of roles. There must be two or more contesting parties, possibly a chairman or at least some overtly agreed upon agenda of possible topics and allocation of rights to speaking, etc. The second description is unmarked with respect to these characteristics and could also be used in referring to an ordinary conversation. Item three definitely suggests an unstructured activity where speakers speak their own mind without any prior limitation on what can be said and who is to speak when.

How are such social assumptions implicit in messages signaled in speech? Clearly, the difference is not merely a matter of the dictionary meanings of the lexical items involved. Linguists will note that the two sentences carry different variable selection rules. While sentence 2 allows:

They're gett'n t'gether to talk it over.

variants such as:

They're hav'n a meet'n to discuss the issue.

or:

They are sitting down to rap about it.

violate ordinary stylistic cooccurrence restrictions. The signaling of social meaning, like the signaling of reference, therefore involves both paradigmatic and syntagmatic constraints.

It has been pointed out that sociolinguistic selection constraints are different from the cooccurrence constraints that apply among syntactic and semantic features, since they cut across the usual levels of grammar and do not allow for rule ordering. Scholars such as McCawley (1968) and DeCamp (1971) suggest that they be treated as discourse features applying to a stretch of discourse as a whole and marking it as formal, informal, polite, or familiar, etc. But so far we have had little in the way of systematic study of such discourse features. Even a casual examination shows that the identification of particular discourse stretches as "formal" or "informal" is considerably more problematic than the identification of a lexical item as carrying semantic features such as concrete or abstract, animate or inanimate, etc. When used in natural conversation sentence (1), for example, may have a variety of situated meanings that are quite distinct from what we ordinarily understand by formality. When it serves to describe a group of children talking in the playground, the effect is humor or irony. On other occasions, it may convey contempt or condescension.

Not that the feature of formality is irrelevant in these cases. In order to understand a message as ironical, we must know (a) that speakers in our culture distinguish among speech activities that do carry procedural norms such as those described earlier and those that do not, (b) that activities of the former type are appropriate for adults and not for children, and (c) that the distinction made in (a) is signaled by choice among referentially equivalent lexical, phonological, and other options. Formality can be seen as a rough, though somewhat imprecise, gloss for the association between linguistic alternants and the social characterization of activities. When the content of what is said meets the speakers' expectation as to what this relationship should be, the interpretation of formality applies, and in that sense formality is an aspect of what we can call social meaning. In arriving at a situated interpretation of a message, the speaker must match the social meaning of an utterance with the content of what is said and with other contextual features incident to the speech act. When these show the expected match, then the description itself signals the fact that the activity is carried out in the prescribed manner. When there is a conflict between the social values of two or more features—i.e., when, as in the aforementioned case, the behavioral norms associated with the form of the message conflict with the context, which refers to children rather than adults—then metaphorical interpretations such as irony are generated. Given the referential meanings, the speakers' situated interpretations, and a knowledge of the possible linguistic options, it should be possible to recover the social meaning of the messages in context, using elicitation techniques and methods of analysis that are equivalent to those used by linguists in building a theory of grammar.

An additional analytical problem in the study of social meaning, one that does not occur in grammatical analysis, is caused by the fact that the social meaning of particular modes of speaking varies from group to group, from generation to generation in ways that are not easily relatable to the usual factors of income, social class, education, etc., and are as yet little understood. The statement:

> *Come at six. We are dining early tonight.*

when made in the context of a dinner invitation, is part of the normal unmarked speech of many older-generation Englishmen. When used in a group of younger people, it is likely to be interpreted as ironical or sarcastic. Although both groups have grammatical competence in English, they attach different situated interpretations to the same message and, to the extent that speech is used to assess speakers' personality characteristics, they differ in their judgment of the same speaker's attitude, ability, etc. Sociolinguistic analysis of conversations, if it is to be valid, must account for such differences.

One of the first systematic attempts to go beyond the grammatical description of isolated sentences and deal with social meaning in language in terms of selection constraints is found in the recent work of Halliday and his associates (1969). Halliday argues that language can be viewed as "behavioral potential," i.e., that social structure and grammar offer a set of options and that spoken utterances are the result of a selection process in which speakers choose among a network of social, semantic, syntactic, and phonological alternatives to express their intent. He cites the example of a mother who wants to keep her child from associating with certain playmates and utters the sentence:

That sort of place is not for playing in.

The content of this utterance can be analyzed at the social level as involving an appeal (a) to authority and (b) to general rather than particularistic norms, and (c) being object oriented rather than person oriented in content, since it refers to playing in a place rather than playing with people. If the mother had chosen to say:

I don't like you playing with those children.

the appeal would have been characterized by (a) affective and (b) particularistic norms, and (c) person orientation. Halliday goes on to point out that the speakers' selection of different clusters of social features also leads to significant differences in grammar.

Category clusters such as those just presented are considerably more detailed than simple dichotomies like formal and informal, and have the advantage of relating the linguist's grammatical categories to the sociologist's content analysis of questionnaire responses. Nevertheless, they are subject to a number of objections when applied to the study of face-to-face situations.

To begin with, the analysis takes for granted the sociologist's analytical categories. It is assumed that these categories constitute a known universal grid. What is seen as problematic is their distribution in particular cases and their linguistic realization. While it is certainly possible to show that, when studied with statistically significant samples, there is a correlation between sociological codings of sentences and language usage, Halliday's discussion gives no indication of how and through what cognitive processes speakers utilize these categories in the interpretation of messages and how it is that two sets of people can arrive at different interpretations of the same message. Nor is there any unambiguous procedure for assigning social meaning features to sentences. On the contrary, writings on social interaction have amply documented the arbitrariness and ad hoc nature of sociological coding procedures (Garfinkel, 1972; Goffman, 1964).

But even if we accept the assumption that such categories are directly applicable, Halliday provides us with no explicit theory of how and by what linguistic signs they are signaled in speech. The implicit assumption is that the analysis of phonology, syntax, and semantics conducted in accordance with the commonly accepted linguistic research paradigms can also provide information on social meaning. Recent work in the ethnography of communication suggests that this is not the case. It has been shown that there exist a number of other linguistic devices not covered in the ordinary type of linguistic analysis that serve to communicate social meanings. Most important among these are (a) the sequential ordering of utterances and the allocation of turns of speaking among participants (Frake, 1964; Sacks, 1972; Schegloff, 1972), (b) the choice of message form or speech event (Hymes, 1972) (e.g., whether to convey a message by conversation or lecture), (c) code switching or selection among cooccurrent clusters of variables (Gumperz and Hernandez, 1971), (d) intonation, stress, speech rhythm, and other paralinguistic cues (Crystal, 1969).

A major important analytical principle to emerge from the recent work in this area is that it is impossible to interpret situated meanings apart from the total context of what has been said before and what is said afterwards. The interpretation of a message is not a constant; it depends on what it is in response to and how it has been received. What is said at one point in a conversation may change the interpretation of everything that has gone before.

William Geoghegan's (1970) study of address rules in Samal, a Philippine language, is the first formal attempt to account for contextual interpretation of messages. Geoghegan distinguishes between two distinct processes for generating appropriate address forms: "code rules," which specify what can be said, and "marking rules," which rewrite the code meanings in accordance with context and social expectations. Whereas the output of code rules can be talked about in abstract semantic terms, marked meanings communicate only by contrast with code meanings. They depend on processes of matching such as those described earlier in which the speaker evaluates the social meaning of alternate expressions against the context in which they are said. It follows that marked meanings can be studied only as part of larger stretches of interaction. Analysis must deal with exchanges rather than with sentences or text, and concentrate on how speakers react to each other through speech.

In view of the novelty of this approach to language and in view of the as yet little understood variability in interpretation rules, there is a case to be made for a method of study that, like the techniques of the older structural linguists, combines analysis with discovery procedure. The starting point of the analysis is the speakers' situated interpretation of verbal exchanges. The purpose is to discover (a) how and by what verbal devices such interpretations are generated and (b) what underlying social assumptions are necessary in order to relate situated interpretations to linguistic form. In what follows we will try to illustrate such a method.

The data for our analysis are taken from two tape recordings, approximately one hour each, made in a Berkeley, California, elementary school. One first- and one second-grade classroom were recorded. Both were taught by an open classroom method, in which children are divided into activity groups, each group being seated around a separate table and engaged in a particular task, such as reading, building models, etc. Classes were ethnically mixed according to the usual Berkeley formula, 40% black and oriental children and 60% white. The two teachers, one of whom was black and one white, were each assisted by several volunteer assistants who helped in guiding the activity groups. The materials were recorded over a period of several weeks, during which time the ethnographer acted as a regular classroom observer (Lewis, 1970). Before making the recordings she spent several days in each classroom familiarizing herself with the children, the physical layout of the classroom, and the teacher's style. No attempt was made to capture everything that went on at a particular time or to make a sample of all interaction. The investigator simply moved from group to group and turned on the tape recorder whenever an interaction sequence caught her interest, sometimes starting the recording in the middle of an encounter, making sure, however, that what was recorded was of sufficient length to permit analysis.

Although all recordings were made during class sessions, not everything on the tape can be regarded as teaching. On occasion a teacher converses with another adult or with a child. At other times children engage in informal play. Learning sessions, likewise, are variously structured. It becomes necessary, therefore, as a first step in the analysis, to divide the tape into episodes, noting natural breaks in the interaction and changes in participants, and to find operational criteria for distinguishing teaching episodes from others. The criteria used in this task were (a) the focus of the activity, i.e., what was done, and (b) role distribution as it emerged from the sequence and illocutionary force of the statements and responses that make up a stretch of interaction. Using these criteria, we were able to define teaching as an encounter involving two or more participants focused about a particular task (i.e., reading, spelling, constructing a model, etc.) and characterized by a division of roles such that one actor, S_1, assumes and is accorded authority to guide the action and is accorded expertise with respect to that task. Thus, S_1 can be seen to command, correct, criticize, etc., while the other actor, S_2, follows S_1's directions, asks for information or confirmation, occasionally protests or disagrees, etc. Given this definition, we were able to isolate a number of teaching events, all of which fall under our definition but vary widely with respect to the way in which participants define their activities and their mutual relationship and in the verbal strategies they use to accomplish the interactional tasks involved. The present analysis will focus on two episodes that differ maximally with respect to these features: a second-grade child giving a first-grader a reading lesson and a teacher conducting a spelling lesson with a group of second-graders.

In line with our analytical goal, to relate situated meanings to the linguistic signs by which they are conveyed, conversational texts are transcribed at two levels (see the Appendix for a complete transcription). The left side of each page gives a verbatim record of what is said, including detailed phonetic transcriptions and intonational markings wherever necessary.[2] The right side comments on the interactional tasks being accomplished, identifying the illocutionary devices[3] used and sometimes the corresponding perlocutionary effects, giving verbal glosses or paraphrases wherever possible. While the comments on the right attempt to capture the speakers' situated interpretations, the transcription on the

[2] The method used for marking intonation is taken from the system presented by John Trim (1972) that is derived from the Kingdom method (Crystal, 1969), with the addition of two symbols of our own. The system adopted is provisional, and in our future work we may wish to incorporate elements of the system developed by Crystal (1969). In the notation of Trim, the utterances are divided into tonal groups in which a nucleus is determined as carrying the major phrase contour. The phrase may consist of one word or a long utterance containing several embeddings, according to the number of breaks or nuclear contours. Normally, the nucleus is the last stressed syllable in a phrase, though it may happen that a large number of syllables or words will follow after it. Trim describes six contours: (1) ͵low-fall, (2) ͵low-rise, (3) ˋhigh-fall, (4) ´high-rise, (5) ˇfall–rise, and (6) ˆrise–fall. Our material required the addition of two symbols, one for sustained tone, → , in low, mid, or high pitch, and one for emphatic, +, which is a diacritic added to one of the Trim tones.

In addition to the nucleus, the phrase may have a head or heads, either high or low, marked by vertical accent marks, ', or ͵, consisting of stressed syllables preceding the nucleus, as well as breaks, prenuclear changes in pitch. The nucleus may be followed by a tail or tails, syllables coming after the nucleus and falling away from the level of the nucleus gradually, or rising, according to the direction of the nucleus. The conventional punctuation marks used in our transcription are placed there for convenience of the reader, they are not part of the analytical apparatus.

[3] The term *illocutionary devices* is patterned on the notion of illocutionary force, introduced by Austin (1965) and developed by Searle (1969).

left indicates how and by what linguistic signs this interpretation is conveyed.

Although we use the term *situated interpretation,* we do not mean to imply that we are giving a detailed account of everything that a speaker may see or understand in a message. Ultimately, any message is open to a number of interpretations, depending on the extent to which personal background knowledge is brought in. The aim is to capture the kinds of judgments that members make when, for instance, they agree on saying that speaker A is being critical of speaker B, is confirming what B has said, is sounding friendly, aggressive, etc., and to show what these judgments are based on.

Since our situated interpretations are couched in everyday language, since glosses or paraphrases are given, and since judgments are directly related to what is said before and after and how it is received by other participants, our right-side transcriptions form an ideal basis for checking the analyst's interpretations against those of others, as well as for avoiding the kinds of ambiguities that arise when the analyst's categories are used or when grammaticality judgments or other evaluations of language are elicited in the abstract or under experimental conditions that differ from ordinary life situations. Whenever possible, our transcriptions were shown to a participant in the situation, as well as to other speakers of different social background, so as to test the extent to which speakers can agree on situated interpretations and to isolate systematic differences in interpretation. Whenever such differences are found, it is then possible through further elicitation to determine the extent to which they reflect differences in language usage rules, whether they can be traced to social values attached to particular linguistic forms or prosodic features, to speakers' use of unfamiliar rhetorical strategies such as code switching, or simply to differences in rules of etiquette.

Although the two episodes studied here seem quite different on the surface, when we examine the interactional tasks that the child teacher C_1 and the adult teacher T perform, we find that these are to a large extent equivalent. Our use of the term *interactional tasks* here is in some sense the parallel of what recent students of classroom interaction call language function when they classify utterances as instances of framing, focusing, informing, directing, responding, requesting, etc. (Forsyth, 1971). But rather than attempting to isolate a limited number of such functional categories, we prefer to give somewhat more discursive and, we hope, more informative descriptions, descriptions that apply to exchanges rather than to individual utterances. Our aim is not to count the incidence of functional categories but, rather, to isolate some similar tasks and use these as a basis for comparing the ways in which various individuals signal the fact that they are performing these tasks.

1. Warding off interference

A. Child teacher (*C1*):

line **A. 38a C3:** (not defined as learner) *,Boy-→*
    A. 38b C2: (defined learner) *Boys-→ and-→ girls-→*
    A. 39   C1: *'Don't, tell 'im, 'I'm ,teachin' 'im.*

B. Adult teacher (*T*):

line **B. 30 T:** *. . . How do you spell Ken?*
    B. 31 A: *Where's 'Ken? K-→C-→K-→E-→ , er . . .*
    B. 32 T: *,A, 'I is ,spelling it . . .*

Line A. 39 and line B. 32 are both responses to an attempt by a student other than the one designated as respondent to participate in the interaction. *C1*'s strategy is an unambiguous direct command to stop participating, followed by an equally direct assertion of her rights in the situation. *T*'s strategy is to disqualify the interruption indirectly by stating that someone else is performing. In fact, it is not the case that *I* is spelling but that *T* wants *I* to spell. *T* is describing a social event, *I*'s turn at spelling, which if understood has the effect of discouraging *A* from attempting to spell. Both *C1* and *T* here employ a social rule that goes "*X*'s performance of an operation precludes *Y*'s (or anyone else's) doing so." However, *C1*'s invocation of the rule follows upon a forceful indication of what she wants *C3* to do, as a backup to her command. For *T*, the very invocation of the rule is expected to have the force of a command, and no specific directive for *A*'s behavior is given.

2. Confirming the learner's response

A. Child teacher:

line **A. 21 C2:** *Page ,thirty-three, where's 'thirty-three?*
    A. 22 C1: *Thirty-,three.*
    A. 23 C2: *Thirty-,three, is 'this 'thirty-three?*
    A. 24 C1: *Thirty-three.*

B. Adult teacher:

line **B. 8   T:** *Of a—*
    B. 9   C: *Girl.*
    B. 10 T: *OK.* (goes on to address another student)

Here, in episode A, *C1* confirms *C2*'s question of line A. 23 by an extract repetition of her own statement of A. 22, using the same intonation and stress pattern. *T*, on the other hand, uses a special lexical item, "OK" to signal her confirmation.

The following episodes are somewhat more complex and require more detailed analysis.

3. Comparative elicitation strategies

   A. Child teacher:

line **A. 1** **C1:**   *'Come ⌄here.*
    A. 2 **C1:**   *'Sit 'down around ⌄here.*
    A. 3 **C2:**   *Do you know— ˈany . . . (you know)—like' this?*
    A. 4 **C1:**   *ˌSit down ⌄here,ˋnow!*
    A. 5 **C2:**   *'I don't wanta read all them ˌwords!→*
    A. 6 **C1:**   *⌄Well (let's see) ˈwhat's this ˋword anyway.*
    A. 7 **C2:**   *'I don't ˇknow!*
    A. 8 **C1:**   *ˌLarge.*
    A. 9 **C2:**   *'What?*
    A. 10 **C1:**   *ˋLarge!*
    A. 11 **C2:**   *ˌLarge.*

   B. Adult teacher:

line **B. 9** **T:**   *'I, do ˌyou see a name on that page that you know?*
    B. 10 **I:**   *Ann.→*
    B. 11 **T:**   *'Hm?*
    B. 12 **I:**   *ˌAnn.*
    B. 13 **T:**   *ˌThat's the one that ˋJ just named. ˌHow do you ˋspell Ann?*
    B. 14 **I:**   *A–N–N→*
    B. 15 **T:**   *How do we say the 'A? (pause, no response)*
    B. 16 **I:**   *(no response)*
    B. 17 **T:**   *ˌJ, 'do you wanta ˌhelp her?*
    B. 18 **C:**   *ˋI know.*
    B. 19 **J:**   *The <u>letter</u> ˌcapital A.*
    B. 20 **T:**   *ˈCapital ˋA–ˌN–N. 'Why do we sayˌ capital, I?*
    B. 21 **I:**   *(no response)*
    B. 22 **T:**   *'Why would we put a capital A on theˌ Ann,ˌ E?*
    B. 23 **E:**   *Because it'sˌ someone'sˌ name.*
    B. 24 **T:**   *It's theˋ name of somebody, ˌI. So we make it ˋspecial.*
    B. 25 **E:**   *A ˌgirl, the ˈname of a ˌgirl.*
    B. 26 **T:**   *Would you see anyˌ other name I, that you know?*
    B. 27 **C:**   *'I see a name, a ^Ben.*
    B. 28 **T:**   *Any <u>other name</u>. Let I find one. Do you ˌsee a name you know there? →'*

B. 29 I: (long pause) ʼ*Ken.*
B. 30 T: ˎ*All right,* ˋ*Ken. That's* ˎ*right.*

Both episodes can be seen as attempts by the two teachers to elicit task-oriented responses. In each case the learner begins with inappropriate answers. The teacher then obtains the desired response by a series of strategies.

The distinction between the situations is that *C1* must define her role, whereas *T*'s role is clear. This also bears on the difference in verbal strategies. *T*'s students are more or less obliged to sit in her presence by the very definition of the task. If *T* is going to give a spelling lesson, then the students must be there; that is why *T* is in the school building in the first place. This is not the case for *C1*. She must make the role relationship clear to her student personally, and she is doing it by means of a direct command, telling him to *Come here* and approximately where to sit, *Sit down around here,* etc. When he does not respond immediately but, rather, directs a question at her, she repeats her command, giving specific time and location: *Sit down here, now!*

Even in this brief sequence *C1* demonstrates a characteristic of her overall strategy, which is to change both form and style of delivery in an escalating series until her purpose is accomplished. Lines 1 through 4 are successively more specific in terms of actual verbal content. *C2* is directed first to approach, then to sit in the general vicinity, then to sit in a specific place at a specific time. Line 4 shows an intonational contrast as well in the raised pitch and volume and high-fall contour on *now!* This sequence embodies a three-stage tactic that reaches its peak in the verbally and intonationally marked *now!* The tactic succeeds to the extent of focussing *C2*'s attention on the task, albeit to protest, *I don't wanta read all them words!* whereas his previous rejoinder was diversionary and unrelated, answering a command with a question. We may also assume that by now *C2* is in fact sitting down, judging by the subsequent dialog. *C1* then narrows further the focus on "words" introduced by *C2* by repeating and intonational foregrounding, as well as by specifying, *What's this word, anyway?* *C1*'s new tactic is the use of the interrogative. Attention is now focused on a single word. *C2* says he does not know in a tone of voice implying *How should I know?* (fall–rise contour), and *C1* then supplies the actual word. We might say she is giving an example of the kind of response she expects from *C2* as the student. *C2* still delays by asking for a repeat, even though *C1*'s first reading was quite loud. She repeats with escalated emphasis—the first time was low-fall, the second is high-fall and high volume. *C2* then repeats the word in low-fall tone and is drawn into the lesson relationship.

Our adult teacher example starts at a point in the discourse approximately equivalent to line A6 in the child–child discourse, except that her focusing question does not have the simultaneous contrastive organizational effect that *C1*'s does. That is, there is no doubt that her students are the students and are expected to respond in the vein of the questions asked. *C1*'s *Well, let's see, what's this word, anyway?* and *T*'s *I, do, do you see a name on that page that you know?* are both attempts to elicit a task-oriented response from a student. *C1* characteristically uses a question form of the type *what's this*, for which a content answer would ideally be the response. *T* uses a more indirect question form, *do you see*, for which a yes–no answer would be appropriate, and further questioning would logically be required in order to elicit a content answer. All of *T*'s subsequent elicitations have this form. The student, *I*, accurately glosses *T*'s question as the functional equivalent of *C1*'s *what's this* and provides, in fact, a content answer. Some interpretative skills beyond the purely lexical–syntactic skills are required in this case to deduce the functional meaning. After *I*'s answer, *T* asks for a repeat and *I* repeats the word *Ann*. We note, however, that *I*'s intonation has changed from a mid-sustained reading type of tone to a low-rise tone, which might be suitable to express tentativeness. *T* neither confirms, denies, nor repeats *I*'s answer but metacomments on it: *That's the one that J just named.*

We infer from this statement, which has no overt value markers in it, a mild criticism of *I*'s answer. To interpret it requires the understanding of a rule: It does not count to give an answer that someone else has already/just given. *T* then asks *I* how to spell the word, foregrounding *spell* with a high-fall contour that serves as a two-way contrast: (1) with *T*'s utterance of line 1, *V, how do you spell Ann?* and (2) with her preceding utterance, glossed: *J just named it, but how do you spell it? I* spells *Ann*. *T* asks a thematic question designed to elicit the "capital initial letter for proper nouns" concept, which has been a focal point in the lesson. Once again the surface form of her question *How do we say the A?* requires some secondary-level interpretation in order to produce the correct response. *I* does not respond, and *T* calls on another child, *J*, with a *do you want to* request form, employing the expression *help her* to indicate that *J* should provide the correct answer. A child, possibly *I*, says *I know* as *J* provides the correct answer. *T* repeats the spelling of *Ann* using the correct case designation for the first letter. She then addresses *I* once more by name to elicit the theory behind "capital letter": *Why do we say capital, I?* I does not respond. *T* addresses another child, *E*, by name, using a hypothetical mood, *Why would we,* and somewhat metaphoric language, *put a capital A on the ANN? E* responds correctly, *Because it's someone's name. T* repeats *E*'s correct response with changed surface structure, *It's the name of somebody, I,* foregrounding the concept "name" with high-fall tone and employing *I*'s name as if to draw her particular attention to it. *T* complements the answer with a pseudo-logical explanation, *So we make it special,* which conveys a somewhat generalized notion of the relation of capital letters to names. A further step of deduction is required to get *T*'s meaning: It's a name, we make a name special, a capital first letter is a way of making a name special. *E* supplements her own correct answer by specifying further that *Ann* is the name of a girl. *T* does not respond to this volunteered information and addresses *I* by name once more, using a hypothetical auxiliary, *Would you see any other name?* Another *C* simultaneously volunteers an answer. *T* continues questioning *I*, repeating *any other name,* then deflects *C*, neither confirming nor denying his answer, employing an imperative form, *Let I find one.* She repeats her question to *I* in the same intonation as all her previous questions. After a long pause *I* responds with a tentative high-rise tone, *'Ken? T* then confirms, foregrounds the answer by repeating it with a high-fall, and repeats her confirmation, substituting a pronoun-copula-predicate adjective construction, *that's right,* for the purely affirmative *all right,* by way of emphasis.

T has now succeeded in eliciting a correct and seemingly original, task-oriented response from *I*. It took a series of exchanges, the length of which may be due in part to the number of children involved. Contrast this with *C1*'s swift and direct interchange with a single student, *C2*. Other contrasts present themselves in addition to length of sequence. We feel that the brevity of *C1*'s sample interchange is no accident, for behind every syntactic and lexical shift we have been able to uncover a tactical purpose and a corresponding effect on *C2*, and this would be equally the case for any segment of the child–child reading lesson we examine. We might attribute this in part to *C1*'s ambiguous status as a child teacher or to other reasons, such as her cultural background and her shared code with *C2*. For whatever reason, *C1* is efficient in her use of language, and at the same time she makes ready shifts in her use of syntactic forms as well as prosodic features to accomplish her purpose.

T also employs changes in syntax and lexicon and uses some intonational devices. But two impressions emerge from her overall discourse. One is that she relies heavily on the interrogative form, both for requests to perform and for actual elicitation of content responses. The other is that the succession of forms she employs in eliciting an appropriate response is in some ways a mirror image of what *C1* does. While *C1*'s strategy is one of increasing specificity of requests, *T* shows a tendency to become successively more indirect, moving from *how do you spell* to *how do we say,* from *do you see* to *would you see.* There is also a lack of intonational variation in *T*'s delivery.

Let us now turn to a more systematic examination of the linguistic devices used by participants in the two episodes. Upon first listening to the recording of the two children in episode A, we were struck by the extraordinary degree of musical and rhythmic relatedness between *C1*'s and *C2*'s speech. To some extent this is exemplified in the "thirty-three" sequence cited earlier, in which a single word forms the pivot for a five-line exchange. We temporarily styled this rhythm "syncopation." A more elaborate example of a similar interactional pattern was discovered upon reading Reisman (1970) at just the point in the tape where we were about to give up trying to transcribe a difficult passage because "everyone was talking at once." Similarly, on first listening to the section for adult teacher examples in this study, the transcribers were impressed with the "monotony" of the interaction, and with how uninteresting it was to transcribe in contrast with the two-children tape.

What kinds of perceptions do these judgments come from? Why is it possible for someone to listen to two people talking and, without understanding the content of what they are saying, know, for example, that they are arguing, romancing, or otherwise intently interacting? There are, doubtless, many reasons. We would like to suggest that the prosodic component encompassing stress, pitch, and timing along with speech features usually termed paralinguistic is as important in interpreting the meaning of interactional exchanges as referential meaning or propositional content, and that it functions to maintain and control interactions in somewhat the same way as the coordination of gestures, facial movements, eye blinks, etc., described in the recent literature on kinesics (Condon and Ogston, 1967). In talking of such things as question intonation, emphatic intonation, etc., linguists suggest that intonation, when choice among alternatives is optional and does not affect the grammaticality of a sentence, carries meaning. What we would like to suggest here is that such expressive meanings, although surely based on some universal signs, are not meaningful in the abstract but are the output of marking processes generated as part of the interactional exchanges. What these features do is affirm, question, emphasize, or otherwise qualify something that has been said or is being presupposed in the message. When seen in this light, prosodic aspects of speech become part of an optional set of communicative strategies that can be used alternatively with syntactic, lexical, or phonological variables. Choice among these alternatives is a function of the speaker's background and his communicative intent. The contrast between children's and adult strategies in our example provides some good illustrations of this phenomenon.

Here are some examples of the children's use of intonational and prosodic features and the meanings they carry. When the child teacher repeats or echoes part of the learner's utterance, using the low-fall stress and intonation contour, the meaning is confirmation or affirmation. See the use of *thirty-three* in item 2. When an item is repeated with substitution of high-rise for low-falling or high-falling tone, the item is being questioned or challenged. When the learner repeats or echoes the teacher's utterance with the same intonation and stress, the meaning is "I am following your directions" or "I am doing what you told me":

4.1. **A. 10   C1:**   `ˋLarge!`
      A. 11   C2:   `ˋLarge.`

4.2. **A. 26   C2:**   *Come-→*
      A. 27a C1:   *The-→*
      A. 27b C2:   *Ba-→ ′The? ′The? The-→*

4.3. **A. 68   C1:**   *Say-→*
      A. 69   C2:   *Sa-→ ′Say?*
      A. 70a C2:   *ˇS⁺ay?*
      A. 70b C1:   *S̲a̲y̲-→*

In the last sequence *C1* begins by prompting. *C2* starts to follow, then challenges her. As he repeats his challenge she simultaneously affirms her original statement. A rise in pitch on a particular item accompanied by shift in stress to that item and special loudness and sometimes falsetto voice suggests special emphasis or surprise, or contrast with a previous statement:

5.1. **A. 1   C1:**   *′Come ˌhere.*
      A. 2   C1:   *ˈSit ˈdown around ˌhere . . .*
      A. 4   C1:   *ˈSit down ˌhere, ˋn⁺ow!*

5.2. **A. 8   C1:**   *ˌLarge.*
      A. 9   C2:   *′What?*
      A. 10 C1:   *ˋLarge!*

5.3. **A. 12 C1:**   *Go⃗ get yo book . . .*
      A. 14 C1:   *ˌGo get yo⃗ book!*

Emphasis often takes the form of a sequence of several statements, each one augmenting the pitch and stress of the preceding one, followed by a resolution that is signaled by a slight drop in pitch, as in the following:

6. **A. 8**   **C1:**   ⌄*Large.*
   A. 9   **C2:**   ⌐*What?*
   A. 10 **C1:**   ⌐*Large!*
   A. 11 **C2:**   ⌄*Large.* (resolved)

Intonation contrasts are also used by the children for more subtle maneuvers, such as bluffing or covering up errors:

7. **A. 32**   **C1:**   *The-→*
   [ðə]
   A. 33   **C2:**   *The-→* ⌐*They!*
   [ðə]
   A. 34a **C2:**   ⌐*At ain't no* ⌄[ðə].
   A. 34b **C1:**   ⌄*No,* ⌐[ðə]
   A. 35   **C2:**   ⌐*At's* [ðə], ⌐*did you say* ⌄[ði]?
   A. 36   **C1:**   *I said . . .*
   A. 37   **C2:**   *The-→*
   [ðə]

Here *C2* has attempted to correct *C1*'s reading. Unable to carry his protest through, he pretends to have said what she said, attributing a different articulation to her. Note how in lines 34a and 35 *C2* quickly changes his mind in the face of *C1*'s repetition, and having already denied that the word was [ðə], he must resort to a purely tonal contrast in order to complete his sentence and at the same time assert the correct form of the reading as his own.

In comparison with the reliance on intonation and stress in episode A, the adult teacher, although she uses similar devices on occasion, makes much more extensive use of lexical and rhetorical devices. Consider the following passage, in which the adult teacher, like the child teacher, attempts to correct and guide the learner's response:

8. **B. 59**   **B:**   *P-→ E-→ T-→* ⌄*E.*
   B. 60   **T:**   *Just P-→ E-→ T-→* ⌄*E? What do you say about the first letter?*

In item 8 the teacher challenges *B*'s answer by repeating it as a question preceded by the qualifier *just*, indicating that it is inadequate. She then asks another question that contains a hint as to what part of the answer has been neglected. In item 9 we see further examples of the adult teacher's use of strategic questions both to signal the inadequacy of a child's response and to provide cues as to the locus of the missing elements of the answer. These cues are contained in lexical indicators rather than direct hints, e.g., B. 41, . . . *Do you see an* [ae]*-sound?, B. 43, What sound do you see?* Contrast *C1*'s repetition and assertion of the right answer, using intonation as an aid, with *T*'s focus on what is wrong with the answer, using lexical items and question forms:

9.　　**B. 37 T:**　*Do ˏyou see any word there that you know, B, any-one's name?*
　　　　B. 38 B:　ˎ*Pat. P-→*
a.　**B. 39 T:**　ˊ*What's that?*
　　　　B. 40 B:　ˏ*Pat.*
b.　**B. 41 T:**　ˈ*Where do you see* ˋ*Pat?* c. *Do you see an* [ae]ᵥ *sound in there?*
　　　　B. 42 B:　ˏ*No.*
c.　**B. 43 T:**　ˈ*What sound do you* ˋ*see?*
　　　　B. 44 B:　ˎ*Pat.*
b.　**B. 45 T:**　*Do you see an* ˏ[ae]*-sound?*
　　　　B. 46 B:　*No.*
c.　**B. 47 T:**　*What sound do you* ˎ*see?*
　　　　B. 48 B:　ˎ*Pet.*
　　　　B. 49 I:　ˊ*Peter?*
b.　**B. 50 T:**　*Is there an* ˏ[ər] *on the end?*

Devices:　a.　request for repetition
　　　　　　b.　challenge cum question: *Where do you see Pat?*
　　　　　　c.　attempt at focusing on salient feature

The following examples illustrate the adult teacher's strategies for confirming learner's response:

10.1.　**B. 7**　**T:**　*Of a__-→*
　　　　B. 8　**V:**　ˎ*Girl*
　　　　B. 9　**T:**　ˎ*OK* . . . (addresses another *C*)

10.2.　**B. 28**　**T:**　*Do you see a name you know there?*
　　　　B. 29　**I:**　(pause) ˊ*Ken.*
　　　　B. 30　**T:**　ˎ*All right.* ˋ*Ken. That's* ˏ*right.*

10.3.　**B. 33**　**I:**　*Capital K-→* . . .
　　　　B. 35　**T:**　ˊ*E-→*

    B. 36 I: ˌ*N.*
    B. 37 T: ˌ*Right.* ˌ*Ken.*

10.4. B. 57 C: ˌ*Pete.*
    B. 58 T: *That's* ˌ*right. How do you* ˋ*spell it?*

10.5. B. 66 T: ᵢ*Can you spell the word* ′*Roy for u͢s, J?*
    B. 67 J: ˌ*R*–ˌ*O*–ˋ*Y*
    B. 68 T: ˋ*Good.* ′*That spells* ˌ*Roy. R*–*O*–ˌ*Y.*

10.6. B. 1   T: *V, how do you* ′*spell* ˌ*Ann?*
    B. 2   V: *A*→ *N*→ ˌ*N*
    B. 3   T: *A*–*N*–ˌ*N*

Note the variety of expressions the teacher uses to confirm and guide her learners: *OK, All right, That's right, Good, That spells Roy.* She also uses the device of repeating the answer. However, echoing the child's intonation is not noticeably a part of her strategy. Nor is exact echoing of the form of the response her method so much as confirming the content. For instance, in B. 24 she repeats the exact meaning of E's answer with a different surface structure and the optional substitution of *somebody* for *someone:*

11. B. 22 T: ′*Why would we put a capital 'A' on* ˌ*Ann,'* ˌ*E?*
    B. 23 E: *Because it's someone's* ˌ*name.*
    B. 24 T: *It's the* ˋ*name of somebody,* ˌ*I* . . .

The adult teacher does, however, make extensive use of echoing elsewhere when repeating and thus developing her own question strategies. Here, as in the case of the eliciting strategies discussed previously, her technique contrasts with that of the child teacher.

A further important aspect of the children's speech is the sharp rhythmic distinction they draw between reading and conversational style and word game style. Compare the following example:

12.1. A. 32a C2: *Boys*→ *and*→ *girls*→

12.2. A. 40   C2: *The b͜oys*→ *and͜ girls*→

In the first item, each word is produced separately as in a list of items, vowels are elongated, and tone is sustained, i.e., neither falling or rising. In the second, elongation of vowels is less but the rhythm is staccato and tone is still sustained. By contrast, a sentence like:

13. A. 35 C2: . . . ′*At's* [ˋdə], *did you say* ˌ[d͢i]*?*

is characterized by normal word sandhi and a wide range of intonational patterns. In:

14. **A. 74 C1:** ˈ*I'm ʼon tell your ˌteacher* —

is pronounced in sing-song style and draws the response:

15. **A. 75 C3:** *You ˌcain' g͡it m͡e* —

where by falling in with the style *C3* signals his competence in the style and in managing peer relationships.

The contrast between reading and conversation style is used for communicative effect in the following sequence:

16. **A. 35 C2:** ˈ*At's* [d̪ə]. ˌ*At's* [d̪ə], *did you say* [d̪i]?
    A. 36 C1: *I said* . . .
    A. 37 C2: *The*→
       [d̪ə]

As described previously, *C2* has challenged *C1*'s reading but, in the face of her repetition, accepts it, asking her if she had said something else. Before she can assert what she really said, he falls into reading style as if to say "Never mind, let's go on reading."

In episode B, on the other hand, while the teacher maintains the same rhythm throughout, the children differ stylistically between interactions with her and interactions with each other. Contrast:

17. **B. 23 E:** *Because it's someone's ˌname.*

in which the child's speech echoes the teacher's low pitch, volume, and lack of tonal contrast and uses standard English variables, with:

18. **B. 34 C:** ˈ*You messin' up the* ˈˈ*raser ˌalreădy!*

Here the rhythmic and intonational contrasts are pronounced. *Already* is emphasized by high pitch, elongated vowel, high-falling tone with 2-stage drop and stress. Note the use of black variables such as copula deletion.

The overall impression gained from our analysis of style and sequencing of illocutionary devices is that the two groups differ in their definition of the teaching task and of their social relationships, i.e., mutual rights and duties. The children see their task as teamwork focused around the task of reading, i.e., producing the printed word orally.

This is illustrated with the following:

19. **A. 45**   **C1:**   *They→*
    A. 46   **C2:**   *'They?*
    A. 47a **C1:**   (to C3) *'Get outa ˏhere.*
    A. 47b **C2:**   *They go→*
    A. 48   **C2:**   *ˏNot ˋthey!*
    A. 49   **C1:**   *Down→*
    A. 50   **C1:**   ı(short pause) *They→*
    A. 51   **C2:**   *ˊThey→*
    A. 52   **C1:**   *Go→* (short)
    A. 53   **C2:**   *Go→* (short)
    A. 54a **C1:**   *'Theyˏgo down→*
    A. 54b **C2:**   *'Theyˏgo down→*
    A. 55   **C1:**   *To−*(low volume)
    A. 56   **C2:**   *To→ the--* (projected volume)
    A. 57   **C1:**   *ˏLunch*
    A. 58   **C2:**   *ˏLunch*
    A. 59   **C1:**   *ˋRoom.*

In item 19 the end of a sentence has just been reached in the ongoing reading. *C1* reads the first word of the next sentence in typical sustained reading intonation and is echoed by *C2*. *C1* turns aside momentarily to deflect interference without breaking pace as *C2* again repeats the read word and augments it with another one. He then contests *C1*'s reading of a previous word, but she continues with the passage, picking up in sequence to the word read by *C2* as she was simultaneously talking to *C3*. Even while talking aside she has not broken the sequence of interaction with *C2*. After a short pause in which *C2* does not speak in his turn, *C1* begins reading the sentence again with *C2* following in word-by-word suit in identical intonation and timing. *C1* repeats the whole phrase and is echoed identically by *C2*. *C1* then introduces a shift in mood by dropping her voice to a low pitch, and *C2* repeats her word but in a contrasting, slightly projecting pitch. *C2* then augments by filling in the next word on the page. *C1* reads a word echoed by *C2*, both in a low-rising tone suitable for signaling the penultimate in a series, and *C1* caps off the sentence with a high-falling tone, ending the sequence. Over all the sequence there is a regularity of time intervals between the utterances of the two speakers. There are no long pauses, and in the event of a short pause, as between lines A. 49 and A. 50, *C1* immediately fills in by starting the passage over again, successfully inducing *C2* to follow suit. Variation in rhythm, such as a double beat, may occur, as when *C2* aug-

ments his repetition with an independently read word, or when *C1* recapitulates a phrase, followed by *C2*. But the intervals between utterances
remain equal overall. In another passage, where one *C* initiates a change
of pace by shortening the interval and raising the pitch level, the other
follows suit. We see that sentences are cooperatively produced. This is a
characteristic of the children's reading throughout. Elsewhere in our
analysis word count reveals that *C1* and *C2* speak approximately an
equal number of words even when they are not reading. In example 3, for
instance, *C1* produces 19 words to *C2*'s 20.

Moreover, we see a certain parallel production in sequential length
configuration. If *C1* makes a long utterance, *C2* is likely to make a long
reply; if she makes a one-word utterance, he will do likewise and vice
versa. In the sample segment of episode B that we used to contrast *C1*'s
and *T*'s elicitation strategies, example 3 (lines B. 12–B. 31), we found
that *T* used 103 words, of which 6 are children's names used in address,
to 25 words for all of the children combined. Almost by definition, then,
her utterances are considerably longer than those of the children. If her
purpose is to elicit responses from the children, her input cost is considerably greater proportionally than *C1*'s. This contrast in relative production, along with the variety of other contrasts we have presented, arises,
we feel, out of differing concepts of participant structure and differing
definitions of the task of teaching held by the child and adult teacher in
our data. *T*'s definition of her task is one of evaluating the learners' ability to read and to verbalize spelling rules:

20. **B. 1 T:** *J, how do you 'spell ⟍Ann?*
    B. 2 J: *'A→ N→ N*
    B. 3 T: *'A − N−⟍N. What ⟋kind of an A?*
    B. 4 J: *⟍Capital.*
    B. 5 T: *'Why ⟋is it ⟍capital?*
    B. 6 J: *ıCause it's a ⟍name.*
    B. 7 T: *Of a →*
    B. 8 J: *⟍Girl.*
    B. 9 T: *⟍OK. I, do ⟋you see a name on that page that you
    know?*

Her technique is one of calling on the children to read and guiding the
children along certain logical or quasilogical lines of induction by lengthy
questioning. She sees the activity as a rule-segregated one in which the
relevance of utterances is determined by her alone and children's production is almost entirely in response to her elicitation. The entire episode takes the form of a sequence of questions and answers. The teach-

er's implicit authority is reflected in the fact that she assumes the right to continue questioning even in the face of no response. In the event of volunteered responses, deemed "inappropriate" or "out of turn," *T* may discourage the speaker by indirectly referring to rules of conduct. The child teacher in episode A is less concerned with evaluation than with making sure that *C2*'s production is faithful to the printed words, i.e., that "reading" is in fact taking place. "Correct" answers are thus unmarked, and she interferes only when production deviates from what is written. Moreover, *C1* appears to see her task not as eliciting performance from *C2* so much as helping him in reading. This is not to say that division of authority is not operating in the situation, for we have seen *C1* in various attempts to gain and maintain control. Also, she has the inherent superiority of one who has mastery of a skill that is being transmitted. However, her actual teaching behavior is fundamentally cooperative rather than hierarchical, and is centered on a certain prosodic style and rhythm of exchange. *C2* is free to initiate topics and even to guide the activity to some extent. He can interrupt, and there are times elsewhere in the material when *C1* assumes the role of playmate. It is this alternation of roles along with the parity of production — the sense of prosodic interplay — that differentiates the child's definition of teaching as a cooperative activity from the adult teacher's focus on evaluation and control.

Conclusion

Although this study is intended to be illustrative rather than definitive, it should be sufficient to suggest that methods based on those of linguistics, when applied to the study of conversations, can yield rich information on social interaction, provided that the analytical framework is adapted to the purpose, and questions asked of the data are properly defined. Frake (1964), Sacks (1972), Schegloff (1972), and Moerman (1972) have shown that the sequential ordering of information and selection of illocutionary devices and content are rule governed. Our own work adds, we hope, to this tradition by showing how the rules of social interaction can be realized in linguistic form.

Our findings suggest that communications of meaning in conversation can best be understood by distinguishing between two semantic processes similar to what Geoghegan, in his study of address terminology (Geoghegan, 1970), has called coding and marking processes. Code rules are the processes by which ideas are encoded into grammatical, i.e., potentially interpretable, sentences. Marking rules take the output of code rules and, by reinterpreting message elements in relation to other cooccurring elements, speakers' presuppositions, and other contextual information, generate situated interpretations. The role and functioning of linguistic features in marking processes is as yet little understood. Only some of these features of language are dealt with in traditional linguistic analysis. Others, such as variable selection, code switching, choice among intonational, prosodic, and paralinguistic options, sequential ordering of content, and illocutionary devices, have only begun to be studied. Where they have been described, they have tended to be treated in taxonomic terms and not as an integral part of the process of linguistic communication.

One reason for this neglect has been the emphasis on sentences and texts as the proper unit of linguistic analysis and on grammars as structurally homogeneous systems. A distinguishing feature of sociolinguistic marking processes is that meaning does not inhere in isolated sentences and, thus, cannot be listed in dictionaries. The creation of social meaning relies on juxtaposition of one utterance with another or with some aspect of the speaker's or hearer's background knowledge. It is this juxtaposition that is used for metaphorical effect and, as Claudia Mitchell-Kernan (1971) has suggested, may account for the persistence of linguistic variables in speech communities.

The other feature of this marking process is the variability of marking rules. Our own examples point to some important differences between children and adults. Some of these may be maturational; others are culturally determined. This variability is an important feature of interaction in any speech community. It can lead to serious miscommunication (Gumperz, 1970). Yet its relation to macrofactors of class, race, ethnic origin, educational achievement is as yet little understood. Further investigation along the lines suggested here may lead to clarification of some of these issues.

Appendix: Texts

EPISODE A (CHILD TEACHER)

C1 is the "teacher," a second-grade girl.
C2 is the "learner," a first-grade boy.

TEXT			GLOSSES AND COMMENTS
A.1	**C1:**	*'Come here.*	**A.1** — *C1*, addressing *C2*, demands that he approach.
A.2	**C1:**	*'Sit 'down around here.*	**A.2** — *C1* directs *C2* to sit down with measured timing and falling tone, as in A.1.
A.3	**C2:**	*D'you know . . . 'any . . . you know . . . like 'this?*	**A.3** — *C2* asks question unrelated in content and conversational rhythm (sandhi

contrasted with measured 1-2 rhythm) and intonation.

A.4 **C1:** ⌄*Sit down ↓here, ˈ⁺now!*

A.4 − *C1* repeats demand of line A.2. *Now* is characterized by high-falling pitch, overloud stress, and separation from the preceding statement by a pause suggesting forceful emphasis. Gloss: Let's get down to business.

A.5 **C2:** ˈ*I don't wanta read all them words!*→

A.5 − *C2* protests, using a sustained tone. The tone level is suggestive of a mid or minor tone and is characteristic of *C2*'s speech.

A.6 **C1:** ⌄*Well, (let's see)* '*what's this* `*word, anyway?*

A.6 − *C1* starts with a vocative followed by a question, in effect directing *C2*'s attention to the material. Lexical item "word" is echoed from *C2*'s foregoing line, but not specifically singular. It is foregrounded by nuclearity, primary stress, and high-fall intonation.

A.7 **C2:** ʼ*I don't* ˈ*know!*

A.7 − *C2* disavows. Falling–rising tone suggests gloss: How should I know?

A.8 **C1:** ⌄*Large.*

A.8 − *C1* informs in declarative low-fall.

A.9 **C2:** `*What?*

A.9 − *C2* questions abruptly in request for repeat.

A.10 **C1:** `*Large!*

A.10 − *C1* repeats with emphatic loudness. A.10 escalates A.8, going from low-fall to high-fall, as if to say "I already told you."

A.11 **C2:** ⌄*Large!* [splice in tape]

A.11 − *C2* repeats with same intonation as *C1*'s A.8 and volume close to her A.10, echoing her intensity.

* * * * *

A.12 **C1:** ⌄*G⃗o get yo book. (Y⃗ou ain' gon' rea⃗d.)*→

A.12 − *C1* commands in "stop jiving" intonation, high head, low sustained fall, vernacular phonology.

A.13 **C2:** [Laughs]

A.13 − *C2* responds by laughing, as if to deflect *C1*'s command.

A.14 **C1:** `*Go get yo* `*book!*

A.14 − *C1* repeats her command with stress shifted to *book,* and higher, more childlike pitch.

A.15 **C2:** *W-w-w, you said you would go . . . the teacher.*

A.15 − *C2*'s high-pitched falsetto voice suggests protest and challenge to *C1*.

A.16 **C1:** ʼ*Come* ⌄*on now.*

A.16 − *C1* shifts strategy to coaxing.

A.17 **C2:** *. . .* ʼ*read a* `*book!*

A.17 − *C2* makes a partly inaudible statement in a falsetto tone suggesting protest.

A.18 **T:** *Can't you get it?* ʼ*Let him get him* ⌄*own book.*

A.18 − *T*'s question, which serves as a directive bears out the (largely intonational) evaluation of *C2*'s line as a protest. *T* then hortatively addresses *C1* with a direction whose function is to make *C2* act.

A.19 **C1:** `*OK.*

A.19 − *C1* expresses compliance.

A.20 **C2:** -*right.*

A.20 − *C2* also complies, in a low voice.

(There is a long pause on the tape; presumably, *C2* is getting his book.)

A.21 C2: *Page ,thirty-thrȩe, 'where's `thirty-three?*

A.21 — *C2* announces the page number, then questions about its location. Note measured rhythm and syncopated timing, projecting tone.

A.22 C1: *Thirty-three.*

A.22 — *C1* repeats the salient item *thirty-three* in a low declarative tone.

A.23 C2: *Thirty-three, is 'this ´ thirty-thrēe?*

A.23 — *C2* repeats the item *thirty-three,* then asks if the page he has found matches that number. He has repeated the number four times, twice as a declaration and twice as a question.

A.24 C1: *Thirty-three.*

A.24 — repeats the item in the same tone as in A.22, declarative low-fall.

A.25 C2: *¡Kay. Well, I was, I was ,over ,here.*

A.25 — *C2* is satisfied, affirms finding place, drops voice level.

A.26 C2: *Cŏme —*

A.26 — *C2* begins to read in sustained, projected "reading tone." High sustained tone suggests tentativeness.

A.27a C1: *The→*

A.27a — *C1* corrects *C2* by producing a different word in mid-sustained tone.

A.27b C2: *Ba→ ´ The? ´ The? The→* [bae?]

A.27b — *C2* simultaneously is following up his first word with a semantically logical sequel. He then picks up on *C1*'s correction, repeating it in question intonation, high-rise, two times, then once again in reading tone, sustained, showing acceptance of *C1*'s correction.

A.28 C1: *Morning→*

A.28 — *C1* continues the reading.

A.29 C2: *Morning→ is→ ´ cŏming?*

A.29 — *C2* repeats in identical reading intonation. He then independently reads the next word in the same sustained tone. A third word is produced in high-rise question tone.

A.30 C1: *`Over!* [r:]

A.30 — *C1* corrects with high volume and high-fall emphatic tone. Tonal emphasis is accompanied by very long final [r:].

A.31 C2: *`Over! The morning i→* (Break in recording).

A.31 — *C2* repeats, echoing *C1*'s tone. He then begins to recapitulate the sentence to himself in reading tone. There is a break in the recording.

A.32 C1: *The→* [dǝ]

A.32 — *C1* reads a word.

A.33 C2: *The→ `They!* [d]

A.33 — *C2* repeats after *C1* in reading tone, then challenges *C1*'s reading by changing a phoneme and using a higher volume and high-fall intonation. He also draws out the vowel [e:] for emphasis.

A.34a C2: *''At ain't no [dǝ],*
A.34b C1: *,No, [dǝ].*

A.34a–35 — *C2* develops his tonal challenge into a statement explicitly correcting

A.35 C2: *"At's* [ɖə]. *'At's* [ɖə], *'did you say* [ɖi]?

C1's reading. *C1* at the same time negates his correction and repeats her reading, such that they are simultaneously producing phonetically identical but intonationally contradictory utterances. *C2* reflects *C1*'s affirmation of her own reading by finishing his sentence with the word he just negated, still using a challenging tone to mark a contrast that no longer exists. He follows up with a repetition of his effective confirmation of *C2*'s reading, and asks her if she said something else.

A.36 C1: *I said . . .*

A.36 — *C1* in normal tone begins to answer *C2*'s question.

A.37 C2: *The→*

A.37 — Before *C1* can finish her answer, *C2* produces the word in a reading tone, resuming the lesson activity.

A.38a C3: *Boy→*

A.38a — *C3* joins in the reading. It is hard to tell from the tape if his onset precedes *C2*'s.

A.38b C2: *Boys→ and→ girls→*

A.38b — *C2* continues reading the sentence, in part simultaneously with *C3*.

A.39 C1: *'Don't tell 'im, 'I'm teachin' 'im.*

A.39 — *C1* addresses *C3* in measured lecturing tone (command), as in line A.2. She makes a negative command followed by an assertion of her rights in the situation.

A.40 C2: *The boys→ and girls→*

A.40 — *C2* repeats what he has read, making units out of the two NPs.

A.41 C1: *Go–*

A.41 — *C1* reads in a low sustained tone, with long w-glide, suggesting exaggeration appropriate for prompting.

A.42 C2: *Go··→ to··→*

A.42 — *C2* repeats what *C1* has read and supplements it with the next word.

A.43 C1: *Lu–* [tə]

A.43 — *C1* prompts *C2* by producing the first part of a word, holding the onset.

A.44 C2: *Lunch. Come→*

A.44 — *C2* quickly responds by producing the whole word; vocalic onset suggests enthusiasm, as do the timing and slightly long, laryngealized first phoneme. *C2* then attempts to read on.

A.45 C1: *They→*

A.45 — *C1* corrects him by producing a different word in reading tone.

A.46 C2: *'They?*

A.46 — *C2* repeats the word with low-rise mild question tone.

A.47a C1: *'Get outa here.*

A.47a — *C1* addresses *C3* with a command in a sustained low-rise tone (dialect typical) related to her tone of line A.12. She maintains a measured rhythm, not breaking the pace of her interaction with *C2*, and employs vernacular phonology.

A.47b C2: *They go→*   **A.47b** — *C2* is simultaneously reading, using the word *C1* gave him and that he previously slightly questioned.

A.48 C2: ˌ*Not* ˈ*they!*   **A.48** — *C2* now openly contests the word they.

A.49 C1: *Down→*   **A.49** — *C1* reads in sustained tone, continuing from *C2*'s line A.46b, ignoring his protest of line A.47.

A.50 C1: *They→*   **A.50** — *C2* has not picked up his cue and *C1* begins reading the sentence again from the beginning, as if to encourage *C2* to read after her.

A.51 C2: *They→*   **A.51** — *C2* repeats after *C1* in identical tone and timing.

A.52 C1: *Go→* (short)   **A.52** — *C1* reads.

A.53 C2: *Go→* (short)   **A.53** — *C2* repeats, identically.

A.54a C1: *They͜ go-down→*   **A.54a** — *C1* recapitulates the sentence, bringing the words together, ending with a mid-rise sustained tone indicating that more will follow and retaining reading tone.

A.54b C2: *They͜ go-down→*   **A.54b** — *C2* reads in chorus with *C1*, with identical timing and other features. In both cases there is a slight pause after *they; go down* is like one word. *C1*'s voice is at a slightly lower pitch and volume, like a support to *C2*'s reading.

A.55 C1: *To→* (low volume)   **A.55** — *C1* here drops her voice still lower.

A.56 C2: *To→ the→*   **A.56** — *C2* uses a more projecting pitch and volume. He follows up his echo by reading another word independently in a sustained tone, but at a lower pitch.

A.57 C1: ˌ*Lunch*   **A.57** — *C1* prompts *C2* with slow onset, long [l:], and low-rise tone appropriate for an item in a series other than the last one.

A.58 C2: ˌ*Lunch*   **A.58** — *C2* repeats quickly in same tone.

A.59 C1: ˋ*Room*   **A.59** — *C1* completes the sentence in high-fall tone suitable for logical conclusion.

A.60 C2: ˈ*I be* ˈ*finish wit͑this book!* ˌ*What's ͗that word?*   **A.60** — *C2* states expectatively in conversational tone that he is/will be finished reading the book. He then returns his attention to the reading, asking *C1* for the next word. Low-rise with slightly sustained tone suggests the gloss "What's that word? I know but temporarily forget." (Or, "What's that word, anyway?")

A.61 C1: *Ann→*   **A.61** — *C1* reads.

A.62 C2: *Ann→*   **A.62** — *C2* echoes.

A.63a C2: *Mother→*   **A.63a** — *C2* begins voicing next word

A.63b	**C1:**	*Mother*→	**A.63b** − *C1* reads in unison with *C2*.
A.64	**C1:**	*Is in*→	**A.64** − *C1* reads in sustained tone with continuity between the two words.
A.65	**C2:**	*Is*⁻→ *in*⁻→ [ʔɪz ʔɪn]	**A.65** − *C2* repeats the same words but with breaks in between as he normally does for reading.
A.66	**C1:**	'Ann's mother is 'in the ˋlunchroom.	**A.66** − *C1* reads the full sentence with continuity.
A.67	**C2:**	*Ann's mother*→ *is*→ *in*→ [ʔɪz ʔɪn] ˌthe ˌlunchroom.	**A.67** − *C2* repeats the words of the sentence but breaks between the words as he would if he were to read alone. However, he makes units of the noun phrases, reflecting advance knowledge of the structure of the sentence. At the end he abandons reading tone and gives normal declarative low-fall to *the lunchroom*. His low-fall contrasts with *C1*'s high-fall on the same word.

slightly before *C1* but otherwise they read in unison.

(There is a break in the recording)

A.68	**C1:**	*Say*→	**A.68** − *C1* prompts in low-fall sustained tone, long vowel.
A.69	**C2:**	*Sa*− *'Say?*	**A.69** − *C2* starts to repeat but breaks off to question.
A.70a	**C2:**	ˇ⁺Say?	**A.70a** − *C2* repeats his questioning of *C1*'s word in emphatic falsetto as
A.70b	**C1:**	*Say*−	**A.70b** − *C1* affirms in reading tone.
A.71a	**C1:**	ˌAnn−	**A.71a** − *C1* starts a word with elongated vowel, low-fall tone.
A.71b	**C2:**	ˌAnn−	**A.71b** − *C2* joins her in reading the word slightly behind. He also elongates the vowel, and uses the same low-fall tone.
A.72	**C1:**	ˌIs (whisper)	**A.72** − *C1* prompts in whisper, long vowel.
A.73a	**C2:**	*Is*→	**A.73a–73b** − *C2* and *C3* echo *C1* in
A.73b	**C3:**	*Is*→	chorus.
A.74	**C1:**	(to C3) 'I'm 'on tell your ˌteacher . . .	**A.74** − *C1* warns *C3* in sing-song rhythm and tone, sustained final syllable, to stop interfering. The tone interval in the nucleus could be characterized as minor.
A.75	**C3:**	You ˌcain' gĭt mē . . .	**A.75** − *C3* responds with sing-song dare, glossed "Try and catch me." His intonation is a development of *C1*'s and also employs a minor interval in the nucleus drop, as well as an even more elongated, musical final vowel.
A.76	**C2:**	'What's this wŏrd?	**A.76** − *C2* asks a question about the lesson in conversational tone, using a slight falsetto sustained or minor interval rise on

the nucleus. In effect, he supports *C1*
here by ignoring *C3*'s interruption.

Episode B (Adult Teacher)

The teacher is represented in the text by *T*, individual children by their initials.
Unidentified children are represented by *C*.

TEXT	GLOSSES AND COMMENTS
B.1 T: *J, how do you 'spell Ann?*	**B.1** — Quiet, almost muffled voice, *T* calls on *J* by name, following with request for information.
B.2 J: *'A→ N→ N*	**B.2** — *J* responds by spelling out word. Her tone echoes *T*'s quiet falling tone.
B.3 T: *A − N − N. What kind of an A?*	**B.3** — *T* repeats *J*'s spelling a little faster, drawing together letters in monotone, follows with request for further information.
B.4 J: *Capital.*	**B.4** — *J* supplements in slightly sustained tone.
B.5 T: *'Why is it capital?*	**B.5** — *T* questions further in slightly sustained low-fall tone, suggestive of question intonation.
B.6 J: *Cause it's a name.*	**B.6** — *J* answers, low voice.
B.7 T: *Of a→*	**B.7** — Same low tone, sustained (prompt) "fill in the blank" request.
B.8 J: *Girl.*	**B.8** — *J* fills in correct word.
B.9 T: *OK. 'I, do you see a name on that page that you know?*	**B.9** — *T* gives lexical confirmation, turns to address another child with a question.
B.10 I: *Ann.→*	**B.10** — *I* answers with sustained reading tone.
B.11 T: *'Hm?*	**B.11** — *T* asks for repeat.
B.12 I: *Ann.*	**B.12** — *I* repeats herself with tentative low-rise.
B.13 T: *That's the one that J just named. How do you 'spell Ann?*	**B.13** — *T* comments on *I*'s reply, gloss: Somebody already gave that answer, but go ahead and spell it. Slight criticism implied, *spell* foregrounded by high fall. (How do you spell it, anyway.)
B.14 I: *A→ N→ N*	**B.14** — *I* spells.
B.15 T: *How do we say the 'A?*	**B.15** — *T* requests more information, as with *J* (B.3), using a slightly different form and with high head followed by high-rise nucleus, possibly indicating a reminder or reflecting the fact that *T* has asked this question before.
B.16 I: (no response)	**B.16** — *I* remains silent.
B.17 T: *J, 'do you want to help her?*	**B.17** — *T* turns back to *J*, gloss: *You* know the answer, please demonstrate an appro-

priate response. Shift of attention may carry implicit criticism.

B.18   C: `I know.

B.18 – A child, possibly *I*, expresses a wish to answer that goes unheeded. Another interpretation is that this is *J*.

B.19   J: *The letter �‚capital A.*

B.19 – *J* stresses capital as the salient part of the answer.

B.20   T: 'Capital `A, ͵N – N. 'Why do we say "͵capital," *I?*

B.20 – *T* repeats *J*'s answer, foregrounding it with high head and high nucleus, supplies the rest of the spelling. She addresses *I*, requesting her to supply the theoretical justification for an answer she was, for whatever reason, unable to give.

B.21   I: (no response)

B.21 – *I* remains silent.

B.22   T: 'Why would we put a capital 'A' on ͵Ann, ͵E?

B.22 – *T* repeats her question with different surface structure, employing hypothetical mood, same intonation. She addresses it to still another child, *E*. Note figurative language "*put* a capital A *on* . . ."

B.23   E: *Because it's someone's ͵name.*

B.23 – *E* answers correctly, echoing *T*'s low pitch and volume and lack of tonal contrast.

B.24   T: *It's the name of somebody, ͵I. So we make it ˋspecial.*

B.24 – *T* repeats *E*'s answer with different surface structure, foregrounding the concept "name" with high-fall, employing *I*'s name to draw her attention, and supplementing an explanation of the answer.

B.25   E: *A ͵girl, the 'name of a ͵girl.*

B.25 – *E* augments her answer, making it more specific.

B.26   T: *Would you see any ͵other name, I, that you know?*

B.26 – *T* once again addresses *I* with a question that is functionally an elicitation, as in B.9. She uses the hypothetical mood and specifies *other*, reflecting both that *I* has answered previously and that her answer had already been given.

B.27   C: '*I see a ͵name, a ˆBen.*

B.27 – A child other than *I* gives an answer. Note that his answer corresponds directly to the surface form of *T*'s elicitation formula, "do you see," filling in the answer to the unspoken further question, "What is the name that you see?"

B.28   T: *. . . ͵any other name? Let ͵I find one. D'you see a name you know there?*

B.28 – *T* meanwhile is still phrasing her question to *I*, repeating the salient portion of it. *T* deflects *C*'s participation with a positively framed command, without changing pace or pitch. She goes on to repeat her question elicitation to *I*.

B.29   I: (pause) ´Ken?

B.29 – After a pause *I* answers with a high-rise question contour.

B.30   **T:**   *ˌAll right. ˋKen. That's ˌright. How do you ˋspell Ken? Don't forget what you ˋsay to that firstˊletter. How do you spell Ken?*

B.30 — *T* gives a lexical confirmation with low-fall tone, repeats the answer, then confirms once more with syntactic and intonational emphasis. She then asks *I* for another stage of the answer, quickly reminding her to apply the capital letter principal, using the expression "*say to that first letter*" to evoke it, and the construction "Don't forget—" as a prompt device. The prompt is sandwiched closely between the two question requests to spell and is marked by higher pitch and greater tonal contrast than is usual for *T*.

B.31   **A:**   *'Where is ˊKen? K-→, C-→ K→ E, er . . .*

B.31 — Another child attempts to answer the question put to *I*.

B.32   **T:**   *ˌA, 'I is ˌspelling it. 'Capital ˌK —*

B.32 — *T* discourages her from spelling by metaphorically stating that *I* is doing so; in fact, she is referring to the social situation, *I*'s turn at spelling, and the assumption that if it is *I*'s turn, then no one else should spell. *T* prompts *I* by giving part of the answer.

B.33   **I:**   *Capital K-→*

B.33 — *I* repeats *T*'s prompt, with same intonation.

B.34   **C:**   *'You messin' up the ''raser ˌalreadyˆ⁺!*

B.34 — A child addresses another admonishingly, using a voice quality, tonal contrast, and phonological register noticeably different from that of *C*'s involved in spelling.

B.35   **T:**   *E-→*

B.35 — *T* continues prompting *I*, ignoring line B.34.

B.36   **I:**   *ˌN.*

B.36 — *I* this time supplies the final letter of the word instead of imitating *T* as in line B.33.

B.37   **T:**   *ˌRight. ˌKen. Do͢ you͢ ͢see any word there that you know͢, B, anyone's name?*

B.37 — *T* gives lexical confirmation, repeats the answer in low-fall declarative tone, then turns to address another child with the thematic question, same low pitch, low tonal contrast.

B.38   **B:**   *ˌPat. P-→*

B.38 — *B* gives an answer in declarative low-fall and proceeds to the next step, spelling the name.

B.39   **T:**   *'What's that?*

B.39 — *T* calls for a repeat of *B*'s answer with high-rise intonation.

B.40   **B:**   *ˌPat.*

B.40 — *B* repeats her answer with same low-fall tone.

B.41   **T:**   *a. 'Where do you see ˋPat?*
                b. Do you see an ˌ[ae] sound in there?

B.41 — *T* asks a question that is in fact a negation or a challenge of *B*'s answer, as we see by her following question. While the form of *T*'s first question could mean a simple request for information, the second question in this context could only mean that there is no [ae] sound in the word. 'Pat' and '[ae]' are foregrounded by high-fall.

B.42 B: ␣*No.*

B.42 — *B* picks up challenging import of *T*'s questions and cue that answer is "no," tentative low-rise. See B.44, where *C*, although agreeing that she sees no [ae] sounds, repeats the word as *Pat.*

B.43 T: '*What sound do you ˇsee?*

B.43 — Note high-rise versus low-rise tone reflecting "do you" question versus *wh* question. Interactional significance carried by change in content; B.41a and b are rhetorical questions, and B.43 is a request for information.

B.44 B: ␣*Pat.*

B.44 — *B* repeats her former answer, not responding to *T*'s cues.

B.45 T: *Do you see an ␣[ae] sound?*

B.45 — *T* repeats her challenge question with identical form and tone as in B.41b.

B.46 B: ␣*No.*

B.46 — Again *B* responds in the negative, as demanded by the context of *T*'s question, although substantively there is as yet no indication that she has gotten the point.

B.47 T: *What sound do you ␣see?*

B.47 — *T* repeats request for information made in B.43.

B.48 B: ␣*Pet.*

B.48 — *B* changes the appropriate phoneme of the answer. Note lack of semantic tie throughout: Where *B* in her answers refers to whole words, *T* refers to letters or phonemes. Evidently they have different implicit notions of what the activity is.

B.49 I: '*Peter?*

B.49 — *I* posits an answer with high-rise question intonation, still referring to whole words.

B.50 T: *Is there an ␣er on the end?*

B.50 — *T* questions, using her former strategy of eliciting sounds. Gloss: "It's not quite right. There's no *er* on the end."

B.51 I: *Is it '*Peter?*

B.51 — *I* repeats her question, using a full sentence and slightly louder, higher voice, high-rise tone. Her question shows that she has not gotten *T*'s strategy.

B.52 T: *I's ˇhelping you. She's given you a ˇclue. But is there an ␣er on the end of that?*

B.52 — *T* speaks without directly confirming or negating *I*'s response, rather, she addresses *B* about *I*'s guess. The first two statements can be understood as qualifying the ensuing question, which reiterates what she has already asked in B.50, using the same semantic approach as in all the foregoing. However, this time she shifts to high-rise tone, possibly to contrast with the two statements B.52a and B.52b, which give indirect acceptance.

B.53 **C:** (indistinguishable)

B.53 – *C* replies inaudibly.

B.54 **T:** ʹWhat's the word?

B.54 – *T* asks for repeat.

B.55 **C:** (indistinguishable)

B.55 – *C* once again replies inaudibly.

B.56 **T:** ʹWhat?

B.56 – *T* once again calls for a repeat.

B.57 **C:** ʹPete.

B.57 – *C* produces an audible answer.

B.58 **T:** That's ʹright. How do you ˋspell it?

B.58 – *T* gives a lexical confirmation and asks for the second stage of the answer.

B.59 **C:** P→ E→ T→ E

B.59 – *C* spells.

B.60 **T:** ʹJust P−E−T−E? What do you say about the first ˈletter?

B.60 – *T* questions, implying that the answer is incomplete, and gives a clue as to what is missing.

B.61 **C:** ˌCapital.

B.61 – *C* supplies the name of the concept *T* is eliciting.

B.62 **T:** How do you ˋspell Pete?

B.62 – *T* once again asks *C* to spell the word, implying that the capital letter concept should be included.

B.63 **C:** Capital P··→ E··→ T··→ ˌE.

B.63 – *C* performs correctly.

B.64 **T:** Do you see a word there, L, that you know, somebody's name?

B.64 – Without responding to *C*'s final answer, *T* turns to another child, *L*, with a question. Her long utterance, although it contains several embeddings, gives the impression of being unpunctuated and maintains an even tone overall, except for a slight rise at the nucleus.

B.65 **L:** (indistinguishable)

B.65 – *L* responds at a very low volume.

B.66 **T:** ˌCan you spell the wordʹ Roy for uˋs, L?

B.66 – *T* uses a question form to request *L* to give the second stage of the answer.

B.67 **L:** ˌR−ˌO− ˋY.

B.67 – *L* spells, using a tone sequence appropriate to seriation.

B.68 **T:** ˌGood. ʹThat spells ˌRoy. R−O−Y.

B.68 – *T* confirms lexically, makes a confirming statement about the answer, and repeats what *L* has said in declarative low-fall contour.

References

Austin, J. L.
   1955   *How to do things with words.* New York: Oxford Univ. Press.
Bellack, Arno A.
   1966   *Language of the classroom.* New York: Columbia Univ. Teachers College.
Condon, W. S. and W. D. Ogston.
   1967   A segmentation of behavior, *Journal of Psychiatric Research* **5.**
Crystal, David
   1969   *Prosodic systems and intonation in English.* New York: Cambridge Univ. Press.
De Camp, David
   1971   Toward a generative analysis of a post-creole speech continuum. In *Pidginization*

and creolization of languages, edited by D. Hymes. New York: Cambridge Univ. Press.

Forsyth, I. J.
1971   *Some preliminary notes on language functions in the classroom.* Mimeo. Univ. of Birmingham, Dept. of English Language and Literature.

Frake, Charles O.
1964   How to ask for a drink in Subanun. In *The ethnography of communication,* edited by J. Gumperz and D. Hymes. *American Anthropologist Special Publication* **66**(6), pt. 2.

Garfinkel, Harold
1972   Remarks on ethnomethodology. In *Directions in sociolinguistics,* edited by J. Gumperz and D. Hymes. New York: Holt.

Geoghegan, William H.
1970   A theory of making rules. Working paper no. 37. Univ. of California, Berkeley: Language-Behavior Research Laboratory.

Goffman, Erving
1964   The neglected situation. In *The ethnography of communication,* edited by J. Gumperz and D. Hymes. *American Anthropologist Special Publication* **66**(6), pt. 2.

Gumperz, John J.
1970   Sociolinguistics and communication in small groups. Working paper no. 33. Univ. of California, Berkeley, Language-Behavior Research Laboratory.

Gumperz, John J. and Eduardo Hernandez-Chavez
1971   Bilingualism, bidialectalism, and classroom interaction. In *Language in social groups,* edited by J. J. Gumperz. Stanford: Stanford Univ. Press.

Halliday, Michael S.
1969   Relevant models of language. In *The state of language,* edited by A. Wilkinson. Univ. of Birmingham, School of Education.

Hymes, Dell
1972   Models of the interaction of language and social life. In *Directions in sociolinguistics,* edited by J. Gumperz and D. Hymes. P. 35ff. New York: Holt.

Kernan, Claudia Mitchell
1971   *Language behavior in a black urban community.* Monograph no. 2. Univ. of California, Berkeley: Language-Behavior Research Laboratory.

Lewis, Louisa
1970   Culture and social interaction in the classroom: An ethnographic report. Working paper no. 38. Univ. of California, Berkeley, Language-Behavior Research Laboratory.

McCawley, James
1968   The role of semantics in grammar. In *Universals in linguistic theory,* edited by Bach and R. Harms. New York: Holt.

Moreman, Michael
1972   Analysis of Luo conversation. In *Studies in social interaction,* edited by D. Sudnow. New York: Free Press.

Reisman, Karl
1970   Contrapuntal conversations in an Antiguan village. Penn-Texas working papers in sociolinguistics, no. 3. Univ. of Texas, Austin.

Sacks, Harvey
1972   On the analyzability of stories by children. In *Directions in sociolinguistics,* edited by J. Gumperz and D. Hymes. New York: Holt.

Schegloff, Emanuel A.
　　1972　Sequencing in conversational openings. In *Directions in sociolinguistics,* edited
　　　　　by J. Gumperz and D. Hymes. New York: Holt.
Searle, John R.
　　1969　*Speech acts: An essay in the philosophy of language.* New York: Cambridge
　　　　　Univ. Press.
Trim, John
　　1971　English intonation. Mimeo. Cambridge Univ., Dept. of Linguistics.

Agreeing to Agree on Genealogy:
A Luo Sociology of Knowledge

BEN G. BLOUNT

Introduction

This work is based on an analysis of a tape recording made among the Luo of Kenya.[1] The tape contains the speech of a group of Luo elders during the course of a day on the general topic of the genealogical reconstruction for their clan. The meeting was arranged by one of the elders and his son, ostensibly for the purpose of filling in gaps in the clan's organization that were due to the inability of some members to recount their genealogies accurately or in depth. Those inabilities had been discovered through the author's efforts to do a more or less routine genealogical history, primarily to work out overall lineage organization for the clan. In addition, the meeting was to synthesize the elder's information about genealogical and lineage relationships to produce the definitive account of their clan organization.

The elders did produce a complete genealogical account for their clan, perhaps even a definitive one, but not in the way in which the author had anticipated. The elders all were reputed specialists in clan history and lineage organization, and they themselves stated, individually, that they would pool their knowledge to solve the problems in specific areas of the genealogy. It was expected that they would concentrate on the structural gaps, but what took place was an interactional process in which individual initiative and ability was the central factor in establishing as correct

[1] Field research was carried out in Sakwa Location, South Nyanza, for 15 months in 1967–1968 and 5 months in 1971. The research was supported by NIMH Grant 12,649-01 (1967–1968) and by NSF USDP GU-1598 (1971).

The original version of this study was prepared for the Conference on the Ethnography of Speaking at the University of Texas, April 20–22, 1972. A revised version was presented at the Colloquim on Art, Artifice, and Reality in African Verbal Experience, UCLA, November 7, 1972, and will be published under the title "Luo lineages: Genealogy, verbal art, and social reality." The present version has benefited from discussion at both of these gatherings. Particularly helpful were comments from Elise Padpug, Mary Sanches, Brian Stross, and Dorothy Wills.

any portion of the genealogy. The initiative and ability was based on speech prowess, knowledge of Luo history and folklore, and social position among participants at the meeting and in the community at large. Combinations of these factors yielded a genealogy that was a product of negotiation, based on Luo history, but history as a partially dictated and a partially arbitrated synthesis. In effect, the genealogies as history were created by the elders in competition, cooperation, and occasionally by fiat within a framework of Luo social interaction.

The meeting of the elders and events preparatory to it revealed features of Luo social organization relevant to but transcending the structural arrangement of lineages. Lineage organization is based on genealogical reckoning, which becomes more difficult as one moves backward through time. The lack of certainty about accurate reconstructions provides the basis on which negotiation can proceed, and the "ground rules" for negotiation reflect dimensions of social organization that, although independent of lineage organization, may impinge directly on it. Conveniently for the ethnographer, the negotiation occurs within the framework of a speech event (as this term is used by Hymes, 1962 and Gumperz and Hymes, 1972), an event that is named—*kwano kware* 'to count ancestors'—and has an internal structure.

The major objective of this study is to identify the structure of the speech event, i.e., the rules that underlie the event and that members may invoke in the course of the event in order to influence its outcome. The central analytic focus is on interaction, and this work draws heavily from the work of the ethnomethodologists, especially Garfinkel (1964), Cicourel, (1964), and Sacks (1972). The sequential organization of conversation, however, is viewed more in terms of background structure and expectancies than in terms of the logical structure of conversational sequencing rules; thus, the intended contribution is toward a sociology of knowledge, where knowledge is a product of a social construction of reality (cf. Berger and Luckmann, 1966). To begin, we need to look at, in turn, the structural importance of Luo lineages, the results of conventional research on Luo lineages, and the unfolding of the interaction at the elders' meeting.

The Structural Importance of Lineages

The concept of lineage has had a long and important role in the study of social organization, especially for African societies. In fact, lineages have often been considered the basic organization unit of African groups (cf. Fortes, 1953, for a historical account). Among African societies, the Nilotes of East Africa—including the Luo—have been recognized as exemplary lineage-based societies. Studies on the Luo have emphasized patrilineal descent as the organizing principle of Luo society (Ogot, B. A., 1967; Southall, 1952; Whisson, 1964). A conventional structurally summary of Luo lineages can be represented as follows.

In traditional Luo society, an individual's social position was intimately associated with his position in a genealogical charter. His rights, duties, and obligations as a member of society were given overt structure by virtue of his membership in successive levels of lineages. Among the Luo, these levels extended, at the maximum, to 9–12 generations. These *gweng,* maximal lineages, had little import for the daily affairs of the Luo, since all of the individuals in a *gweng* congregated only on ritual occasions. The intermediate levels of lineage organization were of more immediate significance. The operational feature at these levels was opposition, i.e., lineages of 6–8 generation depth were identified and named [*libamba* (sg.), *libambini* (pl.)] only in contrast to another unit, equal in genealogical depth. Within these opposable groups, individuals were ranked by status according to generational seniority and age. At both the *libamba* and *gweng* levels, the lineage membership served to locate individuals in internal schemata, reinforced and consolidated by common pursuits and opposition to like and equal groups.

The minimal lineage, of 3–5 generational depth, is the most pervasive in terms of defining the spheres of social interaction and the network of rights and duties. Residence patterns consistently reflect the kinship and genealogical relations that obtain among the individuals. In a given residential area groups of homesteads are spatially arranged, so that clusters represent the unity of the *anyuola,* the minimal lineage. In more traditional times the *anyuola* was a corporate group, owning in common all of the land for grazing and allocating land for agriculture. Within the *anyuola,* men were ranked first, according to genealogical relationship and, second, according to relative order of birth, i.e., an older brother would have more authority than a younger brother, and both would be subservient to all male members of the next-higher generation. Activities of the *anyuola,* as a corporate and residential group, thus, were regulated by the principle of seniority, based on relative age and generational age.

A Luo man's social identity in large part reflects his own particular position in relation to other individuals on the basis of the seniority principle. All elderly men, and especially those of one's *anyuola* and *libamba,* are to be shown respect by younger men. Respect and deference rules apply as well among individuals who are peers in terms of age but who are at different generational positions in the lineage structure. If the great-grandfather of one man is the great-great-grandfather of his age mate, then the first individual will be of superordinate status compared to the second. Theoretically, every man in a *gweng* can trace his relationship to every other male member, even if this requires recounting genealogies over a period of several hundred years (based on the rate 30 years = 1 generation). In this respect, a man's societal position is contingent on his historical or genealogical pedigree but subject to the constraint that relative age among the living is of primary importance.

In summary, the principle features of Luo lineage structure are these: (1) The shallower the depth of a lineage segment, the more direct the effect on an individual's daily activities; (2) the primary ordering principle for super–subordinate relationships among individuals is generational age; (3) the secondary ordering principle is relative age (order of birth at the family level); and (4) among age mates (beyond the extended family), the degree of generational depth to a common ancestor may be invoked as a marker of relative social position. Owing to the social importance of these features, one would predict that an individual in Luo society would have excellent command of his genealogical history, especially at the *anyuola* level, since aspects of his social position are defined by the lineage networks. One would expect, also, that elders would exhibit more interest in and control of the genealogical histories. Both of these expectations are only partially supported by the empirical evidence.

Genealogical Reconstruction: Problems and Background

As a standard ethnographic technique, genealogical information was collected from the oldest adult male in a sample of 50 homesteads. The homesteads were all located in an area defined by the Luo themselves as a clan (*gweng*), and it was expected that the men would be able to retrace the *gweng* genealogy. In actual fact, the number of ancestors any one individual could count varied from a low of three to a high of eight. Three generations of ancestors were not sufficient to link most individuals to the *anyuola* level, much less to the *gweng*. Even eight generations was insufficient to cover the entire clan.

An additional finding was the lack of a direct correlation between the ages of the individual men and the number of ancestors they could recount. It is generally reported in the ethnographic literature that elders have a better grasp of genealogical information, due to accumulated knowledge, their role as protectors of tribal lore, and their positions in the power structure. The Luo have a similar explanation, believing that the older a man grows, the wiser he becomes and the more information he controls. However, the Luo survey does not fully substantiate these beliefs. Not all of the elders outperformed the younger men. Nor was there any direct correlation between performance and social variables such as relative economic position, literacy, or commitment to community development (as indicated by church membership, local political activity, and involvement in self-help projects).

The generational depth of a man's *anyuola* was the best measure of his control of his genealogical history. Thirty-one of the 46 individuals who recited their genealogies (67.4%) counted the exact number of generations in their *anyuola*. In only one case (2%) did an individual report fewer than the *anyuola* number, and in this instance the *anyuola* was relatively large (5-generation depth). Fifteen men (32.6%) could identify ancestors beyond the *anyuola* level, and 4 of the most prestigious elders would not recount any of their ancestors at all. The latter point will be discussed in some detail.

Within the *anyuola,* genealogy appears to function as an organizational principle essentially as described in the literature. The fact that every adult male except one could easily trace the kinship relations within his *anyuola* underscores the viability of the lineage system. Property is inherited according to the descent rules, and in each *anyuola* the men could reconstruct the division of land over the appropriate number of generations by referring to the ordering of genealogical relationships. This is not surprising, given the economic and social primacy of the *anyuola* in the Luo social system.

What was surprising in the survey of genealogical information was, first, that few individuals could retrace their consanguinial relatives for the *gweng* lineage system, and second, that several individuals would not divulge information for fear of making mistakes in the reconstruction. To take these in turn, the majority of Luo men showed little interest in tracing their ancestors beyond the *anyuola*. Common statements were "I only know X-number-of ancestors. Beyond that I lose the path" or "The grandfathers lived long ago; that is history/legend (*sigana*), and I don't know that." The Luo men did not appear distressed or even concerned that their knowledge of genealogies extended only to the *anyuola* level. If asked, they could name the founding father of the Luo, Ramogi, and the founder of the tribe, Alego, but they were not worried about the intermediate levels. This attitude was surprising, considering that these men will state that, ideally, a Luo man should know at least all of his ancestors in his *gweng,* if not for his *piny* 'tribe, nation'. The lack of concern was surprising, also, in light of the fact that the more ancestors a man can remember, the more prestigious he is in the eyes of the Luo. Men who can reconstruct their genealogies back to the migrations from the Sudan into Uganda are famous throughout Luoland.

If most men can trace genealogy only slightly beyond the *anyuola,* what happens to the intermediate levels of genealogical relationships? At the most general level, the Luo do precisely what is common in most lineage systems—they telescope the generations in the upper levels of the genealogy so that the founders/leaders are historically closer to the present generation. For example, some Luo men count to the *anyuola* level, add three or four more ancestors, and then link them directly with the founder of the *piny*, Alego. The degree to which telescoping is effected depends on the individuals conducting the exercise. Some are more able than others to compose a long list of ancestors, but in all cases in this study the lists were incomplete. Several of the men who presented these accounts admitted the inaccuracies and suggested that particular elders should be consulted for a more complete history. They maintained that only a very few old men could remember what the correct order of generations should be. In the Ulanda *gweng,* however, the old men who were reputably knowledgeable about Luo history were precisely the ones who refused to discuss their genealogies. Each of these elders insisted that, although their knowledge was extensive, they were afraid of committing errors if they recited the genealogies by themselves. There are good reasons for their fear. Reconstructing genealogies some 300–400 years into the past without written records would be difficult even if the genealogies were linked in ideal fashion, i.e., if descent were systematic and without intervening variables. History for the Luo is not without complicating factors, such as partial or wholescale migration, warfare, assimilation of other groups, leviratic inheritance, and fictive kinship. In view of these considerations, it is understandable that an elder could feel insecure about recounting the correct genealogical strings.

Since each elder was aware that his genealogical account might not correspond to what others would say, mistakes, misinformation, and inconsistencies could have social consequences. This concern was voiced by most of the elders; they did not want to be placed in a compromising position vis-à-vis the other elders. It became clear that no one wanted to be the sole spokesman for the reconstruction of Luo genealogy and history. It might be noted that aversion to such positions are characteristic of Luo culture. The Luo attempt to minimize personal qualifications that could stereotype them generally as superior or extreme individuals. More will be said on this topic later, but for the present the reluctance to pose as a specialist can be counted as a contributing factor to the refusal by elders to reconstruct their genealogies.

The story of the elders' disinclination to talk individually about genealogies is not yet complete. An additional element must be considered, one that is related to and derived from those already discussed. To recapitulate, Luo men who could recite only limited genealogies recommended several elders in the community as specialists. These elders, however, were reluctant to accept the responsibility as individual spokes-men, even though they admitted that they were indeed knowl-edgeable in the realms of history and genealogies. They stated that, owing to the complexity of the issue, they were afraid of providing inaccurate accounts if they spoke *as individuals.* Several elders suggested that they might be willing to talk about genealogies if other elders were present. The obvious implication is that the topic of genealogy recon-struction is appropriate for discussion only when the proper participants are convened. Inquiries among informants showed unanimous agree-ment that genealogies should be discussed only by a group of elders. Moreover, it was stated that the elders should meet at the home of one elder who would serve as host and provide food and drink for the visi-tors. The proper setting for discussion of genealogy is, thus, a social visit.

Visiting is a daily phenomenon in Luo life, and the basic social posi-tions in Luo society are reflected in the patterns of those visits. The scheduling of daily activities provides for a period of four or five hours every afternoon when visiting with one's relatives and friends is appro-priate and expected. The choice of which homestead one visits on any given occasion is contingent on a host of factors such as kinship rela-tions, mutual interest, business matters, proximity, and availability of beer, to name only a few, but the fundamental organizing principles for visitation patterns are sex and age. Except for adolescents, who frequently visit in mixed male and female groups, sex segregation is gen-erally observed. Further divisions are made according to age, especially for men. Elders' visits are made according to age, especially for men. Elders visit with elders and young men with other young men.

Each social category of visiting groups maintains inventories of con-versational topics related to the societal positions of the participants. Although the domains of topics may overlap from category to category, as, for example, the crops or rainfall, the category itself will delimit the overall range of topics. For instance, according to informants, genealogy could be a topic of conversation for old women and for middle-aged men, but only infrequently. Old men, on the other hand, rely on genea-logical reconstructions as a standard topic for conversations during their social visits.

Genealogies are, thus, appropriately discussed by knowledgeable elders among themselves. The subject is inappropriate for discussion in other social contexts, including tutorial situations. The elders who are recognized specialists act as social participants in a speech event. One would expect, then, that the organization of the speech event as a sociolinguistic phenomenon will have some bearing on the reconstruction of genealogy. Stated otherwise, genealogy as a concept is not independent of the sociolinguistic factors that regulate discussion about it. The genealogies are infused with manipulation of social information.

The Speech Event: Setting and Activity

In response to the elders' suggestion that a meeting be held, arrangements were made for a gathering at the home of one of the field assistants. Fifteen elders who were reported to be specialists were informed of the meeting and invited to attend. They were told that the purpose of the meeting was *kwano kware,* to count their grandfathers, in order that a complete record could be obtained for the clan.

On the appointed day the elders arrived leisurely, over the course of two hours and with no formality except the exchange of greetings. At 10:00 A.M., three elders had arrived and sat around a large table inside the main house of the homestead. Conversation consisted mainly of inquiries about each other's families, about the rains and conditions of the crops, and about recent local events such as Masai cattle raids. These topics — family, crops, and recent local events — invariably constitute the pattern for initial conversation in visiting situations. This gathering was no exception, and the routine was repeated as each new elder joined the group. By 11:30, eight elders were present, and the counting of ancestors began.

The conversational shift to the topic of ancestors was not marked by any ritual or formality. One elder, named Nyanjom, told the host, Okumu, to pay attention to the recounting and to write the names correctly. At this time several independent conversations were under way and were continued for a few moments. Gradually, however, attention became focused on Nyanjom and his speech. At first Nyanjom addressed his remarks to Okumu, naming distant ancestors and telling him to write them down in turn. After several names had been recorded, and after Nyanjom had asked Okumu for a reading of the names that had been written, the other elders began to participate in the speech event.

The opening phase of the speech event was informal. There were no formal announcements of intent, purpose, or procedure, and discussion on the topic of genealogy was initiated by one elder amidst the confusion of several other information conversations. There was no appointed or recognized discussion leader, but once initiated the discussion was dominated by Nyanjom. Participation by other elders began within a few minutes, and the structure of the speech became more complex.

Several themes can be identified in the unfolding of the speech activity, each of which is a factor contributing to the ultimate agreement on the genealogies. The first theme concerns the source and type of information that is made available for the reconstruction of genealogies. Nyanjom began his listing of ancestors with Ramogi, the founder of Luoland, and he quickly traced the sons and grandsons of Ramogi down the genealogical ladder to Alego, the father of *piny* Alego, the "country" of Alego. The audience did not ask for clarification or object to any of this reconstruction, although Nyanjom remarked, near the end, *Ka ariaso to ikwera ni wuon Awedhi iriaso* 'If I falsify it, (you) object that the father of Awedhi (i.e., Nyanjom himself) is lying'. Once Nyanjom began to trace Alego's descendants, the elders raised points of clarification and signaled their agreement by repeating portions of Nyanjom's statements or responding with the general affirmative *ee!* For example, a response to Nyanjom's *Magi nyithind Nyibil* 'These are the children of Nyibil' was Okumu's *Gin nyithind Nyibil* 'They are the children of Nyibil', followed by Nyanjom's *ee* 'yes'. Again, an elder named Mreji followed Nyanjom's *Ara indik Bup gi Mdura* 'All right, write Bup and Mdura' with *Ee, Bup gi Mdura, ee!* 'Yes, Bup and Mdura, yes!'.

As an example of a request for clarification, Okumu asked *Min Alego ni en ng'a?* 'Who was Alego's mother?' in response to Nyanjom's directive *Ara, ndiki min Alego* 'All right, write down the mother of Alego'. Nyanjom's answer was *Ani mana bu min Alego* 'Just the mother of Alego', but, interestingly, he referred to her grinding stone (for maize), which still exists in Alego's Location: *Bi pong nitie kata gonyo* 'The stone for grinding is still there'. In addition, Nyanjom asked another elder, Ochondo, to verify the existence of the stone. Ochondo did, marking the first instance of a practice to be repeated time and time again in the discussion. This practice consists of reference to an object or entity whose physical existence serves to establish the validity of the point made in reference to it. Phenomena outside the realm of descent and filiation can be used to establish the validity of the genealogical claim. Ochondo's response to Nyanjom, in full, was *Ne awinjo, ni pong nitie, ni min Alego en dhuno* 'I understand that the grinding-stone is there. The mother of Alego was a person'. This explanation was accepted by the group.

Nyanjom continued to direct the conversation, and whenever an elder requested additional information, he called on Ochondo or, sometimes, another elder in the group for support. In each instance, reference would be made to some physical object or geographical feature, such as a river, and to some activity in relation to it. For instance, the separation of two brothers, Rado and Odongo, was explained in relation to a glass bead owned by Odongo. In summary, the story is as follows: Rado and Odongo were brothers who lived together in one home. Rado's son, in playing, swallowed a glass bead (i.e., money) belonging to Odongo. Odongo insisted that the bead be returned. Emetics failed to produce the bead, and in a fit of anger Odongo slew the boy and took the bead from his stomach. As a result, Rado separated from his brother and moved away to a new area, and thus two clans were formed.

Although reference at first is to a physical object, the object often is the topic of a folk tale, and the entire tale is recited. The Luo elders occasionally commented after such a story *mano sigana* '[a] history-story'. As the discussion progressed, more and more frequently the genealogy was articulated subject to the supportive context of folklore. In most instances, recourse to folklore was sufficient to establish a point. Difficulties arose, though, when conflicting stories were given to document and support a point. Furthermore, these problems arose as the genealogical linkages of the elders' lineages were called into question. This occurred first in relation to Oluoch, the elder who, judging from the frequency of speech turns, was the third-ranking individual at the gathering.

Three stories were told about Oluoch's grandfathers. Oluoch had remarked that Nyibil was one of his ancestors, and he had said that Ochieng was an ancestor as well. Since it had been established that Ochieng was one generational level below Nyibil, Ochieng necessarily would have been Nyibil's son. However, Nyanjom had not mentioned Ochieng when listing Nyibil's sons. One elder, Onono, noticed this inconsistency and asked Oluoch to clarify it. Oluoch responded by telling how Ochieng's group had been defeated in a war and had scattered throughout neighboring areas. Ochieng settled by a river, where he was found by a neighboring group (Nyibil's lineage) who adopted him into their clan.

Onono took issue with Oluoch, saying that although it was true that Ochieng was discovered by the river, he was ambushed and captured there by Nyibil's group, not merely found there. He then elaborated on the details of the capture.

Oluoch replied by elaborating further on the details of the meeting between Ochieng and Nyibil's group. He then stated that this account was true, and Ochondo, the second-ranking individual, added that he had heard the story before as Oluoch had told it. Then, to clinch the argument, Oluoch quickly recounted his grandfathers from Ochieng, son of Nyibil, referring to the homestead where Ochieng and his sons had lived, and adding that, yes, it was true that Ochieng was adopted by Nyibil. Onono retreated by agreeing that Ochieng had been, indeed, adopted.

The question of how Ochieng was adopted is the important aspect of the issue. The fact that he was adopted at all is sufficient to lower the status of Oluoch's lineage, for the Luo refer to assimilated peoples as "not true Luo," even though the assimilation may have occurred several generations in the past (cf. Ogot, 1967). Onono may or may not have known that Oluoch's ancestor, Ochieng, had been adopted, but Onono's version of the *sigana* (story) implies that his aim was to lower Oluoch's position by insisting that Ochieng had been captured. This meant that Ochieng was adopted as a war captive, making his societal position lower in comparison with that of someone who voluntarily assimilated. Onono's remarks can, thus, be thought of as a ploy to reduce, however minimally, the social currency of Oluoch's lineage. The ploy was not totally successful, mainly because of Ochondo's intervention, and Onono had to be content with establishing Oluoch's position as an assimilated Luo.

Onono's apparent strategy of calling into question Oluoch's origins and thereby reducing his social prestige is consistent with a general theme in Luo speech behavior. Luo speech events are characterized by speakers' self-praise and self-aggrandizement. A speaker calls the audience's attention to his virtues, especially those that have redeeming social value, and indirectly, often by innuendo, calls into question the virtues of the audience. The display may be very direct, as in the case of young men praising their strength and virility, or indirect, by exhibiting one's skill at manipulating information. This feature of speech events is manifested in public gatherings such as church (Whisson, 1964), traditional dances (Ogot, G., 1967), tea parties, court cases, secondary school debates, and school parties. Onono's behavior is an example of the self-praise genre, in which he called attention to his knowledge of Luo history by reciting specifics of a folktale (i.e., by referring to objects that allegedly were present at the scene of the action). At the same time, he called into question Oluoch's story, his specific knowledge of folklore, and his position in the overall lineage structure. Oluoch, however, not to be outmaneuvered, countered with another, still more extensive version. It is entirely plausible that Onono would have continued the exchange, but, as noted, Ochondo lent his support to Oluoch by verifying his account, and Onono did not pursue the issue.

The technique of maximizing one's own position while minimizing those of others becomes more apparent in the third story told about Oluoch's origins. This version was told by Nyanjom, and because he had directed and dominated the discussions to that point, more specific background on his activity and the Luo attitudes relating to such activity are essential to an understanding of the impact of his story and the group's reaction to it.

Nyanjom's dominance in the event can be seen in a number of ways. He was the one who initiated the proceedings, and he spoke more often and generally for longer stretches of time than his fellow elders. As well, he persistently reminded the others that they should be attentive to his speech, but he did not admonish them directly. Rather, he selected Ochondo as his target, criticizing him for interrupting the proceedings, as in *Ochondo, winji wach* 'Ochondo, pay attention to (the) news/information', and challenging him to match knowledge with himself, as in *Ochondo, ing'eyo siganano?* 'do you know that story?' and *Ochondo, ikia?* 'don't you know [that]?' in reference to a *sigana* that he had just related.

Ochondo thus served as the exemplary victim, but the other elders also were occasionally reminded of Nyanjom's superior position. Often, a question or point raised by one of the elders would not be answered immediately. Nyanjom would merely continue with his story, and several minutes later he would return to the question and answer and elaborate on it, but without any acknowledgment as to its author. The implication is that the question was premature and that, left to his own rendering of the story, Nyanjom would have dealt with the issue anyway. Occasionally, Ochondo was directly chastized on essentially that point, with Nyanjom rebuking him for introducing a topic prematurely or out of sequence. There were never any direct, immediate objections by the elders to Nyanjom's actions.

Nyanjom attempted to extend his domination by telling his own, the third version of Oluoch's origins. Strikingly, he withheld comment on the issue until the other elders had expressed their opinions and the question of Oluoch's lineage had been resolved in favor of Oluoch's own account. Nyanjom's revival of the issue provided him the opportunity to correct the others' remarks and maximize his own position at the expense of the second- and third-ranking individuals, Ochondo and Oluoch. Nyanjom's version of the story, in summary, was that Oluoch's grandfather, Ochieng, had indeed been found at his home by the river but that he had not been discovered there. To speak of a man being discovered in his own home was nonsensical, Nyanjom maintained. Nyibil's group were the strangers in the area, who came upon Ochieng at his home and who settled in the area where Ochieng lived. Ochieng then was assimilated by Nyibil's group.

Although Nyanjom's account differs only slightly in content from Oluoch's, the variation underscores an important point, namely, that Ochieng was the host to Nyibil's group but was later assimilated by them. This means that Nyibil's group was dominant over Ochieng and that it was to his advantage to join their lineage. Left unspoken, but nevertheless implicit, is the notion that Ochieng may have joined Nyibil's lineage by marrying one of its women. Oluoch therefore would be linked to the central lineage only as an in-law, or, stated otherwise, as less than a full agnatic member. In the course of the ensuing argument, Nyanjom raises this very point; but it is first necessary to trace the development of the argument.

After Nyanjom presented his version of the story, the other elders had several options in way of response. One possibility was no response at all, allowing Nyanjom to succeed with his delayed-response strategy. In this case, his version would have been accepted as correct. A second option could have been introduction of a new topic and then a subsequent revival of the Ochondo–Oluoch version at an appropriate place. Still a third, and the one actually chosen, was direct confrontation. Nyanjom had concluded his statement by giving an example, saying that if he went to his neighbor's house and found him at home, he could not then say that he had discovered his neighbor. Ochondo retorted with *Ero ema ne okwanyueno* 'Well, then you found him'. Nyanjom replied, *Ok okwany* 'He wasn't found'. Then he proceeded to repeat the example, and asked Ochondo to verify it. Ochondo's reaction was *Awinjo mana wachni kwara* 'I understand just these words, grandfather', i.e., I understand just the example, but not the story itself. At this point Nyanjom raised the issue mentioned earlier, that possibly Oluoch's ancestor Ochieng married one of Nyibil's daughters. This was done indirectly by pointing out that Onono's ancestors had been assimilated through marriage and that perhaps Oluoch's case was similar. Ochondo, however, was not content to drop the issue and continued to force the matter by challenging Nyanjom again: *Ok ine ka koro mano iwacho ka mbaka* 'Don't you see that what you say will start an argument/fight?'. Nyanjom protested, *Awacho bura, kendo kambaka ayanyo ng'ato* 'I am talking meeting-talk [i.e., officially] even if I offend someone.'

At this point the discussion had become charged with tension. Nyanjom's final statement had been another challenge, asserting that the truth of his position was not reduced by someone's taking issue with it. Nyanjom had been challenged, but he was not retreating or compromising. Onono took the first step in defusing the immediate confrontation by pointing out that whenever a person becomes abusive, the essence of truth leaves him—*koro odok kayany aye uru, an mano to adagi e chuny bura*. After some discussion on this point by various elders, Onono cleverly turned Nyanjom's challenge in reverse by stating that he did not want to offend anyone but that he wanted some specific information about Nyanjom's lineage. In the ensuing discussion Onono indicated that some irregularities could have been present in Nyanjom's own lineage, irregularities that could be explained only if the assumption were made that an improper form of marriage had occurred among Nyanjom's ancestors. In effect, Onono had steered the conversation away from a direct confrontation and back into a framework within which he could follow the technique of maximizing his position and minimizing that of his coparticipant, Nyanjom. Onono chose a topic on which all could agree and then used the obtained agreement to bolster his position and render Nyanjom vulnerable to further attack.

The elders were presented with an opportunity to deny, for once, Nyanjom the prerogative of citing the "accurate" reconstruction, and they were quick to press their advantage. Several agreed that the incongruity in Nyanjom's lineage history could indeed be accounted for by an irregular marriage, i.e., by a marriage between individuals of two clans who were forbidden to marry for several generations because a marriage between two of their members had already occurred. Oluoch added that the account could, indeed, be true, and that he had even heard stories to that effect. The mood of the group at this stage clearly was unfavorable to Nyanjom. It was apparent that although they had not agreed to insist that Nyanjom's own lineage had its own irregularities, they were prepared to force that conclusion if Nyanjom did not yield in his version of the Oluoch origin story. Nyanjom acquiesced by stating, in reply to Oluoch's allegation, that he, too, had heard rumors about his lineage. His statement underscored the fact that his ancestry could be called into question, perhaps had been questioned already in some quarters, and he was willing to recognize this possible threat to the authenticity of his lineage reconstruction. His acquiescence marked the end of that phase of the event. Nothing more was said about Oluoch's origins, and the accepted version was Oluoch's and Ochondo's account.[2]

Summary

In structural outline, the following sequence was observed in the Onono–Oluoch–Nyanjom episode: (1) Onono, who ranked fourth in standing among the elders, challenged the third-ranking man, Oluoch; (2) Oluoch responded and was seconded by Ochondo, the second-ranking elder; (3) Nyanjom, the top-ranking elder, in a delayed response, proposed his own version of Oluoch's lineage, calling into question Oluoch's origins and indirectly attacking Oluoch; (4) Ochondo rejected Nyanjom's story; (5) Nyanjom insisted that he was correct and used Onono's lineage as an example of the type he alleged for Oluoch (thereby attacking Onono); (6) Ochondo criticized Nyanjom; (7) Nyanjom retorted that no one should take offence at the truth; (8)

---

[2] In addition to tape recording the speech event, two assistants recorded the events, one taking notes in English and the other in Luo. Each recorded Oluoch's version as the "final, accurate" one.

Onono insinuated that Nyanjom's lineage was not immune from irregularities; (9) several elders agreed to this possibility; (10) Oluoch alluded to rumors to the effect that Nyanjom's lineage was not without blemish; and (11) Nyanjom acquiesced to the threat and abandoned his story.

The interaction episode partially reveals the processes through which genealogy is reconstructed, but additional information is necessary for clarification and interpretation. An immediate problem requiring clarification is the question of rank. One dimension of rank manifested in the speech event was the number of contributions to the reconstruction. Nyanjom undeniably surpassed the others in terms of contributions. He spoke much more frequently than they, recited more stories, and generally directed the discussion. The number two position was held securely by Ochondo, who appeared very knowledgeable as well, but beyond that point the ranking was more amorphous. Oluoch was third solely in terms of frequency of speech, and by the same standard Onono was fourth. The other seven to nine elders were considerably less vocal and spoke primarily to ask for information or to signal agreement to a point. Participation in the discussion appeared to be based, to a large extent, on the historical information an individual had at his control. The more *sigendini* 'histories/stories' an individual could bring to bear in the discussion, the greater his control of the genealogical reconstruction and the more firmly entrenched his rank.

Other considerations are involved in the ranking process. Among these are kinship relations, choosing sides, and the threat of altered genealogies. In one sense, all of the elders at the gathering were kinsmen, since their individual lineages could ultimately be linked together into a master lineage. Reckoning of kinship was, thus, theoretically possible, but exceeded the bounds of practicality. Among the elders, three groups of two men each were kinsmen in the practical sense of tracing their relationships within the same *anyuola*. Conflicting patterns of interaction therefore were possible, one set for peers among elders and one for superordinate–subordinate generational levels within the *anyuola*. Nyanjom and Ochondo fit this pattern. They belonged to the same *anyuola* and, on the generational principle, Nyanjom was Ochondo's grandfather, even though they were approximately the same age chronologically. Ochondo could not have been ranked higher in the gathering than Nyanjom because of their relationship, and it would have been an insult to Nyanjom for Ochondo to have dominated the conversation. His proper role was as a subordinate to Nyanjom, to serve as Nyanjom's exemplar victim, as noted earlier, but also to support Nyanjom's arguments. Ochondo's position in the ranking was, thus, contingent in large part on his relationship with Nyanjom, from whom he derived prestige in exchange for support. Ochondo's position was further enhanced by his ability to provide his own *sigendini* when required.

Occasionally, Nyanjom's and Ochondo's accounts came into conflict, and in most cases Ochondo yielded to Nyanjom. In the story of Oluoch's origins, however, Ochondo was committed to a position before Nyanjom contradicted him. Furthermore, other elders were committed to that position as well. In effect, sides had been chosen and commitments made to those sides, and in this process Ochondo was acting as an elder vis-à-vis the other elders. Nyanjom's rejection of his story was also a rejection of this status, and Ochondo refused to accept this alteration. He was the first to challenge Nyanjom and led the initial rebuttal to Nyanjom's story. The conflict between the number-one and number-two men quickly led to a further choosing of sides, and in this instance all of the elders sided with Ochondo.

The elders' choice to side with Ochondo probably was not so much support of Ochondo as reaction to the hegemony of Nyanjom. In Luo society in general, strong feelings are evoked and sanctions applied whenever an individual dominates an activity to the perceived detriment of others.[3] In primary school, for example, a student who insists on providing answers to the teacher's questions must be careful not to infringe on the rights of others to answer. Otherwise, he will be ridiculed by nicknames and shunned by his classmates. A more dramatic example of the same phenomenon is provided by the case of four young children, all approximately three years old. In an effort to entice them to talk, an adult asked them to name various objects in the environment, pointing to the objects and asking, What do you call that? One child consistently spoke before the others. After several minutes of this activity, one of the boys stood up, walked slowly to the precocious child, struck him in the eye with his fist, and calmly walked away from the gathering. The elders' temporary alliance against Nyanjom appears to represent a symbolic expression of the same phenomenon. The elders reserved the right to deny Nyanjom his rank as leader, expressing their privilege through alignment with a challenger to his rank.

Ochondo's confrontation with Nyanjom provided the opportunity for the elders to apply sanctions against Nyanjom in a culturally appropriate fashion. Ironically, Ochondo himself was subject to their actions in one sense because of his kinship relations with Nyanjom. The suggestions by Onono and Oluoch that Nyanjom's lineage might have its faults was, by

---

[3] Domination of an event is to be clearly distinguished from self-praise. The latter is not only appropriate but required in many contexts. It becomes inappropriate and offensive only when other individuals are not allowed the same opportunity.

implication, a threat to Ochondo. Clearly aware of that potential, Ochondo did not participate in any of the discussion on the lineage irregularities. Rather than supporting his own lineage and, thus, Nyanjom, he tacitly allowed the mild censure of Nyanjom to be completed. Although Ochondo was in danger of guilt by association if he did not defend his lineage, defense was a less desirable option, entailing a reversion to a subordinate kinship role with Nyanjom. Besides, the lineage history was not actually altered. The threat to reinterpret the history was a mechanism to admonish Nyanjom.

The final point, the threat to alter lineage relationships, leads back to the original question of how lineages are reconstructed. Beyond the *anyuola* level, reconstruction occurs in speech events attended by genealogical specialists, elders who maintain an interest in the history of their society. Elders who do not maintain such an interest are less prestigious in their community and are less apt to serve as advisors at the subchief's and chief's political meetings and as the clan elders (*jodong gweng*). The elders who participate in the events are ranked according to a variety of factors. Those who have reputations as effective speakers are accorded status and are more likely to participate actively in the events. Control of information is another factor. The more *sigendini* an individual knows, the more effectively he can participate and the more likely he is to direct the proceedings so as to enhance the position of his own lineage. Kinship relations among the participants influences the ranking and provides the basis for conflicting roles. Conflict thus arises over incompatible roles and over competition for the final version of how the intricate lineage system is structured. Any individual may attempt to reconstruct the system to his own advantage, but he runs the risk of a concerted group effort to alter his own lineage. The historical picture is amorphous to the degree that no one reading is accepted as accurate, and competition arises in a social matrix of the speech event as to which reading should be acceptable for the immediate future. The competition is acted out in the absence of strict rules of procedure, where the privileges of rank are minimal in comparison to individual initiative, and where individual initiative is countered by group pressure according to cultural norms.

Conclusion

Genealogy as a structural principle of organization operates most clearly at the *anyuola*, minimal lineage, level. All adult males can readily recite their genealogies and relate the generational levels to specific issues such as inheritance, division of land, and distribution of cattle.

The question of agreement on genealogical reconstruction as such does not arise. Beyond the *anyuola,* the time depth of genealogies begins to extend into the distant past, from 100 years at a minimum to 500–600 at a maximum. Genealogical reconstruction over such time depths is no simple matter, since the genealogies are subject, through time, to alteration. They are changed, for example, to allow for assimilation of non-Luo and in-laws. As well, continuity of lineages is complicated by factors such as migration and dispersal through warfare.

Reconstruction of genealogies is controlled by the dominant social category of people in Luo society, the elders. The topic is appropriate for discussion when a group of elders is convened, and only elders are allowed to attend. These factors provide the setting for a speech event, named *kwano kwane* (to count ancestors). The counting of ancestors and, thus, tracing of genealogical relationships within the speech event is subject to the manipulation of information according to social relationships and cultural norms. The final version of genealogy for any speech event is the product of what the elders agree to agree upon. Any elder can make an assertion about a given feature of genealogical history, but he has to consider that he may be called upon for clarification. If so, he must be able to refer to some specific objects or events that verify his point. If the object or event is the theme of a *sigana,* his position is strengthened. Other elders may counter with their own stories, and sides may be chosen on the issue. To be successful in reconstructing a genealogy, then, an elder must be cognizant of the potential social effect of his assertions on the group of elders. The more successful an elder, the more he can direct the discussion, establish his reputation as a knowledgeable elder, and structure the genealogy to his own advantage and to the detriment of others. However, he must exercise caution not to be too successful. If the group objects to his domination, they may threaten to rework the genealogy so as to malign his lineage. Whatever the final product of the reconstruction, its acceptability as the accurate genealogy is the end result of a creative process whereby a structure of individual relationships is defined by reference to sets of rules and by individual initiative. An agreement is arrived at such that the participants can agree.

References

Berger, Peter and Thomas Luckmann
  1966   *The social construction of reality: A treatise in the sociology of knowledge.* New York: Doubleday.
Buchler, Ira and Henry Selby
  1968   *Kinship and social organization.* New York: Macmillan.

Cicourel, Aaron
1964 *Method and measurement in sociology.* Glencoe, Illinois: Free Press.
Fortes, Meyer
1953 The structure of unilineal descent groups, *American Anthropologist* **55,** 17–41.
Garfinkel, Harold
1964 Studies of the routine grounds of everyday activities, *Social Problems* **11.**
Gumperz, John and Dell Hymes (editors)
1972 *Directions in sociolinguistics: The ethnography of communication.* New York: Holt.
Hymes, Dell
1962 The ethnography of speaking. In *Studies in human behavior,* edited by W. Sturtevant and T. Gludwin. Washington, D.C.: Anthropological Society of Washington.
Ogot, B. A.
1967 *History of the Southern Luo,* vol. I. Nairobi: E. African Publ. House.
Ogot, Grace
1967 *The promised land.* Nairobi: E. African Publ. House.
Sacks, Harvey
1972 An initial investigation of the usability of conversational data for doing sociology. In *Studies in social interaction,* edited by D. Ludnow. New York: Free Press.
Southall, Aidan
1952 *Lineage formation among the Luo.* Memoranda of the International African Institute, no. 26. London: Oxford Univ. Press.
Whisson, Michael
1964 *Change and challenge: A study of the social and economic changes among the Kenya Luo.* Nairobi: Christian Council of Kenya.

The Child as Practical Reasoner[1]

JENNY COOK-GUMPERZ

"Ahem!" said the Mouse with an important air, "are you all ready? This is the driest thing I know. Silence all round, if you please! 'William the Conqueror, whose cause was favoured by the pope, was soon submitted to by the English, who wanted leaders, and had been of late much accustomed to usurpation and conquest. Edwin and Morcar, the earls of Mercia and Northumbria—'"
"Ugh!" said the Lory, with a shiver.
"I beg your pardon!" said the Mouse, frowning, but very politely: "Did you speak?"
"Not I!" said the Lory hastily.
"I thought you did," said the Mouse. "—I proceed, 'Edwin and Morcar, the earls of Mercia and Northumbria, declared for him: and even Stigand, the patriotic archbishop of Canterbury, found it advisable—'"
"Found what?" said the Duck.
"Found it," the Mouse replied rather crossly: "of course you know what 'it' means."
"I know what 'it' means well enough, when I find a thing," said the Duck: "it's generally a frog or a worm. The question is, what did the archbishop find?"
The Mouse did not notice this question, but hurriedly went on, "'—found it advisable to go with Edgar Atheling to meet William and offer him the crown. . . .'"

Lewis Carroll: The Adventures of Alice in Wonderland

Failure to acknowledge the conventional requirements for maintaining the normal surface of everyday interaction is a recognized way of creating humor. The questioning of what "everyone knows" to be a linguistic convention is, at best, a cause for a laugh or a request to stop fooling around. As surrealists, humorists, phenomenologists, and some sociologists have shown, every time the surface of conventional normality is "breached"[2] we are reminded that the maintenance of what we

[1] Work on this paper was supported in part by National Science Foundation Grant No. NSF GS-30546-Gumperz. Some of the data referred to were collected while the author was employed by the Science Curriculum Improvement Study at the Lawrence Hall of Science, University of California, Berkeley. The ideas expressed here lean heavily on the work of Harold Garfinkel and Aaron Cicourel. I would like to thank Susan Ervin-Tripp and John J. Gumperz for their comments and Linda Veloria for her help with the art work.
[2] For examples and explanation of breaches see Garfinkel (1967); also, David Sylvester's introduction to the "Magritte" catalog for Tate Gallery exhibition (1969).

must take to be a dense actuality—the givenness of the everyday world—is in fact a precarious state of affairs depending in part on constant verbal affirmation that normal activity is going on. To breach the surface of normality can be an upsetting experience, both philosophically and emotionally, from which a return to the commonplaceness of everyday talk can appear to be comforting. But even the normalness of everyday talk is itself achieved. It is achieved through a delicate balance between features that can receive attention in their own right and are open to discussion, and those that must remain hidden. These hidden features can be comprehended and recognized in passing but cannot be singled out for undue attention, or the situation changes from being "normal daily talk" to a joke. All these processes, both the hidden but acknowledged and the expressible and discussable features of speech events, are illustrated in the quotation from *Alice in Wonderland.* In fact, "Alice" can be seen in its entirety as a Victorian child's primer for competent communication. It tells of the conventions, describable rules of good talk and behavior, of politeness and ways of gaining acceptability through taking the other person's needs into account in one's choice of words and topics. It also shows how the backgrounded features do their work by singling them out, allowing their axiomatic status to be questioned and so making the world seem absurd in the process.

The purpose of this study is not to analyse *Alice in Wonderland* but to explore some current ideas and recent evidence showing how the child becomes a competent communicator in the adult world. The theme can best be expressed in Garfinkel's 1967 terms as how the child comes to know a world in common with others and in common with others to be taken for granted. One of the difficulties in studying what social psychologists and sociologists have called "child socialization" is that often it is not *what* the child knows, says, and does that is of interest but what he does not do and does not question (this problem is also encountered when the parents' actions are studied). Since the appearance of competence in daily life is given more by the activities that are not singled out for undue attention by actors, to study the acquisition of the sense of social structure as a normative order is often to upset this delicate balance between the known and expressible and the known but taken for granted (and therefore passed over) features of the everyday world.

We will refer to these features, the discussable and the hidden, as foregrounded and backgrounded aspects of communicative situations. By this we mean that *foregrounded* features are the codifiable rules of etiquette, requirements for politeness, greetings rituals, and other ceremonial features of communicative encounters. *Backgrounded* features are the ways in which the former are accomplished, via features of intonation, stress, and syntactic marking, through what Gumperz has suggested are conversational inferences based on linguistic marking processes (Gumperz, 1974). The foregrounded features can be presented as reconstructed rules to any questioner. The rules tell us what we *must* do to fulfill any social requirements and what we cannot do, but not what we can do, for the accomplishing of the rules is a different matter. In rearing children we have everyday rules of conversation and conduct that are "ad hoc" versions of the cultural rules: "It's rude to interrupt someone when they're talking," "Do not talk with your mouth full," "Reply when someone speaks to you." Backgrounded features are not learned through explicit rules, even of this kind, although something of their social implications could be explained by members if they were asked.

The problem that we will consider is how the child acquires and practices the knowledge that the world of everyday life has the quality we have described as a "dense actuality," an unquestionable existence as given, although it is often apparent that this sense is not as secure as we can imagine. The normality or mundaneness is given by the exercise of practical reasoning (Cicourel, 1972; Garfinkel, 1967; Pollner, 1970). This is the search for the reasonableness of daily life that leads us to fill in any relevant detail and look for the sense of any utterance, assuming that we will find it if only we do our work of interpretation and addition of relevant details adequately. How the child comes to comprehend and exercise the skill of practical reasoning is what we will attempt to give some demonstration of.

Previous studies of child socialization (through the period when the subject was very popular in social psychology in the 1950s and early 1960s) have focused on the normative features, as in the study of moral development and growth of conscience (Aronfreed, 1968). When the guiding model has not been behaviorism, the internalization model has been taken to account for all the seemingly generative aspects of the child's actions, such as the mismatch between the researcher's sets of "normative moral principles" and the child's behavior in tests and observed situations (Cook-Gumperz, 1972). Apart from the Freudian-derived principles, which were never translated adequately into research terms, a theory of internalization that regards social or sociological principles as constitutive of the individual personality through linguistic experience has remained undeveloped. The area of child socialization study has resulted in an awkward shifting of focus, and at best a correlation, between individual behavior, normative principles, and social-sociological pressures. Meadian-derived role theory still mistakes the elucidation or explication of the principles of social regulation for the achievement of that order through daily practice. The intrinsically rationalist model can see no possibility of adequate rules generating inadequate performance (see Cicourel, 1972 and Wrong, 1961 for criticism of these issues). How the social gets "inside" and how the development of an individualized social being can be examined other than through exteriorized displays is a problem that has been formulated by\Garfinkel as follows: "For Kant the moral order 'within' was an awesome problem, for sociologists the moral order 'without' is a technical mystery [1967:35]." In the solution of this technical problem, interest has shifted from the study of the processes of the acquisition of social control as social regulation to that of language acquisition itself, after a long period during which language and speech were neglected. More recently, interest has developed not only in acquisition of grammatical roles but in the child's acquisition of "communicative competence" (Gumperz and Hymes, 1964; Hymes, 1967), that is, the ability to guide interaction appropriately.

Most studies of communicative competence focus on the acquisition of "named," i.e., culturally identifiable, speech events, e.g., insults, jokes, ritual insults, address forms, language games (Dundes *et al.,* Labov in Gumperz and Hymes, 1972). These are aspects of communication that show the child's developing understanding of the explicit communicative rules of his culture. In these events attempts are made to locate the regulative features that act as metacommunicative properties and tell us when a certain speech event is taking place. Descriptive studies in the ethnography of communication have shown some of the requirements and features that any study should examine, such as choices of speech mode, channel, code and genre, etc. (Hymes, 1972; Sherzer and Darnell, 1972). These theoretical studies do not as yet tell us much about the importance in different kinds of speech events of the choice between alternative patterns of features, and so for acquisition by the child there is no order of priority nor developmental sequence suggested.

Studies in the child's acquisition of communicative skills have begun to show possible developmental sequences and have suggested that the child acquires strategies that are both culturally specific and yet seem to account for the universal orders of grammatical development (Mitchell-Kernan, 1970; Kernan, 1970; Stross, 1970; Blount, 1970). Recent work in the acquisition of grammar is moving in a direction similar to the communicative competence studies. Slobin (1971) shows that speaking competence is a more complex phenomenon than the acquisition of grammatical competence alone. In some recent shifts in theory, the study of language acquisition has moved from the earlier concern with charting the developmental acquisition of known grammatical features of a single language, most usually English. Cross-cultural studied have broadened the perspective beyond the study of each language as a separate system to consider the universals indicated by acquisition in many different languages from different language groups. The consideration and search for universals in acquisition, especially for a possible universal order of acquisition, has raised again the consideration of the relationship between the child's cognitive development and the acquisition of potentially universal features of language (Ferguson and Slobin, 1972).

Both grammatical and communicative competence appear to be learned in somewhat similar ways as social skills. There is growing evidence that grammatical development is a context-embedded skill and that the child learns language not as an abstract set of rules for correct grammar and separate rules for correct contextual use but as communicative rules in which grammar is learned in relation to specific contexts. Slobin has suggested that children acquire some very general operating principles for the recognition of some syntactic features and, through the use of these in specific contexts, develop further rules of syntax in gradually growing complexity and abstraction.

What I want to do is to examine and describe what I take to be some of the more general potentially universal *social features* that underlie, in fact underpin, grammatical development. The starting point for this study is in some measure the recent work by Slobin (1971 and 1972), who gives a full cross-cultural survey of the evidence on language acquisition and suggests that universal similarities and differences in development between different languages point to children's having cognitively a set of *simple heuristics,* or operating principles, that direct them in the development of these culturally different grammars. Further, he builds on the idea that the child begins the move into the acquisition of syntax with a well-formed set of semantic intentions. The existence of such prelinguistic semantic intentions has been demonstrated by Talmy (1970) and Stross (1970) and described, from the standpoint of a rather different linguistic theory, by Halliday (1972, 1973).

This work in language acquisition suggests two possibilities for inquiry in social development: (1) The child's social development has begun at a prelinguistic stage and in a way that prepares the child for the development of semantic intentions. It follows that the development of an intent to communicate must depend on certain social understandings of the child. (2) The child may also have a simple heuristics to guide his social development. Although social rules are not of the same codifiable type as linguistic rules, social and cognitive development must probably proceed in rather similar ways in their relationship to early language development.

In bringing together recent work in the field, Slobin has shown that both cognitive development and communicative understanding precede the ability to produce grammatical sentences. Children depend on both a prior intent to produce speech and a social context to interpret it. It appears that children do not make judgments of grammaticality apart from the social situation; that is, knowing something to say precedes the ability to say it correctly. It seems that competence in both language and cognition proceed developmentally in rather similar ways, through the acquisition of context-embedded (dependent) rules that the child develops for himself as a free variation on the general principles that are the developmental universals. Although the cognitive principles lead the way, it appears more and more evident that children develop strategies for communication rather than grammatical rules per se, and develop their grammatical knowledge out of the *practice* of producing and comprehending socially appropriate, or at least acceptable, speech.

In order to consider some of the social understanding that the child develops prior to and concommitant with the early stages of language development, we will have to depend mainly on suggestive anecdotes as evidence. Our lack of social counterparts for the kinds of evidence Slobin has drawn on for his demonstration of the heuristic principles for grammar tells us something about the nature of "social rules." These social rules lack the normative certainties and alternatives of grammatical rules. Grammatical rules tell us broadly what we can do as well as what we cannot do. "Social" rules seem to operate, as I have described, more "in the breach than in the observance." We are not aware of breaking one until after the act. The guiding principles of communicative competence may be more of this nature, although they also depend on the normative "rigor" of linguistic rules. For language acts in two ways, not only as a tool for its own acquisition and understanding, in which the linguistic thought processes must shape the development of syntactic and semantic concepts, but also as a guide for other cognitive coding processes, especially in the processing and storage of iconic information about events and relationships (Miller, 1972). As such, language must act *reflexively* to develop the principles by which it is both learned and practiced in speech events. The position seems to be, as described at the beginning, that some aspects of the communicative situation are more apparent as "normatively described," while others are less available for direct discussion, although both contribute equally to the communicative message.

The gap between what is linguistic and what is social is an abiding problem in child socialization. Existing work in language socialization has brought together two areas of study that intrinsically differ. Since we do not yet have an essentially *social* concept of language, the relation between the acquisition of language as grammar and the acquisition of social rules and/or communicative regulations has seemed somewhat indistinct; apart from an awareness that without language as a means of expression the child's understanding of social principles could not be studied (for example, the critical discussion over Piaget's moral development study as to whether the child possesses and comprehends "moral principles" prior to his ability to express these [Kohlberg 1969]).

If it is the case that language acts reflexively to shape the grounds for its own acquisition and, therefore, for the shaping of social acts of language use, we need to ask both how the process of acquisition gets started through the shaping of prelinguistic social and semantic intentions and how language acts as a guide to further social development.

Language as a Social Principle

I would like to suggest that we need not begin by looking for any specifically *social* principles in language or its use—for example, in the form of certain syntactic constructions, choices of words, acquisition of speech rituals, or ways of speaking as being the social principles that languages introduce into the child's life—although the requirements of syntax will surely influence or express the child's perception of social relationships and communicative encounters.

The thesis of this study is that it is initially language itself that is intrinsically a "social principle" for the child. With the acquisition of syntax the child for the first and major time becomes aware of the *normativeness* of the world of others. In accepting the acquisition of the normative system of language—and it is an acceptance, as Halliday's description of the prelinguistic-to-linguistic stage shows—the child is accepting the normative regulation of his own intentions as a part of the world known in common with others.

The child becomes aware of the normativeness of this world for the first time when he begins to attain the principles of syntax or, rather, what Halliday has called the "stages of wording."[3] The discovery is not immediate but gradual, as the child builds up the specific instances of the regulative principles of syntax as the necessary shape for his semantic intentions, although it must occur as a result of a cumulative awareness that language use means the use of regulative principles. The acquisition of wording means, for the child, the use of syntactic constraints he has observed in others, and the realization that he can adequately share his

---

[3] Wording is a traditional linguistic concept that combines the acquisition of vocabulary with that of syntax.

own semantic intentions only if he uses the form that the principles suggest. This realization brings directly into the child's life, for the first time, the awareness of what it is to accept a social world, that is, a world shared and known in common with others. Previously, in the stages of prelinguistic and private language usage, the child has experienced mis-understanding by others and both frustration and acceptance of his desires and wishes through his own communicative endeavours, but, in an as yet unformulated because prelinguistic way, the child must have a feeling of coming to terms with his environment by himself. As the real-ization of the regulative principles of syntax grows on the child, he is no longer by himself, because, in order to share the world with others, he now begins to know that his observations and comments must be ex-pressed in ways already in existence.

The child begins by learning that different kinds of semantic intentions (e.g., statements versus commands) can be expressed differently, by regularly varying features of his language. This discovery is charted by Halliday (1973), who shows how a $13\frac{1}{2}$-month-old child discovers that his "words" can have varying uses when combined with different patterns of intonation. Previously, both phonemic shape and intonation had been part of each single "meaning" unit; the move into syntax comes with the dis-covery that phonemic shape and intonation could co-vary independently. The next stage of the acquisition processes suggested by Slobin's study, which shows an order of acquisition of the main universal features, begins with regular morphemic variation to express different relationships between features of the environment. Slobin states that one of the child's first speaking principles in the acquisition of grammar is "look to the ends of the words." This indicates that the child already distinguishes between "things" and "their relationship to other things" and that these rela-tionships are expressed in word endings. We must assume that at this stage the child has already perceived many of these relationships before he acquires the rule, but that he then realizes that there is a required way of expressing his observations. This must be a direct realization that there are normative principles governing the social expression of his observa-tions, which is what language is for the child, an understanding that in order to share experiences the necessary form must be used. Early language-syntax development, which begins for the child with variation at about 1 year and continues until $3\frac{1}{2}$ years, is a period of intense activity and is the major time in the child's life when he will be brought face-to-face with the *normative* requirements of the world of others. Both body control and the control of other aspects of social behavior are never quite as constraining because they do not have the cognitively demanding, fine detail of syntactic principles. The acceptance of language norms occurs spontaneously to the child, and he teaches himself these requirements because he wishes to share his intentions with others and enter into a shared world.

The acceptance of language both as syntax and as vocabulary is a realization that the world is already shaped by others who have lived in it before (Vygotsky, 1962). The child's development of the principles of syntactic regularity is an immense cognitive task that the child undertakes in order to be a participating member of this common order. Once the "idea" of normative controls on a shared world has been acquired by the child (as it must be in the early stages of syntax development), the world will continue to be a place that has a normatively "social" structure (i.e., shared–known in common). It may be this idea that we go on to create or recreate in our search for similar social regularities and their normative features. Once the "concept of normativeness" is developed, the world will always keep in its everyday activities (except as a philosophic enterprise or "mental choice") a sense of givenness or actuality. To recap once more, what is social about language socialization is the learning of language. The acceptance and, therefore, use by the child of the regulative principles and vocabulary that others use to express their comments and requests is an acceptance of a common shared view of the world. The perception and use of syntactic rules brings with it the understanding that the world of others that the child shares is governed by *normative* principles and that, in order to share in the world known in common, the child must use these principles.

Never again after language syntax learning will the child have such an awareness of the normativeness of the social world. Since social rules do not have such clear detail, it is only through the acquisition of syntax that the child gets the idea of the normative structure of the world shared and known with others.

While the child's understanding of the normative structure of a shared world is gained through the acquisition of language, the social understanding that develops in the prelinguistic stage is of the utmost importance. It is the existence of this prelinguistic social awareness that encourages the child to attempt the acquisition of grammar because the need to communicate is already felt and understood. Recent work (Bloom, 1971; Dore, 1973; Halliday, 1972; and Slobin, 1972) has suggested that a prior semantic intention exists before the child's move into language. Paraphrasing Dore grammar in this sense is a formal marking of a prior semantic intention. Slobin also suggests that there must be a prior cognitive development. This restating of the principle that cognitive development preceeds grammatical development imputes to the child an intentionality even to his first linguistic acts. The assertion of the primacy of cognitive development questions the innateness hypothesis in that it does impute a conscious intentionality. My suggestion of the primacy of a form of social understanding goes even further in this assumption. It suggests, metaphorically, that the learning of language for the child is not like learning to walk but like learning to dance: a more definite act in a known specified context that depends on recognition of more than one social and perceptual sense of modality. The preceding discussion focuses specifically on different kinds of implications underlying grammatical development. It attempts to show that existing data on the stages of language acquisition can be understood as showing a social development. It suggests that there is for the child a cognitive formulation of social principle, which encourages the child to attempt the more rigorous communication of a shared grammar. I will call this principle the *reciprocity principle* and attempt to show how this principle makes the child willing to accept the normative stipulations of grammar.

The *reciprocity principle* (Schutz, 1964) can be simply stated as the child's understanding that other people can be assumed, for all practical purposes, to be the same as himself. The child's earliest knowledge is formed by his attempts to differentiate the world and its objects from himself as actor upon these objects. But the practice of a life with others also requires a different kind of understanding. It requires the understanding that other people can be assumed to be the same as me, for if they were to share my knowledge and were to see the world from my perspective, they would see it in the same way that I do, so I can assume without changing places with them that *they see the world as I do.* This is a very important realization for the child to make, for without the sense that his attempts at communication would receive reciprocal understanding from others, the child might not be encouraged to move from his "private" communication system to the shared regulations of grammar.

Let us draw on some illustrations from Halliday's recent work to show in some ways how this social principle can occur. Halliday describes his son's acquisition of language from what is usually regarded as a prelinguistic stage, 9 months, to approximately 2 years of age (1972, 1973). From 9 months to 14 months, the language system of the child consisted of phonemes with associated prosodic features, proto-words. At $13\frac{1}{2}$ to 14 months, Nigel began to distinguish the independent variation of the phonemic shapes and the intonational features. Leaving aside the functional theory Halliday uses as a theoretical framework for his observations, he shows that between the ages of 9 months and 14 months Nigel distinguished two broad categories of verbalization: those that comment on events or his feelings and those that require some response of either action or verbalization, the latter being talk that "gets things done." At 14 months, Nigel was able to mark these two kinds of verbalization with different prosodic, intonational patterns, the requests carrying a rising tone. The comments carried a falling tone, indicating that no response was required. The utterance was as though it were self-sufficient. Halliday points out that these distinctions were the indication of the beginning of a new understanding of language by Nigel, the understanding that language could be used not only as an extension of the body's power, e.g., as an extra hand to get things done, but also as a resource in its own right. Furthermore, these distinctions showed an awareness that verbal comments are useful in and of themselves, that we can share our experiences with others by means of language. Halliday expresses his surprise at the large number of "commenting remarks" or "mathetic remarks" that the child makes.

At 18 months, Halliday observed the beginnings of dialogue in Nigel; for example, after a request Nigel would wait for a reply, or after a request made of him he would take up the verbal line and repeat or add some comment of his own. At just beyond 2 years, Nigel added a new and important distinction between information known to the hearer because he was present at the scene of the action and information not known because the hearer was not present. Halliday describes this as paraphrased in the following: "He used the declarative form to give information that he knew was already possessed by the hearer, to respond to experiences that had been shared by both, and he used the interrogative form to convey information that the hearer did not possess, to refer to experience which had not been shared by the two. When the hearer was present, he said 'Daddy the tower fall down.' To his mother entering the room later, he said "Did the tower fall down?" It seems he was marking the information that was necessary for the operation of shared experiences to begin. This seems to indicate that the child was in the process of understanding the reciprocity principle. Having realized that reciprocal understanding could be expected from others, the child tests out for himself the *limits of reciprocity.* The child's semantic syntactic distinction indicates his awareness that the *other person is like himself,* and not, as Piaget suggests, that in the child's world the adult is omniscient. Further, it shows the workings of the child's mind in assuming that we must in some way mark the special information that we wish to be shared in the context of that verbal encounter. As I have stated, there are limits to the reciprocity principle, though our daily exercise of practical reasoning enables us to fill in and make sense of the events we encounter. We recognize and overcome the limits of reciprocity by using a further social principle, which will be described. It may be considered the case that, in marking the distinction syntactically at this point, the child is overgeneralizing a "social rule" that he is in the process of learning. Halliday comments that this distinction is dropped from adult language. This is not quite the case; all that happens is that we learn more complex ways of lexicalizing or formulating the kinds of differences in shared knowledge that are not marked by a direct syntactic principle. Later the child could say, "While you were out, the tower fell down," or "Did you know that while you were making the coffee the tower fell down?" or "I guess you didn't realize it, but the tower fell down."

Once the child has developed the reciprocity principle, he begins to accept the need for language; since he can assume that the other person is like himself, he can find the language system of others acceptable as an expression of his own intentions and understanding.[4]

After this the period of rapid growth of vocabulary and syntax begins, and the child relies increasingly on the reciprocity principle as a form of practical reasoning to interpret speech in context. The acquisition of syntax is a process of extracting rules from specific instances of speech acts. The child builds up the rules from *context-embedded usage* (Talmy, 1970; Moskowitz, 1970). This is corroborated by some recent work on language acquisition using a different linguistic theory, which has shown that very early in the developmental process children learn to distinguish between different "registers," that is, different kinds of speech for different situations, such as speaking to adults versus speaking to children (De Stefano, 1972).

In this process of extracting and building up "rules" from specific contexts, the child has the sense that he is both accepting and yet creating his language at the same time. In Piaget's terms, he *achieves* his language rules.[5] It is possible that if this were not the case the normative power of language would not be so great. But the language-learning situation is in no way a simple one; there is more to the acquisition of syntax than the deduction of language rules in context. In order to deduce syntactic rules from speech, the child has to perceive and interpret a complex communicative message. As I have already described briefly, there are both foregrounded and backgrounded features in any communicative situation. Initially, the idea implies that features of communicative acts that either can be or usually are explicitly described or taught are *foregrounded* features. Those that are used to accomplish the foregrounded features and are not singled out for attention are *backgrounded* features. The foregrounded features are often seen to be culturally variant and as indicators of cultural difference, for example, address forms, politeness, and eti-

---

[4] It is precisely this understanding of the preexistence of a shared world known in common that the interpretation and acceptance of language requires and is described in Helen Keller's diaries (Langer, 1942).

[5] Piaget's description of the acquisition of moral rules is in terms of the *achievement* of rules.

quette rules such as the use of "thank you." These features are all subject to what have been called *alternation rules* (Ervin-Tripp, 1972). Choice between alternative forms indicates differences in the social relationship, and there exists a known set of possible alternatives that are available for discussion by members. These are the features that ethnographers of communication would record as making up different speech events and indicating differences between events.

Backgrounded features are those that operate without such potentially explicit awareness and cannot so easily be given an explicable "social meaning," although they are equally powerful as indicators of social relationships. Ervin-Tripp (1972) has described the situation of delineating the different features of speech events as follows:

> It is not clear how the different realizations of social selectors might be important. Language, address terms, pronominal selection or consistent verb suffixing (as in Japanese) can be consciously controlled more readily perhaps than intonation contours or syntactic complexity . . . Such forms can be taught to children or newcomers. Forms which allow specific exceptions, or which have options so that too great or too little frequency might be conspicuous, cannot be taught deliberately so easily. Such rules can be acquired by newcomers only by long and intense exposure rather than by formal teaching [p. 232].

Ervin-Tripp points out that these features are subject to what Gumperz has called *cooccurrence rules* (Gumperz, 1964). Cooccurrence constraints control the selection of speech variables so that sequences met some deeply embedded "appropriateness condition." While mistakes in foreground features can be corrected, in fact we are often taught specific strategies for the recognition of mistakes in these features and reparative strategies for overcoming them. Mistakes in background features such as an unusual stress pattern or a mismatched intonation contour are much more demanding of attention. The problem with backgrounded phenomena is that their very complexity makes it much more difficult to say what a pattern of normality or ordinary stress and intonation should look like. Although we feel that we know an unusual or nonnormal pattern when we hear one, these features are much more "practice" conditioned.

One of the problems for a child's development of competency may be the recognition of which features are to be backgrounded and which foregrounded. We have chosen these terms precisely because we want to emphasize that communication is *multichannel* and messages are sent through all channels at once; therefore, the meaning of a communicative situation is a compound one (Bateson, 1971). The senses are bombarded by messages from which the speaker–hearers select certain themes, although the selection takes place on several levels of perceptual modalities at once. The relationship between the elements in a communicative situation is a shifting one, in fact a transitory one, because it depends in part on the temporality of the sequencing of speech. At the stage of prelinguistic communication, the child is attendant to signals that, for him, have perhaps a greater foregrounded importance than after the acquisition of syntax. Likewise, during the acquisition of syntax the child attends to some cues more than to others. Recent work in both speech perception and child language development has shown that the child learns some broad intonational patterns before he begins the distinction of phonemic contrasts. Work in the biological basis of language has shown that information on these early-acquired intonational sequences are coded on the right side of the brain along with other "deeply unconscious" behavior control such as digestive tract control, while the information on phonemic perception is coded at a more conscious level on the left side (Wang, 1973). In this sense, the beginnings of the backgrounded features are prelinguistic and of great importance to the beginnings of language, since they are learned as part of a rudimentary form of communication at the beginning of the child's communicative development. In the prelinguistic stage the child learns to communicate through other modalities, through eye contact, smiling and crying, and other body and facial gestures. It seems that the child's desire to communicate with others is a spontaneous act and that the child uses different modalities at different stages of development (Mussen, 1970).

The notion of foregrounded and backgrounded features is to show that the importance of channels and modalities as indicators of meaning is, to some extent, both a learned and a developmental skill. In the case of communicative events, rather than individual acts of communication, the figure–ground relationship of the communicative modalities remains unstable for a long time beyond the development of syntax. The child proceeds to learn syntax by exercising his own practical reasoning, assuming that what is said to him intrinsically makes sense, and it is his job to decide on the meaning even if the filling in of "relevant" details of his own is necessary (the quotation at the beginning of this chapter is a play on this idea). Grammatical rules are extracted from the total message by the child and used as processing rules (Slobin's operating principles) that help him in both encoding and decoding speech. As we know from many grammatical development studies (e.g., Frazer, Brown, and Bellugi, 1963, the first main test of this hypothesis), the child's decoding or comprehension ability outpaces and precedes his ability at encoding and speech production. We can assume, therefore, that the child uses every communicative device that he recognizes in order to discover the sense of the utterances that he interprets, and the child has a great deal of prelinguistic experience to rely on. The child's use of the reciprocity principle continues to guide his search under the assumption that what is *situated* (that is, present to all participants, either as occurring during their association or present in the physical setting) is reciprocally available. As we have seen in the example of Nigel, what is not situated is *marked* as necessary to be made explicit. What is situated is available to all.

In this way we can describe the child's interpretation of speech as *iconographic:* that is, the setting, shared history of the participants as well as presently occurring events for the participants are treated as a single communicative context in which verbal utterances and their prosodic features form a single unit for interpretation by the child. All parts of the message and context contribute *equally* to the possible interpretation. *All components are considered to contribute similarly to the understanding for both the child and his reciprocal partners.*

Children therefore reveal at times a rather different notion of what is backgrounded and what is the foreground in the communicative event, and make a perhaps different grouping, or "chunking," of utterance sequences into speech events and contexts. Many features of a communicative event are recognized but not made explicit by adults and become background. Such features as facial gestures, body gestures, and posture are noticed and coded by us, but in giving a verbal explanation to a fellow member we would not normally remark upon these features as being ones that shaped our interpretation of any speech event. We would give an interpretation that focused on the verbalized aspects of the event and any "history" of previous events or the participants' activities that linked with the event under discussion. Only if the background features are in some way specially marked in the event, or dissonant, or cumulatively disturbing to our sense of "normality" would we foreground them and comment on them as influencing our interpretation. For children, this division is more fluid. This is shown by the fact that in everyday occurrences children are likely to comment on background features as a part of a normal explanation. For example: When a 9-year-old boy wanted to find out what his sister had bought him for a Christmas present, he was told he could not question her. He then said, quite seriously, "It's all right, I'll wear a blindfold and then I can't see what little Jenny is saying." He said this in earnest, really not intending a joke.

The same question applies to the child's grouping of events into sequences such as have been variously called speech events, communicative events, and, in a narrower sense, speech acts. Everyday life

Figure 1.

is made up of a stream of talk and behavior that often has little segmentation in terms of change of actors or scene. Alternation of actors, activities, and physical location can mark a transition in speech event, but in everyday life, especially for a small child, these changes may be few. In our perception of this stream, we group or (to take a term from Miller, 1956) "chunk" these sequences into "speech acts" or speech events. It is the focusing of features that indicates to the participants how to "name" or contextualize the stream of talk. The child is an apprentice in the activity once he has acquired the principles of syntax and begins to use talk to guide his activities and shape his interaction with others.

The child is guided by his own practical reasoning based on the reciprocity principle, and this leads to mistakes in the child's reasoning about the availability of interpretations to others. The child treats each situation as an interpretive icon; that is, he reasons iconographically, by overdepending on reciprocity with others. The child's use of deictic features has often been used to illustrate the child's lack of competency as a communicator. In Figure 1, for example, the whole message is contained in both the picture and the words, including the size of the typography. The same is true when children interpret socially situated talk. There is a reliance on intonation to "carry the sense" and an understanding that words, actions, prosodic features, and setting are all a part of the same *interpretive icon.*

The child groups or "chunks" act and setting as a single context in which, since all actors are present, any reference to the setting or any particulars generated within that setting must be available to all and do not need to be marked as "not to be taken for granted." To the child it would seem unnecessary to express in words what we can take for granted by reason of our presence in the situation. This reasoning may lie behind some children's test performances, for example in the situation described by Hawkins (1970), in which children aged 5 and 7 were asked to tell stories from cartoon strips of pictures. Many of these children told stories that contained unreferenced pronouns because, while it was possible to explicate the reference of the pronoun by pointing to the story character, it would have appeared to children as unnecessarily redundant to have put the reference into words.[6] The child has yet to learn to take into account that setting, nonverbal prosodic cues, and the speech can co-vary independently.

In fact, it can and has been shown that children depend perhaps more on both visual perceptual cues (Haber, 1970; Cicourel, 1972) and on intonation (Gumperz and Herasimchuk, 1973) rather than placing their interpretive reliance on the verbalized features of the interaction alone. An example of this is shown in some recent work in studying children's communication in instructional situations (Cook-Gumperz and Bowyer, 1972), in which pairs of children were asked to give directions to each other, using the tape recorder as a telephone to reach a friend's house marked on a stylized map by a cross. After each of the two had attempted to guide the other to the place using only verbal directions, the two were read a set of directions that were ambiguous and inadequate to reach the house. The children were asked to tell what was wrong with the directions and to say why they would not work. The idea was that since the children had the experience of giving the directions, they would be able to spot the verbal ambiguities that resulted from lack of descriptive detail. (For example, there were two banks in the town, one on either side of the road, and all the directions said was "turn by the bank." In practice, many of the students (fourth-graders) failed to notice the verbal ambiguities. Several pairs worked hard to make the instructions work in spite of having been told by the experimenter three times that the instructions were wrong. Students followed the path as indicated by the experimenter's directions, and when a point of ambiguity arose the students tried by tracing the path with a finger until the correct house was reached. When the experimenter repeated, "Are the instructions all right? Can you get to the house with these instructions?" the students replied "Yes." Their own acquired knowledge was used to compensate

[6] If it is the case that, as Grice suggests, one of the universal principles of conversation is that of economy of means, the "enough is enough" principle, then this example of what Bernstein has called a "restricted code" is in fact the use by the child of the Occam's razor of good conversation. What is at fault is not the child's competence to conduct conversation but the failure to realize that this rule, like all social rules, is subject to exceptions, the exceptions being the more detailed "practice" rules of conduct on which we rely to make the general rules work.

for the inadequacies of the written and spoken directions. We take this to be an example of the child's practical reasoning following from the reciprocity principle. The child looks to make sense of what is said to him, and fills in any relevant detail to the best of his ability. In this case the child could not disembed his knowledge of the workings of the map from the verbal directions he was given and so evaluate these directions on their own merits. This is an example of the child's interpretation of "speech in context" as a single unit, not separating out the verbal message from other features and treating it as a source of information by itself. In fact, in everyday life we do repeatedly require the child to exercise "practical reasoning," that is, to make our comments or instructions appear reasonable and workable. For example, in the data described by Gumperz and Herasimchuk (1972), a teaching situation involving a reading group in a second-grade classroom, the teacher says to the child, "How do you spell Ann?" The child responds "A–N–N." The teacher says "Yes, but what kind of an A?" The child does not respond, but another child answers, "Capital A." From this interchange it becomes clear that the request to spell *Ann* is not in fact a request for the child to literally spell out the word *Ann* but to give the spelling rules for proper names. The child was expected to "fill in" the required detail in order to make the instructions suitable for the kind of reply the teacher expected.

Similarly, in test situations we require the child to know that tests do not follow the usual rules of everyday life; i.e., instructions are to be taken *literally*, to mean so much and no more. For example, consider the previous experiment in which the student was required to give instructions for his friend to get to a house (the stylized map represented a cross between a street map and a diagram, with the houses and other buildings such as stores, banks, etc., sketched in) and the student was supposed to give directions by calling on any features of the town that he could see. When asked to direct his friend to the house, one student replied, "Well, if it's got all these buildings and things this town has just *got* to have street names; I'd tell him the names of the streets and he could find his own way." The task required the student to give instructions by means of descriptive detail only, but this went against the child's experience of life in an urban setting. The experimenter had to reply, "Well, suppose this town hasn't got any streets names. How would you direct someone?," thus placing the test situation outside of the realm of daily events.

The child follows the first principle of practical reasoning, look for the sense, to make the utterance fit within a perceivedly normal course of affairs. But what for the child is the *sense* of the utterance may not be so for the adult, for whom this situation belongs to a different set of activities and therefore indexes different kinds of behavioral possibilities (again, the assumption that in "test" situations words have a literal meaning). Children are aware that utterances are situated and that the knowledge traded upon is within a sequence of utterances and within a particular context, but they assume that the particulars that frame the sequence and the utterance, *being situated,* are reciprocally available.

The child's use of pronouns and other deictic features is an example (as the illustration showed) of the child's situated, iconographic treatment of speech in context. Piaget (1959) suggests that the child's use of pronouns that are not adequately referenced is due to the child's being "shut up in his own point of view." Piaget observes:

> . . . the explainer sprinkles his exposition with such expressions as: "You understand, you see, etc.," which shows that he has not lost sight of the fact that he is talking to a friend. The cause of his ego-centrism lies much deeper. It is extremely important, and really explains all the ego-centrism of childish thought. If children fail to understand one another, it is because they think that they do understand one another. The explainer believes from the start that the reproducer will grasp everything, will almost know beforehand all that should be known, and will interpret every subtlety. Children are perpetually surrounded by adults who not only know much more than they do, but who also do everything in their power to understand them, who even anticipate their thoughts and their desires. Children, therefore, whether they work or not, whether they express wishes or feel guilty, are perpetually under the impression that people can read their thoughts, and in extreme cases, can steal their thoughts away [p. 101].

Piaget explains what he has called the *egocentrism* of children's thought and their expression of it in this way: "These habits account, in the first place for the remarkable lack of precision in childish style. Pronouns, personal and demonstrative adjectives, etc., 'he,' 'she,' or 'that,' 'the,' 'him,' etc., are used right and left without any indication of what they refer to. The other person is supposed to understand, [ibid., p. 102]." But the child's acquisition of language and his use of the many grammatical rules concerned with morphemic variation show that the child can already deal with more difficult problems of reference in speech and language. So the child must (by the age of 5–8) both cognitively and grammatically comprehend that relationships can be expressed through words and grammatical choices.

The examples of the child's unreferenced pronouns are better evidence for the use of the reciprocity principle. The child expects that others will also use iconographic interpretation of his speech the same way he uses speech in context as a single interpretive icon for his understanding of others. I am not disputing Piaget's observations—in fact, he corroborates my description of the reciprocity principle—however, I am suggesting that this is due not to the child's egocentric viewpoints once the existence of the reciprocity principle makes them untenable, but, instead, to the fact that the child has not yet learned how to apply a further social principle. This principle I will call *reflexivity of language.*

This can best be explained as the child's awareness that what is to be treated as *foreground* for the course of the interaction, and what "speech event" this talk is a part of, can be lexicalized and made a part of the talk. The communicative breakthrough for the child begins with the recognition that speech and its associated paralinguistic features *create the grounds for their own understanding.* The reflexivity principle provides the child with the understanding of how speech provides evidence of its own interpretive frame. The social force of this principle is the child's awareness of the limitations of the reciprocity principle, for although people are like each other, they are not the same. Children often begin to comment at about 6 that "everyone is themselves." By 7 or 8, the child is just beginning to be aware that there are at least three different channels for the communication of meanings — setting, nonverbal information, and the verbalized message — and that each can convey different meanings. This is very difficult for the child to accept, as it reverses much of the practice of the early social principle on which language learning is based, the reciprocity principle. The child learns to accept the world and its descriptions as "known in common" and, therefore, as reasonable descriptions of his own experience. The assumption that other people are similar to himself tells him that he can find their sound and word system suitable for the expression of his own meanings.

The child begins his move away from the sole use of the reciprocity principle to guide his social use of language as he begins to learn that setting, prosodic features, and the verbal and lexical message can co-vary independently. We have accepted Halliday's suggestion that children initially learn language when they realize that phonemes and intonations can co-vary, so their further communicative development is continued, after the acquisition of syntax, by the development of more complex communications in which all the features do not contribute *equally and similarly* to the message. The detailed analysis in Gumperz and Herasimchuk (1972) shows how children initially rely more on intonation as a foregrounded feature of a communicative message.

When the child learns that one part of the communicative icon can be foregrounded, he is beginning to learn the possibility that different channels can carry different meanings. This introduces the possibility of meaning more than you appear to be saying, giving the message an additional communicative (or illocutionary) force through the introduction of irony and other means of not meaning what you say or meaning the opposite. The use of ironic jokes or teasing routines, in which what is said is meant to be taken in an opposite way, is an indication that the child is able to see the social influence in shaping a piece of interaction as varying independently of the direct semantic sense of the comment. For example, an 8-year-old girl is taking part in a dinnertime conversation with her family, grandmother, father, mother, and brother. Her brother is speaking, talking mainly to his grandmother about baseball stars in different teams. He mentions Babe Ruth as someone who was talent spotted early in his life. The girl says "My hero." Mother: "What did you say?" Girl: "My hero" (repeated with exactly the same rising intonation pattern and pitch). This time everyone hears and everyone laughs. Grandmother: "Is the Bambino your hero?"

In this incident the intonation suggests that she does *not* think of the baseball player as her hero at all; the effect of the moment is to make an ironic joke, so taking the floor from her brother, achieving a topic switch, and indirectly indicating some disapproval of the topic. Children often start using ambiguous comments or saying the reverse of what is meant at about age 5. But using these techniques successfully with some measure of sureness is an indication of the child's awareness of "meta-communicative" purposes of the reflexivity principle in language – talk used to control and adjust the setting for further talk with others.

Through the reflexivity principle the child understands and uses for communicative ends the social assumption that other people, while similar to me, are *not the same as me:* They do not share the same biography; my own biography is a unique set of experiences of which only some are known to others. The expression of social difference gives an impetus for further language development. The period from age 7 to 8 or 9 is a period of very rapid vocabulary growth in which the child adopts more ways of describing the world and develops concepts that are generic principles for further semantic development (Miller, 1972).

I suggest that one of the main ways in which the reflexivity principle is observable is through the use of *formulating* (Garfinkel and Sacks, 1970). Formulating is the ability to lexicalize the already, perhaps, known but unstated purposes and assumptions made by the participants in the talk. Formulating expressions are "coded tags" and expressions that say "in so many words" what the talk is about or what has just been stated inferentially, as in the following example. An 8-year-old girl has just arrived home from school with a new friend; she is showing her mother something while her friend, not introduced, waits beside her. Mother: "Do you want to go to the bathroom?" Girl: "Yes." Mother: "Well, you look like you'd better hurry up, honey, and go to the bathroom." As the two girls leave the room, the friend says

"Ba(h)throom." Girl: "As you may realize, my mother is English." This is not the first use of this phrase by this girl; it appeared during about a week in lots of contexts such as "As you may realize, Daddy, I had my cast off today."

Piaget's description of the child's use of features like "you see," "you understand" also indicates that these children have learned something about formulating expressions. The reflexivity principle is expressed as an ability to put into words, to lexicalize the purposes of the conversation so that the purpose can be addressed "reflexively" as a topic within the conversation. Children still process speech in context iconographically, and since the figure and ground are not always distinguished as in the adult mode, they are often still treated as a single interpretive unit. During the learning of adult ways of formulating and foregrounding the purposes of the talk (what Garfinkel and Sacks have called "glossing practices or ordered particulars of talk"),[7] often the wrong features are marked or the right ones go unmarked. For instance, children often use the wrong stress pattern when trying to resolve a syntactic difficulty; they "overgeneralize" the use of formulating features, as in the previous example. Adults would not pick up the implications of the friend's comment on the mother's pronunciation in quite such a "formalized" way as the girl did. Adults would probably say something like, "Yes, you're right, she's English." Beyond the realization of the reflexivity principle, children have still to become practitioners in the strategies of communication.

Conclusion

The argument of this study has been that children's social and linguistic development are intrinsically interrelated. Acquisition of syntax is triggered by prelinguistic social understanding, which gives the child grounds for formulating his "semantic intentions." This understanding I have called (following Schutz) the *reciprocity principle*. The child is aware that others have a similar understanding to him and so, for all practical purposes, can be regarded as the same as himself. Based on this principle, the early acquisition of "words" and the slightly later grammatical principles introduce the child, for the first time, to a realization of the *normativeness* of the "social world," that is, the shared world that the child gets to know in common with others. Through language the child comprehends that this world existed prior to his arrival, and its

---

[7] These features can be called "glossing practices" (Garfinkel and Sacks, 1970). An illustration of a kind of gloss is the following "Rose gloss": On entering a new town, perhaps by being picked up by a colleague at the airport, Rose would comment after the first few minutes of the car ride, "It's changed." What *it* consisted of is then revealed by the driver's descriptions, which gave the visitor a way of sharing knowledge of the town.

constraints, the regulations of its means of communication through vocalized symbols, also constrain the expression of his intentions. This social understanding, based on the reciprocity principle, leads the child through the cognitive rigors of language acquisition: the process of building up a set of grammatical rules from context-bound messages in which setting, paralinguistic features, and verbal message all contribute to the meaning. In order to unravel meaning the child, using his own "practical reasoning," fills in any previous experience he has to make sense of the verbal messages he receives, and seeks any way to "make sense" of the message, since the reciprocity principle leads him to expect to both give and receive reciprocal understanding from the other person. From this experience the child gets to know that in different contexts, different parts of the message icon are foregrounded. The child treats the compound message as a single interpretive icon in which the semantic load is not carried only by the words and syntax. The child presents and interprets speech iconographically, as speech in context, in which all parts of the communicative situation are accorded an equal interpretive potential. As the notion of foregrounding develops, the child gains a recognition of the limitation of reciprocity: The other person, while like myself, is *not myself;* he does not share my unique biography. This social awareness leads to the development of what we have called the *reflexivity principle,* in which the child realizes that language use can provide the grounds for its own understanding. The child's acquisition of language leads him to adapt his verbal strategies to the communicative requirements of the situation at hand. The child, through the exercise of practical reasoning and the understanding based on the reflexivity principle, gradually learns that social control can be realized through speech itself, among other ways, by lexicalizing his intentions "in so many words" and by relying on taking the verbal message alone as the foregrounded semantic feature of the interaction.

By accepting the thesis of this work, that language acquisition can be seen as a process of realizing the normativeness of a shared world, rather than as a simply linguistic and/or cognitive process, much of the recent linguistic work in the acquisition of phonological, syntactic, and semantic rules potentially can be integrated into a single framework, and, thus, the notion of "language" as used in language socialization can become an intrinsically "social" one in a rather general sense.

References

Aronfreed, J.
  1968 *Conduct and conscience.* New York: Academic Press.
Bateson, G.
  1971 *Steps to an ecology of mind.* New York: Ballantine Books.

Bloom, L.
   1971   *Language development: Form and function in emerging grammars.* Cambridge, Massachusetts: M.I.T. Press.
Blount, B.
   1970   *Acquisition of language by Luo children.* Working Paper no. 19. Univ. of California, Berkeley, Language-Behavior Research Laboratory.
Cicourel, A. V.
   1971   Basis and normative rules in the negotiation of status and role. In *Recent sociology no. 2.,* edited by H. P. Drietzel, New York: Collier-Macmillan.
Cook-Gumperz, J.
   1972   Language and socialization: A critical review. In *Class, codes and control,* edited by Basil Bernstein. London: Routledge and Kegan Paul.
Cook-Gumperz, J. and J. Bowyer
   1972   *The development of communication skills through elementary school science: An experiment using the SCIS program.* Univ. of California, Berkeley, Lawrence Hall of Science.
De Stephano, J.
   1972   The concept of register in adult–child speech. Typescript.
Dore, J.
   1973   The development of speech acts. Ph. D. dissertation, City Univ. of New York.
Dundes, A., Leach, J. W., and B. Özkök.
   1972   The strategy of Turkish boys' verbal duelling rhymes. In *Directions in sociolinguistics,* edited by J. J. Gumperz and D. Hymes. New York: Holt.
Ervin-Tripp, S.
   1972   On sociolinguistic rules: Alternation and co-occurrence. In *Directions in sociolinguistics,* edited by J. J. Gumperz and D. Hymes. New York: Holt.
Ferguson, C. and D. I. Slobin (editors)
   1972   *Studies in child language development.* New York: Holt.
Frazer, C., R. Brown, and U. Bellugi
   1963   Control of grammar in imitation, comprehension and production, *Journal of Verbal Learning and Verbal Behavior* **2,** 121–35.
Garfinkel, H.
   1967   *Studies in ethnomethodology.* New York: Prentice-Hall.
Garfinkel, H. and H. Sacks
   1970   On formal structures of practical actions. In *Theoretical sociology,* edited by J. McKinney and E. Tiryakian. New York: Appleton.
Gumperz, J. J.
   1964   Linguistics and social interaction in two communities. In Ethnography of communication, *American Anthropologist* **166,** (6).
   1973   Towards an action theory of sociolinguistics. Unpublished manuscript.
Gumperz, J. J. and E. Herasimchuck
   1973   The conversational analysis of social meaning: A study of classroom interaction. In *Proceedings of the 23rd Georgetown Meetings on Linguistics and Language Study,* edited by R. Shuy. Georgetown: Georgetown Univ. Press. (Reprinted in this volume, see p. 81.)
Gumperz, J. J. and D. Hymes
   1964   Ethnography of communication, *American Anthropologist,* special issue no. 6.
   1972   *Directions in sociolinguistics.* New York: Holt.
Haber, R. N.
   1970   How we remember what we see, *Scientific American* **176,** 104–12.

Hawkins, P.
  1970 Social class, the nominal group and reference. *Language and Speech.* Reprinted in *Class, codes and control,* edited by Basil Bernstein. London: Routledge and Kegan Paul.
Halliday, M. A. K.
  1972 Learning how to mean. In *Foundations of language development,* edited by E. and E. Lenneberg. UNESCO and IBRO.
  1973 Early language learning: A sociolinguistic approach. Paper prepared for IXth International Congress of Ethnological and Anthropological Sciences, Chicago.
Hymes, Dell
  1967 Models of interaction of language and social setting, *Journal of Social Issues* **23,** 8–28.
  1972 Models of interaction of language and social life. In *Directions in Sociolinguistics,* edited by J. J. Gumperz and D. Hymes. New York: Holt.
Kernan, K.
  1970 *Acquisition of language by Samoan children.* Working Paper no. 20. Univ. of California, Berkeley, Language-Behavior Research Laboratory.
Kohlberg, L.
  1969 Stage and sequence: The cognitive development approach to socialization. *Handbook of theory and research in socialization,* edited by D. Goslin. Chicago: Rand-McNally.
Langer, S.
  1942 *Philosophy in a new key.* Cambridge, Massachusetts: Harvard Univ. Press.
Miller, G.
  1956 The magic number seven plus or minus two, *Psychological Review* **63,** 81–96.
  1972 English verbs of motion: A case study in semantics and lexical memory. In *Coding processes in human memory,* edited by A. W. Melton and E. Martin. New York: Holt.
  1973 Toward a third metaphor for psycholinguistics. Unpublished manuscript.
Mitchel-Kernan, C.
  1970 *Language behavior in a black urban community.* Working Paper no. 23. Univ. of California, Berkeley, Language-Behavior Research Laboratory.
Moskowitz, A.
  1970 *The acquisition of phonology.* Working Paper no. 34. Univ. of California, Berkeley, Language-Behavior Research Laboratory.
Mussen, P. (editor)
  1970 *Handbook of research on child development.* Chicago: Rand-McNally.
Piaget, Jean
  1959 *Language and thought of the child.* London: Routledge and Kegan Paul.
  1962 *The moral development of the child.* New York: Collier Books.
Pollner, M.
  1970 On the foundations of mundane reasoning. Ph.D. dissertation, Univ. of California, Santa Barbara.
Sanches, M. and Blount, B.
  1975 Sociocultural dimensions of language use. New York: Academic.
Schutz, A.
  1964 Common-sense and the scientific interpretation of human action. In *Collected papers, vol. 1: The problem of social reality,* edited by M. Nantanson. The Hague: Martinus Nijhoff.

Sherzer, J. and R. Darnell
   1972   Outline guide for the study of speech use. In *Directions in sociolinguistics,* edited
           by J. J. Gumperz and D. Hymes. New York: Holt.
Slobin, D.
   1971   Suggested universals in the ontogenesis of grammar. In *Advances in psycho-
           linguistics,* edited by G. B. Flores D'Arcais and J. W. Levelt. Amsterdam: North
           Holland.
   1972   Cognitive pre-requisites for the development of grammar. In *Studies of child lan-
           guage development,* edited by D. Slobin and C. Ferguson. New York: Holt.
Stross, B.
   1970   Verbal process in Tzeltal speech socialization. Paper given to the American
           Anthropological Association Symposium on Speech Socialization, San Diego.
Sylvester, D.
   1969   Magritte, Introduction to the Arts Council exhibition catalog. London: Tate
           Gallery.
Talmy, L.
   1970   *Semantic componentry and Samoan acquisition.* Working Paper no. 35. Univ. of
           California, Berkeley, Language-Behavior Research Laboratory.
Vygotsky, L.
   1962   *Thought and language.* Translated by E. Hauffaman and C. Vakar. Cambridge,
           Massachusetts: M.I.T. Press.
Wang, W. S.-Y.
   1973   Why and how do we study the sounds of speech? Unpublished manuscript.
Wrong, D.
   1961   The oversocialized concept of man in sociology, *American Sociological Review*
           26, 184–93.

II. METACOMMUNICATIVE ACTS
AND EVENTS

Introduction

MARY SANCHES

The studies included in Part II represent another emerging concern of linguistic anthropology. Like the ones in Part I, these developed out of a conviction within anthropology that we must ultimately aim at accounting for *all* language behavior as part of cultural behavior, and not just one segment of it, the "sentence." Metacommunicative events are, in this way, like other communicative events, a large and important segment of our verbal–cultural behaviors; and to ignore them would be to give an unrealistic view of the kind of creatures people are.

Not only has the analysis of metacommunicative events been largely overlooked – if not avoided – by formal linguists, but when it has been approached – principally by anthropologists (and this is so probably because, in the course of their ethnographic investigations, its importance has been impressed upon them by the inordinate amount of time people in most societies spend on metacommunicative activities) – the descriptions of the phenomena resemble very much the description the blind men came up with for the elephant they were investigating. The metacommunicative acts and events I am considering here are but one of our total set of metacommunications. Metacommunications range from quotations, "I said that I saw the cat," through suprasegmental metalinguistic devices indicating a proper reading of an utterance, "Oh, yeah, that's *real* pretty" (read: negative truth value) – to the elaborate rituals of religious and artistic domains. They all have in common the feature of referencing some aspect of the communication system – whether an utterance previously spoken, an element in the code, or the major patterns of the grammar of interpersonal relations in the society.

There are four most important sources of thinking about metacommunication that must be considered for our discussion. The first is the general use of the term *metalinguistic* to refer to mention of an element in the language code rather than to the class of events to which the element in the code itself refers. Thus, in the sentence *I don't see any book,* the form *book* refers to the class of elements that, by virtue of having certain semantic features, are included in the conceptual category "book." However, in the sentence *I don't see any "book,"* "book," though formally the same as in the first sentence, refers, not to the class of items that qualify as books, but to a representation of the linguistic form itself as written in a sentence. This discussion was initially developed by philosophers in the interest of being able to talk about a scientific metalanguage comprising logical notation and rules. However, probably in all language communities, we also have "folk" metalanguage. "Folk" metalanguage is, of course, native – as opposed to scientific – terms to refer directly to the code and elements in it. Sometimes, in our language anyway, these two potentially distinct levels overlap: For example, *sentence* is both a native English term to refer to a specific unit of speech and, at the same time, a scientific term. In fact, one of the processes in the development of a science of language description is that of innovating a set of metalinguistic forms independent from but incorporating their folk counterparts.

A second, and possibly the most important, contribution to our thinking about metacommunication is that of Gregory Bateson and his colleagues, stemming from concern with how the communication of individuals labeled "schizophrenic," and major figures in their interactional network, differed from those of people not so labeled. Their research led to the recognition that in "schizophrenic" communications there was a consistent deletion of certain kinds of signals: those that tell the receiver how to read the message, in combination with messages that are metaphoric, or in some other way "derived." These communicative aberrancies, felt Bateson and colleagues, were a survival mechanism in the face of messages from very important others in the communication network that "reclassified" prior messages as of a different kind of event from that intended by the sender – a kind of evasive action on the part of the schizophrenic, so as to not be pinned down and suffer retaliation for sending a "bad" message.

These insights broaden the extant set of concepts to include metalinguistic events as a subset of metacommunicative events. Whereas up until the time of these insights we were limited to thinking about metacommunication in terms of verbally coded elements (words) that *directly* referred to elements in the code, Bateson and colleagues' (1972) thinking about the problems of schizophrenia allowed us to think also of the signals about the message, i.e., intonation, etc. that tell us *how* to read the verbal message, and are, thus, an indirect reference to the message, as metacommunication. In addition, the verbally encoded "framing" devices that define, indirectly, the type or class of speech event that an utterance is implicitly understood to be give evidence to our recognition — culturally — of a more abstract set of types of speech acts in the minds of native actors (for example, his analysis of the behavior of the schizophrenogenic mother to whom he brought the "beautiful and untidy" flowers [1972: 194].

The third contribution to thinking about metacommunication is that of Jakobson's (1960) and Hymes' (1964) discussion of speech or communication events in the historical context of developing a more natural unit of verbal behavior than the "sentence." As derived from communication theory, these focuses are based on the elements of a communication event — i.e., the necessary components for the occurrence of communication. A communication event is constituted, by definition, by the presence of the following elements: sender, receiver, message, channel, code, and context.

In Jakobson's (1958) conceptualization, any utterance can have a number of referrents (focuses) in addition to its nominal or basic focus on "context," which, in his terms, provides its referential function. The other functions provided by focus on the various elements of the communication event are as follows:

	Focus	*Function*
	sender	emotive/expressive
	receiver	conative
message	form	poetic
	channel or contact	phatic
	code	metalingual

Hymes (1964) has since expanded this framework for developing a theory of communication events as distinct from just speech or language (the ethnography of communication) by an elaboration of the concept of "context" to two items: "topic" and "setting."

The Jakobson–Hymes thinking about the functions of speech is important to this discussion because all of the events to be considered are those whose focus is on the code. They are not, however, simply metalinguistic, because they refer both to the wider cultural code for behavior generally (not just verbal behavior) — the communication system.

A fourth body of discussion about metacommunication — especially relevant to what we are calling metacommunicative events, as distinct from simple communication events — exists in the anthropological genre usually called "symbolism." Symbolic analysts, while not consciously pursuing analysis of their data as communication, have nevertheless given us a great number of descriptions of metacommunicative events. Though a later statement, to be cited, belies it, Geerts (1973), in a recent publication on a Balinese metacommunicative event, does assume a communication model, as the following quotation shows:

> What sets the cockfight apart from the ordinary course of life, lifts it from the realm of everyday practical affairs [read: communication], and surrounds it with an aura of enlarged importance is . . . that it provides metasocial commentary upon the whole matter of assorting human beings into fixed hierarchial ranks and then organizing the major part of collective existence around that assortment. Its function, if you want to call it that, is interpretive: it is Balinese reading of Balinese experience; *a story they tell themselves about themselves* [p. 26; italics added].

and

> If one takes the cockfight, or any other collectively sustained symbolic structure, as a means of "saying something of something" . . . then one is faced with a problem not in social mechanics but social semantics [ibid.].

Geerts thus provides us with an idea of the referent of the communication, the topic, if you will. However, we still do not know what the message, i.e., the comment on the topic, says, in terms that would allow us to compare it with metacommunicative events in other societies in which hierarchy is also of overwhelming importance in ordering human relations. The reason the discussions of metacommunicative events by symbolists are problematic for trying to relate them to the discussions of Bateson *et al.,* Jakobson, and Hymes can be seen in the following quotation, also from Geerts' description of the Balinese cockfight:

> To put the matter this way is to engage in a bit of metaphorical refocussing of one's own, for it shifts the analysis of cultural forms from an endeavor in general parallel to dissecting an organism, diagnosing a symptom, *deciphering a code,* or ordering a system . . . to one in general parallel with penetrating a literary text [ibid.; italics added].

It should be obvious, however, that the interpretation of a literary text, as of a Balinese cockfight, Javanese *ludruk,* Ndembu initiation rite, and any and all other communicative, i.e., cultural, behavior, can be understood only if the code on which it is based is described, thus allowing us to know what is being communicated and how such messages are to be constructed. The major difficulty with these types of metacommunicative events—as distinct from simple communicative events—is that their reference is to aspects of the cultural code that are by nature quite abstract and, thus, unverbalizable.

We would eventually hope for two things from an understanding of metacommunicative events:

1. That through isolating the elements — or mechanisms — that qualify particular communicative events as metacommunicative ones, i.e., their defining criteria, we will eventually be able to set up a scientific schema for isolating different types of metacommunicative events and acts. That is, it seems obvious that genres such as our own terms *joke, drama, baptism,* etc. refer to metacommunicative events and acts among which we can distinguish in terms of both their referents and the devices that distinguish them as metacommunicative. Cross-culturally, if an adequate theory of metacommunication can be established, we would have a basis for formulating and identifying such scientific categories as, for example, "humor" in one society's repertory with an equivalent category in others'. This could be done not on the basis of its evocation of laughter — a functional criterion and noisy at best — but on the basis of shared metareferrents and event structure. We would also be able to specify with accuracy favorite metacommunicative events of different types of speech communities and whether certain types were present or absent. What is involved here is a question of whether a group's metacommunicative events can be predicted from its subsistence and sociopolitical integration levels.

A related goal is to be able to differentiate among the various genres of metacommunicative events in a productive way on the basis of the same criteria. In other words, how does "ritual" differ from "drama" and "religious ceremony"?

2. A second goal we can aim for is the utilization of metacommunicative devices into our theory of how language as a behavior-generating model allows for the production of an infinite number of speech events. The generally recognized mechanisms for generating both infinitely long and an infinite number of sentences from language are recursive devices. Only one metacommunicative device, quotation framing, e.g., "I said I couldn't go," has been dealt with in formal linguistic description (Zwicky, 1971) as embedding, a grammatical process. Other metacommunicative devices involved in framing/embedding must also operate to provide for recursiveness. Furthermore, the multiple levels of reference made available by metacommunicative acts and events is another mechanism providing for infiniteness in speech. Metacommunicative devices allow us to make increasingly complex reference, which adds to our stock of sentences in the inventory of speech. Consider, for example, the referential alternatives of the word *bird* in the following otherwise identical sentences:

a. *I don't hear any bird,* where reference is nonmetacommunicative.

b. *I don't hear any bird,* where reference is to this identical sentence, as a favorite expression, or a salient expression of a famous personality and, thus, to the person noted for saying it.

c. *I don't hear any "bird,"* where reference is to someone's not talking loudly enough for the receiver to get all parts of the message and, thus, to a part of a prior utterance.

In the discussion that follows I would like to use the studies included in Part II to test the applicability of a preliminary set of criteria for cross-cultural understanding of larger metacommunicative acts and events as distinct from quotation, and accompanying truth-value signals. The scheme represented here has been developed from the above-mentioned work of Bateson et al. on schizophrenic communication and Jakobson's and Hymes' discussions of the ethnography of communication and the functions of speech. The characteristics of metacommunicative events so far isolable seem to be the following:

1. *Simultaneous multiple speech events:* There must be two communication events incorporated into one, and they must be occurring simultaneously. That is, there must be two conceptually distinguishable senders and receivers of the message sent, such that one (set of) sender(s) functions in two communication events, labeled 1 and 2 in Figure 1, at the same time. In Figure 1, one set of receivers, those in Event 2, is implicit, while the sender(s) and receiver(s) of Event 1 are explicit. In addition, the "senders" of both simultaneous events are the same people. That is, they hold multiple simultaneous identities.

2. *Indirect reference:* The second criterion that qualifies a communication event as a metacommunicative one seems to be that its reference must be indirect. While this is not so for *metalingual* speech acts, a subclass of the broader category of metacommunicative acts, it is certainly so for the kind of events that most of these studies represent.

3. *Reference to the cultural code:* A third criterion, mentioned briefly

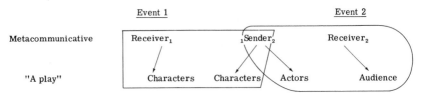

Figure 1.

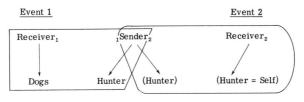

Figure 2.

earlier, is that reference is not limited to the "code" in its narrowest linguistic sense of phonological, morphological, lexical, and syntactic elements and their relations, but to the wider cultural code for behavior in the society. This includes, of course, reference to elements in communication events themselves, as well as values and social organization.

4. *Naming, marking, and framing:* In addition, metacommunicative events seem generally to be named segments of behavior, in contrast to metacommunicative acts, which need not be so. In conjunction with the naming of these events, they seem to need not only to be marked stylistically (more or less marking either by stylistic verbal elaborations or by nonverbal elaborations: use of masks, dancing, manipulation of artifacts) but also to have greater or lesser degrees of framing in the form of introductory and ending activities, temporal and spatial restrictions on their occurrence.

The genres included here range from two forms of "religious" performances: Rosaldo's Ilongot *nawnaw* 'spell' and Fitzgerald's Ga *daimɔ*, 'curing ceremony'; to two examples of "humor": Brukman's Koya *naalumaata* 'tongue play' and Sanches' Japanese *rakugo* 'falling words'; to Mitchell-Kernan and Kernan's thought-provoking discussion of the child's acquisition of "insult" in both Samoan and Black English, an example of "song" in Tzeltal by Stross, and finally, Werner's consideration of some features of the communication genre of schizophrenia.

In the Ilongot genre *nawnaw* 'spell', as described by Rosaldo, the realization of multiple simultaneous speech events seems to be as in Figure 2. The explicit receivers of the message (in Event 1) are nonhuman (the hunter's dogs), while the implicit receiver indicated by parentheses to whom the message is directed is, of course, the hunter himself. Perhaps this special type of interaction among participants will turn out to be cross-culturally definitive of "religious" metacommunicative events. That is, perhaps "religious" events are recognizable by one set of receivers being "gods," "spirits," "demons," or others, where, by definition, the interpretation of what constitutes a response from them must be determined by the other participants in the event.

Nawnaw certainly communicates about a wider set of cultural behaviors than just the verbal. As Rosaldo expresses it, ". . . a small group of culturally significant and contextually desirable themes . . . " constitute the topic of the spell. The way in which indirect reference is made to these themes is very complex and interesting: Both metaphor and punning are utilized within the syntactic framework of simile and imperative. That is, embedded into one simile frame: "Be like_____, dog" and two imperative frames: "Don't, dog,_____, dog" and "Do, dog,_____,dog" are the names of plants that both serve as the topic in the simile frame and are derived to serve as verbs in the proscriptive imperative frames. In the simile frame, forms are used that have associations to violence. More complexly for the imperative frames, the verbs, which have associations of "violence," or at least behavior appropriate to the context of hunting, are derived from the names of plants, which, in turn, have associations with domesticity, so that the associational forms for violence are, in turn, derived from, and thus we may say subordinate to or contained within the domain of, domesticity, as Rosaldo points out. Thus, the grammatical process by which the reference is made is itself a mirror image of the relationship between the two themes in the thinking of the group: violence, as realized in the hunt, must be subordinated to serve the social purposes of the group.

While *nawnaw* can be said to occur within the conceptual framework of "preparatory to the hunt," is a named unit of behavior, and is marked stylistically—both verbally by stress, short lines, etc., and by the accompanying nonverbal behaviors of "steaming" and "switching" the dogs with herbs utilized verbally in the spell—it needs no physically manifest spatial framing nor elaborate verbal framing. That is, unlike our elaborately framed religious "services," neither is a stage needed, nor is it necessary to announce what one is about to do before doing it. It would seem that perhaps everyone in the society so well understands the conceptual scheme of behavior that no overt framing is necessary.

While the lack of framing characteristic of *nawnaw* contrasts with the Ga *daimɔ* described by Fitzgerald, we intuitively feel that both share similarity as "religious" events as contrasted with the two "humorous" ones to be discussed. However, the *daimɔ* does differ from the *nawnaw* in its elaborate framing—verbally both at beginning and end of the total event, and internally among what we can distinguish as discrete parts that make up its syntactic structure, a structure lacking for *nawnaw*.

The feature of multiple simultaneous communication events, which we have postulated for metacommunicative events in general, is realized much more complexly in the Ga *daimɔ* than in the Ilongot *nawnaw* (Figure 3). The participants in the curing ceremony are explicitly communicating with the gods, which is the nominal purpose for which they

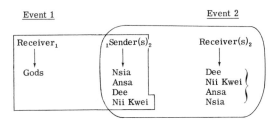

Figure 3.

understand themselves to be gathered. However, as Fitzgerald points out, they are also implicitly communicating with each other. One of the characteristics of this ceremony is the brocaded effect derived from the richly contrapuntal structuring of senders' and receivers' roles (Fitzgerald's principles of "anticipation" and "reversing fields"), to which he attributes the effective "curing" power of the ceremony. As represented earlier, the principle sender shifts are in direct counterpoint with the major receiver shifts.

Like the Ilongot *nawnaw*, there is considerable metaphoric communication in the *daimɔ*, but it is embedded into the event in quite a different way. Here it occurs in the form of proverbs (Fitzgerald's "indexicality of expression"). As in the *nawnaw*, this device facilitates indirection of reference and serves to refer to the relationship between the people and their gods and to the desired action on the part of the latter, as well as to the negative events that have occurred to necessitate the curing ceremony.

The two papers representing "humor" as opposed to "religious" events are different from the former and from each other in ways that may correspond to differences in the evolution of communication systems overall. Brukman's paper on Koya *naalumaata* 'tongue play' and my description of Japanese *rakugo* 'falling words' are two examples of cultural behavior most clearly marked "This is play" in two widely divergent societies: The Koya are a face-to-face community of "hill people" in southeast India and the Japanese a complex, industrialized nation–state.

The commonality between these events is that the participants in the two simultaneous communications are very similar: They demand the recognition of an "audience," and thus, in contrast to the Ga *daimɔ* or the Ilongot *nawnaw*, there is no imaginary participant (Figures 4 and 5). This fact, that the members of an audience, the implicit participants as receivers of the messages, are distinguishable, means that both the participants in Event 1 function as senders in Event 2.

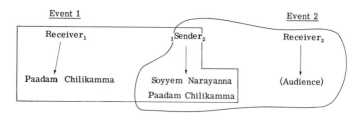

Figure 4. *Koya naalumaata (sender–receiver shifts with audience by episodes). This is Episode 1.*

These two events are further similar in that while the "audience" does not participate in Communication Event 1, they do communicate with the senders of Event 2, the "narrator." That is, the laughter, which is characteristic of these types of events and one of the few message forms allowed from the "audience," refers to Event 1. It is a response to the sender(s) of Event 2 *about* the first event and, thus, also serves as verification for our interpretation of these kinds of events as metacommunicative.

As Brukman demonstrates, one can only "Characterize the manner in which ongoing verbal behavior [is] understood by participants in social encounters" by showing to what the encounter has reference. In this "tongue play" event, the indirect reference is to norms of behavior in relation to social organization. Although reference is also to ideal cultural behavior in the Japanese "falling words," the type of behavior mentioned is quite different. While it is marriage norms in counterpoint to some standard of public behavior for Koya *naalumaata,* what makes for humor in Japanese *rakugo* is talk about rules for communication itself. It is clear that the determinants of what is funny are quite different for Koya and for Japanese. In *naalumaata,* the dominant theme is sexual activity, while in *rakugo* (and in most other Japanese humor with which I am familiar), that is almost never the cause of laughter.

Another difference between these two events, which parallels the difference between the Ilongot *nawnaw* and the Ga *daimɔ,* is that the Koya

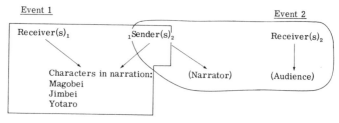

Figure 5. *Japanese rakugo.*

naalumaata is less overtly framed than the Japanese *rakugo* performance. As Brukman explains, the verbal framing that occurred in this particular instance was probably an artifact of the investigator's prompting.
Although the Koya "tongue play" is recognized as an identifiable and
named class of events, this is the only recognition of it as bounded. As
Brukman says, the properties that constitute it cannot be said to have
boundaries, and people do not assemble explicitly to do joking. It can be
performed at any place and at any time. Japanese *rakugo,* on the other
hand, are elaborately framed both by where and when they may occur,
and conceptually, the kind of interaction that characteristically takes
place within this frame being totally unacceptable anywhere else.

In Koya *naalumaata* there are no professional roles of participants to
the event; however, only people standing in certain kinship-defined relationships to each other can successfully participate in the humorous
exchanges, which explains why the first episode fails. One notices also
that in *naalumaata* the event-roles assumed by the participants are stereotyped—they might be prototype Abbott and Costello parts.

Brukman, citing Radcliffe-Brown, brings up one other element
common to, yet handled differently in, these two "funny" events: their
occurrence at points of culture stress or conflict with a "function" of
maintaining equilibrium between conjunctive and disjunctive categories
and relations. In the analysis we are using, however, one can view the
mechanism being utilized to produce laughter as juxtaposition of the
ideal and the real to produce the absurd. This is doubly complex in the
naalumaata third episode, in which not only are the ideal patterns and
norms of marriage contrasted with the real conditions of the individuals
in the interaction, but in addition, a style suitable to one kind of content
(baby talk) is used to talk about what turns out to be sexual activity. In
the Japanese *rakugo* it is the real rules for communication juxtaposed to
the narrated behavior of the "fool," Yotaro, that produces absurdity.

One final parallel between these two events must be mentioned: The
phrase *malla paccatam* 'then lying down' at the end of the third episode
of the *naalumaata* interaction brings into focus the alternative referents
of the exchange and, thus, the definition of the event as absurd. In this
way it is very like the final utterance in the narration of *doguya, zudon,*
"1. bang = sound of gun" and "2. sound of something falling =
rakugo," in that it indirectly makes reference to the kind of event in
which the participants have been engaged.

The Mitchell-Kernan and Kernan study is relevant to this discussion
in that it presents an analysis of a metacommunicative act that is possibly universal: "insult." It also provides us with insight into the
child's acquisition of such acts.

As the acquisition of language requires more than learning just how to string words together into "sentences," it requires learning also the cultural definitions of classes of events, when each is appropriate and of what they are constituted. As Mitchell-Kernan and Kernan demonstrate, children are likely to misjudge what legitimately constitutes the defining criteria of an "insult." Children seem to pick up evaluations expressed about behavior in the form of comment on the behavior as topic, and from these make inferences about what is a member of the "insult" class of metacommunicative acts. As the authors say, "when a child insults correctly, he indicates the cultural value he has internalized; . . . mistakes, however, are informative because they indicate something about the process by which the child acquires cultural values" and also because they indicate something about the way in which children acquire definitional criteria for classes of communicative events and acts. In the description here, it appears that the children first pay attention to the suprasegmental or nonverbal marking features of the act (in this case intonation?) that signal that something is said disapprovingly, overlooking or not paying attention to the contextual framing that distinguishes that particular instance of verbal activity (possibly glossable as "criticism"?) from the more ritualized "insult." For instance, with the examples "You got a baby" or "Your father dove into the sea" or "Your mother sleeps with your father," in the model utterance that the child is using he noticed and remembered the negative intonation features used, but did not know that while doing any one of these things in one social context may be bad, it is not so in all: While diving into the sea for foreigners may be disapproved of, it is not the activity itself that is.

"Insult" is a metacommunicative act by virtue of the fact that its meaning is derivable only by reference to abstract cultural values and rules of behavior. As such, there seem to be two directions in which interaction utilizing them can then develop. As Mitchell-Kernan and Kernan mention, insults that are not referent to very deep levels of cultural rules are only met in kind, but when the insult reaches reference to a very deep level of cultural value—in Samoan this is reference to the position of the receiver on the value of generosity—the interaction quickly loses its ritual quality and the hearer responds with tears. On the other hand, metacommunicative events of insult "duels" (Labov, 1972; Dundes, Leach, & Özkök, 1972), which capitalize on reference to nonexistent standards, and thus absurdity, produce laughter.

The genre "song" shares some of the characteristics of metacommunicative events and acts as we have outlined them here, but as described by Stross it seems to lack others, to have some that are unique, and also to be able to *accompany* other metacommunicative events. The characteristics that "song" shares with the other metacommunicative events are the following:

1. *Indirect reference:* In the example described here, "A young man has license to hum or sing a few measures of (one particularly allusive song) while visiting the home of a young woman, even though her parents are present. *Any direct proposition* by the boy in such a situation will immediately provoke the girl's father to violent anger."

2. *Mention of a cultural ideal:* In the examples cited here, this seems to be, for the most part, by direct reference to their opposites. However, while in most contexts our criterion of multiple simultaneous communication events seems to hold, for a subtype of the songs described here it seems to fail—unless one wants to describe a person singing to himself as constituting two senders and receivers.

Schizophrenia, the subject of our last study, brings us back full circle to consideration of phenomena that gave rise to thinking about metacommunication in its wider sense. In the sense in which we use it, the term *schizophrenia* can be understood as a metaterm for a style of speaking that itself involves metacommunicative acts. That is, it is a folk—and a scientific—term that we give to certain speech styles. However, as Werner points out, it is not too clear just what the characteristics are that enable us to encode a speech style as schizophrenic. The interesting thing is that, like dialect labeling, this is a social phenomenon that we are labeling (maybe idiolectal), and it makes some implications about the internal state of the individual whose speech is so labeled.

There are two points about schizophrenic speech that should be made in relation to the metacommunicative acts and events I have been discussing in this section:

1. All of the "deviant," "schizophrenic" examples of speech Werner cites would not, under other circumstances, be judged to be so. For example, as Bateson has noted, what makes them either acceptable or unacceptable as "normal" seems to be the framing devices we expect. The example of unusual metaphor, e.g., "The therapist is a bus" or "Men are grass," were they framed and then marked as a "joke" or "poetry" (and, importantly, in a setting that was not defined as communication between a "patient" and a "therapist"), would be accepted as "normal" speech.

2. All of this leads us to speculate about the importance of context, and the elaboration of various kinds of context in interpreting speech in different types of societies (sociocultural communication systems). In

earlier discussions of some of the other studies, it has been noted that some events, in comparison to others, principally the Ilongot *nawnaw* as compared to the Ga *daimɔ*, and the Koya *naalumaata* as compared to the Japanese *rakugo,* were relatively "unframed." That is, they can occur at any time and place preceded by *no* verbal statement informing onlookers of what is about to take place. While it is impossible to be conclusive from a few cases, I think it would be valuable to explore further the implications they suggest: As sociocultural systems become more complex, and people have less and less information about each other, it is increasingly necessary to have physical manifestation of conceptually understood metacommunicative event categories, in terms of the event-internal marking features and *especially* in terms of the framing devices that identify them.

References

Bateson, Gregory
  1972   *Steps to an ecology of mind.* New York: Ballantine Books.
Geertz, Clifford
  1972   *"Deep play" Notes on the Balinese cockfight.* Daedalus, inter, 1972.
Hymes, Dell H.
  1964   Introduction. In *The ethnography of communication,* edited by Gumperz, John J. and Dell Hymes. Special publication of the *American Anthropologist* **66** (6):1–34.
Jakobson, Roman
  1960   Concluding statement, linguistics & poetics. In *Style in Language,* edited by Sebeok, Thomas A. Cambridge: MIT Press, 350–377.
Zwicky, Arnold M.
  1971   On reported speech. In *Studies in linguistic semantics,* edited by Fillmore, Charles J. and D. Terrence Langendoen. New York: Holt: 73–78.

It's All Uphill: The Creative Metaphors of Ilongot[1] Magical Spells

MICHELLE ZIMBALIST ROSALDO

While offering only part of a solution, Malinowski gave an apt and revealing name to a problem when he spoke of the "creative metaphor of magic [1966:238]." Malinowski's goal was to characterize the power and function of a ritual language that had a structure and purpose very different from that of ordinary everyday speech. Though he failed to account for the content of magical metaphors, Malinowski's key observation, that magic relies on the use of repeated and redundant metaphorical expressions, paved the way for a good deal of subsequent research. Since his time, Turner (1962), Levi-Strauss (1963, 1966) and others (Tambiah, 1968; Strathern and Strathern, 1968) have explored relations among metaphors in magic and implicitly directed attention to the questions of why spells use some metaphors rather than others and how the practitioners' choice of particular metaphorical expressions can help us understand the effectiveness of spells. Munn, in a recent paper (n.d.), reexamines Malinowski's materials and suggests that magical metaphors highlight perceptual attributes, qualities of feeling and acting, that correspond to the practitioners' experienced goals.

My purpose in this study is to apply the results of a number of these earlier studies to a particular ethnographic example, first, by showing that metaphors in spells are systematically and meaningfully related, and second, by discussing the ways in which these relationships are made salient and compelling through the spells' expressive form. Like

[1] "Ilongot" is the name that, since the 18th century, has been used in the ethnographic literature to designate a Philippine group of Malayo–Polynesian speakers who refer to themselves and their language as *bugkalut* (untranslated) or *qiruNut* 'from the forest'. In 1967–1969 my husband (R. Rosaldo, 1970, 1971) and I (M. Rosaldo, 1971) did the first systematic work on their social organization and culture, my work being funded by a National Institutes of Health Predoctoral Fellowship and a National Institutes of Health Research Grant (5 FI MH-33, 243-02 BEH-A). The study has benefited from critical discussions with Jane M. Atkinson, Bridget O'Laughlin, Sherry B. Ortner, and Renato Rosaldo.

Levi-Strauss, I argue that the effectiveness of spells depends on the fact that they invoke images from a number of diverse areas of experience and that these images, in turn, are regrouped and organized in terms of a small set of culturally significant and contextually desirable themes. At the same time, following Malinowski, I show that this new organization, the creative product of the spell, itself depends on the repetitive and formulaic quality of magic. Each magical expression, taken by itself, can be seen to highlight some attribute of the experienced world, which serves as a model for the spell's desired outcome; each suggests a variety of associations that relate the practitioner, his objective milieu, and his immediate goals. But the "power" of the spell as a whole depends less on the originality or uniqueness of these particular expressions than on the ways in which they work together. Stereotyped and formulaic lines in magic provide a vehicle through which a wealth of concrete imagery is ordered, and very different images can come to be examplars of the associations that they share. Through the use of diverse images in repeated formulaic lines, the practitioner highlights similarities among things that are ordinarily unrelated. By combining rich and vivid imagery with a limited and formulaic use of language, he creates a metaphorical order that conforms to his aspirations. He subordinates the natural world's diversity to a simple and compelling conception of a world that he, through magic, can control.

Before continuing, I should say something about the Ilongots, whose spells provide a basis for discussion. The Ilongots, who number over 2500, are hunters, headhunters, and swidden agriculturalists, inhabiting the fertile hill country of Nueva Vizcaya, Nueva Ecija, and Quezon Province, Northern Luzon, Philippines. Ilongot women are gardeners, who produce, prepare, and serve the rice that forms the staple of the family diet. Ilongot men see themselves primarily as hunters – of animals and of men. Hunting for game is seen as a complement of women's agricultural activities; often, in the center of a room when food is being distributed, women will be dishing out rice portions while men cut up and distribute bits of meat. In this, as in a number of other details, the texture of Ilongot social life is casual, egalitarian, and familiar. Neither politics nor kinship, age nor sex, establish enduring hierarchical relationships between geographically scattered families, individuals, or larger social groups.

In areas of belief, ritual, religion, as in social relations, Ilongots recognize no authorities. While Ilongots say that in the past they had frequent recourse to the knowledge and techniques of religious specialists and shamans, missionary influence and the ravages of World War II have eliminated the few families who were known for their familiarity with spirits, or for their special abilities to treat the ill. But the absence of specialists does not entail an absence of belief and of practice. By the time he reaches his late teens, every Ilongot, male or female, has some knowledge of the words and herbs, rhythms and gestures of magical spells, or *nawnaw*. Each has the opportunity – in the course of hunting or gardening, tending a headache or curing a feverish child – to call, quietly, for the help of a spirit, to slip off to where the necessary herbs are found growing, or to suggest new metaphors to a companion in the hope of improving his spells.

'Magical spells', or *nawnaw,* range from a whispered "Now, now, go, go away, cold" when swallowing an aspirin to a prolonged and excited performance accompanied by as many as ten or twenty magical herbs. While the latter, the real or "true" *nawnaw,* can be distinguished as 'medicinal spells' (*sambal*), 'headhunting charms' (*kuiri*), and 'preparations' (*qaimet*) for gardening or hunting, all use the same syntax and rhythms, and all use images and gestures that most adult Ilongots recognize and understand. No one is taught these spells, and no one is felt to be an expert. Nor do Ilongots believe that any one spell or performance is certain to take effect. As the practitioner yells to the steam on a hearthstone, spits away evil, or spills a "poison" onto the ground, children cry, dogs bark, and other adults in the vicinity continue with their everyday activities. All are familiar with and may even add a line or so to his imagery, but for the most part his performance goes unremarked.

The spells themselves draw upon a wide range of experiences and images; practitioners say they use whatever words, herbs, or metaphors come to mind. "There is nothing," I was told, "we won't mention, if it helps to remedy what is wrong." So, in a hyperbolic tone, men may conjure an absurd image of good fortune – asking to have diarrhea from the quantities of meat their hunt dogs will catch. As suppliants, they ask for pity; or, boasting, they may lie to the spirits and tell them that soldiers will come in the morning and catch them in the body of the sick. When trying to banish a spirit, the practitioner gathers plants with names like "chase," "twisted," "skewed," or "toothless." At other times, he may call upon birds in the mountains, bananas, houseposts, or arrows. He might, for example, gather red-sapped plants to cure his bloody diarrhea, or call on running rivers to wash away a disease. He may wish to be as hard to find as a flea is, as strong as metal, or as well defended as the thorny trunk of a tree. And he names a multitude of such images – fleas, rice, a knife in rotten meat, a car in the lowlands – and steams, smokes, and spits upon a wide assortment of plants in the course of a single spell.

Metaphors in spells derive from the stuff of physical experience, the ordinary categories of everyday life; and, as Levi-Strauss would have predicted, these categories are interrelated in a way that permits the

magical practitioner to find new meanings in his world. Concrete experience provides the practitioner with a resource from which to construct a
metaphorical reality. A pun on a name, or the physical characteristics of
some real or imagined object — these provide him with a repertoire from
which he constructs a model of his illness or of a desired cure.

So, for example, in a spell for sore throats, the facts that hair is a thing
of the body, that roof thatch belongs to a housetop, and feathers are associated with birds are less important than the fact that all of these
(along with betel husks and deer skins) are fuzzy, scratchy, itchy kinds
of things. Taken as a set, they, in effect, define an ailment in terms of its
most salient characteristic; sore throats too are itchy, and when itchy
things are burned together, a sore throat may be cured. Or, to take
another example, in ordinary ways of thinking plants are not readily
related to what salt is, and plants as botanical objects are not thought to
be the same kinds of things as their names. But in a spell for the "salt"
affliction (which comes from violating the "salt oath" of peace), the following plants were selected: three that are known for their "white"
leaves, four with a sweet taste or pungent odor, and two whose names
could be construed as puns on the words for "to flow" or "to dissolve."
In other words, three attributes — whiteness, flavor, solubility — that are
associated with salt for the Ilongots are used to invoke it as a cure.
These attributes serve as a matrix for a kind of magical schema; they are
used to reconstitute or reorder experience in a way that confirms and
articulates the assumptions underlying the spell.

In these and a number of more complex examples, the Ilongot magical
practitioner resembles Levi-Strauss' savage bricoleur:

> Consider him at work and excited by his project. His first practical step is retrospec-
> tive. He has to turn back to an already existent set made up of tools and materials, to
> consider or reconsider what it contains, and finally and above all, to engage in a sort of
> dialogue with it, and, before choosing between them, to index the possible answers
> which the whole set can offer to his problem. He interrogates all the heterogeneous
> objects of which his treasury is composed to discover what each of them could "sig-
> nify" and so contribute to the definition of a set which has yet to materialize
> . . . [1966:18].

So, in the salt spell considered, a "treasury" of plants is examined.
And three white plants are chosen because each can "signify" that
quality — much as we might speak of clouds or sheets or flour as sig-
nifying the notion "things white." Where we (and the Ilongots) usually
think of "whiteness" as a characteristic of diverse and unrelated items of
experience, in the new grouping "whiteness" itself defines a conceptual
unit, of which the different objects, equally, are a part; finally, that
"whiteness" enters a more complex set in which a color, a taste, and

an operation together order a number of previously unrelated objects as exemplars and concrete realizations of the magical power of salt.

This ability of magic to recode or reorder experience is at least implicit in much of the work mentioned earlier. Munn (n.d.), for instance, has recently made an elegant statement concerning the ways in which certain qualities of objects (like the "whiteness" of salt and of plants) are foregrounded in magical contexts. When unrelated things are treated as similar, their shared characteristics become the defining features of a new and purposive system of meanings; old objects, the bits and pieces of the bricoleur, lose their conventional senses and come to stand, instead, as exemplars of a desired order. What once appeared an incidental likeness becomes the basis of a new orientation toward the experienced world.

Observations like these concern the relations of relatively unsituated symbols, and, with one or two possible exceptions (Levi-Strauss, 1963; Tambiah, 1968), they have been detached from consideration of the spell as a performance, and, in particular, a performance with a special linguistic form. Textual structure, so important to Malinowski, has been subordinated to the study of abstract symbolic relations. Yet, especially in the traditions (and the Ilongot and Trobriand are among them) in which the language of spells is felt to be of crucial importance, it seems useful to pay more attention to the formal structure of that language itself.[2]

In the discussion that follows I suggest that formulaic constraints, constraints on rhythm and syntax, contribute to the metaphorical artifice of the practitioner—much as form and meaning are linked in any good poem. I do this by considering at length two versions of an Ilongot hunting spell, which were chosen as suggestive examples of how expressive form is intimately related to the rich imagery used in magic. A consideration of the texts that follow will indicate how the formal structure of a magical performance contributes to its creative force.

The Preparation of Dogs for Hunting

Major Ilongot hunts are cooperative and call for the participation of most of the men of a settlement. Plans are communicated in a chorus of calls that run from house to house during the early morning; when all is settled, the men set off in the arranged direction to prepare an ambush and wait for the dogs and the game. In the meantime, one individual,

[2] A similar consideration seems to have informed the "symbolically" oriented linguistic analysis of Jakobson (1956, 1966), Fox (1971), and Hymes (1968), and my debts to these thinkers should be obvious in much of the following.

usually an older man, will feed and ready his hunt dogs. When his companions have departed, he asks his wife, if food is available, to prepare a meal of sweet potatoes for his animals, and he himself may wander off into the woods above their garden to find the magical herbs, the "true preparation" (*qaimet*), that will excite and whet their scent. These herbs, with names that sound like "she boar," "meet," "surround," "encounter," will make the dogs become alert, move quickly, and chase the game downhill into the area the hunters have prepared. The plants themselves are named and punned on (starred items in the text that follows) in the course of the old man's spell. Because dogs are supposed to set off as soon as the spell is completed, the hunter waits until all have eaten. Then he takes a hot stone from the fire and sets it at the feet of a dog that he fears may be sluggish or one that he counts on to lead. Holding his herbs on the stone in his right hand, he pours water over them, so that steam rises up to meet the dog in its face. Ilongots say that the stone stands for the household and the steam is the animal's scent; together, they tell the dogs that they need not go too far in trying to track down their prey. While the rock is steaming, the hunter hits the dog's nose with the herbs (this will anger him), blows on him, beats him (to brush off his "innocence," his "not-having-taken-a-head"), spits, and then steams the leaves once again. The dog may twist, bark, act restless, but the hunter pays no attention. In a low and steady voice, he tells him that he is steaming, awakening, preparing; he recites words that will excite him, that create for the dog and its master the image of a good hunt. When finished, he throws the leaves away with a "whoosh" that banishes bad fortune, then hoots and sets off with his dogs.

Here I give the abridged texts of two such spells, both "staged" for me, taped, transcribed, and translated with the help of the performers themselves. They strike me as fairly representative of some eight hunt dog spells recorded, and numerous others whose actual performance I saw.

Hunt Dog Spell 1[3]

qinaNranakanande:kan qatu nun   they like you dog, my dog, "Lady"
be:kur

---

[3] The spells given here were performed by two speakers of the same Ilongot dialect, that spoken in the central portion of the Ilongot region, where I conducted most of my research. Strictly speaking, then, the spells and comments that follow should be considered as representative for that region and not for the Ilongots as a whole. While there are at least four distinguishable Ilongot dialects, differing primarily in phonetic preferences and a few lexical items, all can be represented by the same phonological system. The symbols used all have conventional interpretations, except that /N/ is [ŋ], a velar nasal; /r/ is a voiced velar fricative; /e/ is a high mid vowel; and /V:/ indicates vowel length.

makararawmu ma gipnan	really go after the male boar
qinaNranakanande:kan qatu	they like you, dog
simaqeNkan qatu nuy beaweta qatu	be like, dog, a harpoon arrow, dog
qinaNranakanande:kan qatu	they like you, dog
simaqeNkan qatu nu kire: rekpa nu sineNdera qatu	be like, dog, the falling of pollarded branches, dog
qinaNranakanande:kan qatu	they like you, dog
kabuyubuyun ma rawenyun Nunsin qatu	keep in a pack as you're going, dogs
qinaNranakanande:kan qatu	they like you, dog
kata qatu peNirawmun qatu	bite, dog, as you go for it, dog
qinaNranakanande:kan qatu	they like you, dog
qiNatNatku dimu tuy ma raqeka qatu	I rub you with the herbs, dog (rubs herbs on head, nose of dog)
qinaNranakanande:kan qatu	they like you, dog
simaqen nuy menipaduN* nu kaberetmun qatu	be like one meeting (or dueling with) an enemy, dog
qinaNranakanande:kan qatu	they like you, dog
qentataqenaNkan qatu ma rawenmun Nunsin qatu	stay close on it, dog, as you are going, please, dog
qinaNranakanande:kan qatu	they like you, dog
qipatakumbaNyun* qatu tuy ma rawenyun Nunsin qatu	encircle, dog, as you are going, please, dog
qinaNranakanande:kan qatu	they like you, dog
qiNatNatku dimu ma talagan qaimetmun qatu	I rub you with your true "preparation," dog (rubs dog with plants)
qinaNranakanande:kan qatu	they like you, dog
qiNaliNika qatu tud ma paNapuwana qatu	you are steamed, dog, on the hearthstone, dog (pours water on stone)
qipaNapuwanmu dimun qatu qiraw qidepam nu qima gipnana qatu	may it steam up to you, dog, as you go for the scent of the male boar, dog
qinaNranakanande:kan qatu	they like you, dog
qed ka Nunsin qatu nambe:ntade* qatu	please do not, dog, straighten* out, dog
qinaNranakanande:kan qatu	they like you, dog
qinarak qaimesin qatu	that I have "prepared," dog
simaqeNkan nuy takmar nu buayan* qatu	be like the bite of a crocodile,* dog
mambuayakan* qatu tu maqawa qatu	be a crocodile* today, dog

qinaNranakanande:kan qatu	they like you, dog
qed ka Nunsin qatu nakite:teNkadi tuy ma kaberetmun qatu	please do not, dog, chase your enemy uphill, dog
be:likuneNkan nud qapuma qatu	spin (like a bug seen in whirlpools?) around your "grandfather," dog
qinaNranakanande:kan qatu	they like you, dog
pff pff pff	(blows on herbs)
qipaliget dimuy qitan qatu	may this make you angry, dog
qinaNranakanande:kan qatu	they like you, dog
tataqeNkan Nunsin qatu	stay close on it, please, dog
qinaNranakanande:kan qatu	they like you, dog
qipansisiwinanmu tuy ma rawenmu Nunsin qatu	get ever closer, as you are going, dog
qinaNranakanande:kan qatu	they like you, dog
manqe:qetuqtukayim tuy ma depay nu gipnana qatu	sniff and sniff for some trace of a male boar, dog
qinaNranakanande:kan qatu	they like you, dog
simaqeNkan qatu nuy pendalaqda nuy kade:Nyana qatu	be like, dog the hooting of a hornbill bird, dog
qinaNranakanande:kan qatu	they like you, dog
paNilampisawim ma rawenmu Nunsin qatu	hurry and bite, as you are going, please, dog
qed ka Nunsin qatu mekite:teNkadi tuy ma rawenmu Nunsin qatu	please do not, dog, chase uphill, as you are going, dog
pambelukugmu nud qapum tuy ma rawenmu Nunsin qatu	shove it down to your "grandfather," as you are going, please, dog
qinaNranakanande:kan qatu	they like you, dog
qituNedmu qabeNa qatu	make it sit as you plunge for it, dog
qinaNranakanande:kan qatu	they like you, dog
qipapalaNpaNenmu ma belagibeg qimenqabeNanmun qatu	sweep the moss off the trees as you leap through them, dog
qinaNranakanande:kan qatu	they like you, dog
pff pff pff	(blows on herbs)
maNayapNedkan* qatu tuy ma rawenmun qatu	shorten,* dog, as you are going, dog
qiNatNatku dimun qatu tuy qayapNede* qatu	I rub you, dog, with the "shortening,"* dog

sayden nu qima nemu*
meninemukin* qatu tu qima kuwa
 nu qima qitarun qatu
qinaNranakanande:kan qatu

and also, with the "meeting"*
may you meet*, dogs, the path of
 the wild game, dogs
they like you, dogs . . .

HUNT DOG SPELL 2

pff pff
qige:liNitakan qatu nud kuaq-
 meta* qatu
makakuakuaqmetkan* qatu
 peNre:reputmun qatu
binarakade qatu ma
 peNrarawmun qatu
qinaNranakanande:kan qatu
qed kan qatu qinare:reNita qatu

(blows on herbs)
I steam you, dog, with the "quick-
 ening,"* dog
quicken,* dog, your scent, dog

as if it were tied to a stake, dog, as
 you are going, dog
they like you, dog
do not, dog, let go (of the scent),
 dog

simaqeNkan qatu nuy pentakmar
 nuy lamege qatu
simaqeNkan qatu nuy buliwed nu
 bikrat nud qita makbeta qatu
qinaNranakanande:kan qatu
qisimaqeNkan qatu nuy
 penqe:qegarqegar qatu nuy
 kade:Nyana qatu
peNirawmun qatu
peNitaNirku Nu dimu qatu nu
 qima raqeka qatu

be like, dog, the bite of a crocodile, dog
be like, dog, the twisting of a
 python round a male deer, dog
they like you, dog
and be like, dog, the screeching,
 dog, of a hornbill bird, dog

as you go for it, dog
now I beat you, dog, with the
 herbs, dog (beats herbs on dog's
 nose)

qinaNranakanande:kan qatu
medinaqeta* qatu nuy ma ra-
 wenmun qatu
qinaNranakanande:kan qatu
tatan likuNan qatu ma peNibug-
 kutanyun qatu nu qima gipnana
 qatu
tuqmeg kata qatu ma peN-
 irawmun tan qatu
qed kan qatu na NawaNawan
 qatu
simaqeNkan qatu nu qipen-
 duwaduwa nuy kiat mad qawak
 nima tawena qatu

they like you, dog
may you meet* it, dog, as you are
 going, dog
they like you, dog
just one small ravine, dog, will you
 run over, dog, to catch the boar,
 dog
you'll bite right away, dog, when
 you go for it, dog
do not, dog, get all confused, dog

be like, dog, an explosion of lightning in the middle of the heav-
 ens, dog

kabuyuniyu tuy ma rawenyun qatu   move in a single pack, as you go
                                       there, dogs
qinaNranakanande:kan qatu . . .   they like you, dogs

DISCUSSION

Whatever their apparent differences, the two spells given reveal a number of similarities, some of which distinguish *nawnaw,* as a genre, from ordinary Ilongot speech.

To begin with, all spells are composed of short lines that end in a vocative or address term, like "dog" in the examples above. All spells are addressed to something—at times a spirit, at others a disease name or a charm. The gardener speaks to the rice she has planted; the hunter addresses his dogs or his hand. In a sense, any spell can be seen as a process that creates a relationship between the practitioner (in this case the hunter) and some agent, a hand, a rice bundle, a dog, or whatever, that effects the desired result. Thus, the spells presented here are addressed to the "dogs" of the hunter, and "dog" as a vocative ends each phrase and each line. The spell names the hunter's actions on his object—he steams it, rubs it, beats it—and tells what the object must do in turn. Even the refrain lines, *qinaNramakanande:kan* . . . or, sometimes, *nakaramaktakan* (which I translate "they, I, like you . . .") because of their apparent derivation from the root *ramak* 'to like, want, desire', function primarily as relational elements, establishing a formal connection between the dogs and the single hunter ("I") or between them and the spirit world ("they"). These lines (which are limited to use in magical utterances and appear in most Ilongot spells) are among the few magical phrases that Ilongots themselves were unable to interpret; yet I think I am right in assuming that, like some of the "weird" expressions Malinowski encountered (1966:211–250), they serve to define a relationship between the practitioner and the object of his spell.

Beyond that, many of the lines in the spells are formulaic, and syntactic variation is slight. We find, for example, repeated use of a simile frame (*simaqeNkan qatu* . . .), a proscription (*qed kan qatu* . . .), the durative "as you are going, dog," the use of plant names in verbal expressions (starred in the text), and a few other kinds of commands.[4] All of these are short and rhythmic; all guarantee that the spell sounds like a spell, which, unlike ordinary discourse, is limited to two to six

---

[4] Malinowski suggests that the same may be true of Trobriand magic when he speaks of the regular use of "metaphors, oppositions, repetitions, negations, comparisons, imperatives and questions with answer . . ." that make "the language of magic unusual and quaint [1966:222]."

(usually four) main stresses in each line. This is illustrated in a fragment like the following:

> *qinaNránakanande:kan qátu*
> *simáqeNkan qátu nuy beáweta qátu*
> *simáqeNkan qatu nuy kerè:rĕkpa nu sinéNdera qátu*
> *káta qátu peNiráwmun qátu*

There also seem to be rules for the number and placement of secondary and tertiary stresses (as in the third line just given) but these cannot be dealt with here.

Finally, spells of any single type seem to be limited in their contents. Hunting spells have a number of fairly straightforward things to say about what dogs should do when hunting: Stay together in a single pack; catch the scent; chase the game downhill and not up, toward the hunters and not away from them; move quickly, but manage not to go too far. Dogs are told to bark, to bite, to find the game and hold it, to make their "enemies" slow down in their tracks. Each line (and each gesture), taken singly, says something about the hunt dog or object; it names an action that is desired or forbidden, or a thing to which the object is compared.

Yet the spell does more than provide a list of desired behaviors. The various imperatives are felt to be powerful and convincing because they are related to one another through the formulaic structure of the spell. In the discussion that follows, it will be seen that all images associated with a single frame or formula are related, that they are, in effect, articulations of some one underlying theme. All images that enter the simile frame, for example, are linked by a web of implicit associations to a covert theme or key idea that is central to Ilongot conceptions of the hunt. The same is true for the set of all possible proscriptions, and for all plant names that can be used as verbs. Implicit connections among images used in a single formulaic context become obvious and salient because they are expressed in lines that themselves are similar; the repetition of lines of the same form highlights associative relations among their terms.

Stated otherwise, the language of magic is limited to a small number of formulaic modes of expression because these provide a way of organizing diverse images and highlighting some of the semantic associations and thematic orientations that underlie, and are activated in, the spell. In the analysis that follows, three such formulas are considered:

1. The simile "Be like, dog, _____, dog," in which the images used in the empty slot all suggest positive associations with hunting. These will, for illustrative purposes, be considered in greatest detail.

2. The proscription "Don't dog, _____, dog," whose possible images are verbs illustrating behaviors that must be avoided.

3. Lines in which plant names are mentioned, typically in the form of verbs in a positive command. These vary somewhat syntactically, yet I consider the fact that all plants used in hunting spells are treated in a similar manner—through both the actions of the practitioner (who beats them, steams them, and so on) and the use of their names in the spell—sufficient evidence to consider them, too, as a single collection, exemplifying a single thematic concern.

Each of these formulas, I will argue, is a vehicle through which the world of the magical practitioner is subordinated to a single conception; each is associated with a variety of concrete images that exemplify some underlying cultural theme. Three recurrent formulas provide the mold through which the spell constructs its metaphorical reality—a vision of a world that can be organized in terms of three powerful and relatively independent themes. While actual performances of hunting spells may differ in their particular images and details, all can be seen to reflect this shared core of models and assumptions; and all make use of a limited and formulaic language to realize, or recreate (in a variety of concrete images), three shared and critical ideas.

Similes

Much as the speaker of English says "Your eyes are like stars" and "Your lips are like roses," the Ilongot magical practitioner likens his dogs to arrows and a number of other things. Explicit comparisons, or similes, like these are spoken and understood under the tacit assumption that, out of a world of possible comparisons (eyes are also like pebbles and boulders, twins, hollows, and the deep blue sea), the one chosen is based on a likeness or shared characteristic that is relevant to the context at hand. Thus, when the hunter says, for example,

> *simaqeNkan qatu nuy beaweta qatu*
> be like you dog a harpoon arrow dog

he is, quite clearly, not suggesting a comparison between the physical characteristics of hunt dogs and the ("distinctive") features that would, say, distinguish arrows from spears, and harpoon arrows from flat ones, in a traditional semantic account. Rather, Ilongots explain, harpoon arrows *siNed,* they "catch onto" things—and hunt dogs, like arrows, should "catch onto" and hold the game. In other words, hunt dogs will be like harpoon arrows if they act like them, and so the image calls forth a model, a kind of action-schema, for how the hunt dogs are to behave.

Of course, similes are not always based on actions (we can say "You are like a ghost," which means "You look white"), but Ilongot spells are concerned with the ideal action of some object, and their similes are consistently interpreted as action schemas – which provide complex models for how an object ought to behave. Thus, dogs are compared to fire, because fire "leaps" through the grassland, and they are told to "bite and hold on" like a crocodile, "to hoot" like a hornbill bird. Or, to take a very different example, the headhunter asks that his body "slip by" like a feather and "hide" like a flea on a dog. In each case, what is most important about the predicate, the second term in the simile, is that it provides a very specific (and readily verbalized) model for the action of the first one. It suggests verbal associations that relate both the object of the spell and the predicate to an idealized conception of action, which is relevant to a successful endeavor.

But the world offers infinite possibilities for such metaphors. We can never know all the things that an arrow can stand for, nor can one know to what a hunt dog may be compared. The power of metaphor in spells (and I take simile to be the most explicit kind of metaphor[5]) lies in the fact that its images are a good deal more than apt, incidental comparisons. In particular, a harpoon arrow is a good metaphor not only because it "catches onto" things but also because it is an arrow, a weapon, that is violent, an instrument used to kill. In the discussion that follows it will be seen that all images – lightning, fire, crocodiles – that, in hunting spells, appear in the conventional frame:

> *simaqeNkan qatu nuy* . . .
> be-you dog like . . .

are related. The images, or predicates of the comparison, appear to comprise an open collection of possible or likely realizations of a single underlying notion: All speak of violence, and in this they are all different ways of saying the same thing. What is more, the fact that they occupy the same position in a frame leads the analyst, and also the Ilongot practitioner, to attend to their similarity. Such implicit interconnections make each image doubly appropriate, as if to say, "Violence is a conception that emerges naturally from our experience of reality; and hunt dogs can

---

[5] Metaphors are expressions that establish relationships of similarity among conventionally unrelated categories of things. Following Barfield (1947), I take similes to be the most explicit kind of metaphor because they specify an equation of unlike objects; other kinds of metaphorical expressions – as when, in English, the supports of a table are called legs – are often more difficult to identify and so are more covert.

be like lightning, crocodiles, and so on, because they are violent as well." I can think of no better rhetorical procedure for garnering faith in one's dogs.

The power and ramifications of this device are revealed in a complete listing of all similes found in hunt dog spells. While no individual uses all of them, all are generally familiar and can, for the most part, be seen to have much the same underlying theme. All of the following are, then, possible completions of the Ilongot version of "Be like, dog. . . ." They are followed by explicit interpretations that my Ilongot informants offered, as well as whatever additional ethnographic notes are needed to illuminate their cultural meaning. The first four images are probably the most common; beyond that, I have ordered them in a way that reflects my sense of the relevant associations by which all are interlinked.

1. *beawet* 'harpoon arrow'. The fact that it "catches onto" things is cited in folk interpretations as crucial, though it also seems important that arrows are weapons, used to kill men as well as animals, and that, among arrows, the harpoon is a highly valued type.

2. *menipaduN nu kaberetmu* 'meeting your enemy'. Dogs are told to go right up to, to "meet" the game, and the same word can be used to describe a ritual duel. One of the plants used in hunt magic is called *padupaduN,* or "meeting," so not only an action image but also a plant is here invoked.

3. *pendalaqda nu kade:Nyan, penqe:qegar nu kade:Nyan.* Both mean "the hooting, howling, screeching of a hornbill bird." The explicit comparison concerns the hunter's wish that his dogs stay on a scent, and signify it by barking (elsewhere, he may say "Don't be silent, dog . . ."). *Kade:Nyan* is an example of what Ilongots call 'beautified language' (its everyday form is *kaw*); words like this can be used at any time, though they seem to contribute to the sense of importance or power associated with particular speech events. Since hornbills are used by Ilongots only in the manufacture of headhunting ornaments (earrings and a headpiece worn only by one who has taken a head), the image involves a more general invocation of headhunting, and so, of a violent theme.

4. *pentakmar nu buaya, pentakmar nu lameg.* Both mean "the grasping bite of a crocodile," where *lameg* is a somewhat unusual and, thus, "beautiful" name for the animal.[6] The idea here is that the dog, like a

---

[6] While my data are inconclusive, it seems likely that *lameg* and most other "beautiful" expressions used in spells are in fact borrowings from the Northern Ilongot dialect, which is different from the Central one considered here (M. Rosaldo, 1971). That the use of words from distinct but related languages and dialects may, in fact, be characteristic of "ritual languages" and codes in a number of cultures has been suggested by Fox (1975).

crocodile, will bite and hold onto its catch. Crocodiles are feared and, again, suggest headhunting, both because their teeth are used in safety charms, giving strength to the killers, and because the crocodile is one of the few animals that men like to behead. Two men I knew who had been on a headhunting raid together called one another "fellow crocodile" (cf. R. Rosaldo, 1971) to commemorate their adventure.

5. *pendalaqda nù me qamet* 'the howling of a monkey.' Many Ilongots think that the word *Meqamet,* 'large male monkey', is related to *qamet,* 'spirit of the beheaded.' The explicit image in this line again concerns noise, but it is significant that monkeys are pests that destroy crops, and they are also animals that men like to behead.

6. *pentakmar nu bikrat, buliwed nu bikrat.* These mean 'the grasping bite of a python' and 'the twisting of a python', respectively, referring either to the tenacity of its bite or to its ability to surround and hold onto its prey. I am not aware of any additional associations with the python, except that, in general, it is feared.

7. *maNat* 'biting ants'. The verb *kaat* 'to bite' is embedded in this name. The dog's bite, like theirs, should be painful.

8. *beaki* 'roaches'. This was given two interpretations. They are named either because they "bite" or because they "clump," moving in groups to their food, as dogs are to move in a single pack.

9. *sabud nu putyukan* 'the sting of a honeybee'. Again, a painful bite is described. It also seems relevant that honey is gathered only by men.

10. *kirekpa nuy sineNder, kirekden nuy sineNder.* Both mean "the falling or collapse of pollarded branches," although the second employs a more "beautified" form of the verb. Pollarding trees is a man's primary contribution to garden activities. Swinging high on rattan tightropes, men say they are "raping" the forest; and, as they slash away, branches crash to the ground amid headhunting boasts and victorious yells. Ilongots interpret this image as one of quick violence (like the action of dogs, who disrupt the undergrowth as they race through the forest) or loud noise.

11. *ruNuy* 'fire, forest fire'. Fire is said to "leap through the grasslands," as dogs are to cover the forest in a flash (in a riddle, for instance, "fire" is the "name of a man who eats a whole rice field in a single day"). Burning a swidden can be described as an instance of *ruNuy,* and it is men's work; I imagine that this kind of fire is opposed to the more feminine "flame" or "hearthfire," an image used in agricultural spells to "warm" the heart of the rice.

12. *kirekpa nu rumun* 'the falling of overhead branches'. This has much the same standard interpretation as the pollarding image. It suggests suddenness and clamor by alluding to the fact that often, in the forest, high masses of dead vines, leaves, and branches will, for no apparent reason, collapse onto the ground.

13. *penduwaduwa nu kiat* 'the flashing, blasting of lightning'. This is interpreted as an image of loud barking; I imagine that it also implies speed.

14. *peminatpinat nu quriyan* 'the pulling back and forth of a whirl-pool'. This is like dogs that surround the game and force it to "circle" their master.

15. *penlinek nu kabe:ktege:n* 'the rushing of rapids'. This is explained as an image of speed and, sometimes, precision. In rapids one has the feeling that the water has no choice but to move on its violent course; here it is hoped that the game will be forced through an ambush as water is forced over rough rocks.

16. *peNkareNken nima taqnur* 'the splashing forth of an emergent stream'. This is interpreted as an image of quickness and sometimes, again, of precision; the water spurts forth in a single direction from a single source.

17. *paysipit nu matanek* 'the twisting, shaking of a small fish'. This suggests quickness.

18. *quNraw nu sinaqdeN* 'going for hanging (meat)'. This tells the dogs to leap as they do when they jump for meat drying in the house-hold. Dogs often do manage to consume stored provisions, and people feel angry but helpless against their persistent attempts.

19. *mentaktakande beNubeNeta* 'beating on cooking pots'. This is an image for noise, but it was also said to suggest an abundance of prepared food — that is, a successful hunt. The only contexts in which I am aware that people may beat on cooking pots are headhunting celebrations and domestic quarrels.

20. *kuwatu nu pinutud* 'the path of a prepared chew of betel'. This suggests that the dogs will be as close to the game as men who hand betel quids to one another. While I am not sure if Ilongots intend it, the image makes me think of those tense situations in which people do, in fact, hand prepared betel chews to one another — in meetings of enemies and strangers, people one might be tempted to kill.

21. *pemugkut nu berun qinadalana bakidu di naynay* 'the running of a newly taught carabao in the lowlands'. This is an image of speed, and it is more common in headhunting than in hunting spells.

22. *bugkut nu qutumubil* 'the running of a car'. Again, this is more common in headhunting spells, and also suggests speed.

23. *pentaked nu qula, pentaked nu kamurat* 'the regular spacing of sweet potatoes', 'the regular spacing of *kamurat*'. *Kamurat* is a wild plant often gathered for these spells, which, like the sweet potato, sends its runners at regular intervals into the ground. In like manner, Ilongots say, the dogs will follow close on one another and hold a constant scent.

The same image is used in agricultural spells to suggest the regular spacing of healthy rice.

Perhaps the first thing to remark about all of the images given is that each can be construed as "like" a hunt dog in terms of some quality of action; in each case, speed, sound, precision, bite, and so on provide very specific models, or schema, for how a hunt dog ought to behave. In this way, each of these similes is rendered accessible to folk interpretations that highlight a similarity, an attribute, a characteristic action or quality shared both by hunt dogs and some of the things of the world. That shared characteristic may, as in the case of, say, "pollarded branches," be more complex than the sort of thing linguists usually intend when they speak of "semantic features"; but, like a feature, it can be used to specify a new field of meaning, to which both dogs and falling branches belong.

Yet, as suggested previously, the effectiveness of the spell seems to depend on more than a number of reasonable comparisons; and, in particular, the fact that all images given occupy the same slot in a single, repeated syntactic formula suggests that they themselves are linked by a set of associative connections to some shared thematic core. Such associations are implicit, and more difficult to specify than the explicit action-schema that informants readily discuss. Yet I think we are justified in inferring these interconnections. In particular, five (1–5) and possibly nine (19–22) of the images just presented suggest killing or headhunting; nine (3–9, 17, 21) name animals, of which all but one (17) are generally considered inedible (some, like pythons and monkeys, are edible only for people of certain social categories); and at least six (4–9) are destructive or dangerous to man. Cross-cutting these groupings, we note that the images that speak of nature name its violent, destructive aspects (4–9, 10–16); and, with the possible exception of the last three entries (the only similes that are found in other kinds of spells), those that suggest human activities (9–11, 19, 20) point to violent acts, performed, for the most part, by men.

In other words, the various images stand, not simply as models for particular modes of action, but also as reflections of an implicit sense that hunting, like headhunting, is a form of killing; a covert sense of violent destruction seems to underlie them all. This is why people who use different images can be felt to be saying the same thing, and it is why certain kinds of images — "a crying baby" for "loud noise," or "sucking" as a model for "holding on" — are not introduced at all. From the point of view of the practitioner, these similes are much more than appropriate descriptions of hunt dogs; they are felt to be effective because they exemplify an ideal of violence that interrelates the collection as a whole. Because words that occupy the same position in similar or juxtaposed lines are, and are experienced as, related, the similes effect a reorganization of wide and diverse aspects of experience in terms of a single cultural ideal.

The same theme is, of course, heard elsewhere in these spells, as when dogs are told to "bite your enemy" or "sweep the moss off the trees." It is heard, too, when the predicate noun in one line is treated as a verb in the next:

> *simaqeNkan qatu nuy takmar nu buayan qatu*
> be like dog the bite of a crocodile dog
> *mambuayakan qatu tu maqawa qatu*
> be a crocodile dog today dog

In such sequences, the use of a single root in two syntactically distinct predicates creates a feeling of conviction, as if the structure of language itself could be subordinated to a single dominant idea. Finally, "violence" as a theme is reflected in the notion that plants rubbed on the nose will "anger" (as they do, in fact, aggravate) the hunt dog, or that beating the dogs with herbs will chase their "innocence," their "not-having-taken-a-head."

Hunting spells are rich in violent connotations. Yet I would like to suggest that it is the simile frame itself that provides for the primary or focal expression of the theme of violence in the hunt. Because they occur in a formula that is repeated, recognized, and salient, the images used in hunting similes are experienced as exemplifications of a single orientation; and because so many images are so related, they give an aura of plausibility and necessity to the hunter's violent goals. More generally, it seems likely that all spells are realizations of a few core themes, ideas, or orientations and that each of these is given primary articulation in some one expressive form. So, similes in hunting spells speak of violence (and in agricultural, headhunting, or medicinal spells, they are used to highlight other key ideas), and other lines and actions are used to echo and confirm this theme. In the sections that follow, it will be seen that other formulas—the negative command and the plant name—introduce new thematic considerations; and it will be suggested that the meaning and impact of the spell derive, ultimately, from the interaction of their different, and contextually relevant, key ideas.

The Negative Command

If similes can be said to give positive content to the concept of "ideal dogs," another frame defines its boundaries, or limits, by saying what it is not. The frame:

> *qed kan qatu . . .*
> don't-you dog . . .

is the source of these proscriptions. Negative sentences employing this
frame in hunt dog spells include the following:

qed ka Nunsin qatu nambe:ntade qatu	please, do not, dog, straighten out, dog
qed kan qatu qinantaratarawtawa qatu	do not, dog, get lost, dog
qed kan qatu nansawasawan qatu	do not, dog, go aimlessly, dog
qed kan qatu na NawaNawan qatu	do not, dog, get confused (crazy), dog
qed kan qatu nantalaNyaw kayqanupmun Nunsin qatu	do not, dog, disperse (get lost) in your hunting, please, dog
qed kan qatu qinanwakata qatu	do not, dog, go out in all directions, dog
qed kan qatu nanwaNita qatu	do not, dog, spread out, dog
qed kan qatu peNiqaqasiweklaNa qatu	do not, dog, disperse, dog
qed kan qatu qinatensiyesiyetan qatu	do not, dog, go one by one, dog
qed kan qatu qinaNgigimapasin qatu	do not, dog, let go (of the scent), dog
qed kan qatu nanle:lekikiyi nun qatu	do not, dog, tire (of the scent), dog
qed kan qatu qipenNelaqNelan qatu	do not, dog, give up, dog
qed kan qatu qinare;reNita qatu	do not, dog, break off (the scent), dog
qed kan qatu mekite:teNkadi nun qatu	please do not, dog, force it uphill, dog
qed kan qatu qinaNkayube qatu	do not, dog, be afraid, dog
qed kan qatu qinayquliki qatu	do not, dog, let it (your catch) be small, dog

In general, these commands tell the dogs not to separate from one
another, not to give up the scent (and so lose the pack), not to spread
(straighten) out, get lost, confused, or dispersed. As with the similes discussed earlier, each line has a single, specific interpretation (though their
sense is more "transparent," less "metaphorical" than with the similes),
and yet, when taken together, each appears to be a variant realization of
a single, underlying theme. All of these proscriptions are concerned with
the fear that the dogs will lose their sense of mission and, in particular,
that they will act as individuals and lose their collective orientation to

the hunters as a group. As was the case with the similes, I believe that this constitutes a single thematic orientation and that its general impact is foregrounded by virtue of its repetition in a number of formally equivalent lines. Finally, this theme too has its echoes, or confirmations, in the various commands for dogs to push the game downhill, to stay in a single pack, and so on elsewhere in the spell.

It is worth noting that negative command forms are not unique to the spells of the Ilongots. They are found in Trobriand and Malay spells as well. I imagine that this is because spells are, in part, devices for defining ideal concepts, and part of defining a concept involves specifying what it is not.[7] In fact, the Malays, too, are specifically concerned that their dogs will forget that they were hunting, and a dog spell recorded by Skeat begins with the lines "Let not go the scent; formidable you were from the first . . . [1965:181]."

Plants and Plant Names

A third formulaic context has to do with the incorporation of plant names into the spoken spell. The method by which plants are included involves both physical and linguistic manipulations. First, a small set of possible and appropriate hunting plants are collected, and these are held together and used to steam, beat, rub, and agitate the dog. Second, these plants become metaphors, which are named or punned on in the course of the hunter's spell. Unlike the images used in the other formulas considered, vegetal referents are embedded in seemingly conventional verbal expressions. Much as the English "table leg" can be recognized as a metaphor only if one knows that "legs" are conventionally parts of an animal body, it is only because we know that these verbs are also plant names that they can be considered metaphors at all.

Depending on the semantic content of their names, plants can be incorporated in lines that differ somewhat syntactically. They appear in similes:

simaqen nuy menipaduN* nu kaberetmun qatu
be like meeting* your enemy dog (*padu paduN* is the name of a plant)

and in negations:

---

[7] For a discussion of negation as a poetic device in folk literature, see Jakobson, who speaks of "traditional Slavic negative parallelism — the refutation of the metaphorical state in favor of the factual state [1960:369]." Spells seem to use the same device, but in reverse: A likely (or "factual") but undesirable state is negated in favor of an imagined (abstract, and in a sense "metaphorical") desirable one. A similar process is suggested by Burke's (1961) discussion of the uses of negative expressions in establishing a sense of the supernatural.

  qed ka Nunsin qatu qinambe:ntade* qatu
  do not please dog straighten out* dog (*mabe:tad* is a plant)

But by far the most common are plants that are used as verbs in simple commands:

  paNayapNedmun* qatu ma rawenmun qatu
  shorten,* dog, what you are going for, dog (*qayapNed* is a plant)

meninemukin* qatu tu qima kuwa nu qima qitarun qatu
encounter,* dogs, the path of the wild game, dogs (*nemu* is a plant)

  makakuakuaqmetkan qatu peNre:reputmun qatu
  quicken (intensify)* dog, your scent, dog (*kuaqmet* is a plant)

The particular plants used and named in any one performance are something of a chance selection from a much larger collection including some 30 or more possibilities. As was the case with similes and negations, each has its own particular significance, and there are also some meanings they share.

A full discussion of the use of plants in these and other spells is beyond the scope of this paper (cf. M. Rosaldo, 1971, 1972; Rosaldo and Atkinson, n.d.), but a few observations are relevant. To begin with, the relations among plants used in hunting are somewhat more complex than the images in earlier examples. Some plants are used because their physical characteristics evoke the desired outcome. So a plant called *mabe:Nru,* or 'flavoring,' in fact has a sharp or pungent odor, and another, called *buayaqen,* or "crocodile" (for no reason I am aware of), has a pleasant and spicy flavor. These are thought to invoke the good taste of fresh game. Again, *takumbaN* 'encircling' has verticillate leaves, which are said to suggest dogs rushing around their master's feet. But for the most part it is the names, rather than the physical characteristics, of plants that are felt to be most important. Some, like "she boar" and "straightening," have names that are specific to hunting. And the vast majority, "bad luck," "beckon," "base," "near," "shorten," "meet," "encounter," "filling," "addition," and others, have names that make them appropriate to both agricultural and hunting spells. In any case, in all but a few examples all of these plants can be used to signify some important characteristic of hunting. Each plant is a concrete metaphor, a physical realization of some quality shared by the hunt or hunt dog and its appearance or name.

Each plant can be assigned its particular magical significance. At the same time, it is possible to discover shared and significant associations among most, if not all, of the plants used. In terms of their physical characteristics, most of these plants come from the forest, grow near water (which is associated with the notion of "fattening"), and have many and tiny leaves; in this, at least, they are similar. The names of the plants, too, are suggestive. Most speak of nearing, surrounding, coming closer. Where the similes speak largely of violence, the plant names, taken together, stress closeness, even sociability, and the behaviors on the part of the hunt dogs that will enable the hunter to stay near and bring lots of game to his home. This theme is echoed in the lines that bid the dogs to stay near their "grandfather" and bring the game to his feet; it is also reflected in the symbolism of the steaming hearthstone, which signifies a scent near the home. Finally, most of these plants are used in spells for agriculture as well as for hunting, where they suggest, again, that fruitfulness, a good harvest, will "meet" and "near" and "fill" the gardener's hand. As in the case of the hunter, the gardener asks that the rice "heart" come to her, that it surround her, that she be able to spend an entire day reaping the rich yield of a single spot. (Her language, in fact, recalls that of the Trobriander, who would "anchor" his garden and yams.) I would like to suggest, then, that the general theme, or covert concern, underlying the use of plant verbs in hunting is almost diametrically opposed to the violent theme of the simile frame. It highlights the domestic and social uses of hunting, which complements the agricultural activities of women in providing food for the home.

Thinking about Meaning

According to my analysis, both of the spells considered can be seen as devices for creating the image of a good hunt dog by defining what a good hunt dog should be. Three themes, key ideas, or orientations were important: On the one hand, dogs must be violent; on the other, they should be almost social, domestic, and meet the game somewhere close by. Finally, they should know what is forbidden: to disperse, to be individualistic, to lose track of the point of the hunt. Each of these themes is realized or articulated in the spell through a number of diverse images: names of plants and prohibitions, crocodiles, lightning, hearthstones, and so on. And sets of these images are associated with a single formulaic mode of assertion, which is used repeatedly in the course of the spell. Thus, to return to our first example, images found in the simile frame almost all suggest violence, and, because lines of the same form are felt to be similar, their thematic unity is brought forward in a manner that appears to confirm and give life to its salience as a way of ordering the world. So similes do not merely "suggest" the idea of violence; they seem to "create" violence as a conceptual imperative, a real and necessary mode of experience, to which the hunt dog must necessarily comply.

Of course, not all similes are about violence, and more kinds of things than similes, negations, and plant names go into a spell. Each of the dominant themes associated with a single formulaic context is, we have seen, echoed elsewhere. The idea of violence, for example, is heard in commands about "biting"; it is reflected in the notion that rubbing a dog's nose with plants will make it angry and strong. Again, the social and domestic theme of the plant verbs is strengthened by the fact that many of the plants used are also associated with gardening; it is heard in the one simile that equates hunt dogs and sweet potatoes, and even in the notion that "steam on the hearthstone" equals dogs finding scent near home. Finally, the proscriptions or negative commands have their positive counterparts in commands to stay close together and the like. These "echoes" do not undermine the methodological assumption that underlies the preceding analysis: that words and things occupying the same position in a fixed context or formula can be assumed to be related, and that such formulas, in fact, provide a focus for the articulation of core and underlying themes. Rather, the fact that themes are found else-where provides additional evidence for their importance, salience, and necessity (for practitioner and analyst alike). In the end, it seems reason-able to say that the spell organizes itself as it organizes experience, in terms of these dominant ideas.

The analysis of images associated with particular formulaic contexts isolates three themes that are communicated in Ilongot spells for hunting: the ideas of violence, sociability, and cooperation. Still, two issues remain to be examined. First, to say that the spell "tells" the hunt dogs to be violent hardly explains why a hunter should believe his words to be effective, why they should have a transformative force. It will be helpful to speculate as to what the spell "does" for the hunter. A second question has to do with the relation of these spells to "creative" linguistic performances elsewhere; in the concluding section I suggest some general connections between the "creativity" of magic and other creative uses of words.

Thinking about the effect or meaning of a spell is a difficult matter, because Ilongots themselves take a very practical attitude toward their magic. They are reluctant, without seeing its consequents, to say how a spell might succeed. For Ilongots, a spell is no more than an *attempt* to make certain things happen, and whether one is verbose or indifferent, enthusiastic or skeptical, one cannot be sure it will work. Nor does the sequencing of images within a performance, or the way a spell is situated in relation to the everyday activities around it, determine its impact or force. Rather, what force the spell has or makes available depends on its power to remold and reorganize experience, to show that everything from the plant world to the structure of language itself can support and be related to one of its dominant themes. What is more, these themes themselves do more than define a good hunt dog. In the end, I think, they characterize Ilongot conceptions of hunting, and so, orient or intensify the sense that the hunter has of his own activities and goals. All of the themes discussed have meaning, ultimately, because they locate the hunter in terms of cultural concerns and social tensions that give meaning to his everyday world.

This can be illustrated by considering some of the human implications of each of the three themes considered. First, violence as a statement about dogs relates hunting as a human activity to the headhunting exploits through which one "becomes a man." These are associated, not only in spells but in a wealth of other forms of cultural expression—in rituals that compare the young hunter to the killer, in jokes that link game to the human victims of a raid. In a sense, headhunting is an extreme form of hunting, hunting as a male activity par excellence. At the same time, of course, hunting is also like gardening. As suggested earlier, they are seen as complementary techniques by which men and women, equally, provide for their kin. And so, the plea for dogs to "meet," "encounter," and so on, phrased in plant verbs, also talks to the domestic meaning of the hunt. Finally, the negative commands define the boundaries of the category "good hunt dog" and, I would suggest, invoke a problematic area of human activity as well. In Ilongot society in general, and especially in hunting, the pursuit of individual wealth or renown is looked down upon, and competition is inhibited and even feared. It seems, then, that proscriptions on individualistic behavior on the part of hunt dogs may correspond to a social taboo.

These connections are no more than my speculations, yet they suggest that the spell is felt to be effective, that it speaks to the hunter, because, in defining a hunt dog and reclassifying a range of experience to that end, it also relates hunting to certain crucial dimensions of cultural and social experience. In effect, the spell exploits a number of details, models, dimensions of sensuous experience in order to articulate, or intensify, the hunter's logico–meaningful experience of himself in his cultural world.

Creativity and Constraints

As I said earlier, no two performances of an Ilongot spell are apt to be identical, and yet Ilongots tend to speak of them as substantially the same. They say this not, as might a Trobriand magician, because spells are defined as somehow frozen, as truths man has acquired from a perfect and powerful nonhuman force. Ilongot spells, on the contrary, are felt to be human products, and various performances are comparable insofar as they have the same meaning, express and give form to certain underlying cultural themes. While each performance of a spell is an individual outcome—governed by whatever chance associations led the practitioner to choose among stereotyped lines—it is, at the same time, a general statement that creates, as it were, a feeling of necessity, a sense of the "right" organization of the world. Somewhat paradoxically, one might say that Ilongot spells are creative because they are ultimately the same.

The creativity of spells lies, I have argued, in their ability to reorder the categories of common-sensical experience, to group a wealth of objects, sensuous details, and chance similarities in terms of a small set of culturally and contextually meaningful themes. This is achieved in spells by minimizing possible variations in syntax, by dictating the formulaic structure that most assertions must take. Similarity of structure highlights implicit relationships within a flood of concrete and sensuous imagery, enabling it to take on new sense. So constraints on form highlight, or create, associative relationships among images so different that they could not be recalled, interpreted, or organized except in terms of (what then become) the spell's dominant and compelling themes.

This sort of creativity seems to be related to a recent observation by Friedrich (n.d.):

> The poetical quality of ordinary language and the creative use of language particularly in poetry, are not independent of "immediate stimulation" . . . but, quite on the contrary, depend on maximizing interconnectedness between the fine grained symbolism for sensuous and "immediate" detail and, on the other hand, the underlying semantic structure of language [pp. 44–45].

This happens, he goes on to say, through devices "partly, if not largely independent of the usual system of rules for clause and sentence formation [*ibid.*]." In terms of Ilongot magic, I would take this to mean that the spells can be creative—they can create new relationships among the sensuous things of the world, their physical identities, and their names—because their form itself is limited. Creativity in spells, and perhaps in a number of other formal linguistic genres, is apt to be greatest when syntactic variation is most constrained.

Of course, it is hardly surprising that creative uses of language may be associated with constraints on expressive form. From our earliest years we learn to think of poetry in terms of constraints on sound, rhythm, and the like. And Jakobson (1960, 1966) speaks at length about the ways in which similarities of form (or of sound) lead us to discover relations of sense. The same point is made by the literary critic Empson, who is concerned to show how certain kinds of formal strictures may lead us to hear juxtaposed images "ambiguously," both as statements in themselves and as complementary expressions of their "highest common factor"—which activity he aptly describes as adopting a "poetical attitude toward words [1947:91]." Finally, and at some reach from poetics, the relationship between formulaic constraints and creativity is at least implicit in some of Bernstein's (1972) elliptical comments about the "metaphorical" capacities of people who command a "restricted" code.

A common intuition runs through the work of all of these thinkers. And it is an intuition that Ilongots readily exploit in performing their magic—using language to create what is, for them, a world that is different from the one they are given, a world that conforms to the needs of the practitioner, to cultural meanings and cultural controls.

References

Barfield, Owen
  1947 *Poetic diction and legal fiction, essays presented to Charles Williams.* London: Oxford Univ. Press.
Bernstein, Basil
  1972 A sociolinguistic approach to socialization: With some reference to educability. In *Directions in sociolinguistics,* edited by J. Gumperz and D. Hymes. Pp. 465–497. New York: Holt.
Burke, Kenneth
  1961 *The rhetoric of religion.* Berkeley: Univ. of California Press.
Empson, William
  1947 *Seven types of ambiguity.* New York: New Directions.
Fox, James
  1971 Semantic parallelism in Rotinese ritual language, *Bijdragen Tot de Taal— Land—en Volkenkunde,* 215–255.
  1975 Our ancestors spoke in pairs: Rotinese views of language, dialect, and code. In *The ethnography of communication,* edited by J. Sherzer and R. Bauman. Cambridge: Cambridge Univ. Press.
Friedrich, Paul
  n.d. The lexical symbol and its non-arbitrariness. In *Festschrift in honor of Carl F. Voegelin,* edited by M. Dale Kinkaid. The Hague: Mouton (to appear).
Hymes, Dell
  1968 The "wife" who "goes out" like a man, *Social Science Information* 7(3), 173–199.
Jakobson, Roman
  1956 *Fundamentals of language,* with M. Halle. The Hague: Mouton
  1960 Linguistics and poetics. In *Style in language,* edited by T. Sebeck. Pp. 350–377. Cambridge, Massachusetts: M.I.T. Press.
  1966 Grammatical parallelism and its Russian facet, *Language* **42**, 399–429.

Levi-Strauss, Claude
1963 The effectiveness of symbols. In *Structural anthropology*. Pp. 186–205. New York: Basic Books.
1966 *The savage mind*. London: Weidenfeld and Nicolson.
Malinowski, Bronislaw
1966 *The language of magic and gardening* (or, *Coral gardens and their magic*, vol. II, first published in 1935). London: George Allen & Unwin, Ltd.
Munn, Nancy
n.d. The symbolism of perceptual qualities: A study in Trobriand ritual aesthetics. Paper presented at the meetings of the American Anthropological Association, New York, 1971.
Rosaldo, Michelle Z.
1971 Context and metaphor in Ilongot oral tradition. Ph.D. dissertation, Harvard University.
1972 Metaphor and folk classification, *Southwestern Journal of Anthropology* **28**(1), 83–99.
Rosaldo, M. Z. and J. M. Atkinson
n.d. Man the hunter and woman: Metaphor for the sexes in Ilongot magical spells. In *Interpretation of Symbolism*, edited by R. Willis. London: Malaby Press, Ltd. (in press).
Rosaldo, Renato
1970 *Ilongot society: The social organization of a non-Christian group in Northern Luzon, Philippines*. Ph.D. dissertation, Harvard University.
1971 Fellow-bulldozer: How not to name an in-law. Paper presented at the meetings of the American Anthropological Association, New York.
Skeat, Walter William
1965 *Malay magic*. London: Frank Cass & Co. Ltd. (first published in 1900).
Strathern, Andrew and Strathern, Marilyn
1968 Marsupials and magic: A study of spell symbolism among the Mbowamb. In *Dialectic in practical religion*, edited by E. Leach. Cambridge: Cambridge Univ. Press.
Tambiah, S. J.
1968 The magical power of words, *Man* **3**(2), 175–208.
Turner, Victor
1962 Themes in the symbolism of Ndembu hunting ritual, *Anthropological Quarterly* **35**(2).
1964 Symbols in Ndembu ritual. In *Closed systems and open minds: The limits of naivety in social science*, edited by M. Gluckman. Edinburgh: Oliver & Boyd.

The Language of Ritual Events among the GA of Southern Ghana

DALE K. FITZGERALD

Introduction

In the sizable ethnographic literature on folk religion and magic, one will often find mention of the rich ways in which language is used in ritual performance. But careful study of ritual texts has been undertaken by very few anthropologists. Of the traditional ethnographers, perhaps only Malinowski (1935) provides detailed analysis in this area.

Recently, a number of works have appeared that provide a variety of interesting approaches to the subject. Tambiah (1968, 1970) and Horton (1967:157–161), in their concern to understand the "magical power of words," take up one of the central matters of the field. Work in other, more specific areas has also appeared: glossolalia (Goodman, 1969; Samarin, 1969, 1972), religious genres (Fabian, 1971), religious argot (Zaretsky, 1969), preaching styles (Crystal, 1972), and prophetic speech (Fitzgerald, 1970), to mention a few. Most relevant, because of its breadth and style of analysis, is the recent work of Marks (1972) on the interpatterning of linguistic and musical styles in Afro-American rituals. Finally, the programatic article by Samarin (1971) is important because it formulates some of the central questions by which research and analysis may be guided.

In this study I have found it more appropriate to speak in terms of ritual rather than religion or magic. This is because communicative behavior rather than beliefs is taken as the starting point for analysis. I will use the word *ritual* to indicate a broader referent than intended by Durkheim (1969), in that it will here include actions motivated by both religious and magical beliefs, but a narrower referent than intended by Goffman (1967), in that I will be concerned only with face-to-face interaction enacted in a specified context.

Primary data for this analysis are provided by transcriptions of tape-recorded ritual performances, supplemented by written notes covering nonverbal aspects of these performances. Field work was conducted among the Ga[1] during two periods: February 1967–September 1968 and April–November 1971.

Ritual Events and Ritual Communication

This section outlines the field of study, indicating the range of ritual events found in Ga culture and the modes of communication employed in their construction.

RITUAL EVENTS

In delimiting the field of ritual events in Ga culture, it will not be possible to work only from lexically encoded Ga concepts, for there are no general terms in the folk lexicon used consistently to refer to the ritual domain at large or to mark major subdivisions within it. The widely used Ga term *kusum* 'custom/ritual/ceremony', itself almost certainly a loan word from English (*custom*), comes closest to indicating the area of interest. But its referent is considerably broader than the field I wish to indicate. What do exist in the folk lexicon are numerous terms for specific rites, plus a number of somewhat more general terms that show a great deal of variation both across speakers and within the same speaker's usage (cf. Sankoff, 1972). Under the circumstances, we must proceed from the starting point of a definition derived intuitively from a general knowledge of Ga culture. The following is, thus, a working definition, necessarily tentative, pending further analysis of ritual phenomena:

Ritual Event: A human undertaking involving a complex of words and actions[2] aimed at communication with spiritual entities

---

[1] The *Ga* people number approximately 350,000; their homeland is the Accra plains of southeastern Ghana. About three-quarters of the *Ga* population live in urban or semiurban conditions in and around the city of Accra.

Major ethnographic work on the Ga has been done primarily by two people, Margaret Field (1937, 1940) and Marion Kilson (1967a,b,c, 1968a,b, 1969, 1971). There is also an important and growing literature in the *Ga* language, published largely by the Bureau of Ghana Languages and the Presbyterian Book Depot, Accra. The *Ga* language is classified by Greenberg (1963) as a member of the Niger–Congo family of languages, of the Kwa subfamily. *Ga* is a "tone language," which is to say that the tonal component of the spoken language is semantic.

[2] Tambiah (1968:175) quotes a statement by Leach (1966:407) as follows: "Ritual as one observes it in primitive communities is a complex of words and actions . . . it is not the case that words are one thing and the rite another. The uttering of the words itself is a ritual." Then, in what appears to be a lapse of good sense, he lifts the phrase "complex of words and actions" and makes of this his "definition" of ritual (1968:184). While this phrase is obviously inadequate as a definition, my use of it in the present definition was suggested by Tambiah's article.

or motivation of cosmic principles, whose purpose is transformative and whose manner of performance is culturally prescribed.

Using this definition, the corpus of ritual events among the Ga may tentatively be divided into four categories: (1) annual rites, e.g., ŋmaa dumɔ, the ritual planting of millet; (2) life crisis rituals, e.g., kpodziemɔ, the ritual recognition of human birth; (3) initiation rites into special statuses, e.g., oselɛ hamɔ, the rite that ends a spirit medium's period of apprenticeship; and (4) rituals of affliction, e.g., daimɔ, a rite performed to remove the effects of a curse.

As may be seen, this four-part division is based essentially on *functional* considerations and in itself says nothing of the range of *structural* types that may be found in ritual events. Thus, for example, while both *yala* 'funeral' and *kpodziemɔ* 'christening' are life crisis rituals, the former is much more complex and polyfocused than the latter. Since one of the ultimate goals of my larger study is to determine the units from which ritual performances are constructed, I am not now in a position to discuss specific structural variations in ritual events. Some manner of closure is, however, needed in this area. I would, then, exclude from our definition of ritual events (1) related sequences of events that, taking place over a relatively long period and often set in different localities, form an extended *ritual process* (for example, the extensive series of events that are enacted during the period of a spirit medium's training) and (2) specific *ritual acts,* microperformances that may or may not be set within a larger undertaking (for example, the purification with incense of those entering a shrine area). In the broad range of ritual events that remain, I prefer to begin by discussing the performances that fall into the general category "rituals of affliction." This choice is dictated by both analytical preferences and wealth of available data.

RITUAL COMMUNICATION

Having outlined our area of concern, we may now turn to a discussion of the place of communication in ritual. As will be seen, my analysis of ritual is based on the communicative modes and mechanisms employed in it. The following provides a preliminary inventory of these communicative modes, together with some consideration of the settings and actors associated with them. In accomplishing this I have made use of the series of analytic components suggested by Hymes (1964) for the study of speech events.[3] It should be noted here that I have purposely

---

[3] I am aware that the particular construction of this grid has gone through a number of revisions since the 1964 article appeared. Since I do not believe the subsequent alterations have substantially changed the basic framework, I have chosen to use the early form.

chosen not to deal in this section with the question of "speech functions." The reasons for this will be made at a later stage of the analysis.

1. *Channels:* Apart from the human voice, a number of other means are used to convey messages in ritual. Most important of these are (a) percussion instruments: drums, gongs, bells, wooden sticks, and hand clappings; (b) body gestures, used especially in the dance routines of spirit mediums; (c) physical objects, or sets of objects, such as used in divination (cf. Bascom, 1969).

2. *Codes:* In addition to major, recognized languages such as Ga, Twi, and Fanti, there are also a variety of "cult languages" such as *Ga sɛɛ sɛɛ* 'ancient Ga' that employ archaic forms and a variable amount of borrowings from other languages. The drum and gong languages, while based on spoken languages, must be considered separate codes. Also, in that there exists an extensive corpus of established "gesturemes," there is a code of body language. Finally, there is a code associated with the sets of physical objects manipulated in ritual performances.

3. *Message forms:* Message forms of major significance in the ritual context include song (*lala*), libation-prayer (*ŋkpai yelɛ*), prayer (*solemɔ*), proverb (*abɛ*), oath (*kita*), prophetic speech (*wɔdzi aywiemɔ*), and incantation (no folk term). These genres or styles should by no means be considered discrete fields, for in performance considerable "embedding" occurs. Thus, for instance, proverbs may be considered one feature that marks (occurs in) prayer style.

4. *Topics:* Since the variation here is so great, there would be little point in generalizing about types of topic common to ritual. However, because of (a) the highly metaphorical manner in which language is commonly used in ritual and (b) the common device of employing different channels simultaneously to convey messages (even different or contradictory messages), considerable subtlety must be employed in determining what is being communicated in ritual events. In short, the student of ritual communication must be sensitive to the multileveled nature of messages: The reading of "referent" depends on which message level is focused upon (cf. Bateson, 1968a,b).

5. *Participants:* In the study of speech events, it has been most common to deal with the dyad sender/receiver. Aside from these situationally determined roles, it is necessary to specify whether the participants are corporeal or noncorporeal. Of the noncorporeal participants, it is important to distinguish among *Ataa-Naa Nyɔŋmɔ* 'God', *dzɛmawɔdzi* 'great gods', *wɔdzi* 'gods/powers', *sisa* 'ghost', *otɔfo* 'unrequited ghost', *susuma* 'soul', *gbeʃi* 'soul's companion', to name the most important. Of the corporeal variety, it is important to distinguish among ritual specialists, such as *wulɔmɔ* 'priest', *wɔŋtʃɛ* 'spirit medium',

tʃofatʃɛ 'medicine man', as opposed to *gbɔmɛi fodzi* 'regular people'.

6. *Settings:* As with topics, there is little that can be said in general about types of setting for ritual events. However, in addition to questions of immediate spatial, temporal, and social setting, it is necessary to specify what place, if any, the particular rite has in an ongoing sequence of ritual events.

7. *Events:* Hymes suggests the "events themselves, their kinds and characters as wholes" as the final component to be considered (1964:13). While there is a certain logical awkwardness about this (something being a component of its own category), there is an important sense in which such a view is justifiable. For it might be said that ritual events have two types of existence: (1) as a set of performance rules in the minds of those whose job it is to guide their enactment (or, in a broader sense, as a "model" of such performances shared in general by members of the culture) and (2) as definitions ascribed in retrospect to properly enacted performances. By making this distinction, we can understand that a ritual event (as a set of rules) preexists (and, in a sense, serves as a component of) an actual performance. Failing to make this distinction, we lose sight of the constitutive nature of events and end by assuming a positivist viewpoint. Empirically, such a view would be contravened in at least two ways: (1) Ritual events can themselves be generated, seemingly out of nowhere, by the emergence of particular message forms with their associated behavior (cf. Marks, 1972: passim). An example of this is provided by cases in which a spirit medium, in the course of her daily (mundane) affairs, may suddenly go into possession-trance, a state most definitively marked by the emergence of prophetic speech style in her utterances (cf. Fitzgerald, 1970). From the moment of her switch into this message form, a ritual event is generated: People in the immediate area assume participant roles, and an entire set of rules for social and verbal interaction are called into play. (2) In a somewhat similar way, a given ritual event, once under way and existing, temporarily at least, as a "defined situation," may be transformed into a different ritual event (or aborted entirely) through changes in the communicative modes employed. Of course, some events are, by nature, inherently volatile, while others are neatly planned in advance and have scripts that all participants know and plan to act out.

Before passing to the next section, two general points should be made about the components just discussed. First, it should be quite clear that very few of the specific communicative modes inventoried here are limited in their occurrence to ritual events. Thus, for example, proverbs (a message form) and body gesture (a channel) are, of course, used outside the context of ritual. Perhaps somewhat less obvious is the fact that communication directed to spiritual entities may occur outside the context of ritual events as I have defined them. This may happen, for instance, when a person entering a room in which there is a god's shrine extends greetings to the god as well as to the humans present there: a very common, at times expected, gesture.

Performance

This section is devoted entirely to the analysis of a single ritual performance.

CASE #82: *Naabu Daimɔ* (SUNDAY, OCTOBER 31, 1971)

Introduction. The rite chosen for analysis is of a specific type called *naabu daimɔ* (literally, "mouth cleansing"). In providing background information for our analysis, I will present the broad framework wherein the performance of this rite emerges as one point in a sequence of related events.

Synopsis. A young Ga woman, past full term of pregnancy, is worried about her failure to commence labor and deliver her child. A decision is made to visit a spirit medium and, through her, consult the family god about the matter. In the ensuing seance it is revealed that people have spoken evil against the young woman and that this has resulted in her being bound by invisible ties that prevent her child's birth.[4] In order to free her from this state, the god indicates that the rite of *naabu daimɔ* should be performed. A date is set for this, and instructions are given as to what articles should be brought for its performance. At the appointed time the young woman, accompanied by her father, returns to the medium's house and the rite is performed. A few days later the woman gives birth to a healthy child. Some time after this she returns to the medium's house and performs a small *ŋkpai bɔmɔ* rite, expressing thanks to the medium's god for his assistance.

---

[4] The state in which the woman finds herself is usually brought about in one of two ways: (1) She has been properly cursed (*loomɔ*) and had a "sensible" god choose to respect the curse and do evil to her, or (2) bad things have been said against her and the spoken words have triggered some less sensible "powers" into action. In either case the rite of *loomɔ daimɔ* (curse cleansing) would be performed to untie her; in the second, the rite of *naabu daimɔ* (mouth cleansing) would be performed. Of the second it is said *naabu emɔ lɛ* 'mouth grabbed her'.

According to the relevant folk actors, the trouble-free delivery of the child was made possible by the prior performance of the *naabu daimɔ* rite.

The task. Perhaps the central question posed by this case is (1) In what way, if at all, is it justifiable to view this ritual performance as the efficient cause of the woman's successful childbirth? For the student of language and ritual, two further questions are posed: (2a) How, and to what extent, is language used in constructing the ritual performance? (2b) Can anything about the way in which language is used in the event suggest an answer to question (1)? In the following analysis an attempt will be made to answer these questions. More explicitly, I will attempt to show that this ritual event is a highly structured communicative performance, guided to completion by specialists with an ability to manipulate symbolic systems so as to make them have a real effect in the treatment of pathology. In one sense at least, the analysis presented here may be taken as support for assertions made by Claude Levi-Strauss (1967) regarding the "effectiveness of symbols."

Analysis. In the following pages the ritual performance will be viewed as emerging from a "normal" interactional setting. The entire span of this interaction may be represented as follows:

$$[NC \cdot RE \cdot NC_2]$$

Here, the brackets stand, respectively, for the arrival of the clients at the medium's room and their departure from it. NC and NC_2 stand for the "normal conversation" that precedes and follows the ritual event, RE. The major segments of this interaction will be discussed separately.

INITIAL INTERACTION ($[NC$)

Early in the evening the pregnant woman, Dee, and her father, Nii Kwei, arrive at the medium's room. As they enter the room there are already three people present: the performing medium, Nsia, another medium, Ansa, and myself.

Two important features mark the initial interaction that takes place as the clients enter the room: (1) the visitors are offered seats, and (2) an extended form of greeting is used, which employs a welcoming device known as *amaniɛ bɔ* 'news telling'. These two features mark the occasion as a "proper visit," distinguishing it from greetings exchanged in "passing by." In themselves, they specify nothing pertaining to a ritual event. In the *amaniɛ bɔ*, indirect reference is made by both parties (visitors and visited) to the purpose of the call, but there is no actual discussion of the ritual they are about to perform.

The greetings over, Nsia (who serves throughout as the person ultimately in charge of guiding the interaction) checks to see if the proper articles have been brought. Satisfied with this, she instructs Ansa as to the manner in which Dee is to be prepared for the ritual. Essentially, this involves the removal of the pregnant woman's clothing and the tying of black and white thread and raffia strings around the major joints of her body. Over approximately the next 10 min, this process is carried out in the middle of the room.

Verbal interaction during this period consists of two kinds of exchanges: (1) instructions from Nsia to Ansa (and questions asked by Ansa of Nsia) regarding the manner in which Dee is to be prepared for the rite and (2) informal conversation among Nsia, Nii Kwei, and myself, mostly concerning family affairs (Nsia is a maternal relative of Nii Kwei), with some discussion of the hardships caused by the Accra municipal tax. There are periods of silence in the conversation, and it is clear that we are all waiting for the preparations to be completed. At one point Nsia calls her grand-daughter into the room and instructs her to go next door and buy a small bottle of gin. The girl returns in a few minutes with the bottle, then leaves the room.

For a number of reasons, we would not want to consider the interaction taking place during this period as itself part of the ritual performance. It is, rather, a particular kind of "backstage" preparation for such a performance. While the tying of threads and raffia is governed by ritually specific rules, the act of tying them is not ritually marked in any way. The threads indicate the state of "tiedness" in which the woman exists and has existed for some time; they are a concrete metaphor representing a spiritual reality. Tying them on her body transforms nothing.

That this segment of the interaction does not partake of the ritual event is clearly indicated by the nature of the verbal interaction that takes place during it. For throughout this period focused communication passes primarily through voice channel, is entirely in Ga, and employs only unmarked speech style. Further, verbal exchanges are dyadic, discursive, and passed only among the human participants in the room. The brief questions and comments passed between the two mediums regarding the preparation of the pregnant woman are entirely matter-of-fact. Nsia could conceivably have performed the preparation without Ansa's assistance, in which case there would have been no reference made to the tying process.

When Ansa has completed tying the threads, Nsia checks to make

sure it has been done properly, then asks Ansa if she has the blade
handy for cutting the threads. A coconut shell cup (*potowa*) of gin is
then poured for Nsia by Nii Kwei. This section of the interaction ends
with the following exchange between Nsia and Ansa:

NSIA: *Where's the blade?*

ANSA: *It's with me.*

NSIA: *It's with you?*

ANSA: *Yes*

NSIA: *Well, ahhh* . . .

Holding the *potowa* in her hand, Nsia then begins the recitation of a
libation-prayer. At particular points in the prayer, she pours drops of gin
from the cup onto the floor as an offering to the gods she is invoking.
With this prayer the ritual event opens.

RITUAL EVENT (*RE*)

Introduction. In beginning our analysis of the ritual event itself, we enter
a realm where, if justice is to be done to its rich meaning, complex
analytic and notational devices are needed. To the best of my knowledge, however, such devices are not now available. Under the circumstances, I will have to proceed in the manner of Levi-Strauss' *bricoleur*
(1966:16–36), building from available oddments a contraption for which
there are no blueprints.

One of the major points, and one of the major problems, of my analysis is that ritual performance displays a highly elaborate structure, involving all levels and means of message production. This includes what
might be called metarhythmic and metatonal (hence, musical) structures
that serve to reinforce structures developed in other ways. A major
handicap in my presentation is that I have yet to develop a notational
system that could adequately represent the "musical" structure of the
performance. In the following analysis I will simply assert its existence,
indicating in very general ways the means of its production.

In the analysis, constituent segments of the ritual will be represented
in algebraic notation. By using this notational device I do not mean to
deny the essentially analogical nature of the performance at a phenome-
nological level. However, while it would not be accurate to claim that
the performance is actually constructed by stringing together neatly
discrete units, neither would it be wise to ignore its analytically dis-
coverable structure.

The major sequential elements apprehendable in the ritual event may be represented as follows.

$$RE$$
$$[P\text{-}I + S + N]$$

Here, the brackets stand for libation-prayers that begin and end the performance. *P–I* stands for prayer-incantations, *S* for song, and *N* for narrative.

Libation-prayer ([). The libation-prayer (hereafter called simply "libation") that opens the ritual event may be viewed as (1) a single point in a developing process, as in the diagram, (2) itself a process with a particular "surface structure" composed mainly of phonological, tonological, and rhythmic elements, or (3) a complex message, developed over time, with a particular semantic content.

Viewing the entire prayer as a single point in a process, we might speak of it as a *context marker* (Bateson, 1968a), setting off what follows it as being, in some significant way, different from what precedes it. We would then be interested to know *how* the libation achieves its status as a context marker. An answer to this question can best be arrived at by careful study of its surface shape, its semantic content, and (in the interrelationship between these two) what might be called its meta-semantic content. As will be seen, careful analysis of the libation can provide a preliminary means for understanding the ritual event as a whole.

Here the libation, as a simple context marker, may be made to produce a more complex structure:

$$[$$
$$(p + n + i_0)$$

where (stands for the highly formulaic opening of the libation (line 1 in the following transcription), *p* for proverb (line 2), *n* for narrative (lines 3–14), i_0 for incantation (lines 15–17), and) for the formulaic closing of the libation (line 18).

Opening line (( ). The opening line of the libation (see transcription and translation) must now, itself, be considered a context marker. The most significant features that distinguish this line from the speech immediately preceding it (see page 216, 217) are as follows: (1) prosodic utterances, (2) loudness of speech, (3) rapidity of delivery, (4) emergence of over-all rhythmic and tonal pattern, and (5) multiple senders.

In order to stress the extent to which the libation's opening line marks a shift in the nature of the interaction, I may here refer to a number of the analytic components introduced earlier. While this might be thought inappropriate (in that they were meant to be used in the study of speech events and not isolated utterances), their analytic utility is required to make my point. In later discussion the adequacy of these components for the study of ritual communication will be more critically considered.

Code: The first line of the libation is marked by a switch from Ga to a cult language, in which the descriptive nicknames used in addressing the gods display a combination of Fanti and Ga word forms.

Message form: Taken together, the five features noted earlier (pro-sodic utterances, etc.) may be said to mark a switch in message form.

Topic: The gods (here considered the topic, or referent, of the utter-ance) addressed in the opening line have in no way been men-tioned in the previous interaction.

Participants: By addressing the gods, a new set of "receivers" are introduced to the scene.

Setting: With this line, it may be said that the setting of the interac-tion changes from "backstage" preparation for the ritual to its "front-stage" performance.

Proverb (p). The second line of the prayer contains a proverb translated as "A forest doesn't help you and you call it evil." The proverb refers to the relationship between the people and the gods[5] and, in a sense, defines the entire ritual scene now unfolding. As message from people to gods, its meaning in this context may be summed up as "Acknowledge the gift by reciprocating" or, more explicitly, "We are acknowledging your existence and your power by giving you a gift; acknowledge our gift by helping us make this woman well."

Narrative (n). Lines 3–14 contain what I have called a narrative, in which relevant background information is provided on the three major figures involved in the performance: Nsia, Nii Kwei, and Dee. While

---

[5] In a ritual context, *koo* 'forest' is often an allusion to the gods. As I understand it, the proverb stated here indicates a reciprocal relationship between people and gods. In the present context I have isolated it as a message from people to gods.

Libation Text (GA)*

1a. *ahhhh eeee Aplese* [---],† *eeee Blase* [---], *Akrɔmɔbii* [---]
 b.   *Nii Oʃraa*

2a. *naa. wɔ kɛɛ kɛʃi, amɔtɔnɛɛ, kooko helee boɛ eee, ni otʃɛ lɛ kooʃa.*
 b.   *yao*

3. *Nowɔɔ, oʃaa yeemɛi, kɛ obii, kɛ ohɔi, kɛ mi* [xxx]‡

4. *nuubi dzi mi, Okai bi dzi mi.*

5. *ni Amatʃoo bi dzi Nii Kwei.*

6a. *tʃutʃuɛ akɛɛ 'otʃɛsɛɛ gbɛ dzi gbɛ,'*
 b.   *yao*

7a. *ʃi ŋmɛnɛ ŋmɛnɛ onyɛ sɛɛ gbɛ hu, lɛŋ gbɛɛ eko ka dzei.* [xxx]
 b.   *nakai*

8. *agbɛnɛɛ, beni aba ni abaa fee nɛkɛ nii nɛɛ,*

9. *ebi yoo, ni dzi Dee, lɛ hu aba na noko ʃioo yɛ ehe ni aba fee.*

10. *gbɛkɛ kɛɛ 'eee, loo ni dzeɔ saa mlamla adzɛɔ a yeɔ.'*

11. *nowɔɔ, lɛŋ ehiɛ eklalaa kɛ eʃika, ʃɛlɛŋ edzwɛ,*

12. *atʃɔɔ lɛ tʃɔ, gbɛkɛ bibioo dzi lɛ;*

13a. *kɛ elɔŋ, kɛ eblɔfɔ kpaa diŋ, kɛ eblɔfɔ kpaa yɛŋ,*
 b.   *enyɔ*

14a. *ni eba ni eba flɔ naabui eeee.*
 b.   *nakai*

15a. *naabu ni yeɔ ʃitɔ ni yeɔ ŋoo.*
 b.   *yao, yao, yao*
 c.   *naabu ni yeo ʃitɔ ni yeɔ ŋoo*

16a.   *abonsai anaa, akpasoi anaa. ŋmɛmɛ wɔ baa flɔ ʃɛɛ*
 b.   *ayei anaabui*
 c. *ayɛi anaa, abonsai anaa*

17a. *ni wɔ ʃa naabui fɛɛ naabui yɛ Tʃɔkɔ.*
 b.   *yao*
 c.   *ayɛi anaa, abonsai anaa,*

18a. *nowɔɔ, naa odaa ni eba ha bo. tʃwaa, manye aba.*
 b.   *yao*
 c. *akpasoi anaa.*

 * a = Nsai's speech.
   b = NiiKwei's speech.
   c = Ansa's speech.
 † [---] = portion of utterance untranscribable.
 ‡ [xxx] = portion of utterance deleted.

1a. *ahhh eeee Aplese* [---], *eeee Blase* [---], *Akromobii* [---]
 b.   *Nii Osraa*

2a. Behold. We say "A forest doesn't help you! and you call it an evil forest."
 b.   amen

3. So, your in-laws, and your children and your unborn children, and me [xxx]

4. I am a man's child; I am Okai's child.

5. and Nii Kwei is Amatsoo's child.

6a. Formerly, it was said "Look to your paternal side"
 b.   amen

7a. but these days your maternal side is open as well.   [xxx]
 b.   right on

8. Finally, when they came to do this thing,

9. his daughter, called Dee, she too was found to have some small trouble which should be taken care of

10. The child says, "Rotten meat is eaten swiftly!"

11. So, she has brought her white cloth and her money, four shillings —

12. she wasn't charged much for she is a small child —

13a. and her raffia, and her black thread, and her white thread,
 b.   *two*

14a. and she has come to cut the mouths!
 b.   right on

15a. mouth that eats pepper and salt
 b.   amen, amen, amen
 c.   mouth that eats pepper and salt

16a.
 b.   witches' mouths
 c.   witches' mouth, devils' mouth

17a. and burn all the mouthes at Tsɔkɔ†
 b.   amen
 c.   witches' mouth, devils' mouth

18a. So, take the drink that she has brought you. Hail, let blessings come
 b.   amen
 c.   witches' mouth

---

* *ayɛi* and *akpasoi* are synonymous; both mean "witches' " *Akpasoi* is Fanti, I believe.
† Tʃɔkɔ is the name of the village where Dee lives.

careful analysis of the form and content of the entire narrative would reveal much of interest, such an endeavor would take us beyond the limits of this study. For this reason, two rather lengthy portions of the narrative (dealing with Nsia's relationship to her god and with Nii Kwei's recent misfortunes) have been deleted (end of lines 3 and 7). I have, however, deleted nothing from the portion of the narrative that concerns Dee.

In lines 8 and 9 Dee is introduced to the gods: They are told who she is (Nii Kwei's daughter) and why she has come ("found to have some small trouble"). In line 10 a proverb is stated, translated as "Rotten meat is eaten swiftly." It refers to the pain (rotten meat) associated with childbirth and to the hope that it might be minimized (eaten swiftly). In lines 11 and 13 Nsia itemizes the materials that Dee has brought for use in the ritual. In line 12 the gods are assured that the pregnant woman has not been charged too much.[6] Line 14 states what will be done in the ritual: Mouths will be cut. The reference is to the evil spoken against Dee, which has bound her.

Incantation (i_0). With line 15 a different type of utterance is begun. While the content of the speech follows directly from the preceding line, the style of delivery changes quite dramatically and we have the emergence of an incantation. The content of line 15 specifies which kind of "mouth" is meant. Such a specification is, in a sense, necessary because the *Ga* word *naabu* (and especially its contracted form, *naa*) is extremely polysemous. Stylistically, not only does the line receive marked support from Nii Kwei (who adds three "amens"), but it is repeated by the other medium, Ansa. Here we see an increased level of participation in the speech act, the growth of a feature that was noted in the first line.

In the three parts of line 16, a further elaboration of this can be seen. Here Ansa, now taking the lead, says the first segment of the incantation (*ayɛi anaa*), while Nsia is silent. The second segment (*abonsai anaa*) is said in unison. The third segment (*akpasoi anaa*) is said only by Nsia, while Ansa is silent. Nii Kwei, however, says his part simultaneously, but out of phase with theirs. Further, instead of using the short form (*ayɛi anaa*), he uses the long form (*ayɛi anaabui*). At the end of line 16a and on into line 17a, Nsia is no longer saying the incantation but has picked up where she left off at line 14, repeating that the mouths will be cut and adding that they will be burned. Ansa, however, continues in

---

[6] Among the *Ga* it is widely known that if a ritual specialist overcharges for services rendered, his or her curing powers will be rendered ineffective.

lines 17c and 18c with the incantation and overlaps with Nsia's last line (18a).

Closing lines ( )). The libation is ended in a formulaic manner (18a). Nsia tells her god to take the drink that Dee is giving him, then says the phrase that marks the end of all libations: "Hail, let blessings come." To which Nii Kwei adds an "amen."

Performance rules. My purpose in this section is to indicate that *all* of the major performance principles to be utilized in the remainder of the event are displayed (albeit in embryonic form) in the opening libation.

Redundancy in coding. This principle, whose broader meaning is discussed in Bateson (1969), is used at this point in the ritual in at least three quite separate ways: (1) The boundary-creating function of the libation is redundantly coded by switching five salient features of speech style. (2) The fact that "divine" cooperation is being solicited is redundantly coded by calling the names of a long list of gods at the opening of the libation. (3) The message of the incantation is redundantly coded by having three people participate simultaneously, all saying essentially the same thing.

Indexicality of expression. This principle, extensively discussed by Garfinkel (1967), is most clearly exemplified in the use of proverbs (lines 2 and 10), which sum up complex situations in highly condensed form. Moreover, in varying degrees throughout the libation (see especially lines 6 and 7), language is used in a metaphorical manner to parsimoniously convey a great deal of information.

Multiple message senders. In the first and second lines of the libation, we see Nii Kwei's immediate participation in the speech act, first by adding to Nsia's list of gods (*Nii Osraa*), then by adding a supportive exclamation (*yao*). In lines 15–18 we see the further elaboration of this device. Viewing the libation as a whole, it may be said that three individuals, playing their respective parts, produce an essentially unitary message.

Interdependence of words and actions. This principle may be exemplified in the present context by recalling that, as the libation is recited, Nsia pours small amounts of gin onto the floor. As with almost all ritual enactments in Ga culture, a proper libation necessitates bringing together the appropriate words and actions. For it can be understood that pouring gin onto the floor is, in itself, an action open to many interpretations.[7] Here, the words that accompany the pouring of gin explicitly define the act, making of it an offering given to particular gods for a specified purpose.

Anticipation. Taken out of context, the incantation phrases that occur in the last lines of the libation might seem anomalous, for there is no ritual action associated with their use. Embedded in the libation prayer, they simply anticipate what is to come. In one sense at least, their appearance here may be seen as a "tuning up" for the central part of the ritual.

Reversing fields. Characteristics of this principle, as it operates in the visual domain, are discussed by Attneave (1971), who calls it "multistability in perception." In the present context this principle is brought into operation on the level of message production and hinted at on a semantic level. In message production it is most clearly in evidence in line 16, where a "crossover" occurs: A single person begins an incantation phrase, then is overlapped by another who then completes it alone. Semantically, its use is hinted at in the juxtaposition that occurs between lines 13 and 14. Nsia first refers to the threads and raffia strings that Dee has brought for the ritual performance, then refers to the purpose of the ritual as cutting not threads but "mouths."

Prayer-incantation (P-I). What I have called a "prayer-incantation" follows the opening libation. As will be seen, this is the most complex speech act of the ritual, and it is within and through this act that the most significant event of the ritual is made to occur. For analytic purposes, the constituent segments of this act have been factored out as follows:

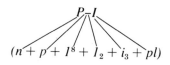

$$(n + p + 1^8 + 1_2 + i_3 + pl)$$

Here the parentheses stand for the opening and closing of the entire speech act, n for narrative, p for proverb, i for incantation, and pl for plea.

Invocation (( ). As with the libation just analyzed, the prayer-incantation opens with an invocation. There are, however, two significant differences: (1) Ansa, rather than Nsia, takes the lead part, and (2) whereas in her libation Nsia addressed the gods associated with her shrine (her

---

[7] Aside from accidental spillage, one might, for instance, pour gin onto the floor as a silent offering to one's own soul (*susuma*).

family's gods, for whom she is the medium), Ansa calls upon the paternal ancestors at large (literally, "grandfathers and fathers") and three major gods of Accra. The style of speech is, however, similar to that used by Nsia in her libation, though somewhat less rapid.

Narrative (n). From the opening invocation, Ansa moves to what I have called simply a narrative, the essential message of which is summed up in the first lines:

GA	ENGLISH
gbekɛbii dzi wɔ, kɛ wɔ naa fufɔ saa.	We are children, with our mother's milk still on our mouths.
nɔni wɔ hiɛ mii nɛ, dzee wɔ gbɛ ni.	What we are working on is not our work,
ʃi nyɛ nɔŋ, nyɛ kɛ wo wɔ de.	but you (gods) have yourselves put it in our hands.
ni, ni nyɛ kɛ wo wɔ deiɛ, wɔ hiɛ mii.	And, since you have put it in our hands, we are working on it.
wɔ ŋmɛɛ he, wɔ ŋmɛɛ he.	We will not abandon it. We will not abandon it.

Her mode of delivery here is extremely rapid, and the utterance as a whole displays a highly formulaic tonal and rhythmic pattern, usually associated with much shorter message forms such as proverbs. Its structural complexity is enhanced by the manner of Nsia's and Nii Kwei's participation: Both, at different points, interject phrases that variously chorus, coincide with, or anticipate the lead speaker's lines. Ansa ends the "narrative" by embedding an excerpt from the incantation that will be used in the next portion of the ritual:

GA	ENGLISH
biantɔnɛ, wɔ nfo lɛ ye kpaa mii.	Now we are cutting her free from the ties.
aʃiʃɔmɔ, eʃite.	May her squatting be her standing up.
	If at night, let it be at night.
kɛ nyɔŋ, nyɔŋ.	If in the afternoon, let it be in the afternoon.
kɛ leebi, leebi.	If in the morning, let it be in the morning.

Proverb (p). This segment of her recitation completed, Ansa states a proverb: *kɔyɔɔ tʃwa ni wɔ ywieɔ*; literally, "The wind blows and we speak." In this context, I believe the proverb should be understood as follows: "In this ritual, we are about to do something with our words; but our speaking them is not sufficient in itself. We rely upon the help of the gods[8] to make our words effective." Use of this proverb here once again makes explicit the need for cooperation between people and gods.

Incantations (i[8]). The ritual actors now move to the central part of the performance: the recitation of incantations accompanied by cutting the seven sets of threads and raffia from Dee's body. Eight variants of a semantically unitary incantation are spoken: Two incantation phrases are used with the first cutting and one each with the successive cuttings. While it would be interesting to analyze the pattern that develops in the variations, we must here content ourselves with transcribing a single incantation exchange. I have chosen as an example the least complex of the eight variants (the third phrase used in cutting the second set of threads), for it may be viewed as a paradigm of the others.

GA	*ENGLISH*
ANSA: *Dee Akoʃia*	ANSA: *Dee Akosia*[9]
DEE: *yee*	DEE: yes
ANSA: *wɔ nflɔ kpaa mii eeee*	ANSA: We are cutting the ties away!
DEE: *ndze mii*	DEE: I am free.
ANSA: *ayɛi anaa,* *dzɛmawɔdzi anaa,* *nɔ ʃɛɛ nɔ anaa,* *wɔ nflɔ blublu.* *oʃisɔmɔ, oʃite.*	ANSA: Witches' mouth, gods' mouth, everything's mouth. We are cutting thoroughly. May your squatting be your standing up.
NII KWEI AND NSIA: *yao*	NII KWEI AND NSIA: amen

As the incantation exchanges are repeated, Nsia's participation mounts to the point that her "background" interjections come to assume a "foreground" saliency. Her most significant interjections may be noted

---

[8] *kɔyɔɔ* 'wind' is a common metaphor for the gods.

[9] Akoʃia is a 'day name' given to Sunday-born females.

as follows: (1) As Ansa is cutting the third set of threads and simultaneously incanting her part (as shown), Nsia loudly interjects: *edze mii, edze mii, edze mii omo*. 'She is free; she is free; she is free already'; (2) on the fourth round of cutting, she again comes in loudly, taking up the chant, *ayɛi anaa, abonsai anaa, naabu gbonyo* 'witch's mouth, devil's mouth, rotten mouth', first anticipating, then overlapping out of phase with Ansa's part; (3) on the sixth round of cutting, she enters at the very end of the incantation phrase, using a type of utterance unique in the entire performance: She here curses (*loomɔ*) those who have brought misfortune on Dee, summoning this misfortune to fall back on their own heads. In this she is joined, belatedly, by Ansa.

Further incantations (i_2). The cutting completed, the threads and raffia are gathered, placed in an earthen pot (*kukwei*), and burned. As they burn Nsia says the following:

GA	ENGLISH
eeee Kwesi Atʃeampɔŋ, o naabilɛ wɔ	eeee Kwesi Atseampon, we are cutting your
nflɔ lɛ yɛ kpaa mii, wɔ wɔ nʃa.	grandchild from the ties and we are burning.
abonsai anaa, ayɛi anaa,	Devil's mouth!! We are burning all, we are burning.
wɔ nʃa eeee, wɔ nʃa, wɔ nʃa fɛɛɛɛ.	We are burning!! We are burning, we are burning all!!!

Harmonizing, Ansa joins her in this. Then, as the threads smolder to extinction in the pot, Ansa goes on in a brief monolog to praise the powers of the god, Kwesi Atseampon. During this, Nsia interjects five "amens."

Further incantations (i_3). Gin is mixed with the ashes of the burned threads, and from it a paste is prepared in the pot. Ansa smears the paste over Dee's protruding stomach in a direction from top to bottom, three times. While doing this she and Nsia chant, out of unison, *eʃisɔmɔ, eʃite* 'May her squatting be her standing up'. Ansa then begins a more elaborate utterance, which I have translated as follows:

> She (Dee) is not among those who say this (ritual) isn't pretty.[10] . . . Whether it is a good thing or not a good thing, we are working on it. For the ancestors (grandfathers and grandmothers) have put it in our hands, so we are working on it. What we came and saw, and what they told us, this is what we know.

[10] Meaning that Dee is not one of the many self-righteous Christians who, publicly at least, disparage traditional religious practices.

Nsia picks this up, repeating parts of it out of unison with Ansa. Nii Kwei also joins in as follows: "Those who say this is foolishness, it is their own problem. And it is their own mouths that say it as well."

Plea (pl). The last of the incantations over, Dee takes the pot with its remaining ash paste and places it at a particular spot on Nsia's shrine. Standing in front of the shrine she prays aloud as follows:

GA	ENGLISH
ntʃɛ miŋkpa ofai	My father I am begging you.
ntʃɛ miŋkpa ofai	My father I am begging you.
ntʃɛ miŋkpa ofai	My father I am begging you.
nʃisomo nʃite	Let my squatting be my standing up.
nɔni fɛɛ nɔni ntaoɔ	Everything I wish help me to
oha ma naa.	have.

As Dee prays Ansa adds supportive remarks from the background, also addressed to the gods. I have translated these remarks as follows:

> There are those who do not respect gods, but my "brother" seated here (Nii Kwei), whatever is being done he is there to help. Everything he wants should be given to him. And Dee, she is not an arrogant person. Whatever is told her, she is not arrogant about it. So, since she is not arrogant, take care of this matter for them. So that people will say "Atʃɛampɔŋ is great." It will be pretty. So take care of this matter and her mother's illness as well. You gods take care of this. So that people will say that this Fanti god is not a pleasant one, but is truly bitter.

Nii Kwei participates by adding "amens" and occasionally chorusing one of Ansa's phrases.

Closing lines ( )). Having waited for Ansa to complete her extensive interjections, Dee ends her prayer, and this entire portion of the ritual. Her last words are *n kɛ ha bo. n kɛ ha bo. n kɛ ha bo.* 'I am giving it to you. I am giving it to you. I am giving it to you.' The immediate referent here is the pot of ash paste that Dee has placed on the shrine; more broadly, it indicates her turning the case over to the gods for their judgment.

Nonritual speech. Thus far, at particular places throughout the performance Nsia has interjected instructions to the other participants, telling them what should be said and done to allow the ritual to proceed properly. For ease of presentation, I have avoided mentioning this type of speech until this point. Instances of its appearance are as follows: (1) Immediately after Nsia completes the libation that opens the perform-ance, Ansa asks, "Well, should I begin the cutting?" Nsia responds, "Yes, you will call her name . . .," then turns to Dee and asks her "day name." When it is learned that her day name is Akoʃia, there is com-ment on what a nice coincidence that is, for "today is also Sunday." (2) When Ansa has completed the opening part of the prayer-incantation, Nsia instructs Dee as to her lines in the incantation exchange. (3) Imme-diately after the last set of threads has been cut, Ansa asks Nsia, "Do you have the matches?" (4) In the midst of her incantation over the burning threads, Nsia directs Ansa, "Bring the knife over here." (5) As Ansa begins the incantation that accompanies her smearing the ash paste on Dee's stomach, Nsia interjects instructions on how the paste should be applied. (6) After the paste has been applied, Nsia tells Dee how to place the pot of ash paste at the shrine.

The speech employed in these instructions (and questions), devoid as it is of stylistic markings and metaphorical referents, provides a dramatic contrast with the ritual speech that surrounds it. Through this contrast we can see that changes from "frontstage" to "backstage" behavior (in other contexts dependent on shifts in spatial or temporal setting) are here controlled entirely by features of speech style. These backstage in-terjections, all of which come from Nsia (or are directed to her), are nec-essary because the other participants do not know the details of the "script" for this particular ritual.

The preceding statements notwithstanding, we must here note that by the end of the prayer-incantation the boundary that has been maintained between ritual and nonritual speech is collapsed. For, after instructing Dee (in unmarked speech style) how to place the pot at the shrine, Nsia recites for her the prayer that she is to say while doing so. While her in-tention here might be said to be purely instructive, the style of speech used is governed by the inherently ritual nature of the utterance. Taken out of context, it would be difficult to distinguish her "instructions" from their "performance." Again, just as Dee is about to begin her own reci-tation Nsia interjects further "instructions," which, in that they are highly marked and ambiguously addressed, become in some sense part of the prayer. Her interjection here is as follows:

GA	ENGLISH
o nyɛ hu, ehe ye.	Your mother too is ill.
ena wala eeee, ena wala	Let her live!!! Let her live!
ʃi kɛ enaa wala, ni ewa!!	For, if she doesn't live it will be extremely difficult!!

nowɔɔ, kɛ fɛɛɛ,	So take all these matters and
kɛ onɔ fɛɛɛ ha lɛ!!!	give them to the god!!!

The significance of this merging of ritual and nonritual speech will be discussed.

Song (S). The central part of the ritual completed, Nsia breaks into a short song in *Fanti.* While I do not understand all the words, it is recognizable as a praise song addressed to her god, Kwesi Atʃɛampɔŋ. She adds a joking comment about the song's paradoxical nature, which Ansa elaborates upon, saying "All of us, song is our elder. If it is said in song, it needn't be said again."

Narrative (N). As Dee stands in the corner of the room putting her clothing back on, Nsia narrates a story. She addresses it to Nii Kwei ("Your nephew stopped by briefly this afternoon . . ."), but speaks loudly for all to hear. Nsia's story recounts the manner in which her god successfully diagnosed and treated a recent case. She describes the case in some detail and ends by complaining that, although the treatment was successful, the man had not returned to perform the rite of thanksgiving (*ŋkpai bɔmɔ*) as he should have.

Closing libation (]). Her story completed, Nsia passes the coconut shell cup to Nii Kwei, saying, "Say[11] a libation so that what we have come to do can be completed."

Nii Kwei's libation is brief, his words spoken softly. He invites the gods to come and partake of his offering, then asks that all in the room may be blessed and the illness cured. Nsia adds the final "amen."

POSTRITUAL INTERACTION (*NC₂]*)

Just as there was no discussion of the ritual prior to its performance, there is none after its completion. However, whereas the preritual interaction was rather stiff and punctuated by periods of silence, there is now an abundance of conversation and much joking. My participation in the conversation is encouraged as Nsia recounts in detail a humorous incident that occurred during our recent visit to an inland village. In a joking manner Nsia informs me that my *gbeʃi* (soul's companion) had then caused me to commit a social misadventure. Ansa and Nii Kwei join in, laughing at Nsia's way of scolding me. Nsia then calls her granddaughter into the room and asks her to help find a missing cloth. In a

---

[11] Could be translated "Say/pour . . ." or "Libate [vt] . . . ."

marked departure from her usual stern treatment of the child, Nsia jokingly compliments the girl when the cloth is found.

Nii Kwei mentions that it is getting late, brief farewells are said, and he and Dee leave for home.

DISCUSSION

Thus far, I have been concerned primarily with displaying the structure of the ritual as it can be seen to emerge through its enactment. While my presentation has necessitated use of an analytic framework, an attempt has been made to minimize interpretative discussion and, to the greatest extent possible, allow the ritual actors to speak for themselves. I believe the data presented do, themselves, provide a sufficient answer to one of the central questions posed at the outset: How, and to what extent, is language used in constructing the ritual performance? For, as should be clear by now, every major enactment in the ritual is achieved through and defined by the use of language. Were it necessary here to select a single example in support of this contention, I might quote Nsia's final instruction to Nii Kwei: "Say a libation so that what we have come to do can be completed."

Before taking up the more difficult question of the efficacy of the ritual performance in achieving its intended purpose, two preliminary matters must be considered: (1) the theoretical disposition that underlies my analysis and (2) my attitude toward the methodological devices used in organizing the presentation of data. My purpose in this is to clarify a stance that has to this point been largely implicit.

Theoretical perspective. My analysis of ritual phenomena is guided by a theoretical perspective wherein "reality" is understood to be socially constructed (cf. Berger & Luckman, 1967). Simply stated, this view necessitates accepting the "objective" truth of "subjective" beliefs.

When applied to the study of human pathology, this orientation leads one to suspect that illness is largely a matter of "subjective" perception. If this is so, we could suppose that much illness could be cured by changing the perception of the afflicted. This assumption, in fact, underlies the basic contention of this portion of my analysis.

Methodological devices. For our purposes to this point, the component grid developed by Hymes for the study of speech events has proved a useful methodological device, allowing a more detailed analysis of performance *structures* than might otherwise have been possible. However, since we are now seeking a fuller understanding of the existential *content* or meaning of the event, our frame of reference is considerably altered. As discussion develops within this altered context, we will come to see that the component grid, at least in its present form, is ultimately inadequate for the study of ritual communication. Nonetheless, in the following pages I will continue to use the terms associated with this grid as a means for organizing the presentation. Here I will concentrate almost entirely on the incantation exchanges that compose the central portion of the ritual.

Channels. On first view it might be said that the only channel employed for conveying messages in the incantations is the human voice. In the absence of *manifest* musical features (i.e., singing), use of the human voice as channel would usually be understood to mean simply the "spoken word" as opposed, for example, to the "written word." However, because of the particular manner in which the human voice is used in the ritual context, where orchestrated participation of four speakers, as well as rhythmic and tonal patternings, appear, an essentially musical structure is created. If we accept the proposition that musical structures, almost by definition, convey some message, we may see that use of the human voice here provides two essentially separate channels for conducting messages. Further, we must understand that the physical objects (threads, knife, ashes, gin) manipulated during this part of the ritual are also made to serve as message conductors.

Codes. At the most obvious level of analysis, it might be said that the Ga language is *the* code through which messages are conveyed. As with our analysis of channels, however, we must look beyond this immediate level and understand that (1) the consistently metaphorical use of the spoken language transforms its nature as code, creating what is essentially a "cult language," and (2) the musical features mapped onto the utterance create a separate code in which a message is conveyed. Finally, the set of physical objects employed in the ritual also provide a code. That is to say, by the particular way in which the various objects are employed in the ritual, meanings are conveyed to the participants.

Message form. Since the boundaries of the complex "prayer-incantation" are clearly marked in its performance, it must be accepted as an essentially unitary speech act. When we come to discuss the features of message form that mark this act, its complexity presents some difficulty. Some degree of organization may be provided, however, by making use of the performance principles isolated earlier.

In the present context, we may simplify our discussion of these principles by (1) subsuming the first three principles (redundancy in coding, indexicality of expression, and multiple message senders) under the fourth (interdependence of words and actions); (2) setting aside the fifth (anticipation) for treatment in a later section, and (3) speaking in only a limited way of the sixth (reversing fields). Again, we will limit our discussion largely to the incantations embedded in the larger speech act.

Interdependence of words and actions. The message form employed in the incantations is distinguished by the simultaneous use of both the spoken word and the actions performed on concrete symbols. Manipulation of both words and physical objects is used together to send what should be seen as the single, underlying message: "You are free from the spiritual ties that bind you." Viewing message production as created in this way, we see a fuller use of the principle of redundancy in coding. For not only are the incantation phrases repeated and spoken by different speakers (as we saw in the opening libation), but two quite distinct channels and codes are used to carry the message. In a somewhat similar way, we now have a more extreme use of the principle of indexicality of expression: Not only are words used in a highly metaphorical or indexical manner, but a number of simple objects, and the actions performed on them, are made to represent complex entities and processes. Further, we may now understand the principle of multiple message senders to have a broader applicability, in that messages are sent both through multiple speaking roles (all four of the ritual actors do, in fact, have spoken roles to perform in this portion of the event) and through the manipulation of physical symbols.

Reversing fields. In the present context, this principle is used to produce at least one important feature of message form. This can be seen in the particular way different speakers' roles are patterned. At the outset of the incantations, Ansa has the lead role and is the only person speaking. During the development of this portion of the ritual, we have noted that Nsia, originally in a supporting role in which she merely choruses Ansa's speech, emerges for a time as a lead speaker, at which point Ansa provides the supporting role. Then, at the end of the incantations, both Ansa and Nsia take supporting roles as Dee becomes the lead speaker. Overall, this produces a reversal of foreground and background roles.

That this principle is also used in developments at the tonal and rhythmic level of speech will, as noted earlier, simply be asserted here. Its proper proof would require the development and use of analytical devices not yet within my competence.

Topic. When we come to discuss the topic of the incantations, we are confronted with a major problem, one that has in fact been with us from the very beginning of our analysis. For the utility of the concept of topic assumes a context in which language is used referentially. While the words and other symbols used in this portion of the ritual do (almost by definition) have referents, it should be clear by now that their use is not *referential,* but *performative.*[12]

Our task is, thus, transformed: We must now seek to answer questions not of what is referred to in the incantations but of what is performed through their enactment. To simplify an otherwise complex argument, I will here claim that what is performed in this portion of the ritual is a transformation of the pregnant woman's perception of her condition and, ultimately, that condition itself. In achieving this transformation, use is made by the ritual specialists of the principle of reversing fields, whereby the act of cutting cloth strings (*kpaa*) is consistently identified as the act of cutting the spiritual ties (*kpaa*). In a very real sense we thus have the reversal (or, perhaps more appropriately, the fusion) of metaphor and reality, wherein the cloth strings (as metaphor) *become* the spiritual ties (as reality). While it may be said that the ability of the ritual to achieve this transformation is dependent on the ritual recipient's culturally determined (preexisting) religious beliefs, there is a very real sense in which, through the particular way communicative forms are continually manipulated, such beliefs are imposed upon her in the course of the performance itself.

Participants. In the previous analysis I have ascribed participant roles in accordance with manifest markings given separate speech acts. Were we to continue in this way in discussing the incantations, a major complexity would arise, for embedded in a speech act manifestly addressed to gods there are dyadic exchanges between two ritual actors, establishing a rather disjunctive pattern of sender/receiver relationships. This complexity dissolves, however, when, from our present point of view, we see that the afflicted woman, Dee, is in fact the "intended" receiver not only of the incantations (which, if they are manifestly addressed to anyone, are addressed to her) but of all "ritual communication" in the performance. This would include her own "performative," "I am free," which—taken together with Nsia's interjection, "She is free. She is free. She is free already."—could be viewed as the most important single utterance of the entire ritual.

---

[12] What might not be clear is why I have waited so long to introduce the idea of "performative utterance." My reasons are as follows: Simultaneous use of a component grid *and* a speech function grid is analytically extremely awkward, since the two grids operate in a cross-cutting manner that frustrates systematic description and discussion. Further, questions of speech function inevitably require dealing with the motives that intend the utterance (deep structure), whereas I have to this point wanted to deal only with manifest features of speech (surface structure). Finally, I have not wanted to enter the theoretical stew over the term's proper application.

Setting. Viewing the ritual performance as constructed in such a way as to have a real effect on the afflicted woman, the specifics of its temporal and spatial setting at large take on a significance that they would not otherwise have. We have noted that the rite is performed on a Sunday and that Sunday is Dee's "birth day." In *Ga* culture, the day of the week on which one is born has a particular relevance, for it is associated with one's soul. As noted in note 5, the state of affliction in which the pregnant woman exists involves her soul's being tied. That the ritual aimed at untying Dee's soul should take place on her "soul's day" necessarily takes on significance for her. This is in fact played upon in the incantation exchanges, in which she is addressed by her day name.[13] Further, in terms of spatial setting, the particular shrine at which the ritual is enacted is one that "belongs" to Dee's family.[14] In the incantations her relationship to the gods at the shrine is repeatedly emphasized, and she is made to feel that "the gods are on her side."

Event. Here we may expand our frame of reference and seek to provide an overview of the event as a whole. The major point I wish to make here is that some of the more specific "reversals" that have been seen to take place at structural and semantic levels within the incantations are paralleled by larger-scale shifts that occur throughout the course of the entire event. And, further, these shifts create an experiential environment wherein a transformation of the ritual recipient's perception of her condition can be more fully achieved. Some of the more outstanding of these may be itemized as follows:

1. In the opening libation Nsia has the lead role; the final "amen" is added by Nii Kwei. In the closing libation Nii Kwei has the lead role; the final "amen" is spoken by Nsia.
2. In the prayer-incantation (a unitary, though complex, speech act), Ansa says the opening line of the prayer, Dee the closing line.
3. The highly marked distinction between ritual and nonritual speech seen in the first parts of the performance have entirely collapsed by its end. This is most clearly realized in the contrast between Nsia's speech style at the opening of the event and Nii Kwei's in the libation that closes it.

---

[13] Among the *Ga,* one's day name is often only used in an intimate context such as private ritual. It is considered private information by many *Ga,* for day names are used by sorcerers against their victims.

[14] While *Ga* society is generally patrifocal, kinship reckoning must be viewed as bilateral. Eticly, Dee is Nsia's father's half-sister's son's daughter; emicly, she is Nsia's daughter and Nsia's shrine "belongs" to her.

4. Through Nsia's curse, the evils that have tied Dee are "thrown" back upon those who inflicted them.

5. Through Dee's last line of the prayer-incantation ("I am giving it to you . . . [repeated three times]," the troubles that she brought to the event are given over to the god.

All of these points can, I believe, be seen as further realizations of what I have in this context called the principle of "reversing fields." The realization of this principle in performance is achieved through use of another (perhaps "subordinate") principle, which I have called "anticipation." In the foregoing we have made explicit reference to this principle only once, when it was used to explain the appearance of incantation phrases in the opening libation. Looking back over the data presented earlier, we may now see that much of the embedding that occurs (including utterances made by speakers in "supporting" roles) may be viewed as generated by this performance principle. Thus, for example, we see that Nsia's praise song to her god is anticipated by a number of brief interjections that Ansa makes to the same effect as the threads are burned.

The principle of anticipation, when combined in performance with the principle of multiple message senders, creates a scene of apparent disorder. However, once the underlying performance principles have been properly understood, the ritual performance may be viewed as what it is: an island of structure in an otherwise rather disorderly social world.

Conclusion

The analysis presented here of a single ritual performance should be understood as a somewhat tentative handling of extremely rich and rather complex data. While there are clearly other, and hopefully less cumbersome, ways in which to isolate the performance principles at work in the construction of events such as this, there has emerged, for the author, a quite fundamental conviction which is not likely to be altered by stylistic reworkings: It is necessary in dealing with rituals of this type (1) to take seriously claims made by participants as to their efficacy and (2) to see these events as aimed (intended) by their directors at the achievement of actual curative functions. While doing so entails asking a more extensive range of questions than is conventionally undertaken, it is only in this way that the intricate structure of the events can be fully perceived.

References

Attneave, Fred
  1971 Multistability in perception, *Scientific American* **225,** 6, 62–71.
Bascom, William
  1969 *Ifa divination.* Bloomington: Indiana Univ. Press.
Bateson, Gregory
  1968a *The logical categories of learning and communication and the acquisition of world view.* Wenner-Gren Symposium on world views: Their nature and role in culture.
  1968b (and Jurgen Ruesch) *Communication: The social matrix of psychiatry.* New York: Norton.
  1969 Redundancy and coding. In *Animal communication,* edited by T. Sebeok, Bloomington: Indiana Univ. Press.
Berger, Peter L. and Thomas Luckmann
  1967 *The social construction of reality.* New York: Anchor Books.
Crystal, David
  1972 Non-segmental phonology and sociolinguistic distinctiveness: The importance of religious language. Paper given at Georgetown Roundtable Session on Language and Religion, 1972.
Durkheim, Emile
  1969 *The elementary forms of the religious life.* New York: The Free Press.
Fabian, Johannes
  1971 Genres in an emerging tradition: An anthropological approach to religious communication. Paper given at American Anthropological Association Convention, New York City, Nov. 1971.
Field, Margaret
  1937 *Religion and medicine of the Ga People.* London: Oxford Press.
  1940 *The social organization of the Ga People.* London: Crown Agents
Fitzgerald, Dale
  1970 Prophetic speech in Ga spirit mediumship. Working paper no. 30. Univ. of California, Berkeley, Language-Behavior Research Laboratory.
Garfinkel, Harold
  1967 *Studies in ethnomethodology.* Englewood Cliffs, New Jersey: Prentice-Hall.
Goffman, Erving
  1967 *Interaction ritual.* New York: Anchor Books.
Goodman, Felicitas
  1969 Phonetic analysis of glossolalia in four cultural settings. *Journal for the Scientific Study of Religion* **8,** 227–239.
Greenberg, Joseph
  1963 *The languages of Africa.* Bloomington, Indiana.
Horton, Robin
  1967 African traditional thought and Western science. *Africa,* **37,** no. 2.
Hymes, Dell
  1964 Introduction: Toward ethnographies of communication. *American Anthropologist,* special publication **66,** 3, part 2.
Kilson, Marion
  1967a Urban tribesmen. Ph. D. dissertation, Harvard Univ.
  1967b Continuity and change in the Ga residential system, *Ghana Journal of Sociology* **3,** 81–97.

1967c Variations in Ga culture in Central Accra, *Ghana Journal of Sociology* **3**, 33–54.
1968a Possession in Ga ritual, *Transcultural Psychiatric Research* **5**, 67–69.
1968b The Ga naming rite, *Anthropos* **63**, 904–920.
1969 Libation in Ga ritual, *Journal of Religion in Africa* **2**, 161–168.
1971 *Kpele Lala*. Cambridge, Massachusetts: Harvard Univ. Press.

Levi-Strauss, Claude
1966 *The savage mind*. Chicago: The Univ. of Chicago Press.
1967 The effectiveness of symbols. In *Structural anthropology*. New York: Anchor Books.

Malinowski, Bronislaw
1935 Coral gardens and their magic, vol. 2. New York: American Book Co.

Marks, Morton
1972 Performance rules and ritual structures in Afro-American music. Draft of Ph. D. dissertation.

Samarin, William
1969 Glossolalia as learned behavior, *Canadian Journal of Theology* **15**, 60–64.
1971 The language of religion (manuscript).
1972 *Tongues of men and angels*. New York: Macmillan.

Sankoff, Gillian
1972 Cognitive variability and New Guinea social organization, *American Anthropologist* (to appear).

Tambiah, S. J.
1968 The magical power of words, *Man* **3**, 175–208.
1970 *Buddhism and the spirit cults in north-east Thailand*. Cambridge: Cambridge Univ. Press.

Zaretsky, Irving
1969 The message is the medium: An ethno-semantic study of the language of spiritualist churches. Ph. D. dissertation, Univ. of California, Berkeley.

"Tongue Play": Constitutive and Interpretive Properties of Sexual Joking Encounters among the Koya of South India[1]

JAN BRUKMAN

Introduction

In *Speech Acts* (1969), John Searle gave the first full-length, developed analysis of the Austinian concept of the speech act (Austin, 1962). Searle divided Austin's notion into three parts: (1) uttering words (morphemes, sentences), i.e., performing *utterance* acts; (2) referring and predicating—i.e., performing *propositional* acts; and (3) stating, questioning, commanding, apologizing, welcoming, etc.—i.e., performing illocutionary acts (1969:24). The distinction clearly seems to be between linguistic form (utterance act) and content or meaning (propositional and illocutionary acts). Searle's object was to characterize how it comes about that certain speech acts of the illocutionary sort have the semantic structure they do, and he chose the particular speech act of "promising" for analysis. In this study I want to follow Searle's line of reasoning and discuss the category of speaking, or illocutionary speech act, that the Koya call *NaalumaaTa* 'tongue play' or *Paraaskam* 'joking.' In particular, I hope to show what constitutes the activity the Koya identify as joking and, beyond this, to lay out the beginnings of an analytic framework for characterizing the manner in which ongoing verbal as well as nonverbal interactions are understood by participants in social encounters.

One of the points I will want to bring forward is that what will be construed as orderly and appropriate in the context of the ritual of joking is contingent on the particular historical and personal biographical circumstances within which the joking takes place. This situatedness of

[1] I would like to thank the editors of this volume for their helpful and patient comments and criticisms. The research support on which this paper is based was supplied by the Committee on Sociolinguistics of the Social Science Research Council, and I gratefully acknowledge their help.

joking will be seen to have certain properties that transcend the particular and, thus, to have more than merely idiosyncratic interest. In addition, I want to show that acts that appear disorderly on one level can be seen to be orderly at another; thus, the notion of competing underlying orders is introduced, illustrating that, perhaps even to native actors, order is difficult to see, given differing individual and group bases for action. This latter is true even in the small face-to-face community in South India in which I lived.

The community itself is a village of about 150 people, consisting primarily of members of a tribal people who call themselves Koya. The Koya number about 200,000 and live in the states of Madhya and Andhra Pradesh along the banks of the Godaavari River in southeast India. For some cultural and political purposes, they are treated by the central government independently from the caste Hindu system and are thereby given certain rights and privileges denied to caste Hindus. In the areas in which they live, however, they are integrated into the caste system for ritual and interactional purposes. For these purposes, they are generally accorded the status of castes that are low in the idealized ritual hierarchy, and the roles they perform in relation to the larger Hindu society are coordinate with this ascribed status.

The languages spoken by the Koya are related Dravidian ones, and in the village from which the following report comes, male speakers of the dominant regional literary language of Telugu far outnumber female speakers. Both men and women speak Koya, a Gondi-related language whose historical and, most important, cultural affiliations are quite distinct from Telugu.[2] Further remarks that frame the cultural background of the Koya appear in the body of the study as part of the theoretical apparatus of the work itself.

Some Background Remarks

Elsewhere (Brukman, 1972), I have analyzed a religious ritual annually performed by the Koya in the hamlet of Raaticeruwu 'stone tank.' In this analysis the essential question asked was why the ritual had the character it appeared to have on the occasion I saw it performed. Put another way, what was the genesis of the behavior displayed in the context of the ceremony?

---

[2] Gondi is the generic name for a group of closely related dialects spoken in south and east central India. It is one of the many nonliterary languages that continue to be used by sizable populations in India.

I want now to take the ritual of *Naalumaata* and ask the same questions of it. There is no doubt that it is of equal importance to Koya life as that of *Waana Boojanam* 'rain festival.' Yet joking is not extraordinary in the way that the rain ceremony is; joking is a ritual of everyday life, and like that life — and unlike *Waana Boojanam* — the properties that constitute it cannot be said to have boundaries. There are no beginnings, middles, and ends as such, and people do not normally assemble explicitly to do joking.

Nonetheless, *Naalumaata,* like *Waana Boojanam,* has the necessary properties one ascribes to all ritual — it regularly recurs (people do it all the time), and it is, of course, ceremonial. That is, both the form and the content of the ritual are conventional, having properties that define the category of behavior called *Paraaskam* 'joking' and that distinguish it from other categories. What is striking about joking in general is that, rather than personal intentions interpenetrating the normative structure and action of the ritual (as in the case of the large-scale and "formal" ritual of *Waana Boojanam*), they *are* the content of the ritual, expressed in conventional, symbolic form.

Joking and Joking Relationships

Radcliffe-Brown, in two classic studies on the topic of joking relationships (Radcliffe-Brown, 1952), has outlined in the broadest of terms what may be called the sociocultural parameters of "joking" behavior. His main point is that, for a variety of reasons specific to particular cultures, structural relations exist between groups that are manifested in particular kinds of verbal behavior, either between individuals who are members of different structural groups or between people who differ on some other dimension than group membership but who nonetheless embody sets of roles that place them distinctly apart. Furthermore, these role relationships are not random; there appear to be certain dyads in which ritual joking relationships are never realized anywhere in the world — for example, the father–son pair.

Generally speaking, Radcliffe-Brown follows the systemic view of the functions that joking behavior fulfills in society. That is, joking occurs at a tension point in the social structure of a society, and it serves — as do many other kinds of social behavior in Radcliffe-Brown's functional outlook — to maintain an equilibrium between the *conjunctive* and *disjunctive* components of intrasocial relationships (1952:95). According to him, the conjunctive component of the joking relationship is almost always associated with "friendship relations"; at least, it is never associated with "solidarity," "[which is] established by kinship or by membership of a group such as a lineage or clan [1952:112]." On the other hand, in any "alliance" or "friendship" relation there is potential antagonism (its source is not spelled out), which is the disjunctive component.

In many respects, precisely what it is that Radcliffe-Brown is arguing is unclear, but the main points he makes appear to be the following: (1) solidarity relationships are antagonistic to joking relationships; (2) relationships between adjacent generations are antagonistic to joking relations (if no other factors are operating), while relationships between alternate generations are conducive to joking relationships; (3) friendship relationships are conducive to joking relationships; (4) friendship relationships are of many kinds, and one of the most important is the marriage alliance; (5) the marriage alliance can take varying forms, one of which is realized in the joking relationship between MB–ZS, and another of which is realized in the joking relationship between cross-cousins.

In summary, Radcliffe-Brown's most important contribution was to show that there are *social* relationships of two types, solidarity and friendship, and that the *interpersonal* relationships that are realized within these structures are of very different sorts. In a more recent attempt to try to account for joking behavior, Douglas opposes her analysis (1968), cast in the symbolist mode of recent British anthropology, to that of Radcliffe-Brown. She underscores the arbitrariness of social structure to illustrate her thesis that the joke acts to control the individual's cognition of social reality by introducing novel ways of perceiving reality. The joke or joking behavior can act to symbolize death and rebirth, pollution and purification, the general state of the world and/or the universe in man's perception. The joking behavior operates within what Douglas calls "an undifferentiated field of friendship and acquaintance." In this field "roles are ambiguous, lacking hierarchy, disorganized . . ."; ". . . laughter and jokes, since they attack classification and hierarchy, are obviously apt symbols for expressing community in this sense of unhierarchical, undifferentiated social relations . . . [1968:370]." It is readily apparent that the undifferentiated field, the absence of hierarchy, the lack of organization are all characteristics of Radcliffe-Brown's friendship relations.

Douglas' analysis elaborates dimensions of joking behavior that function within Radcliffe-Brown's framework but go far beyond it. However, while such structural considerations may form the ground against which interpersonal ritual is carried out, they do not by themselves determine the course or quality of the interaction in interpersonal encounters. What

I hope to make clear is that, for the Koya, everyday social intercourse is not intelligible in these terms, and the realities each individual must deal with have a very different character indeed than the "desiccated perspective" that Douglas attributes to Radcliffe-Brown.

I would suggest that it is, in any case, misleading to maintain a distinction between, on the one hand, an "institutionalized" form of joking and, on the other, "all other kinds of joking." This is because we must accept the fact that wherever men live together the play element can penetrate every form of social interaction, and can reduce even the most formally prescribed and serious encounter among individuals to play, to the nonserious, and even, therefore, to the inherently humorous. Any social relationship has the potential to become ludicrous, and one might suggest that the serious nature of certain kinds of ritual encounters is maintained just because the potential of any encounter's becoming ludicrous must be guarded against, lest the denial of serious reality come to the fore.

The Koya, no more nor less than other social groups, display the ludic side of human behavior in the ongoing nature of social interaction. If we consider joking behavior as one aspect of the ludic or play element in culture, how might we characterize its role in the total social life of the Koya? Put another way, how must social relations be perceived by native actors for joking (and laughter) to be accepted as appropriate in some contexts, and further, how shall we characterize "acceptable" and "appropriate" as properly describing real behavior in actual encounters?

Waana Boojanam and NaalumaaTa

I indicated earlier that it is fruitful to distinguish two contexts of ritual encounters among the Koya. *Waana Boojanam* represents a kind of large-scale ritual within which actors, for the time being, play roles that are highly visible and extraordinary. Both what is done — such as talking to the village gods through the medium of a goat, painting the body in unusual ways, the public sharing of food, and the fact that the activities themselves rarely occur — serve to bring into consciousness the extraordinary framework of the event for the Koya, regardless of the other activities that take place over the span of the ceremony.

In contrast, there is a small-scale ritual, in which individuals play themselves, not "headman" or "member of the Kunja lineage." The joking ritual is one in which the "real self" is not, even ideologically as in the *Waana Boojanam Pandum,* hidden behind the "social self." Beyond this, *NaalumaaTa* or *Paraaskam* is part of everyday life, a frequent activity for a large segment of the hamlet population.

What I hope to demonstrate is that these rituals are tied together not only by their formal properties but also by the individuals who bring them off. In whatever ritual context individuals find themselves, the definition of the situation in terms of the rules that, from one standpoint, may be said to apply abstractly will be crucially affected by such fundamental aspects of social relationships as kinship ties and shared background information. These necessary components endure over the life of all such episodic events like joking encounters. They are the interpretive properties that operate in every situation of face-to-face interaction, however that interaction is constituted. That is, it is the realization of individual plans and purposes that constitutes the reality of the rituals and provides much of their meaning. The continuity of individual biographies obviously exists independently of ritual performance, and in face-to-face communities such as that of the Koya hamlet of Raaticeruwu it has consequences quite different from those in Western culture. In the minds of the hamlet residents I am concerned with here, what links the particular occurrence of the *Waana Boojanam Pandum* and the following analysis of *NaalumaaTa* is precisely this unavoidably shared storehouse of biographical knowledge.

The Data of the Joking Encounter

The following is an attempt to analyze in detail part of a tape recording made of what I have glossed "joking behavior." The total recording is 44 min long from the time the first utterance is heard to the time the recorder was finally turned off. It was made by a group of my closest informants at my request; I was not present during the time of the recording. It represents, although it is admittedly not "natural," the native view of what is entailed in joking behavior. The situation is defined by them and by the presence of the tape recorder. To that degree, it is open-ended and unstructured. Thus, whatever structure there is to this particular slice of verbal interaction is supplied by the actors as the session proceeds, and the primary purpose of this analysis is to recover and account for that structure.

In addition to the tape, which is entirely in the language of the Koya, I have a transcript of the tape made immediately after the session with the aid of the informants who participated in it, and a parallel translation of the tape into Telugu, the superimposed language of the surrounding caste Hindu society. The latter was also done with the aid of these informants at the time the transcript itself was made.

I have available to me, therefore, three kinds of data that, by one criterion or another, characterize the "reality" of the joking behavior of the

Koya. First, I have the tape, a real-time stream of verbal interaction to which I can return again and again, in so doing perhaps sampling the verbal stream at a particular moment on a practically endless number of occasions. Second, I have a "transcript" of the verbal stream. This does not fit a strict definition of a transcript; the closest description of it that I am able to give is that it is an *interpretation* of the occasion recorded. The interpretation is given by the native participants in the recorded occasion and is based, at least partially, on memory of the occasion. Although the task I had set was for my informants to repeat exactly what was said on the tape, this was manifestly not done. Some of the conversation was not transcribed, and some was transcribed incorrectly. We are aware in general that in transcript making, exact replication is never achieved, because we can only approximate the "real" verbal data when we translate it into some other form — in this case, writing. For some kinds of verbal materials, we suppose our transcripts to be approximations that are, as they stand, sufficient for the purposes at hand.

There is, third, the Telugu translation of the Koya transcript. Just as the Koya transcript does not literally render the content of the verbal material, so the Telugu translation is incomplete. Much of the Koya went untranslated, and some of the translation is not faithful to the Koya text. In sum, the process of transcription and translation of the tape is a strictly Koya procedure, apparently unaffected by Western notions of literal translation and accuracy.

Joking as Interaction: Processes and Settings

We know that talk has consequences for both talkers and hearers. These consequences have many of the properties of *convergence* that Sacks has proposed (Sacks, 1967) for members of a particular culture who are attempting appropriately to characterize talk by other, fellow, members. Sacks was concerned with showing that convergence operates to produce labels used by participants interacting in some scene on some occasion to know what and who they are talking about.

In the interchange analyzed here the participants continually monitor their own and each other's behavior, determining, as the occasion progresses, *who* they are for the purpose of engaging in the encounter, and *what* is being talked about, by the consequences of the talk itself. The complexity of the talk lies in the continually progressing definition of the situation at each moment of the occasion. What that definition is and how it comes about is the task for analysis, since the participants in the talking do not say in so many words what the occasion is about, except initially in the *stage-setting episode*.

I use *stage-setting* here, and other dramaturgical terms in what follows, after Goffman (1959, 1963), because the joking encounter has, of necessity, many of the qualities attributable to drama and play-acting. Considering the task I set for the participants, and the way in which the performance progressed, this characterization is especially apt. It does not, however, make the encounter *false,* as I shall try to show. Indeed, in "natural" settings the roles that individuals take and the ways in which they are played have, again as constitutive properties, dramatic qualities that stand alongside and independent of everyday life. There are serious and nonserious roles, and each has its well-defined script. The interpenetration of these two types of roles is one of the properties of this encounter that I want to examine. Thus, I have divided the following account into *episodes,* partly for convenience and partly because they are in fact independently identifiable on the tape. Some of the slices of verbal interaction herein described are naturally bounded because those who made the tape stopped and started the tape recorder wherever they chose. The external boundaries of the tape are, of course, its beginning and end; the internal boundaries are part of the supplied structure of the total encounter.

In the stage-setting episode it is difficult to say whether the talk about joking is unusual; clearly, one of the informants tells everyone directly that "what is wanted is joking" (*paraaskam*). We might call this a meta-stage-setting episode. It is highly unlikely that any such consciously formulated (i.e., overtly expressed) statement of the form of this particular kind of talk had ever been made before in all of Koya society. This is quite different from querying one's informants about a particular kind of behavior, verbal or otherwise. Here, in what is essentially a task I had set for the residents of Raaticeruwu, the whole form and content of a repertoire previously "unrationalized" is brought into the awareness of the participants in the interchange.

The encounter is primarily between two young men and three young women; the recording was done by a third young man, who is the classificatory brother of one of the other men participating in the encounter. My initial suggestion was simply that the men find some girls and do some joking. Although many other requests of this sort had, for a variety of reasons, proved difficult to carry out, this task was taken up with relish and, I can note in retrospect, with a complete understanding of what I wanted.

The kind of joking recorded here rarely occurs in the context of a *focused* encounter (Goffman, 1963). There is, in fact, only one independently constituted social encounter in which such joking takes place as an accepted and expected subroutine of the larger social encounter; this is in the marriage ritual. At all other times, sexual joking is literally a catch-as-catch-can affair, occurring in the interstices of daily activities, such as at chance meetings going to and from the village well, fields, or forest. Every such casual encounter is a small ritual, with prescribed sorts of stereotypes that serve to set the boundaries and the rules of the joking game. Within the rules, however, every player has the chance to use whatever creative resources he has in order to bring laughter, mock disgust, shame and anger, and/or incredulity from the other player or players. Although sexual joking does take place between same-sex players (about each other's sisters or mothers, for example), cross-sex joking has a special piquancy and, moreover, has potentially very real consequences if the players choose at any time to back up their words with actions.

STAGE SETTING

The joking episode takes place among young men and women who have grown up together in Raaticeruwu. At the time of day this recording was made (in the early afternoon), the women had just returned from *kuuli* labor — transplanting rice — in the fields of a local Kapu cultivator. During the early part of August, at the height of the rainy season, virtually the entire village is engaged in some agricultural activity. *Kuuli* labor is a major source of income for the residents of Raaticeruwu, and women especially hire out their labor at rice-transplanting time. The young women's work had been completed by the heat of midday, and when the men approached them about doing *Paraaskam* they were either doing household chores — pounding millet, washing clothes, and so on — or relaxing in the compounds of their houses.

For all of the young men involved, the girls who took part in the *Paraaskam* ritual were women with whom they considered it appropriate to engage in generally ribald repartee and to make repeated sexual advances no matter how many times they were rebuffed. In addition, these women were frequent topics of discussion among the men themselves, each man detailing his progress and setbacks, the geography of his encounter with one or another girl, what had taken place, and so on. As a leisure time topic of conversation, discussion of women ranked high on the list of popularity. While taking part in these discussions, I was struck by the similarities to like discussions among their counterparts in the United States.

The tape begins with an episode I call stage setting. This was done by two of the participants, one peripheral and one central to the action. The peripheral young man, Soyyem Malluru, is slightly older than the rest of

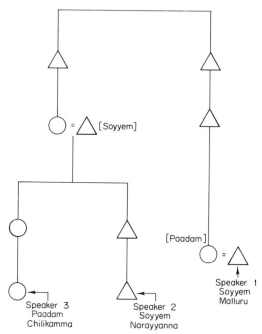

Figure 1. *Kinship relationships among the first three speakers on the joking tape.*

the participants, and stands in the relationship of mother's brother to the first young woman, Paadam Chilikamma. This young man and the first two of the major participants are related in the manner indicated in Figure 1. The diagram also shows that the first two *major* participants stand in a preferred marriage relationship, i.e., MBS/FZD (Mother's, Brother's, Son, Father's, Sister's, Daughter). The older man stands in an approved marriage relationship to the third speaker, i.e., MB/ZD (Mother's, Brother/Sister's, Daughter). Such a relationship is not determinable strictly from the genealogical specifications shown here, but is also dependent on the series of marriage relationships that obtain between Speaker 1 and Speaker 3. In particular, in this case the reciprocal terms used by the two speakers to refer to and address each other are determined solely by the sib of Speaker 3's father. Since the sib of Speaker 3's father is not that of Speaker 1, Speaker 3 uses a cross-relative term of the appropriate generation to address and refer to her. Note, also, that Speaker 1, though married, begins the encounter with a sexual reference, illustrating the point made earlier that the appropriateness of the sexual references in joking behavior does not depend on the marital status of the speaker — at least in certain contexts.

The older man not only helps set the stage for the following encounters, he sets the tone as well. Unfortunately, I do not have a record of the "stage directions" given by the tape technician (the director, if you will), but it is clear that Speaker 1 took seriously the suggestions of the director, since his opening statement is clearly a preparatory comment on what is to follow. He makes two statements, one directed at the gathering and the other directed at his "son."

EPISODE 1

(1a) SOYYEM MALLURU:

> *Narayyanna   kinda,   Chilikamma   miida*
> personal name   below, bottom   personal name   above, top
> "Narayyanna will be on the bottom, Chilikamma on the top."

This statement and those that follow in the first episode are Telugu translations provided by my informants; one sees immediately that the Koya are presenting what they feel to be the essence of statements made in the context of the encounter. The Koya equivalents that appear on the tape use personal pronouns, or such locutions as "my son" (K = *maa peykaDi*). The translators have moved to the use of a kind of third-person narrative. Given the context of the encounter, this phrase is not difficult to interpret, and it evokes laughter from the audience, with the exception of Chilikamma, who protests.

(1b) SOYYEM MALLURU:

> *Nii   kinda   paNDu   pilla   payna*
> you   below   fruit   girl   top
> "Your fruit will be underneath and the girl's will be on top."

The phrase is repeated, with the girl on top and the young man on the bottom. Here, the speaker's reference to "fruit" is a metaphor, first for his "son's" genitals and then, when reversed, for the girl's breasts. Such turns of phrase, known as "sweet" (*tiiya*) talk, are highly valued in this kind of verbal play, and a man's reputation as a "sweet" talker is closely related to his (putative) abilities as a seducer of women. Throughout this series of encounters such attempts at "sweet" talk are frequent (if sometimes constrained by the circumstances) and expected components of the structure of the joking talk.

Speaker 2 then immediately takes up the subject of the interchange by addressing Speaker 3.

EPISODE 2

(2a) SOYYEM NARAYANNA:

> *Waytinnaa!?tisaytaanu*
> Will you come (question/imperative; 2nd per. sing.);
> I will take (progressive)
> "Will you come with me? I will take you away."

As a conversational opening this is unclear, and perhaps only marginally appropriate, but it expresses an intent aggressively stated, that if the girl does not come he will take her (somewhere). The statement as translated into English has no particular resonance for an alien hearer (or reader), yet for a Koya it can have a number of intentional ramifications, and for this speaker and his hearer it has an additional importance. The statement reflects clearly for the "knowing" hearer how personal biographies and background information come into play on the occasions of personal interaction. No naive hearer without additional knowledge could rationally account for what the "meanings" of these imperatives might be. Yet they must be accountable, since they elicit a totally appropriate response from Speaker 3.

(2b) PAADAM CHILIKAMMA:

> *Nanna warraanu!   Nimmaanu!*
> I come (neg. imp.)   You go (imp.)
> "I won't come! You go away!"

This is said in the imperative mode by the girl, and sets the tone for the episode, which in fact is terminated shortly thereafter. I am unable to say what precisely precipitated the termination; one interpretation will be given, but first a more general account of the interchange is necessary.

To begin with, it is possible to give a *conventional* account of the interchange (a question and a reply) in Episode 2 set totally against a background of cultural norms. In Koya society marriage is arranged through negotiations between representatives of the lineages of the prospective bride and groom. A man is prohibited from marrying anyone whose phratry membership coincides with his. Given tribal endogamy, all other females within a certain age range are potentially acceptable spouses. Within the group of women who may be acceptable is a much smaller group who are definitely preferred as spouses. These are women who stand in the relation of first cross-cousin to a particular man. It is generally assumed that at the appropriate time the children of brothers and sisters will marry, and over a long period after a brother and sister have married and have established households of their own (from before the birth of children until their maturity, in fact), discussions are carried on between the siblings and their spouses as to the bride price to be paid, the length of the wedding, and other matters of concern to the families and lineages involved.

From the time of their early childhood, children of cross-sex siblings understand that they are to be wed and behave toward each other in specified ways. This behavior includes a certain amount of deference toward and avoidance of each other in the presence of adults (especially their parents), as befits their future relationship as husband and wife. But it also includes a certain amount of overt sexual activity outside the purview of adults. This activity includes sexual joking and bantering as well as clandestine sexual contacts. The latter behavior is sometimes verbally disapproved by adults but more often is indulged by them as being in the natural order of things.

Sometimes, when the time for the agreed-upon marriage comes about, the family of the groom or of the bride (and usually both) is not capable of paying the costs entailed in a marriage. For most Koya families the cost of a marriage is the largest one-time capital outlay they will ever make. This lack of funds occurs most often when the groom's family has insufficient capital goods (land, bullocks, pigs) or labor to sell, and cannot raise sufficient funds by borrowing from relatives or a local non-Koya money lender. In these cases the prospective spouses are encouraged by their parents to elope, thereby alleviating the necessity of an expensive wedding. The young man and woman prearrange a meeting place — perhaps in the forest during the day, or outside the girl's house late at night — and then escape to the village and the house of some "neutral" and usually distant relative, although the house of a married sister is often preferred by the man. The couple stay at this house for a period of a week or a month until the feigned anger of the parents has cooled. They then return to the house of the husband and he pays a small fine to the father of the girl (and to her lineage), whereupon the two are free to set up a household as a married couple.

Because the young man and woman in the recorded verbal interchange were related as preferred marriage partners (FZD/MBS), they were behaving appropriately toward each other. The man, jokingly, has threatened to take the girl away (a possible elopement is implicit in the threat), and the girl has refused his advances and told him to go away. The interchange is, therefore, an accurate and appropriate reflection of a set of Koya cultural norms.

I call the foregoing a straightforward, if somewhat abbreviated, conventional account of a bit of behavior. It relies on a set of cultural norms (the sources for which are implicit) to make intelligible the perceived verbal behavior, and it is not being too unfair to say that this is the kind of description we accept as the normal form of ethnographic discourse. The proximate cultural norms operative in the situation are the following:

1. Cross-cousins are preferred marriage partners.
2. Joking is an expected part of the cross-cousin relationship.
3. If cross-cousins are in an appropriate situation, then they will joke.
4. The topic of the joking under these circumstances will be sexual—covertly as well as overtly—reflecting one of the primary functions of the conjugal union.
5. Marriages are arranged between the parents and lineages of the individuals concerned.
6. If a prearranged marriage cannot be formally held because of the financial burden placed on the parties, then the couple is encouraged to elope.

At least these six norms must be assumed to be operating if the ethnographer is to make intelligible the verbal interchange under consideration here; they are, therefore, assumed to be operating for each pair of individuals for whom this set of norms is relevant. If the relevancy of the norms for participants is taken into account, it is necessary to move beyond a conventional ethnographic description. That description is deficient in at least two ways: It fails to take into account that communication is necessarily a chain of statement—response/statement—response/statement—etc., in which an initial opening establishes a contingent relationship with an alter; and it fails to reckon with the past history (the biographies) of the individuals engaged in some interchange.

In addition to the cultural norms, there are idiosyncratic, yet no less cultural, factors operating that are strictly nonconventional and must also be included in any analysis of the meaning of the interchange. These are nonconventional in the sense that they are *historical* factors, the factors that Goffman has called background information. These data are not hidden; they are there for every knowing individual to note and to use, if he so desires, as a resource for his participation in the interchange.

In what way can these idiosyncratic features be expressed as cultural as well? Let us take the case of Narayyanna, the male speaker involved in this question and response. N is the only child of K and M. He is about 17-years-old and is a member of the Soyyem clan, a representative in Raaticeruwu of a subtribal, quasi-endogamous (i.e., putatively) group called Kammeri, 'blacksmith', in Koya. Of the thirteen Koya clans resident in the village while I lived there, two were Kammeri clans. Within the village, the Kammeris are differentiated from the Baasa Koyas in a number of ways. In ideal circumstances, the Baasa and Kammeri Koyas would occupy distinct residential areas, loosely organized around the heads of the localized lineages of the two groups. Such a pattern is reflected, but not strictly observed, in Raaticeruwu. In addition, commensal relationships between the two groups are basically unstabilized. On ritual occasions where both groups are present, certain kinds of food are not usually shared between them; essentially, this is a way of maintaining interaction distance and group distinction within a common public gathering. In everyday activities outside the eye of public ("normative") scrutiny, however, this pattern does not necessarily hold; food can be shared. Whether it is in fact shared depends on the personal relationship between the specific individuals involved as well as on the circumstances of the immediate occasion. Note that the norm in fact replicates the kind of commensal relations that are supposed to obtain both between the various Hindu castes and between Hindu castes and "untouchables," but that among the Koya, as opposed to the Hindu, commensal relations are not bound by this norm, although, of course, they are carried out against this normative background.

Social relations between the Baasa and Kammeri groups show considerable strain at present. A complex series of events in the recent history of the village have combined to accentuate the strain, which is in any case inherent both in the views each group holds about the other and in the self-definitions of the members of each group. The Kammeris, as their name implies, are considered by the community to be primarily blacksmiths, a service adjunct to the Baasa Koyas, who are conceived to be farmers by the community.

The continued Teluguization of the Koyas, and the subsequent hardening of hierarchical relationships between them and other outside communities, have only exacerbated the division between the two groups. This is because the Telugu influence has brought to individual Koya an increasing awareness of the radically inegalitarian nature of the society that surrounds them, an ideology counter to the aboriginal tribal structure of which they are now only marginally a part. These changes are certainly not new, because they have been going on since tribals have been in continuous contact with the larger Hindu society. Yet in the past five years radical changes in the physical and social environment surrounding the village have highlighted these changes and accelerated them to an extreme degree. One of the effects of the changes is that, of the 20 men who own or have owned land in the village, 12 have had to sell varying amounts of their land. Eight of the 12 have sold *all* their land (never large holdings in any case), and of these 8, half are Kammeri Koyas. There are 12 Kammeri households in the village; only 3 heads of these households now own land. There are 18 Baasa Koya households; of the heads of these households 7, a much larger proportion, own land.

Narayyanna, the young man in the recorded episode under discussion, is the son of a man who has never owned land, in Raaticeruwu or elsewhere. He is a relatively recent migrant to the village and, as such, maintains a marginal role, economically speaking, in Raaticeruwu. N and his father, along with other men who do not own land, as well as younger men who cannot be maintained on the income derived from their fathers, form part of a group that gets its income from varying kinds of *kuuli* labor extending over varying periods. Actually, there are in fact, very few men in the village who have not performed *kuuli* labor at one time or another; all able-bodied women in the village (including those in this encounter, as I have noted) work at *kuuli* labor when it is available. Even without land, N's father is the village's ranking lineage head of the Soyyem clan. This is because he is the eldest representative of the clan resident in Raaticeruwu, as well as because of his personality: He is, by general agreement, the most flamboyant resident of the village; he is not only a good hunter but a great womanizer and drinker as well. His wife, M, is good-natured, gentle, and kind, a perfect foil to her husband and one of the best-liked people in the village. N follows in the footsteps of his father and emulates his life-style.

An understanding of the foregoing cultural factors, which lie behind Narayyanna's implicit offer to elope with Chilikamma, is a necessary prerequisite to an understanding of the cultural *force* of the brief interchange between the two young people. These factors are known to all the participants in the joking encounter; they are the knowledge that the actors can use to interpret the meaning of the interchange. The meaning of the interchange makes concrete these historical, biographical factors. The economic marginality of Narayyanna's father, and consequently Narayyanna himself, makes the meaning of the elopement more than simply normatively appropriate. Narayyanna is a Kammeri without land and without a job—he could not afford a conventional wedding. His marginal economic position, in turn, is partially a product of the fact that the Soyyems are Kammeri Koyas and all that this means in their relations with the Baasa Koyas. Narayyanna is a young man who should be married by all Koya standards, but is not. His life is a perpetual timeout from the concerns of the more "responsible" members of the hamlet. He goes where he pleases and is always in the company of young women. In short, he is the son of his father, and carries the weight of what this means in the way he is living his life.

Thus, by one set of standards Narayyanna is not a good choice for a partner in marriage, and in this public performance it is this set of standards that Chilikamma is acknowledging in her refusal to go with him. The standards apply to real circumstances, and every individual present in the encounter knows in exact detail Narayyanna's circumstances. It is a fact brought to the interaction by everyone that Narayyanna's mother does not want him to marry Chilikamma, the reasons she gives being precisely those applying to Narayyanna as a potential marriage partner — no income, no land, no future, sexual promiscuity. This episode is the delicious situation of two forbidden fruits confronting each other, for posterity, and the ambiguity inherent in the situation is not lost on any of the participants.

EPISODE 3

The *persona* that Narayyanna displayed in this public encounter probably had much to do with the fact that the interchange was quickly terminated. Some or all of the participants felt that what was being produced did not suit the purposes of the gathering — to produce *NaalumaaTa*. Chilikamma's cold reception, her apparent refusal to take part in the ritual caused the tape recorder to be turned off, and when it was turned on again two new participants took their places in the performance.

The fourth speaker is another young woman, Wiike Mangamma, who is unrelated genealogically to any of the male participants. Since she is unrelated to them, she is for them all and equally a potential sex partner — at the very least. She responds to physical bantering from the fifth speaker, Kunja Sahadev, who has taken her hand, in the following manner.

(3a) WIIKE MANGAMMA:

Nii   *akka*   *ley*
(p.p. your)   elder sister   no!

Nii   *akka*
(p.p. your)   elder sister   (idiom)

This is a kind of idiom for the Koya, and incorporates a diffuse and implicative set of meanings whose interpretation is always context-determined for the hearer or hearers. One of its meanings, for example, is parallel to that of "your mother" in American English when it is used as an indicator of disbelief and disdain toward one's interlocutor; as such, it can represent a challenge as well, but usually is so in very special circumstances only. This idiom is a truncated form of *nii (y)akkandenga!*; '(Go and) fuck your elder sister' could qualify as one gloss of it. In this context, a gloss for the idiom might be "Hey! Stop that, dammit!" It is said in extremis as a response to what, for her at the time, is unwanted physical contact. As I shall try to show, this idiom, or variants of it, has additional connotations that are, again, equally situation specific. I label this imperative interjection as an episode because it stands by itself. It is, at least in its overt context, not an invitation to engage in a normal round of conversation. Besides being an insistent request that the young man stop touching her, it is a kind of metacomment that obviously expresses her feelings about the content of the interaction so far.

EPISODE 4

Kunja Sahadev, the fifth speaker, ignoring the girl's feelings, takes up the last line used by Soyyem Narayyanna and adds the inverted form of Narayyanna's first utterance:

(4a) KUNJA SAHADEV:

> *Tiswaytaanu*   *wa* (pause)
> take will I   come (imp. part.)
>
> *tiswaytaanu*   *waytinnaa*
> take will I   come will you?
> "I'll take you! Let's go! Will you come?"

At first glance, there does not appear to be anything of interest — that is to say, "unusual" — in this utterance. Since one speaker used the phrase, perhaps this speaker just retained it for use when it was his turn. The girl replies like the first girl, saying that she will not come and implying that Sahadev should go.

(4b) WIIKE MANGAMMA:

> *Nannu*   *warranannu*
> I   come (neg. particle) I
> "I won't come!"

Regardless of the similarities between the two exchanges, the analyst must make several decisions for this brief interchange that differ from those made with regard to the previous encounter; this is despite the fact that linguistic evidence *from the transcript* contains no information that would make it possible to distinguish the second episode from the fourth. Here, at least, a judgment must be made about the seriousness of the expressed intentions of the girl, given her initial outburst and other aurally communicated, but nonlinguistic, cues such as the laughter on the tape. An alternative is to postpone making any inferences from this question/response and to judge what has occurred here only when the episode has concluded. However, since the participants cannot postpone their reactions, analyzing interchanges of this sort would seem to require that we try as best we can to make the same assessments that the participants must make—that is, as the dialog continues. If we do so, we make intelligible the verbal communication that occurs, hopefully the same way the actual participants do.

It is significant that Soyyem Narayyanna, the first speaker in the joking episode, was not present during the transcription and translation of the tape. Although he was asked to join in making the transcription, he chose not to do so. I can only speculate on what the reasons may have been for his refusal. A possible explanation could have to do with the current status of his personal relations with the women involved. With his joking partner—recall, the *most* appropriate from a formal, structural point of view—relations were at that time strained because of the negative feelings of his parents about the propriety of marriage to that girl. On the other hand, he was at this time carrying on a well-publicized sexual liaison with Wiike Mangamma—Kunja Sahadev's joking partner. It may be that Sahadev was equally sexually involved with the girl, but if he was, it was discreet. I could obtain no information from him or anyone else who would know whether he was in fact having sexual relations with her, even though on numerous occasions he had freely talked about the possibility as well as the strategies he was currently using to lure her into a sexual relationship. The available evidence is that at the time the tape was made he had been unsuccessful.

There remains a possibility that Sahadev (the second speaker) *did* have a sexual liaison with the girl in the *first* encounter on the tape—again, the girl with whom he did not joke. Three weeks after the tape was made, the father of the girl *formally* accused him of impregnating the girl and demanded some form of indemnification, among other things.

I do not think it an accident that the first joking partners of the two men were *not* the girls for whom there is at least circumstantial evidence that they were actively carrying on illicit sexual relationships. And as the nature of the joking encounter changes with the introduction of new partners, so, too, does the character of the joking.

To summarize: The fact that the two interchanges so far discussed do not seem to square with our expectations on strictly structural grounds requires explanation. At the most abstract level of analysis, no rule is being violated—each participant jokes with an individual whom he or she calls cross-cousin (granting that the situation has been so defined that joking is what is occurring). For certain investigations—for example, those of Radcliffe-Brown—this fact alone would be all the information required. However, the ethnographer's task is different. Since he assumes that the interaction is patterned, he seeks some structure in how particular partners are chosen, and looks for ways in which this structure affects the content of the interchanges. For example, one factor that may help explain the rather brief and tense first encounter is the circumstance of the strained personal relations between the parents of the two young people. These circumstances are probably not, to be sure, sufficient in themselves as an explanation of the variance from an anticipated norm, but they do bring us closer to understanding why the interaction appears faulted in some way. The exchange continues between Sahadev and Mangamma.

(4c)   KUNJA SAHADEV:

> *Warreynae*
> come?
> "Will you come?!"

Here the simple present/future question becomes expressed as an imperative question.

(4d)   WIIKE MANGAMMA:

> *nanna   warranannu*
> I   come (neg. particle) I
> "I won't come!"

> *Barey   waadawaa*   *ley*
> why   come must (imp. particle)   not (neg. particle)
> "Why should I have to come with you?"

The girl first repeats her earlier statement, but she then proceeds with her next sentence to produce an opening for the young man. By asking a question, the girl relinquishes the floor to her interlocutor. Since the start of the exchange, no like opportunity has yet been offered to any of the men involved for stating their business. Clearly, the preliminary phase of the episode has now passed and a new one begins.

(4e) KUNJA SAHADEV:

> *Warrey*   *tiseyweltaanu*   *pelli*   *aadanankii*
> come (imp.) take will (fut.) I marriage doing I for
> "Come! I will come and take you and marry you!"

The speaker now has revealed to his audience what he sees the purpose of the encounter to be. He has given an offering of marriage. It is regarded as a joke and is in the open. How can we understand "I will marry you" as a joke? There is, first of all, an obvious fact: that the speaker is already married. But as analysts we must now ask how in Koya society this fact can make the speaker's statement nonserious. Recall that an utterance has the status of a joke if it is nonserious, i.e., not intended as implementable.

Polygyny is not unknown in Koya society. The men I knew all expressed an interest in having more than one wife, and sororatic marriages are especially desired. Yet of the 455 marriages for which I have some information, only 11 are plural marriages (less than 3%). There are no plural marriages in Raaticeruwu, and in fact I was personally acquainted with only one Koya who had more than one wife. Many men who do have more than one wife are relatively wealthy and powerful lineage or village heads. In no case do I know of a plural marriage of a man under forty, and all polygynous marriages appear to be of long duration. A young man today in the area in which I lived has little chance of acquiring a second wife, primarily because of the economic infeasibility of such marriages. Land is scarce, and individual landholdings are becoming smaller and smaller as time passes. I do not suppose, however, that there has been a radical change in the attractiveness of the possibility of polygyny; it is only that the probability of such marriages occurring *today* is approaching zero. The young man engaged in the encounter here is neither wealthy or powerful; he owns three acres of dry land and two acres of wet land. However, he has an 8-year-old son and expresses a wish to have more children. His wife can no longer bear children, and he told me on several occasions that because of this he was considering acquiring a second wife. Under these circumstances, a valid question is whether it is correct to consider Sahadev's offering of marriage entirely a joke, given his earnestly expressed wish for a second wife. To ask this question is to say that it is problematic, not just for the analyst but for the participants as well.

The girl responds to this offer as follows.

(4f) WIIKE MANGAMMA:

> *Ley   baawa   naytini*
> no/not   male cross-cousin   being pleasing,
>   being sweet,
>   wooing, you (sing.)
> "No, baawa, you're just sweet-talking me."

At this point the "offer" is in the open, and the term of reference/address appropriate to a sexual joking relationship—*baawa*—is used for the first time. Her response is "No," but we may interpret this "no" as a qualified rejection of the offer. Whether or not we, as analysts, take the offer of the young man seriously, the girl apparently does not. At least, she has seemingly suspended judgment about the seriousness of the offer by giving him an opportunity to show her that in fact he is not just "wooing, being pleasing, or being sweet." The young man takes up the option presented him by the girl:

(4g) KUNJA SAHADEV:

> *Nijaamaa   ottadaa   aasaalu*
> true/truth hugging, pressing really, in fact
>
> *worrinaa   kella*
> go you (sing.)   speak (imp.)
> "I'm telling the truth! I'll hug and squeeze you! Come on!
> Go with me. Speak up!"

He says not once but twice that he has been speaking the truth, that the two of them really will go. He implores her to speak, after giving a rather oblique hint about what would be done if they *did* go.

(4h) WIIKE MANGAMMA:

> *Nanna (w) orraa*
> I   come/go (neg. imp.)
> "I won't come!"

Mangamma refuses the offer, so Sahadev, apparently undaunted, takes another line.

(4i) KUNJA SAHADEV:

uccuDu   pooga   iimu
a little bit   tobacco   give (imp.)
"Give me a little tobacco!"

This is a significant utterance in the context of the encounter because it is Koya not only in formal structure but in idiom as well. Earlier, I tried to indicate the ways in which the Koya are a marginal people. They are marginally tribal both geographically and culturally. However, if we seek to define the ways in which we might characterize the Koya as tribal, as having a way of life that is cognitively distinct from the life styles of the castes that surround them, we might find no better way than through the language of the Koya. I do not mean particularly the grammatical structure of the language but, rather, the distinctive ways language is used. Here, it is the reference to tobacco by the young man that is significant. Tobacco is a metaphor for sexual intercourse and has other, more diffuse implications in Koya culture as well. As far as I can determine, none of the neighboring Hindu castes with whom the Koya share cultural similarities use tobacco as a metaphor in this way. The continuity of Koya culture over time and space is, thus, marked in increasingly subtle ways. The unknowing or uncaring observer who is a member of a Hindu caste community living in contact with the Koya tends to lump them socially and culturally with the lowest "unclean" castes of Hindu society. But the young man asking for tobacco here indicates clearly to the young girl that he is speaking to her as a member of his group and, thus, distinguishing the two of them from the dominant Hindu society. If he were joking in Telugu with some *non*-Koya girl, this metaphor would not be part of his verbal arsenal; the metaphor and its appropriate use are a small part of the definition of Koya culture.

Elwin (1947) has reported the use of this metaphor in several related contexts by the Maria Gonds, the northernmost representatives of the Gondi-speaking tribes. The metaphor appears especially in songs and ceremonies. A song sung while the marriage booth is being built has the lines, "That girl is beautiful, give her some tobacco/Take her, press her [cf. *ottadaa*] [1947:578]." And when the two fathers-in-law meet for the first time during the actual marriage ceremony, they say, "Let us eat the powdered tobacco [together]! [ibid.; p. 541]." A song used in a game in which young girls touch parts of their bodies successively at each line — i.e., ankles–waist–breasts–shoulders–hands over head — goes: "Brother has gone to his village/In his purse is sweet tobacco/ Will he eat the sweet tobacco? [ibid., p. 578]."

Also, tobacco is used as a love charm, and tobacco leaves are used in village sacrifices on the return to the native village of young men who have been visiting neighboring villages. These visits are often for the express purpose of finding suitable mates. The tobacco is tied in front of a sacred platform by the girls of the village, and when the boys return home the tobacco is taken down ceremonially and smoked (ibid., p. 442).

Note particularly the contexts in which this metaphor is used. They are all either overtly sexual or, as in the marriage preparations and ceremony, indirectly but obviously related to sexuality. The evidence is clear that the young man is using the metaphor quite appropriately. Mangamma's answer is an emphatic denial, in which she recognizes the metaphor by refusing to acknowledge it.

(4j) WIIKE MANGAMMA:

  pooga ille   baat(a) ille
  tobacco no/not what   no/not
  "What are you talking about?! I don't have any tobacco!"

This is a very typical couplet and is used in everyday conversation, the second part acting as an intensifier. Then the following interchange ensues. Sahadev speaks first.

(4k) *Pooga uccuDu iimu   iimu*
   tobacco a little bit give (imp.) give (imp.)
   "Give me a little tobacco!"

(4l) *ille*
   no/not
   "There isn't any; I haven't any; I won't give any."

(4m) *pooga iitiney neem(u)*
   tobacco give will (2nd per. inf.)

   weytinney
   you (inf.) give will you (inf.)
   "Will you give me some tobacco? Will you give me some?"

(4n) *pooga illey nanna warraanu*
   tobacco no/not I come (neg. imp.) I
   "I don't have any tobacco; there isn't any tobacco! I won't come!"

(4o)   *ta   taa*
     "ta! ta!"   (sound made while touching Mangamma)

At this point in the exchange Sahadev is tickling Mangamma and feeling her breasts. He then says:

(4p)   *weytinnaa   marri*
     go will you   then (q. intonation)
     "you'll go, then?"

This is said in a question form but is not a question. The intonation pattern and the offhand way the question is used with the addition of "then" make it clear that the speaker's intention is analogous to that of a man who has picked up a girl, is claiming that an agreement has been made, and has told the girl to get her coat: "Are you ready to go?" In American society, it can be the climax of a successful pickup or, if the girl says "No," can end the attempt. Here, there is realistically nowhere to go—it is a joke, but the joke has consequences analogous to the American scene.
   The girl answers matter-of-factly.

(4q)   *worra*
     come/go (neg. imp.)
     "I won't come with you!"

The man makes a further brief and feeble attempt, but the girl says "No" once again. Each participant, including especially the recording engineer, recognized the question "Are you ready to go, then?" to be the climax of the interaction. In a natural setting, obviously, the girl need not have so foreclosed on her options; she could have said "Yes." But no nice girl says "yes" in public.

Episode 5

   Kunja Sahadev then initiates another encounter. This time it is with a girl with whom he has quite a different relationship from the one he has with the previous girl. She is an unmarried member of the Kaniti clan, a lineage that is currently considered a wife-exchanging clan with the Kunja lineage. Such clans are called *viyyan kulu* (exogamous groups that have mutual marriage relationships or alliances, literally "seed castes"). The two speakers, therefore, are related as classificatory cross-cousins (she is his FMBSD—or Father's, Mother's, Brother's, Son's, Daughter).

The girl with whom Sahadev had previously joked was also of *viyyan kulu* (Wiike), but he did not use the same approach toward her that he uses toward the girl in this encounter. What culturally relevant data must the analyst know before he can say why this is so? It will do no good to say that he takes a different approach because the first was unsuccessful. We know that *any* approach must be ultimately unsuccessful because of the rule: No nice girl says "yes" in public. Yet we also know that success in these encounters need not be a sexual (coital) liaison. It is not even true to say that the real function of such joking (for the male participant at least) is to come to some – perhaps implicit – agreement with the girl. The analyst needs to know or believe only that on some occasion such behavior is appropriate. The behavior is given; *why* it is that the behavior manifests itself the way it does then becomes the task for analysis. (That on some occasion such behavior is itself appropriate is problematic for the analyst *as well as* for the participants will become apparent.) In this new encounter, Sahadev takes the following approach. He speaks lines 5a and 5c, and Siitamma speaks line 5b.

(5a)   *mii   evva*
       your (formal)   mother (q. intonation)
       "Where is your mother?"

(5b)   *cuuDattey*
       in the seeing (idiom)
       "She is seeing."

(5c)   *cinemattey*
       (cinema hall in the)
       "Oh – she's at the cinema hall."

This exchange is a rather startling and incongruous example which serves to bring dramatically into awareness a problem that is endemic in ethnographic analysis, that of specifying the context within which events occur and explanations are offered. Thus, the fact that there is a cinema hall available to this isolated tribal group provides a category of cultural experience which expands considerably the interpretive horizons of the ethnographic analyst and his audience.

The following exchange has several interesting properties that I would like to explore in depth. Sahadev speaks first, and then he and Siitamma alternate (5d is the second part of utterance 5c).

(5d)   *dooDa   tittiinaa*
       cooked rice   eat will you (q. intonation)
       "Will you eat cooked rice?"

(5e) *dooDa   tittinaa*
cooked rice   will eat I
"I will eat cooked rice."

(5f) *baata   kusiri*
what   vegetables/greens
"What kind of greens will you eat?"

(5g) *kiike   kusiri*
fish   vegetables/greens
"I will eat fish and greens curry."

(5h) *baata   dooDa*
what   cooked rice
"What kind of rice will you eat?"

(5i) *wanji   dooDa*
crude rice   rice
"I will eat cooked *paedi*."

(5j) *mannam   cutaatinaa*
we (exclusive)   see will you
"What will we see then?"

(5k) *windivvu*
hear belching we (personal pronoun proximate: here)
"Then we'll hear belching."

(5l) *aaDitinaa*
play with you
"Will you play with me?"

(5m) *aaDitaanu*
play will I
"I will play with you."

(5n) *nijamaa*
true/truth
"Are you telling me the truth?"

(5o) *awn*
yes
"Yes I am."

(5p) *dooDa   tintaaDaa*
cooked rice   eat will you (q. intonation)
"Will you eat some rice?"

(5q) *awn*
      yes

(5r) *naa   tintaraa   iriwata   tintanaa*
      you   eat will you   we two (incl.)   eat will can

      nimma ninna iriwata   tintdakkanaa
      you   me   we   two (incl.)   eat will can go
      "Oh – you'll eat cooked rice. Well, you and I can eat a little
      bit and go."

(5s) *awn*
      yes

(5t) *malla   paccaTam*
      then   lying down (verbal n.) (q. intonation)
      "Then we'll lie down together?"

(5u) *niih!*
      your (expl.)
      "Your sister!"

Utterances (5a–5u) represent an *episode* that is concluded by the girl's
expression *niih*. Within the episode there are several touch points that
seem to mark it as a unit, bounded by *mii evva* (5a) and concluded with
the expression *niih*, "your sister!" The form that this episode takes is
worthy of examination, since it is quite distinct from the previous one in
which Sahadev has participated.

The episode opens with the expression *mii evva?*, which is interpretable as a question by intonation only. The usual question word itself has
been deleted. Thus, Sahadev's interlocutor must now decide or understand from past experience what the implicit question is: (How/state of
health) is your mother? (Who is) your mother? (Where is) your mother?
are possibilities. We discover from the following exchange that the
truncated question is interpreted as "Where is your mother?" How shall
we account for that interpretation?

There are at least two different and probably interinfluencing ways in
which an interpretation might be made. The first concerns the status of
the relationships obtaining among the man, the girl, and her mother.
Since there are specific question forms in Koya both for inquiring after
the health of someone or for discovering the physical whereabouts of
someone, we might expect an individual's intentional inquiry about
either condition to be overtly marked in some manner. In this situation,
however, failing a crisis in the state of health of the girl's mother, there

can be only one thing about her that the young man does not know. Sahadev has, after all, lived in her presence for his entire life, and it is altogether probable that he knows much more about her than an American would care to know about a lifelong next-door neighbor. There is, therefore, literally only one question that it is reasonable to ask in this situation – where someone is, physically, if he or she is not co-present. However, there is some evidence, external as well as internal, to show that he *does not care* where the girl's mother is or, to put it another way, that he is not asking where she is at all. He has some other proposition in mind.

The external evidence stems from recorded interactions between children, and between children and their mothers, in which the expression *mii evva* also appears. In trying to induce young children to speak, an open-ended frame is often utilized by the child's interlocutor. It consists of the second-person possessive pronoun *mii* and, in the slot following it, a kinship term. So the child is queried, in just the form used here: *mii evva?, mii poyye?, mii anna?, mii akka?*. The child is asked to locate, in turn, each relative ("in the market" or "in the forest" are among the appropriate responses). When a satisfactory answer is given, the questioner moves on to another relative. The object of the game is to elicit some response, not information about the world. It should be noted, of course, that such responses can be treated as imparting information. "In the movies," from an outsider's point of view, contains quite novel information.

In the encounter under consideration here, the opening question *mii evva?* is also a form of play; yet it differs from child's play because it is only the beginning of a more complex set of questions and responses. But regardless of whether the players are young children or the two young adults here, the question is a familiar part of a Koya elicitation routine; the answer is less important than the initiation of an interaction.

The next set of questions (5d–5i) deals with food. Food as well as sex is given extraordinarily high value in Koya culture, perhaps because both are scarce commodities. Whatever the reason for this high valuation, it is true that food, its nomenclature, preparation, and consumption, is often, in appropriate contexts, a metaphor for sex. Recall the earlier use of tobacco as a metaphor for sexual intercourse. Food is equally a metaphor for nonsexual friendship and affection (in the case of same-sex adult age mates), and in phatic or metalinguistic communications in the case of eliciting routines with children. These, too, are occasioned, just as the use of *mii evva?* is, in the sense that individuals in interaction must recognize which of the metaphorical uses of food is *intended* and *appropriate* in any given context.

There are several interesting points in this interchange about food. First, the interpretation of the question routines (cf. Ervin-Tripp, 1964:86–102) as a set of idiomlike formulas for initiating interaction seems to be validated by tapes of at least two other occasions in which the questions asked of young children are precisely those asked here. Second, the redundancy of the responses is of interest. *Wanji dooDa* 'rice rice' is a case in point. Although *doda* is cooked rice, *wanji* can refer either to the seeds of *paedi* (a poor grade of local rice) or the *paedi* itself; but *dooDa* is only the cooked form of *wanji,* although it is possible that at some time another kind of *wanji* would be available to the Koya.

The most obvious conclusion from this evidence is that Sahadev is addressing the girl as if she were a child. Even the intonation contours and the volume of his voice are radically different than they were in the previous episode. Why is this? It is, first of all, true that this girl *is* younger than the previous girl, yet she is postpubescent, and decidedly of marriageable age (about 14, plus or minus one year). However, she has apparently had less worldly experience than the previous girl. In addition, she, of all the women in Sahadev's world, would be the single most appropriate marriage partner for him. Given this background, we might make the initial inference that Sahadev would be considerate of her innocence; and indeed, there is evidence within the episode that this is the case (to be discussed).

But in addition to this consideration, there is something else occurring here — Sahadev is "sandbagging" the girl. All this preparatory byplay is leading up to something, and, with what we already know about the nature of such encounters, we may guess with a good deal of confidence that what that will be is a proposition. To "sandbag" is to conceal one's intent, to practice deception. In these first few moments of the episode, it is as if the real nature of the encounter is purposely put out of mind in order to engage in a child's game. The girl, by making the expected and appropriate responses for some *other* game, acquiesces, if somewhat diffidently, in the playing of *this* game, whatever its definition will be *in the next moment.* But since intent cannot be concealed and deception cannot be practiced — she knows what the game is really about — this preliminary byplay cannot be serious; it is clearly marked "This is play." In what way, then, can we say that Sahadev is sandbagging the girl? To the degree that she cannot anticipate how or when the real game will be made evident, the girl is being deceived and, therefore, sandbagged. And since the deception is not covert but overt (i.e., known to the participants to be taking place), there is a natural tension created while the girl tries to anticipate at what point the encounter will become a different game. Coupled with her shyness (attested to on the tape by the other participants, who remark on the girl's shyness sotto voce in the background), this tension induces nervous laughter, tentative responses, and a low vocal volume on the part of the girl.

As the episode proceeds, then, the young man says (5i) "We (exclusive) what will we see?" And the girl replies "Hear belching" (5i). A more idiomatic gloss for "see" might be "experience." The girl's reply is apparently part of the set routine but novel to me. *Devu* has an interesting etymological derivation among the speakers of the unwritten languages of various Dravidian-speaking groups, meaning, in general, to belch or belching—an approved action, since the number and volume of belches is supposed to be directly related to one's appreciation of a meal. However, among the major written Dravidian languages, it generally means nausea or stomach rumbles—which are not approved. The implication of the response is that the meal would have been quite satisfactory—an implicit parallel to postcoital sensations.

Then S asks (5l), "Will you play?" and the girl says (5m), "I will play." He then moves to the plural exclusive "we two"—*mannam*—and duplicates it with *iru* ("us, a couple, two things"), and asks if the two will drink and eat rice and *kusiri*. The girl agrees. He asks again if "They (the two of them) will eat rice." She agrees once again. He asks a third time, varying the form slightly (5r), if the two ("you and me") of them will play and eat, if they (the couple) will eat and go. His speech has become more rapid, and the volume of his voice has increased. She agrees for the third time, and then the sandbag hits: *malla paccaTam* "then lying down" (5t).

Although his strategy here has been quite different from that of the previous episode, the young man uses "then" once again, the same way he had used it before, to suggest that in the normal order of things, after eating and playing, they, the couple, would lie down. The "then" is intended to close the encounter, to finish the narration of a story that has an inevitable end, a particular foregone conclusion. The girl, however, does not accept the inevitability of that conclusion.

Malla paccaTam draws an immediate *niih* (5u) from the girl. Once again, *niih* is an abbreviation for *ni akka* and is often used in speaking to animals or children as a warning to stop some behavior that is annoying, with the clear implication that further pursuance of that behavior will result in action—a clout on the head, perhaps.

So the sandbagging episode is closed. It is closed because the covert deception is over, and, once again, the object of the encounter that brought all of the participants together is out in the open, because it was finally made overt by the unambiguous statement of the purpose of the encounter.

It is important to note that this entire episode does not appear on the transcript made in the field at the time the joking encounter occurred.

That is, when my informants and I sat down to transcribe the tape, we passed by the entire section analyzed here. It was a taken-for-granted, obvious sort of interchange that we all intuitively understood and believed required no elaboration or comment at the time. I believe this adds credence to the idea that this particular interchange was viewed by the native participants (and by me) as being preliminary to the real nature of the encounter, and unimportant just because the formulaic nature of the question and responses is intended only to create interaction, not to produce substance. If we view the joking as being nonserious, it would seem that this episode and its attendant routine are at the limits of nonseriousness, because the entire encounter is, after all, nonserious. Indeed, it may be that the highly overlearned character of routines precludes their ever being very significant in overt communicative terms, since they are invariably initiators or terminators of interaction, rarely standing by themselves but, rather, serving to ensure the orderly nature of some larger interaction in which people really are supposed to be engaged.

Some Conclusions about the Analysis of the
Joking Ritual

The view expressed here has been that what is *not* said is just as important for the ways in which "joking talk" is accomplished as what is said (see Garfinkel and Sacks on "mock-ups," 1969). It is not technically possible to have as explanations/descriptions replicas of behavior that reproduce in every detail that behavior. Even if a machine existed that could call up on demand a three-dimensional oral, aural, olfactory, and spectographic recreation of some behavioral event, it would not thereby be an adequate description of that event. The advent of the sound tape recorder and the videotape recorder brings us closer to being able to reproduce events, and the problem of understanding how an event is accomplished may be, to that degree, made less difficult. Yet the analyst of the event as interaction must learn to stand at some point that can be used as a kind of explanatory fulcrum in relation to the phenomena. My fulcrum has been language in extended discourse. My object has been to see what initiates interaction, what maintains it, what channels it in specifiable ways, and in what ways it may be terminated. Self-monitoring, the process whereby individuals attend to and adjust accordingly their ongoing behavior, has played an important role in these interaction sequences. I have tried to show that self-monitoring includes calculations about the other participants that help one determine, from moment to moment, what kind of behavior will be most likely to produce some desired state of affairs. Implicit in this formulation is that some states of affairs are desired more than others, and that it may be possible to enumerate or list these desires as terms in the calculation of motivations from moment to moment in any well-understood interaction.

On the tape, once the purpose of the encounter has been brought into the open, the rate of interaction increases greatly, and the nature of the verbal interchange becomes correspondingly complex once the routineness has passed. The episode truly becomes a dramaturgical scene with stage directors and prompters clearly audible on the tape, although absent from the interpretation of the tape by informants. Thus, attention to *substance* or *relevance* becomes important to the native's definition of the situation, considering the nature of the instructions given at the time the transcript was made.

The analysis presented here covers only slightly more than the first 7 min of the 45 min or so of tape recording. The tape remains an incredibly rich source of data for analysis; I have not covered such topics as the native view of stage directions, which, among other things, make explicit what the appropriate *content* of joking behavior should be, nor have I dealt with the interesting use of kinship terms to manipulate the structure of the various encounters. Nonetheless, what I hope to have made clear in this analysis is the need for attending to biographical and historical information—background expectations—if the analyst is to make sense of the interaction in the way it proceeds, as the native actor must. If there were different participants, then there would be a different structure to the interaction within the same framework—and this must be accounted for. Every constellation of individuals in interaction utilizes, as well as produces, a unique combination of standing procedural and biographical information. This standing information takes many forms. It includes cultural rules about what behavior is appropriate in particular contexts; it includes, as well, native knowledge of the native language, which knowledge has as one of its properties the ability to use language in extended discourse.

References

Austin, J. L.
    1962   *How to do things with words.* London: Oxford Univ. Press.
Brukman, Jan
    1972   Strategies of ritual interaction among the Koya of South India. Unpublished doctoral dissertation, University of California, Berkeley.
Douglas, Mary
    1968   The social control of cognition: Some factors in joke preception, *Man* **3**, 361–376.
Elwin, Verrier
    1947   *The Muria and their Ghotul.* London: Oxford Univ. Press.

Ervin-Tripp, Susan
  1964   An analysis of the interaction of language, topic, and listener, *American Anthro-
           pologist* **66**(6)2, 86–102.
Garfinkel, Harold and Harvey Sacks
  1969   Formal structures of practical actions. Unpublished ms.
Goffman, Erving
  1959   *The presentation of self in everyday life.* New York: Anchor.
  1963   *Behavior in public places.* Glencoe: The Free Press.
Grigson, Wilfred (Sir)
  1949   *The Maria Gonds of Bastar* (2nd ed.). London: Oxford Univ. Press.
Radcliffe-Brown, A. R.
  1952   *Structure and function in primitive society.* Chicago: The Free Press.
Sacks, Harvey
  1967   Membership categorization devices. Unpublished ms.
Searle, John R.
  1969   *Speech acts.* New York: Cambridge Univ. Press.

Falling Words: An Analysis of a Japanese *Rakugo* Performance[1]

MARY SANCHES

I. The Cultural Context

As you approach it, the 'variety theater', the *yose,* appears rather like one of the ingredients in a closely-packed urban sandwich. It is almost externally indistinguishable (to the novice) from the bars, restaurants specializing in one-dish cuisine, burlesque halls, movie theaters, 'pinball' (*pachinko*) and mah-jong parlors, and coffee houses. The narrow, telephone- and utility-pole crowded street is further made difficult of passage by clusters of *sarari-man,* 'office workers', seeking appropriate contexts for solidarity rituals with fellow-employees and sometimes momentary oblivion from their day's work. Vendors of hot chestnuts, sweet potatoes or *oden*[2] may be offering their autumn specialties, to be eaten while sitting at their carts. Bicycles and occasionally taxis make their way as best they can through the crowd while the myriad neon images overhead visually echo the human bustle.

If you are Japanese you know that you are, conceptually as well as physically, in a particular district—the *kanrakugai,* the 'entertainment world'. Traditionally—that is, up until the end of the Tokugawa period (officially 1886)—the *kanrakugai* of any city was a district physically separate from the rest of the community; the equivalent of what we would call in English the "redlight" district. In the last hundred years several elements have served to wipe out the actual physical separation

[1] Support for this chapter's research was made available through NSF-USDP Grant GU-1598 to the University of Texas at Austin. I wish to express my gratitude to Takagi Kiyoko, Fujiwara Hisako, Omae Yaeko, Kimura Mari, Hattori Yukimasa, and Hattori Yasuko in particular for their patient help and explanation. I have benefitted from the comments of the following people on various aspects of the text and its analysis: Ben Blount, Fadwa el Guindi, Nick Hopkins, Henry Selby, and Brian Stross.

[2] This listing does not pretend to show the internal structure of the domain of *kanrakugai,* which must be rather complex. The object of this outline is simply to place *rakugo* in its appropriate context cognitively by showing some of the other inclusions in the general domain.

between these traditional "pleasure districts" and the surrounding areas of the city: Firstly, the early Meiji period civil code changes eliminating the official socio-conceptual distinctions between the *hinin* 'outcaste, non-human' residents of the pleasure districts and the fully human social classes removed the necessity for physical segregation, although the traditional connotations of these areas remain—for example, Tokyo's Asakusa district. Also, the tremendous expansion, especially in the last 30 years, of large urban centers like Tokyo and the resulting incorporation by them of smaller cities, towns, and villages has contributed to a blurring of local demarcations. In addition, with "modernization" and industrialization, increasing numbers of people do not live where they work and consequently must commute. Since a major part of the commuter burden is carried by the intra- and inter-urban train system, new clusters of *kanrakugai*-type establishments have grown up around local train stops, where they can be most available to men (particularly) between work and home.

What one comes to the *kanrakugai* for is *asobi*, 'play', and the establishments found there represent the different kinds of ways one can play. The *yose*, 'variety hall', and the performances which take place within its physical boundaries contrast with the physically realized cultural settings within which other kinds of *kanraku*, 'pleasure', take place. The following is a partial list of the kinds of entertainment establishments to be found in any *kanrakugai* district, as well as the type of fun one can expect to find there (see Footnote 2, p. 269).

Name of place:	Type of pleasure to be had:
A. *gekijō* 'theaters'	
kabukiza 'Kabuki theatre'	*kabuki* 'traditional drama'
bunrakuza 'puppet theatre'	*bunraku* 'puppet show'
gekijō "theater"	*shibai* (modern) 'plays'
yose "variety hall"	*rakugo, manzai*, etc.
sutorippu gekijo 'strip theatre'	*sutorippu* 'strip show'
konsāto horu 'concert hall'	*konsato* 'concert'
B. *eigakan* 'movie house'	*eiga* (Western) 'movies'
C. *bakuchi suru tokoro* 'places to gamble'	
keibajō 'horse track'	*keiba* 'horse races'
keirinjō 'bike track'	*keirin* 'bicycle races'
majanya 'ma jong hall'	*majan* 'ma jong'
D. *yŭgijō* 'amusement hall'	
pachinkoya 'pinball shop'	*pachinko* 'pinball'
E. *inshokuten* 'eating and drinking places'	Eating and drinking;

bā 'bars'
  sutāndo ba 'stand bar'
  kyābare 'cabaret'
  ba '(Western-style) bar'
  nomiya, '(Japanese-
    style) bar'
  kissaten 'coffeehouse'
  ryōriya '(Japanese-style) res-
    taurant'
  resutoran '(Western-style) res-
    taurant'

in the case of *kyābarē*
and *bā:* entertainment
by *hosutesu* 'hostesses' in the case
of *ryōriya,* possibly by
geisha.

If you are Japanese you will also know that the kind of entertainment performed at a *yose* is currently relatively less prestigeful than that which takes place at the *kabukiza,* '*kabuki* theatre', or the *bunrakuza,* 'puppet theatre'. The entertainment which takes place at the *yose* still carries a connotation of being *shomin-no-koto,* 'common-people's stuff', having been developed in response to the interests of the merchants' of the large urban centers during the Tokugawa period (approximately 1615–1868). *Kabuki* and *bunraku* admittedly also share these origins but they, unlike *rakugo* and the other entertainments of the *yose,* were "discovered" by foreigners early in the modern period. The foreigners' fascination with and high evaluation of *kabuki* and *bunraku* impressed upper-class Japanese that there must be something of worth in these forms. Consequently *kabuki* and *bunraku* have, along with the *Noh* (which is not an event that takes place in the *kanrakugai*) been given state support and thus crystallized in social amber, effectively kept from developing into forms that might have contemporary social relevance. Not having been "discovered" by foreigners, *rakugo* has not as yet suffered—or benefited from, depending on one's point of view—such institutionalization.

As one buys tickets and enters the unimposing building, it is evident that while the street outside surely belongs to the twentieth century (some would maintain the twenty-first) the inside of the yose keeps its identity with the past and its origins in the life of the *shitamachi,* 'downtown', merchant people of pre-modern Japan. A *yose,* while probably smaller, has much in common structurally with other traditional *gekijo,* 'theaters'. It has a 'stage', *butai,* which faces the sections of the theatre while the audience sits: the 'pit', *hirodōma,* and the 'galleries', *masuseki,* running on either side of the pit. The physical difference between the *hirodōma* and the *masuseki* reflected the status of the audience who sat there: The *masuseki,* 'galleries', which were furnished with padded *ta-*

tami mats cost more than the *hirodoma*, 'pit', where the masses sat on bare boards.

Within the physical context of the *yose*, "variety hall," *rakugo* performances contrast with a variety of other entertainments.

Kinds of performances taking place at a *yose*.

A. Performances organized into the same program:

    kyokugei   'acrobatics'
    tejina   'juggling, sleight-of-hand'
    shinnai   'comic singing'
    kodan   'rhythmic traditional moral monologues'
    manzai   'humorous dialogues'
    rakugo   'humorous monologues'

B. Performances organized into a separate program:

    ryokyōku 'epic chants, accompanied by a *shamisen*'

Of the performances taking place at the yose, only *manzai* and *rakugo* qualify as humorous, principally *verbal*, behavior. That is, their qualification as "entertaining" performances is determined by the speech usage of their performers.

Of these two *rakugo*, "humorous monologues" is valued as the more prestigeful. Although *rakugo* performances have not yet suffered the fate of the other prestigeful traditionally *shomin* entertainments, i.e., *kabuki* and *bunraku*, it is acknowledged as the most traditional, prestigeful, standard-governed, socially respected of the performances at the *yose*. Informants have reported that although just about anyone can try his hand at *manzai, rakugo* is a "discipline," requiring years of study and training, in addition to talent.

Given the tradition of training and accomplishment, and the connotations of cultural conservatism associated with *rakugo*, it only follows that the social, off-stage relationships among the people in its world should be organized on the basis of the same traditional social concepts and institutions universal in Japanese society in the premodern period and still dominant in other culturally conservative domains – especially the "criminal" world and the traditional arts. Just as one cannot be a professional *rakugōka* without training, so also one cannot exist alone – without institutional affiliation – in the professional world of *rakugo*. In order to get professional training in *rakugo* one apprentices – becomes a *deshi* 'pupil, disciple' – to a *sensei*, 'teacher', who represents the *ie*, 'house, lineage', of which the student wants to become a member. Upon being certified competent in their profession, the *deshi*, "apprentice", takes the *ie* name, is thenceforth its representative, and bears responsibility for the honor and continuation of the "house".

The performer narrating the *rakugo* text analysed in this paper is Katsura Shinji, Katsura being a well-known "lineage" or "house" in the world of *rakugo*. Probably the most famous *rakugo* house in Japan is the Kōkontei "family," of which Kokontei Shincho, now about eighty, is the master representative. Successful *rakugo* performers gain personal popularity just as do movie stars and popular singers and are greeted with applause on appearance.

There are also stylistic differences among the different "houses" of *rakugo* performers, and much of the variation can be accounted for by two features: (1) What the location and, hence, the dialect of the area in which the "family" is located is — for example, is it Edo (Tokyo) or Kamigata (Ōsaka) *rakugo;* and (2) Whether they perform according to the traditions of *Koten* 'classic' or *Shinsaku* 'modern' *rakugo.*

The *rakugoka*, 'narrator', appears on the stage of the *yose* alone, except for his *zabuton*, 'cushion', arm-rest, and fan, the effectiveness of his narration depending entirely on what he can communicate without the use of extensive props. While some nonverbal accompaniment — gestures and manipulation of his fan — heighten certain parts of the story, they are not necessary for an understanding and appreciation of the humor.[3] This is reflected in their occurrence in other media: They are sold as printed texts and read and appreciated; with the development of radio they began to occur there, in whose schedule of listings they are represented as, for example, *kinyo no yose,* 'Sunday's variety-hall', indicating that conceptually, if not physically, they can be viewed as still occurring in the same context. *Rakugo* narrations can also be purchased on records.

Rakugo performances are not spontaneous. There are a number of set pieces or topics around which humorous narratives are built. Apprentice performers learn these narratives, and, through practicing them over a period of years, infuse them with their own individual style. Some of the titles of *koten rakugo* performances are: *natto uri* 'the fermented soybean seller'; *mame uri* 'the bean seller'; *daiku* 'the carpenter'; and — the one which forms the data for this analysis — *dōguya* 'the antique store'.[4] Like the other narratives, and indeed the entertainment form itself, this monologue is linked in the minds of Tokyo-ites with the merchant-class life of Shitamachi — the "downtown" area of Tokyo — with its tradition of small shops and enterprises, the underworld, and generally intimate, crowded, communal activities.

---

[3] For some description of this aspect of *rakugo* with pictures, see V. Hrdličkova, 1969. Japanese professional storytellers. *Genre* **3**: 179–210.

[4] The Japanese title *doguya* could be glossed variously as 'junk store/seller', 'second-hand store', or 'antique dealer'. Glossing it as "antique dealer/store" seems to communicate some of the absurdity of the original.

II. Background to the Text

The *rakugo* narration which forms the data for this study was first watched while being tape recorded from a television presentation. Thus the audience reaction was included in the text from which the analysis was made. The tape was subsequently transcribed and worked through with four separate native-speaking informants.

The story line of the monologue is simple: It involves a central character—Yotarō—and five minor characters. Magobei is the old man with whom Yotarō is interacting at the beginning of the narration and by whom he is given a basket of "merchandise" to take to the shop of Jimbei. Jimbei is also an old man, a friend of Magobei, and has agreed to help Yotarō get set up in the "antique" business. The final part of the narrative involves Yotarō's interactions with three would-be customers.

The text itself has presented major translation problems. I am convinced that this is an irresolvable problem in the context of a study like this one: to make the monologue funny, one would have to employ devices that are humorous to American-English speakers and thus lose the point of explicating the mechanisms that make it a humorous performance in Japanese. Abandoning attempts at humor, I have tried to make the translation intelligible by including a running commentary on "what is going on." This is to be found in the form of explanations after each misunderstanding.

It is important to remember that the story, which is represented in translation as being spoken by characters, is actually a monologue narration in the original Japanese. That is, it is spoken by one person throughout, and all understanding of which character is being represented as speaking at any given moment, as well as background information about locale and spatial changes, is made by the listeners on the basis of indirect information given by the narrator.

III. The Text

The Antique Store

NARRATOR: *Well, . . . thanks* (acknowledging applause). *Y'know, when it comes to* **rakugo,** *we don't see very many clever characters. It seems we always hear about these guys who're missing something.*
Here the narrator switches into dialect, and, by so doing, signals the beginning of the narration.

MAGOBEI: (calling) *Hey, Yotarō!*

YOTARŌ: *Ummmm?*

MAGOBEI: *Where are you goofing off* (**asobu**)?

YOTARŌ: *I'm not goofing off.*
MAGOBEI: *Well, what're you doing?*
YOTARŌ: *I'm loafing (burabura suru).*
By failing to recognize that *burabura suru* 'to loaf, laze around' is included in the Japanese semantic system as a kind of *asobu* 'play', as opposed to *hataraku* 'work', Yotarō gives the first clue that he is not all there.

MAGOBEI: *That's what I mean—goofing off. Hey, last night your mother was over here complaining (kobosu) about your shenanigans.*
YOTARŌ: *Well, when y'got bad eyes, I guess you're bound to knock things over (kobosu). Did'ya pick everything up for her, uncle?*
Magobei is not, genealogically speaking, Yotarō's uncle. I have retained the Japanese extended use of this form, both in Yotarō's and Magobei's references to Magobei.
Yotarō has read /kobosu/ as *kobosu* 'knock over, spill', instead of, as is Magobei's intention, *kobosu* 'complain, cry over'.

MAGOBEI: *Not "knocking things over." I said she was crying over you (omae no koto naita).*
YOTARŌ: *Ah, I don't wanna be one of those lady-killers.*
MAGOBEI: *What're you talking about? What's this about a lady-killer?*
YOTARŌ: *Making an older woman (toshima) cry. . .*
MAGOBEI: *What d'ya mean, "an older woman," I thought we were talking about your mother.*
YOTARŌ: *Well, y'know what they say, "love is blind."*
Yotarō has made a series of confusions here: First of all, he equates *toshima*, 'male speaking, older, unrelated female with whom there is the possibility of erotic relationship', with his mother, an inappropriate reference. Magobei does not know, however, that it is his mother that Yotarō is talking about. The ambiguity and confusion are developed as follows:

1. *omae no koto-o naita* '(she) was crying over you' has, similar to English, a connotation that there is some romantic relationship between the person crying and the person being cried over, though this is not the necessary implication;

2. Yotarō then says he doesn't want to be a lady-killer. For Magobei, this switches the topic to some woman, other than his mother, which might be the cause of her crying; in the next sentence, Yotarō seems to confirm his thoughts by saying that he made a *toshima* cry.

3. Yotarō then indicates, however, that for him

"mother" equals *toshima,* and when Magobei's question, *I thought we were talking about your mother,* implies that this is an impossible equation, Yotarō justifies it, logically, by retorting that erotic love overrides all distinctions, including kinship relations (*kono michi bakkari betsu da*).

MAGOBEI: *Hopeless! . . . I'm trying to tell you I'll take you on as an apprentice. How about it, won't you give uncle's old line of work a try?*

"Uncle" here is a term of self-reference used by Magobei.

YOTARŌ: *What's that? Uncle's old line of work was . . .*
MAGOBEI: *Don't you know?*
YOTARŌ: *Well, now that y'mention it, I have an idea what it is . . .*
MAGOBEI: *What? What d'ya mean, an "idea"?*
YOTARŌ: *Yeah, I was watchin' the other night when you came home late carrying all that stuff . . .*
MAGOBEI: *And what did you think was goin' on?*
YOTARŌ: *Well, I wonder what to say, y'know . . . What uncle calls his "work," it's* (whispering) *burg . . . lar, . . . heh?*
MAGOBEI: *What?*
YOTARŌ: (whispering) *burglary . . .*
MAGOBEI: *What? Speak up!*
YOTARŌ: *I should speak up?*
MAGOBEI: *Yeah, speak up!*
YOTARŌ: *Well, in that case I'll speak up! Uncle's work is BURG-LA-RY (**dorobo**)!*
MAGOBEI: *This guy's something else. You think I'm doing something so bad as that, do you?*
YOTARŌ: *Wha'dya mean, "do I think"? Your expression didn't even change. You must be the head of the gang (**ōmono**).*

In this case Yotarō is overextending a rule of nonverbal communication, that if you accuse someone of doing something and their expression does not change, they must be guilty of it. He has accused Magobei of being a burglar, and Magobei makes no response at all in terms of facial expressions, so that Yotarō concludes that he must be the head of a gang of burglars.

MAGOBEI: *What're ya talking about? What uncle has been working at is the antique business (**dōguya**).*
YOTARŌ: *Aha, there's a "**do**" in it.*

Yotarō has made the association that because both *dorobo* "burglary" and *dōguya* "antique business start with the syllable *do-,* they must also be similar in other ways.

MAGOBEI: *What d'ya mean there's a "**do-**" in it? There's a lotta difference. The antique business is tough. It takes a real man to know the ropes. Y'see that big basket over there? In it there's some "garbage" (**gomi**) I've gotten together. Shoulder it and go do some business.*

YOTARŌ: *Garbage (**gomi**)? People are buying garbage (**gomi**)?*

MAGOBEI: *That's antique business talk. Things that are all that's left of a set are called "garbage" (**gomi**).*

YOTARŌ: *Then whole sets of things must be called "refuse" (**hokori**).*

Yotaro has made an unwarranted analogic extension, based on the social distinction in the use of the words *gomi* and *hokori,* which both refer to 'trash, rubbish, garbage'. The distinction between them is that *hokori* (basic meaning, 'dust') is, by extension, more euphmistic and thus more elegant and refined than *gomi,* "garbage, trash." Yotarō concludes that because complete items in a set are better than items from broken sets, which, he is told are called *gomi* "garbage," they must be called *hokori* "refuse".

MAGOBEI: *There's no such word as "refuse." Open the basket and have a look.*

YOTARŌ: *Ah, there's lotsa stuff in here, isn't there. What's this?* (picks up a scroll)

MAGOBEI: *That's a wall-hanging (**kakemono**).*

YOTARŌ: *A ghost (**bakemono**)?*

MAGOBEI: *Not "ghost" (**bakemono**)! Wall hanging (**kakemono**)!*

YOTARŌ: *There's something drawn on it, Uncle. There's something interesting drawn on it. Ah, is it a mullet? Is he eating noodles?*

MAGOBEI: *What are you talking about? It's a "carp fighting his way upstream." Ya' have to hold it lengthways, not sideways.*

Yotarō has picked up the scroll and held it so that the picture of a fish going up a waterfall looks like a fish eating something long and stringy—to him "noodles."

YOTARŌ: *I should look at it this way?*

MAGOBEI: *Yeah.*

YOTARŌ: *Uncle, what's this?*

MAGOBEI: *It's one of a set of five ornaments for Girl's Day* (a holiday on the third of March).

YOTARŌ: *Ah, a doll. The head is loose.*

MAGOBEI: *Oh, the glue has come off, I guess. Well, it doesn't matter today, just take them and go. You probably won't sell them all—I mean, it would be great if you did but . . . well, tonight I'll fix it with some glue, so . . .*

YOTARŌ: *Hey, uncle, this doll has a missing nose. Looks like a mouse ate it. Wouldja like to hear how to catch a mouse?*

MAGOBEI: *I don't need you to tell me. You're probably talking about some kind of mousetrap, huh?*

YOTARŌ: *Uh uhn. Ya don't use a mousetrap.*

MAGOBEI: *You mean you use 'Catless'* (*nekoirazu*, brand name of a mouse poison).

YOTARŌ: *And ya don't use catless, either; it's non-catless* (***nekoirazu irazu***).

MAGOBEI: (intrigued) *What kind of thing is it?*

YOTARŌ: *Uncle, y'know the horse-radish grater, doncha? Well, ya take some cooked rice grains and stick them to it like this, ya know, and stand it up someplace handy for the mouse. In the middle of the night the mouse comes out — squeak, squeak, squeak — he thinks: "Today, I don't have to go all the way to the rice bowl; here's rice right here!" When he tries to eat the rice his nose gets grated, and as he eats he gradually gets all grated away. By morning he's nothing but a tail. Hey, elder, isn't that an invention!*

MAGOBEI: *Better you should try not thinking.* (Switching to the previous topic) *That place uncle was talking about was Shamisenbori* (place where Shamisen are made). *When you get there, there's a public toilet, y'know. If you look off to the side you'll see Jimbei's shop. Just say, real polite like, that you're Yotarō from Magobei's place in Toshima-cho and they'll take care of you. So go on . . .*

YOTARŌ: *O.k. I'm going.* **Sayonara.**

MAGOBEI: *Who in the world says "**sayonara**" when he leaves his own place? You mean **itte mairimasu**, "I'll go and come back."*

YOTARŌ: *"I went and returned" (**itte mairimashita**).*

          Yotarō has done two inappropriate things here. First of all, as Magobei points out, he uses the wrong closing form; when (temporarily) leaving one's own place, the appropriate thing to say is *itte mairimasu*, and not *sayonara*. Secondly, when he is told this, he demonstrates his unfamiliarity with the proper form by repeating it in its perfect aspect inflection, which is absurd because (1) it removes the phrase from membership in that class of phatic phrases used as openers and closers in Japanese (*aisatsu*) and (2) at the same time, makes its meaning, a literal one, "I've gone and come back," absurd in the context of his just leaving.

MAGOBEI: *You mean you've already come back? Hey, close the door after you!*

YOTARŌ: *Please, don't bother on my account (okamai naku).*
This is an incongruous response on Yotarō's part, as is evident even in English: one doesn't respond to a command as though declining an offer. At this point, Yotarō leaves Magobei's and proceeds to walk through the town to Jimbei's, and the following portion of text is his reverie as he goes.

YOTARŌ: (out in the street) *Ah, how about it, there are certainly lots of people around. Since it's people I guess it's o.k.; if they were dogs they might bite, y'know. Wow, uncle was talking strange—said he was a rag collector (kuzuya).*
Yotarō has mis-remembered what he heard. He has confused Magobei's reference to *gomi,* "trash, garbage," explained as slang in the antique business to refer to merchandise, with the business of being a trash collector, i.e., one who walks from street to street shouting for people's old junk.

YOTARŌ: *Well, I'll bet there are some hoods in that business. Calling, "Raaaaags, OOOOOOld paaaaapers," (kuzui, oharai mono), and then ducking into an alleyway when no-one is around and walking off with a wash basin or something . . . They shouldn't be calling kuzui, but zurui.*
This is a play on words: *kuzui* 'rags, newspapers' is the call of the *kuzuya.* *Zurui,* 'devious, sneaky, treacherous' is what Yotarō says the kind of people he is describing should yell instead. The second form is an adjective and the first, while it has the form of one, is not.

YOTARŌ: *Yeah, and there're even worse ones who'll go sneaking into peoples' houses, y-know. Bad characters. They're not the real rag collectors. They go: "Rags, rags and papers, "Rags an' . . . ." "RAAAAgs and papers".*
In the last sequence he is imitating the sound of the calls of someone who stops to sneak into a house. One can tell what he is doing by the duration of silence because the "rag collector" stops yelling and ducks into a house, resuming his call when he's out on the street again.
Yotarō, meanwhile, has become so engrossed in his fantasy about theives that he has forgotten to look where he's going . . .

COP: *Hey, Hey! Whadaya think you're doin' comin' into the police box like that?*

YOTARŌ: *I'm terribly sorry.* (to himself) *What a shock! Nose to nose with a cop!* (looking about and seeing that he is close to his destination): *Ah, guess it must be around*

	here. Suppose I should ask somebody . . . (steps into a shop): *Hello . . .*
JIMBEI:	(thinking Yotarō is a potential customer) *Welcome! Can I give (**sashiaŋeru**) you something?*
YOTARŌ:	*Hm? Well, I'm pretty strong* (to himself). *He says, "Lift (**sashiaŋeru**) something . . .* (to Jimbei): *Shall I lift that big rock over there for you?*

Yotarō has made the mistake of decoding *sashiaŋeru* in its basic meaning of 'lift, raise above the head', and appropriate meaning of 'give, first person to second person, polite.' In doing so, he demonstrates that he is not aware of the rules of social usage, and, in addition, overlooks contextual cues in decoding.

JIMBEI:	*What? What's this?*
YOTARŌ:	*What is it, you say? Ah,* (remembering what he is supposed to be there for) *ya wouldn't know Jimbei, huh?*

Here, Yotarō violates his first address rule: He should suffix Jimbei's name with *-san.*

JIMBEI:	*I beg your pardon. I'm (**temae**) Jimbei.*

Jimbei is using a self-reference term, humble, whose meaning is derived from spatial relations: *te* 'hand' plus *mae* 'in front of', thus, '(the thing) in front of (your) hand'. The word still has its spatial relations meaning in talking about directions, however, which is: 'just this side of X, or just in front of X', depending on the context.

YOTARŌ:	*Just "in front of my hand" (**temae**)? Shit!* (to himself) *Must've gone too far.* (to Jimbei) *In which direction?*

Yotarō has, predictably, read the wrong representation of this lexeme. This adds to our information that he is unfamiliar with personal reference term-usage.

JIMBEI:	*No, no. I'm (**watakushi**) Jimbei.*
YOTARŌ:	*Oh, so you're a **jimbei**. A pretty dirty **jimbei**, y'know. I guess ya don't wash, huh.*

What has happened here is that Yotarō equates Jimbei₁ — personal name — with *jimbei*₂ 'sleeveless article of clothing worn over a kimono'. He adds insult to injury by breaking a basic rule of interaction in making a derogatory comment on the other's personal cleanliness.

JIMBEI:	*What, whadaya want here?*
YOTARŌ:	*Ah, I came from Magobei's place in Toshima-cho, y'know. I'm **Yotarō-san**.*

He breaks two more rules of self-and-other reference: As with Jimbei's name, he should have added, at least *-san* to the end of Magobei's name. He omits any honorific suffix for other-reference, and, instead, does something no Japanese-speaker would ever do: He adds *-san* to his own name.

JIMBEI: (realizing who he is talking to and laughing through his nose). *Oh, yeah, I heard about you . . . from Magobei . . . He said there was this real stupid—I mean, real strong, stupid guy over at his place. You came in place of uncle, huh? Well, is that so . . . Well, this is the place.*

YOTARŌ: *eh?* (he doesn't believe that this kind of a place could be a store)

JIMBEI: *Yeah, you're gonna open shop here* (starting to give Yotarō directions) *Put down your basket. Spread out that mat you're carrying on top of it.* (Jimbei is having Yotarō arrange the stuff from his basket onto the mat he has spread in the street in front of the store). *Put the important stuff over here towards the front. You sit here. Line the stuff up over there. o.k.? You sit here. That's nothing but trash; lean that stuff up in the back . . . When you've got it all arranged . . . It's all dusty . . . Didn't you bring a rag or dust-cloth or anything? Isn't that a duster stuck in there? Just take the duster and clean them off a little. It's cause we keep at it so busily (**akizuni**) that it's called business (**akinai**) . . . o.k.. . . . if there's anything you don't understand, just call me . . .*

YOTARŌ: *Thanks a lot. You're being very good to me* (to himself) *This should attract customers. But since I'm just opening shop today, I should make some special effort . . .* (shouting) *Welcome! A just-finished antique store! A piping-hot antique store! A steaming antique store! Hey, mister . . .*

               He has inappropriately extended to this situation the things he has heard the food vendors shouting.

JIMBEI: *What's this? Stop shouting, stop shouting! That guy was on a motorbike . . .*

YOTARŌ: *On a motor-bike?*

JIMBEI: *Shut up! You don't understand about customers . . .*

CUSTOMER 1:   *Antique-store man . . .* (addressing Yotarō)

YOTARŌ: *Welcome! Just step up to the second floor, please . . .*

CUSTOMER: *Whadya mean "second floor." I don't see any second floor.*

YOTARŌ: *Huh, that's so, isn't it. Well, how about the public toilet?*

CUSTOMER: *Pretty weird antique store . . . Hey, won't you show me that saw (**noko**) over there?*

YOTARŌ: **noko?**

CUSTOMER: *I said show me the saw!*

YOTARŌ: *Well y'know . . . where (**doko**) could it be. . . .*

               Yotarō, not being able to decode *noko* as anything in his lexicon, re-maps it phonologically to *doko* 'where'.

CUSTOMER: *What are ya talking about! The SAW (**noko**)!*

YOTARŌ: *Salmon-eggs (**kazunoko**) y'mean?*
              His second attempt is no more successful. Thinking
              that *noko* might be short for *kazunoko* 'salmon roe', he
              tries that. The customer, in turn, realizes that he isn't
              getting his message across to Yotaro, and so he tries a
              new word.

CUSTOMER: *"Salmon eggs," he says. Now, what would salmon
              eggs be doing here? That two-handled saw (**yaritori**)!*

YOTARŌ: *To the death?*
              However, in Yotarō's lexicon, this item, *yaritori*, also
              has only one readout 'a duel', which is obviously not
              what his customer intends.

CUSTOMER: *A duel to the death? Why in the world? . . . It's a saw
              (**noko**) I want!*

YOTARŌ: *The scrub brush (**kamenoko**)?*
              Again, Yotarō tries to relate *noko* to something he
              knows, coming up with another inappropriate response,
              kamenoko 'scrub brush'.

CUSTOMER: *"Scrub brush" . . . SAW (**nokogiri**)!*

YOTARŌ: *Ah, the saw? (**nokogiri**) If y'want a saw you should say
              saw (**nokogiri**). It's a **noko**, it's a **noko** — ya musn't drop
              the **giri**!*
              To Yotarō, saying, "You musn't drop the *giri*," means
              literally just that with reference to the shortening of
              nokogiri to *noko*. To the customer, as to the audience,
              it has another meaning: "mustn't fail to observe your
              (*giri*) 'social obligations'.

CUSTOMER: *What're you talking about? What is this? Looks like its
              dull (**amasō**).*

YOTARŌ: *Maybe there's saccahrin in it.*
              The adjective *amai,* to the stem of which *-so* "Looks X"
              is added, has a "basic" meaning, "sweet", which by ex-
              tension:

              a. in the environment, "constructed things" — "not
                 put together well";
              b. in the environment, "social role X" — "not a very
                 good X"; etc.

              Yotarō obviously knows only the basic meaning, or
              doesn't know how to read contextual rules, and there-
              fore interprets *amaso* as 'looks sweet', responding
              inappropriately to both the intention of the customer's
              statement, and to the possibility of a saw having sac-
              charin in its composition.

CUSTOMER: *I mean it looks dull (**namakura**).*

YOTARŌ: *Kamakura (place name) is it?*
              Another lexeme with which Yotarō is obviously unfa-
              miliar, and he translates it into one with which he is,
              and which phonologically resembles the customer's.

CUSTOMER: *Naw, I'm saying it doesn't look properly forged (**yakeru**).*
YOTARŌ: *That's not possible. It's done to a turn.*
CUSTOMER: *Done to a turn? . . .*
YOTARŌ: *Yeah, Uncle picked it up from a place that'd burned (**yakeru**) down.*

In this last try at comprehending what the customer is talking about, the misunderstanding is due to the fact that, as in the other instances, Yotarō's readout does not contain any alternative meanings–lexemic representation, and, thus, he can not produce the "correct" one. In addition, this time he reveals, or convinces the customer, that the merchandise is worthless.

CUSTOMER: *Huh, you're selling ferocious stuff. How could anyone use such stuff.* (Walks away).
YOTARŌ: *He left!*
JIMBEI: *Don't stand around saying, "He's gone." I was in a cold sweat just sitting back there listening to you! It's cause you said that fool thing about picking up the saw from where there'd been a fire that he left without buying (**shōben**).*
YOTARŌ: *He pissed? (**shōben**) The guy who was just here? That was quick! Just like a bug. It's not even wet.*
JIMBEI: *No! You don't understand. **Shōben** means he didn't buy anything.*
YOTARŌ: *Then if he'd bought something he'd have shitted (**daiben**)? From now on, I'm wise: Don't let them leave without buying. Just tell them, "You mustn't **shoben**!"*

The first error Yotarō makes in this exchange depends on his having read /shōben/ as $shōben_1$, 'to piss, urinate', when Jimbei intends it as $shōben_2$ 'to break off negotiations'.

To understand Yotarō's second, more creative error, one must know the derivational meaning:

$$shōben \rightarrow sho\text{-} \quad \text{"small"} \atop + ben \quad \text{"evacuation"} \Bigg\} = \text{"urination"}$$

Yotarō extends this, by analogy to:

$$*diaben \rightarrow dia\text{-} \quad \text{"large"} \atop + ben \quad \text{"evacuation"} \Bigg\} = \text{"defecation"}$$

CUSTOMER 2: *Hey, antique-store man.*
YOTARŌ: *Ah, here comes somebody. Welcome!*
CUSTOMER 2: *Show me that **tako** there.*
YOTARŌ: *Huh?*
CUSTOMER 2: *I said show me that **tako**.*
YOTARŌ: *Huh? **tako**? What's that? Uh, if it's octopus ya want, it's at the fish store.*

As with the last customer, Yotarō can not understand what is meant by **tako**. The only thing he knows **tako** as is 'octapus', which, he replies, can not be found in his store.

CUSTOMER 2:   *I'm telling you to show me the pants (**momohiki**)!*

YOTARŌ: *Pants? Are you calling pants **tako**? You shouldn't use English!*

CUSTOMER 2:   *It's not English! They're called "octapus" because they have legs. Remember it! You're pretty new (**toshiro**) aren't you?*

YOTARŌ: (thinking that *toshiro* must be a name) *No, I'm Yotarō.*

CUSTOMER 2:   *I'm not asking your name. Hmph, a fine business-man. How much is this?*

YOTARŌ: *yeah . . .*

CUSTOMER 2:   *I'm asking you "how much."*

YOTARŌ: *Um . . . "how much," . . . I'll have to refuse, but . . . you . . . that . . . here, you mustn't go away without buying (**shōben**).*

CUSTOMER 2:   *What d'ya mean, I can't piss (**shōben**)?*

YOTARŌ: *Um, I'm saying you mustn't go away without buying (**shōben**).*

CUSTOMER 2:   *You mean these? It doesn't seem possible . . .*

YOTARŌ: *You can't!*

CUSTOMER 2:   *But . . . it looks like I could.*

YOTARŌ: *Well, it might look like you can, but . . . if you think it over, you'll see that you can't.*

CUSTOMER 2:   *That's pretty inconvenient. There's no point in buying something you can't even piss in. Well, I'll come back some other time . . .*

Through this entire exchange, Yotarō has been using *shōben*$_1$ 'break off negotiations', while the customer has been thinking he means *shōben*$_2$ "piss"; a situation not only funny in itself, but even more ludicrous when considered in the context of a pair of underpants.

YOTARŌ: *"Come back some other time?" Hey, what about? . . . Um, . . . its . . . just a minute, y'know. Huh, guess he meant a different **shōben**. That's why its so awful hard when you're just an amateur. Even when they tell you not to, ya just keep on doing the wrong thing.*

With the introduction of the next customer, the narrator switches into another dialect, that of the Northeast of Honshu, known in Japanese as *zūzū-ben* 'zūzū dialect'. In the minds of most native Japanese speakers, this represents a most devalued dialect. It in itself is considered reason for laughter, but here it has additional functions: It signals the approach of an individual, a yokel or country bumpkin by definition, who can't be much better off, in terms of comprehension, than Yotarō himself. It must also add to Yotarō's difficulties in decoding what he hears the customer saying.

CUSTOMER 3: *Hey, antique-store man! Mr. antique-store . . .*
YOTARŌ: *Welcome!*
CUSTOMER 3: *Wonder if you ain't got something rare (**tsun**) here??*
YOTARŌ: *Welcome!*
CUSTOMER 3: *Somethin' unusual, ain't ya got somethin' unusual? Doncha unnerstan' (**wakarankē**)?*
YOTARŌ: *An exhibition??? (**hakurankē**)*

In Yotarō's dialect, '(You) don't understand-question-tag' is represented *wakaranai kai.* In his customer's dialect *ai* goes to *ē* and the sequence *-nai* on the end of the verb is shortened to *-n,* producing the unintelligible, (to Yotarō), *wakarankē.* Yotarō can only come up with another lexeme resembling it: *Hakurankē*

CUSTOMER 3: *No; don't you have anything special. I'm saying, don't you have any rarities? (**tsunbutsu**)*
YOTARŌ: *Huh, you've come for sight-seeing (**kenbutsu**)?*

Another feature of the customer's dialect is that *č* goes to *ts* and *i* goes to *U,* transforming Standard Japanese *čin* to *Tohoku*-dialect *tsUn. Čin* (or *tsUn*)+*butsu,* "thing" is another expression meaning approximately the same, "rarities." Yotarō's attempts to decode this is to read /tsUn/ as *ken-* 'to see', and ask the customer has he come for "sightseeing"

CUSTOMER 3: *NO! I'm asking if you haven't got some rare things (**tsun**)!*
YOTARŌ: *A pekinese (**tsun**/**chin**) is it? We haven't got any. There's a cat over on yonder roof . . .*

Trying this time on *tsUn* alone, which he has managed to equate to *čin,* Yotarō again reads out the wrong interpretation:

$chin_1$ — oddities, rare things
$chin_2$ — Pekinese dog,

and replies accordingly.

CUSTOMER 3: *NO! that's not what I mean. I'm asking haven't you got something unusual?*
YOTARŌ: (crying)
CUSTOMER 3: *If you have any, how's about showin' me somethin', y'know.*
YOTARŌ: (tentatively) *No, I don' wanna.*
CUSTOMER 3: *Cut it out! Show me something!*
YOTARŌ: (crying) *Uncle, help!*

By this point, Yotarō, unable to successfully decode what the customer is saying, breaks off interaction completely and violates a basic scene-rule: Although he is nominally there to show his merchandise and sell it to the buyer, he refuses to do just that.

CUSTOMER 3: *Ya stupe! That thing over there! How about showin' me that book (**tōsen**)?!*

YOTARŌ: *Excuse me?*
CUSTOMER 3: *Show me that book (**hon**) over there.*
YOTARŌ: *Pardon me?*
CUSTOMER 3: *I say, woncha show me that book (**hon**) over there?*
YOTARŌ: *Oh, is it this book? Even if I show it to you, you won't
                      be able to read it.*
CUSTOMER 3: *Naw, I can read.*
YOTARŌ: *Not this one. Its only a binding . . .*
CUSTOMER 3: *How about that candlestick holder (**šokudai**) in the
                      back, huh?*
YOTARŌ: *That two-legged one?*
CUSTOMER 3: *Naw, I don't want it; it's only two legs; what use is it?*
YOTARŌ: *It used to have three legs . . . but, it lost a leg . . . If
                      you were to buy that brick wall over there it's propped
                      up against, y'know . . . You could talk to the owner
                      about it . . .*
CUSTOMER 3: *What nonsense! Show me that short-sword (**tantō**) over
                      there.*
YOTARŌ: *Huh?*
CUSTOMER 3: *I said show me the short-sword (**tantō**)!*
YOTARŌ: *Lots (**tanto**) or a little, I can only show you what's
                      here.*
                      Yotarō obviously does not know the name of an item
                      of his own merchandise, and associates it with the only
                      lexeme he has resembling it: **tantō**, 'a lot'.
CUSTOMER 3: *Naa, that's not what I mean. That — the little sword
                      (**tsusē katana**).*
YOTARŌ: (handing it to him) *"Little sword . . . "* (**tsusē katana**).
CUSTOMER 3: (looking at the sword) *Ha, this looks like some maker's
                      name (**zaimei**), doesn't it?*
YOTARŌ: *Huh?*
CUSTOMER 3: *I said, there's a signature (**mei**) . . .*
YOTARŌ: *I got no niece (**mei**) . . . I've got an aunt in
                      Kanda . . .*
                      In this sequence, *mei$_1$* 'name, signature' is undoubtedly
                      too literary a word for Yotarō. He can only interpret
                      the form as *mei$_2$* 'niece'. Unlike many of the forms
                      which he misinterprets, these are, the homonymous,
                      distinct lexemes sharing no basic meanings.
CUSTOMER 3: (trying to pull the sword out of its sheath) *Ya gotta
                      keep the merchandise cleaned. Ya can't let it get all
                      dirty. Ya gotta clean it. It's 'cause ya let it get dirty
                      that it's all rusty . . . I can't get it out . . .*
YOTARŌ: *Ah, it takes more than one person to pull* that *out. . . .*
CUSTOMER 3: *Gimme a hand, pull there. Yeah, but we gotta pull
                      together. O.K., a-one, a-two and a-threeee* (both
                      pulling) *Ugh, and a-four. . . . This one just won't
                      come out.*

YOTARŌ: *It may never come out. . . . It's a wooden-sword* (***bokutō***) *y'know.*

CUSTOMER 3: *Y'mean you've been trying to have me unsheath a wooden sword?*

YOTARŌ: *You asked me to give you a hand. . . . I was only trying to save your face. . . .*

CUSTOMER 3: *You moron! Haven't you got one that comes loose?*

YOTARŌ: *Yeah, that doll over there has a loose head.*

Yotarō, in attempting to apply *nukeru* 'come loose', does so inappropriately and, in so doing, violates the reference of the previous sentence.

CUSTOMER 3: *Show me that gun* (***tanegashima***)

YOTARŌ: *Huh?*

Tanegashima was another name for the island in the harbor of Nagasaki where, during the Tokugawa period (1616–1868) the Dutch were confined as the only Europeans to have trading relations with Japan. One of the traded items was guns, thus the name came to be associated with, and used as slang for, the item. Yotarō, unfortunately, doesn't seem to know this. In the next question, the customer drops this referent and switches to the common word for gun (***teppō***).

CUSTOMER 3: *I thought I said show me the gun* (***teppō***).

YOTARŌ: *Heh?*

CUSTOMER 3: *How much is this gun, huh?*

YOTARŌ: *Huh?*

CUSTOMER 3: *I said, how much is this gun, huh?* (***nanboka tsuŋu***)

YOTARŌ: *bokatsun is it?*

The customer is using, instead of the more "standard" word for "how much," i.e., *ikura,* a slang word, *nanbo.* Yotarō's response is at first nothing, which forces the customer to repeat his question, adding, "I said," which in his dialect comes out /tsuŋu/ instead of, as in Yotarō's dialect, /teitteru/, or /teitten/. This sequence of the unfamiliar /nanbo/ plus /tsunu/ is so bewildering to Yotarō that he can only reply with a sequence that sounds like it might be a word, but actually has no meaning, /bokatsun/.

CUSTOMER 3: *I'm saying how much is this.........*

YOTARŌ: *How many bo?* (***nanbo***)

The form *nanbo,* "How much," which the customer is using, is being decoded at this point by Yotarō, as would be a numeral classifier: the form *nan-* "how many" plus-*bo* "how many *bo?*" and Yotarō doesn't know what a *bo* might be.

CUSTOMER 3: *It's how much?* (***nan bo n***)

YOTARŌ: *One* (***ippon***)!

This line of interpretive confusion is pushed even further when in the customer's dialect he repeats his question, nominalizing the phrase he has just used, *nanbo?* This emerges, instead of /*nanbo no*/ (Standard Japanese representation), /*nanbo n*/, which is picked up by Yotarō as *nanbon*, "how many (long, thin objects)": *nan-* "how many" plus-*hon* 'long, thin objects', and he answers accordingly, *ippon* 'one (long, thin object)' — obviously with reference to the gun.

CUSTOMER 3: *No, that's not what I'm talking about. What about the price (**dai**) of the gun?*

YOTARŌ: *Its oak!*

Customer's intention: dai_1 'price, value'

Yotarō's interpretation: dai_2 'stock of the gun'

CUSTOMER 3: *No, no, I mean money (**kane**)!*

Customer's intention: $kane_1$ 'money'.

Yotarō's interpretation: $kane_2$ 'metal'.

YOTARŌ: *It's iron!*

CUSTOMER 3: *What about the price (**ne**)?*

Customer's intention: $ne_1 \rightarrow nedan$ 'price'

Yotarō's interpretation: $ne_2 \rightarrow neoto$ 'sound'

YOTARŌ: ***zudon** 'bang' sound of gun going off; also, sound of something falling.*

IV. Analysis

I have been motivated to account for *dōguya* in two ways: (1) to specify what makes it "funny" to a native Japanese speaker, and (2) to account for it as an instance of that class of events known as *rakugō* as a total communication event. This includes an accounting of the identities of sender(s) and relations among and receiver(s), channel(s) in use, code(s), context, and how and about what reference is made.[5]

When one views this *rakugō* performance as a communication event it becomes apparent that there is not just a single set of senders and receivers, as in communication events like, for example, a "conversation." Rather we must recognize *two* sets of senders and two sets of receivers. The first one is the identities of "narrator" and "audience." While they alternate as both sender and receiver in the interaction, their communication is for the most part one-way: The narrator tells a story — an almost exclusive control of the verbal channel of communication. The audience is much more restricted as sender: They laugh, and clap at structurally determined points in the narration. They might also remain silent or leave as a way of sending negative messages.

[5] See Hymes (1962, 1964).

The second set of identities which we must recognize as senders and receivers is that within the narration itself: Yotarō, Magobei, Jimbei and the "customers" who occur therein.

By this criterion, i.e., recognizing these two sets of senders and receivers forces us to conclude that there is not just one simple communication event taking place. That is, that the structure of this communication event *needs* the occurrence of two simultaneous communication events: one between identities filled by "real" people, the narrator and the audience, and one among identities within the narration who are "imaginary," or at least not present.

The way in which reference is made and what is referred to is also related to the nature of these two events: Within the narrated event—the interaction between the characters in the story—reference is made in a direct, nonmetalinguistic, nonmetacommunicative way to "real world" meanings. However, communication between the narrator and the audience refers to (1) the messages being sent between senders and receivers within the narration, e.g., the laughter of the audience, and (2) the cultural concepts of competent sender, receiver, and well-formed message. These references are made indirectly by the narrator constructing the dialogues between the characters within the narration. Because they refer to elements of communication, they are metacommunicative.[6]

Thus, in order to account for this particular *rakugō* narration as a communication event (and not just a text), we must recognize the following elements:

1. Two simultaneous communication events: (a) a metacommunicative event between the narrator and the audience, and (b) a nonmetacommunicative event involving the characters invented by the narrator in the context of the monologue.

2. Messages within event (a), the metacommunicative, concern the components of the communication events represented within event (b).

3. Manipulation of the different components of the linguistic code—that is, the phonological, referential semantic and sociolinguistic—by the narrator in patterning the messages within event (b) to both create humor and make the indirect metacommunicative reference to the communicative code (including cultural values).

In what follows I have first outlined the ways in which the humor is linguistically determined by the structure of the messages and interaction in event (b). That is, I have shown how the narrator manipulates the

---

[6] The concepts of metacommunication developed here rely heavily on those of Bateson. See Bateson, 1955.

phonological, referential semantic, and sociolinguistic components of the language code with which he constructs utterances for the characters he creates. I have then tried to show how these elements are patterned within the structure of the narration as an event; how and about what the narrator communicates to the audience; and, finally, how these messages from the narrator to the audience serve to define the total event in which both are participating, and to place it in the wider context of Japanese thinking about different kinds of cultural behaviors and their characteristics.

The characterization of Yotarō, the fool, is critical to the humorousness of the monologue. This is because, behind a definition of what is "funny" in *rakugo,* there is the requirement of an incompletely transmitted or misinterpreted message. It follows that only with a fool, that is, a socially incomplete human being, can this happen. This characterization is accomplished here in two ways: (1) in the misinterpretation by Yotarō of messages sent by others, and (2) in Yotarō's general misapprehension of the sociophysical world in which he lives.

I. Yotarō's lack of information about the sociophysical world: This characteristic is demonstrated in his behavior in several scenes.

A. Yotarō doesn't know how to hold and look at a scroll. He holds it sideways, making it look like the fish painted thereon is "eating noodles," when, in fact, he is swimming upstream. In addition, he fails to recognize the fish as a carp, a never-eaten symbol of bravery and persistence — highly valued traits — in Japan. He thinks it is, instead, a mullet, a common and often-eaten fish. This kind of lack of information puts him outside the pale of human, that is, Japanese, society.

B. He tells how to catch a mouse — that is, by letting it grate itself away to nothing by trying to eat some rice stuck to a grater — also demonstrates this basic lack of understanding about the physical world.

C. He tries to get as a customer for his new "store" a man riding by on a motorcycle.

D. He tries to sell the wall of a building against which a candle-stick with only two legs is propped, ostensibly, so that the customer could use the candle-stick.

II. Beyond this show of general stupidity on Yotarō's part, we can recognize a series of messages, which either were not received by him, or we might say, having been "received" were improperly decoded. These fall into several types, as determined by the component of the language being manipulated in their construction; in other words, the component at which the message fails to be decoded, as indicated by the response made by Yotarō.

A. On the lowest level there is simply no response from Yotarō. An example of this is seen in his interaction with Customer 3:

CUSTOMER: *ano tanegasUma-o misē.*
          Show me that gun.
YOTARŌ: (silence)

The reason for his response is simple enough: Yotarō can not relate what he is hearing to anything in his language model.

B. The next kind of error involves simple phonological play. Most of the instances of these errors seem to be defineable within the context of the narrative as follows: Yotarō is unable to match the form presented by his opposite to anything identical to what is in his phonological component. However, he tries to do so, usually by finding a form with one phoneme different from the one he is presented with, and a meaning that is consequently quite different and sometimes hilarious in the context.

1. He associates *dorobo burglary* with *dōguya antique business* on the basis of their both beginning with the syllable *do-*.

2. He does not recognize *kakemono wall-hanging scroll* and produces in response *bakemono ghost*.

3. He doesn't recognize *namakura dull, blunt* and produces instead, *Kamakura* (place name).

4. He has no phonetic representation matching Customer 3's dialectal *wakarankē (You) don't understand?* and produces the phonetically close *hakurankē an exhibition* — with question intonation. This is one of the more successful examples of this type because of the way in which Yotarō's response serves to answer the question negatively.

5. He has no idea what *tsunbutsu rare or unusual item* could be, and through scanning his phonological component can only come up with *kenbutsu sightseeing*. This play is amusing in the context of the fact that the customer with whom he is interacting is not native to the city and might well be there for sightseeing.

6. A customer asks to be shown a *noko* (→ *nokogiri*) *saw,* and Yotarō, not being able to decode the form, understands it as *doko where*.

7. When the customer tells him that he is *new, an amateur, toshiro,* he doesn't recognize this form and, because of its formal similarity to the general pattern of male first names, responds with his own — Yotarō.

All of these examples utilize sequences which Yotarō has no trouble in recognizing as lexemes, although he can not recognize *which* lexemes they are. However, at the end of the narration, in his interaction with the Tohōku farmer with the impossible dialect, not only can he not match-up the phonetic sequences with any lexemes in his repertoire, but he can not recognize the boundaries to the lexemes which would enable him to identify units. Thus:

> CUSTOMER 3: ***nanbo ka tsunu.***
> *I say, "how much"?*
> YOTARŌ: ****bokatsun deska?***
> *Is it "bokatsun"?*

That is, while the customer's construction is ***nanbo*** *how much* plus ***ka*** *question tag* plus ***tsunu*** *I say/said*, because of the foreignness of the sequence to Yotarō's ears, it is impossible for him to decipher as a unit anything but the initial /*nan*/, which he interprets, as becomes clear later, as *how many*. He thinks the central portion of the customer's utterance: /*nan*/ /*bokatsun*/ /*u*/ might be a word.

In addition to these examples, there are two others, which depend on phonological play linked with shifts in meaning. In addition, these examples are not presented by the narrator within the frame of "unreceived message."

8. As Yotarō is making his way through the streets and soliloquizing about the evil people to be found in the *rag-collecting* business (***kuzuya***), he transforms ***kuzui,*** the call of the rag-collectors, into ***zurui,*** *sly, foul, dishonest.* These are related phonetically in that the second syllable of the first form is repeated in the first syllable of the second form, and that they both end in *-i*, which usually marks a subclass of inflecting adjectives in Japanese, though it is a false marker in the case of ***kuzui.*** Thus:

> *ku   zu   i*
> *zu   ru   i*

9. The humorousness of the *akizuni–akinai* play on words depends on the knowledge that (a) Both *-zu* and *-nai* are negative inflections for verbs and thus:

> ***akizu-ni***   *not giving up*
> ***akinai***

and (b) There are two readings for the verb *akinai:* (1) ***akinai***$_1$ *not grow tired of, not give up* and (2) ***akinai***$_2$ *business, commerce, trades.*

These are the only two instances of this kind of play which do not involve the idea of an uncommunicated message. The second, *akinai/akizuni,* is also almost the only instance in the narrative that did not produce laughter.

C. Punning: the referential semantic component. This is the major humorous form of the narrative. We can define it as having Yotarō's interpretation of a lexeme made, not on the semantic reading intended by the sender of the message, but, because he can not match it properly, to some other meaning. All but one example in the narration involving the semantic component of the language can be considered to fit this definition.

There are two kinds of devices responsible for these lexemic mismatchings.

1. *Whole-form homonymy.* The form the sender intends is identical phonetically to the one the receiver interprets, but they have different possible semantic readings. These form the bulk of the puns in this narration.

   a. Magobei's intention: **$gomi_2$** *leftovers of sets of things,* slang for *merchandise*
      Yotarō's interpretation: **$gomi_1$** *garbage*
   b. Magobei's intention: **$kobosu_2$** *complain, cry about*
      Yotarō's interpretation: **$kobosu_1$** *spill, knock over*
   c. Jimbei's intention: *$Jimbei_a$ man's name*
      Yotarō's interpretation: **$jimbei_b$** *article of clothing*
   d. Customer's intention: **$yaritori_3$** *two-handled saw*
      Yotarō's interpretation: **$yaritori_2$** *duel*

One can see that the forms in (d) are ultimately related semantically through the idea of back-and-forth motion. The basic meaning of *$yaritori_1$* probably being "exchange" of action.

   e. Customer's intention: **$amasō_2$** *looks blunt, dull*
      Yotarō's interpretation: **$amaso_1$** *looks sweet* (taste)
   f. Customer's intention: **$yakeru_2$** *forge*
      Yotarō's interpretation: **$yakeru_1$** *burn, cook*
   g. Jimbei's intention: **$shōben_2$** *break off interaction*
      Yotarō's interpretation: **$shōben_1$** *to piss*
   h. Customer's intention: **$tako_2$** *underpants*
      Yotarō's interpretation: **$tako_1$** *octapus*
   i. Customer's intention: **$tsun_a$** *rare, unusual items*
      Yotarō's interpretation: **$tsun_b$** *Pekinese dog*
   j. Customer's intention: **$tantō_a$** *short sword*
      Yotarō's interpretation: **$tanto_b$** *a lot, large amount*
   k. Customer's intention: **$nukeru_2$** *unsheath* (of swords)
      Yotarō's interpretation: **$nukeru_1$** *come loose*
   l. Jimbei's intention: **$temae_2$** *self-referent, humble*
      Yotarō's interpretation: **$temae_1$** *spatial relations, "in front of"*

m. Customer's intention: ***dai*$_a$** *price, value*
   Yotarō's interpretation: ***dai*$_b$** *stock of a gun*
n. Customer's intention: ***kane*$_2$** *money*
   Yotarō's interpretation: ***kane*$_1$** *metal*

Note that within this category of puns, there are two kinds of whole homonymy; that, as with all of the examples *except* numbers c, i, j, and m, the lexemes, in addition to being phonetically identical, also share some basic meaning, or are related by a process, even though it be historical, of metaphorical extension. The kind of homonymy involved in examples c, i, j, and m we might call "other-domain homonymy." That is, the lexemes are unrelated as to meaning and, in fact, are in completely different semantic domains, and only accidentally sound alike.

2. In addition to the examples above, there are a few puns determined by what I have called "part-form homonymy." That is, the fool's opposite presents him with a form that is either homonymous to a whole lexeme in itself, or to part of a variety of other lexemes.

a. Customer's intention: ***noko*** → ***nokogiri*** *saw*
   Yotarō's interpretations:
   noko → ***kazunoko*** *salmon roe*
   noko → ***kamenoko*** *scrub-brush*
b. Customer's intention: ***mei−zaimei*** *maker's name*
   Yotarō's interpretation: ***mei*** *niece*
c. Customer's intention: ***ne−nedan*** *price*
   Yotarō's interpretation: ***ne*** → ***neoto*** *sound*

The only item that involves the semantic component of language and is *not* a pun is the error Yotarō makes in the initial exchange of the narrative. He replies to Magobei's question as to where he is playing, goofing-off, with a response that lets us know he does not consider the inclusion relation:

   asobu (*burabura suru*, . . .) to hold

The errors described are all determined by the fool's inability to match incoming information to whatever language model he has in his head—and one of the messages the audience is supposed to get is that his language competence is not too great. However, one item in the narrative was dependent on Yotarō's improper *encoding:*

   Yotarō's intention: ***-giri*$_a$** (morph) *cutter*
   Customer's (and audience's) interpretation: ***giri*$_b$** *social obligations*

There are two other features which function to create humor from the "errors" committed here. First of all, as can be noted from all the examples of same-domain puns, the interpretations made by Yotarō are the primary, or dominant, meaning of the lexemes; the reading intended by his interlocutors is always the secondary or less-common meaning. Compounded with this is the fact that Yotarō must ignore contextual clues as to proper decoding in order to make these interpretations.

In most of the examples of "punning" error in the narrative, the misunderstanding is a simple one: one lexical confusion. However, there is one place where the confusion crosses grammatical boundaries. At the end of the narration, when Yotarō is in the midst of his phenomenally unsuccessful interview with the farmer from the Tōhoku, he is asked:

> CUSTOMER 3: *kono..teppo-wa* (almost whispering) *nanbo?*

Yotarō, as described above, after initially not responding, makes several attempts to relate the customer's question to something he knows. These fail and the customer repeats:

> CUSTOMER 3: *nanbo ka tsunu, kore-wa*
> *How much, I'm saying, (is) this.*
> YOTARŌ: (to himself) *nanbo . . .*

At this point the customer unwittingly provides Yotarō with another phonological clue by nominalizing what Yotarō has just said:

> CUSTOMER 3: *nanbo n*
> *It's "how much?"*

which Yotarō can only match to a completely different grammatical derivation:

> *nanbon* → *nan-*   *numeral form, how-many*
>   plus *-hon*   *classifier: long, slender objects*

This, of course determines his response: *ippon* *one long, slender object.*

Although some of the puns in the narration stand by themselves, the exploitation of the pun as a humorous device in *rakugo* is not limited to their serving to produce misinterpreted ambiguity alone. The whole point of the use of puns, in fact, is their elaboration, and I will show why later in the discussion. That is, the fool—the misinterpreting receiver of the message—must develop them in some way.

There are seven points in the narrative where these developments of puns take place:

1. When Yotarō confuses *Jimbei*$_a$, *man's name* with *jimbei*$_b$ *article of clothing,* it leads to a violation of another rule, this time a basic rule of interaction: by stating that "it"/he looks like *jimbei*$_b$ is never washed.

2. One of the most successful puns, in this sense, is on /*gomi*/. Yotarō, after making his initial mistake of not knowing that Magobei meant *gomi*$_2$ *mismatched merchandise,* then extends it in a false analogy so that: *gomi*$_1$ *refuse,* less elegant: *hokori*$_1$ *refuse,* more elegant, and *gomi*$_2$

partial sets of merchandise: **hokori$_2$ whole sets of merchandise.* However, this is not the only way this lexeme is used. Later, when Yotarō is walking through the streets, talking to himself, and tries to recall what Magobei has said to him about his work, he recalls *gomi$_1$*, that is, not its slang meaning. This determines his recall of *kuzuya rag collector,* instead of *dōguya antique dealer,* as Magobei's trade.

3. Yotarō's comments in response to *yakeru* are developed in the sense that his first response leaves us not quite clear as to how his decoding is inappropriate. When he says that the saw was picked up at a place that burned down, it becomes clear that he is inappropriate in two ways, both (a) to the customer's meaning of *yakeru$_2$ forge,* and (b) in the context of his own expression, *done to a turn,* applicable, of course, only to food. In this case he is not talking about food, nor is food cooked or saws forged in burning buildings.

4. The development of *tako underpants* goes further than the simple counter-message from Yotarō, indicating that he does not understand the same form his customer intends. It allows for the message that he thinks the form is English, a situation probably humorous to the audience because the rapid rate with which English forms are being borrowed currently tends to cause just such situations to actually occur.

5. *Temae* is an interesting form because the error here involves a shift between two of the components of the language code. As explained above, Yotarō's confusion with regard to this form is due to the fact that /temae/ is "basically" a spatial reference form—with a "secondary" meaning of pronominal reference. In showing that he is unfamiliar with its secondary meaning, Yotarō also demonstrates that he does not know this set of social rules for language usage.

6. The play on *noko — nokogiri saw* also involves development in that it leads to the presentation of /giri/ → *giri$_a$ -cutter* and *giri$_b$ obligations.*

7. Probably the most amusing, certainly the most elaborated, pun in the narration is that built on /shoben/. The first time around the misunderstanding over this form takes place between Yotarō and Jimbei. Jimbei intends it as *shōben$_2$ to break off interaction,* and Yotarō understands it as *shōben$_1$ to piss.* To show his misunderstanding, Yotarō must comment: *The guy who was just here? That was quick, just like a bug.*[7] *And it's not even wet.* The second time around, Yotarō is the one intending *shōben$_2$* while his customer, who is considering buying a pair of

---

[7] I have translated *semi* as "bug", although, strictly speaking, it is a particular species of insect, usually glossed *cicada. Semi* do not have the connotations in Japanese that "bugs" have in English, but are, rather, asthetic images. For example their crying is associated with the end of summer, hence, sadness. They are mentioned with this implication in poetic forms. Their dying and leaving a shell or husk has been used as an image in Buddhist writings. Yotarō's utterance in this context is incongruous because of these connotations and because his statement *semi mitai like a cicada* usually implies refinement. It might be said, for example, of a woman's dainty eating habits.

underpants, understands *shōben*₁. In addition, /*shōben*/ is elaborated by Yotarō in the same way that /*gomi*/ was developed, that is, on a false analogy:

> if   ***shoben***₁ → ***sho-*** *small* + ***-ben*** *evacuation* = *urinate,*
> then   ****daiben*** → ***dai-*** *large* + ***-ben*** *evacuation* = *defecate.*

Rules of Social Usage: The Sociolinguistic Component

Under this heading I have grouped three separate areas in which deficiencies in Yotarō's language model show up:

1. kinesic interpretation
2. violation of discourse rules
3. lack of familiarity with paradigms for honorifics

First of all, Yotarō misunderstands the implications of facial expression. He interprets the fact that Magobei has not changed expression, when accused of being a thief, to mean that he is the leader of a gang of thieves, the *ōmono.* Generally, there are two meanings to *ōmono:*

1. *ōmono*₁, "someone who is a 'great human being' because of their human qualities or virtues; a saintly person." An index of this is that they react little to outside, social stimuli, and one of the ways of indicating this is by not registering with facial expressions.

2. However, *omono*₂ means 'someone of importance within the structure of the social group to which he belongs (e.g., bank president, department chairman, or, head of a gang of thieves).'

Thus in this case Yotarō has taken the cues for *ōmono*₁ and deduced *omono*₂.

He breaks discourse rules. There are three instances of this kind of violation:

1. He shouts that he has a *piping-hot antique store.* He is modeling his behavior on summonses he has seen in other settings defined as "selling merchandise." However, as in the mistakes he makes in referential semantics, he has failed to note contextual restraints on the linguistic interpretations to be made: the settings in which he has heard this form used as summons were where the merchandise being sold was cooked food.

2. When finally getting a customer, again inappropriately applying a rule from a similar setting, Yotarō invites the customer to *Please, step upstairs,* although his "store" is nothing but a mat spread in the street. When this is pointed out to him, he tries again with a different line: *Well then, how about the public toilet?*.

3. He fails to observe opening rules in his interaction with Jimbei: he addresses Jimbei as an inferior although Jimbei is older than himself and Yotaro is seeking his help in "setting up business."

4. He also fails to observe proper closing rules: He says *sayonara* when leaving his own "area" and when corrected by Magobei and told to say *itte mairimasu,* a phatic form whose meaning is its function as a closer, Yotarō replies, not with the identical form which would be correct, but by changing it to a perfect-aspect inflection: *itte mairimashita.* This makes his utterance incongruous for two reasons: (a) It takes the utterance out of the class of openers and closers (*aisatsu*) and forces a decoding of its literal meaning, *itte mairimashita* '(I've) gone and come back,' which (b) is, of course, physically and temporally out of place, as he has not yet left.

5. He responds inappropriately to a command. On leaving Magobei's he is told: *Close the door behind you* to which he replies: **okamainaku** *Don't bother on my account.* In doing so, he replies as though Magobei's last utterance were in fact just the opposite of a command—an offer to do something for him.

In addition to the discourse rules violated, and thus referenced Yotarō's "fool"-ishness is used to produce misinterpretations in two paradigms involved in distinguishing honorific speech in Japanese. Although these paradigms are quite developed, invading many lexical domains, only two are utilized in this narrative. They are (1) verbs for "giving," and (2) self and other reference.

I have already mentioned that, in his interpretation of /temae/ as **temae**$_1$ *spatial relations, in front of X,* and not as **temae**$_2$ *self-reference, humble, anonymous,* Yotarō has demonstrated that he is not familiar with at least this form. Quickly following this, he blunders again: He omits the required suffix, *-san,* from the names of Magobei and Jimbei. While this might be done with the names of same-age, intimate, same-sex friends, it would never be done in referring to elders, especially if one of the referrents is present. In almost the same breath, Yotarō *adds* *-san* to his own name and completes the reversal of prescribed usage rules.

The other paradigm, which has a social rather than a purely referential meaning and whose rules are violated by Yotarō's decoding process, is that of verb usage for "giving." In Japanese, in talking about the direction in which actions or "things" move, whether for example, from the speaker to a second or third person, pronouns and even subjects are usually not used. Instead of the use of pronouns, one can tell who the behavior or the "things" are going toward and who they are coming from by the use of particular verb forms belonging to paradigms that encode features of the "relative height" of the end points of the transaction. A partial representation of the paradigm of verbs for "giving" in Japanese is as follows:

Verb form	Implied height of end points	*Gloss:* 'I give to':
sashiaŋeru	much lower to much higher	'guest, boss, customer'
aŋeru	low to high	'anyone, honorific'
suru	slightly higher to slightly lower	'anyone, nonhonorific'
yaru	much higher to much lower	'dogs, children, wives'

Thus, to choose a proper verb form we need to know the relative status of the participants to the interaction. Conversely, hearing the choice of a verb form will let us know how the speaker conceptualizes the relationship between the people he is talking about. In the narrative, Yotarō, however, demonstrates that he is not familiar with this paradigm and nullifies Jimbei's politeness by decoding /sashiaŋeru/ as **sashiaŋeru₁** To *raise, lift above the head.* This also points up the basic meaning from which the honorific form was derived.

I would next like to consider the way in which all of the above-mentioned elements of rule violation are patterned within the structure of the narrative as a whole. The first feature of patterning noticeable is that there is a gradual increase or concentration of points of humor in what might be called the space of a unit within the monologue. This can be seen graphically in the following chart:

Segment of narration	Kinds of rule violations
A. Events at Magobei's	*kobosu* — referential semantic
A.1. discussion of mother	*asobu* — referential semantic
A.2. Magobei's trade	*dorobo-dōguya* — phonological
	ōmono — kinesic-semantic
	gomi — referential semantic
A.3. looking at "merchandise"	*bakemono* — phonological
	koi — referential semantic
	nekoirazu irazu — phonological
A.4. closing	*sayonara* — discourse rules
	okamainaku — discourse rules
B. Interlude of walking through town	*kuzui-zurui* — phonological-semantic
C. Events at Jimbei's	
C.1. Opening	*sashiaŋeru* — semantic-sociolinguistic
	inappropriate reference — sociolinguistic

C.1. Opening (cont.)   *temae* — semantic–sociolinguistic
                                    jimbei — semantic
                                    akizuni–akinai — phonological-
                                       semantic

C.2. First customer interac-
     tion
                                    inappropriate customer
                                       opening — discourse
                                    inappropriate discourse rules
                                    noko–doko — phonological
                                    giri — referential semantic
                                    amasō — referential semantic
                                    namakura–
                                       kamakura — phonological

C.3. Customer 2 interaction
                                    shōben — referential semantic
                                    tako — referential semantic
                                    toshiro — referential semantic

C.4. Customer 3 interaction
                                    tsunbutsu — phonological
                                    tsun — referential semantic
                                    wakarankē — phonological
                                    violation of interaction rules
                                    tanto — phonological–semantic
                                    mei — referential semantic
                                    nukeru — referential semantic
                                    bokatsun — phonological
                                    nanbon — grammatical–semantic
                                    dai — referential semantic
                                    kane — referential semantic
                                    ne — referential semantic
                                    zudon — referential semantic

In addition to there being more items of humorous involvement per sequential unit toward the end of the narration, the complexity of their relatedness becomes more involved. That is, in the opening sequences, the play made or the incident of rule violation stands by itself without leading into another lost message. Toward the end, however, more inappropriate decodings made by Yotarō are followed by responses that elaborate the puns.

There are other devices within the narration by which the *rakugōka* indirectly metacommunicates with the audience. Some of these messages are very superficial: Within the context of the narration, in the form of communication from one of the characters — usually Jimbei, Magobei or one of the customers — the narrator gives information about the messages being sent to another character, usually Yotarō. Typically, this is information about the proper decoding of a message. It tells the audience what mistake Yotarō has made, seemingly just in case they did not catch it.[8] Thus, at the beginning of the narrative, Magobei, in response to Yotarō's saying that he is not *loafing* about, *asobu,* but that he is *goofing off,* **burabura suru,** informs the audience that they are related. Later on, where it most certainly counts for more, the customers tell what they mean by the slang they are using, and these are forms that the audience might well not know: *We call them* **tako,** *"octapus," because they have legs,* says the customer of **momohiki** *underpants.* Even the yokel from the Tōhoku lets us know at the beginning of the interaction that he equates **mezurashii mono** *unusual things, Standard dialect* with **tsun** *unusual things, Tōhoku dialect.*

Another important way in which the narrator communicates with the audience is by framing. There are several features to the event by which this is accomplished. The first of these is in the naming of the characters. The names Magobei and Jimbei are nothing more than old-fashioned, merchant-class, Shitamachi—i.e., downtown Tokyo male names. "Yotarō" however, connotes more than just this. The last syllable -*ro* is one affixed commonly to males' names of the recent past. *Yota-,* however, has a bad connotation. It is associated with the epithet *yotamono,* a man who plays around, that is, is given to drinking, gambling and playing with women. The label for a socially-defined non-man, in other words, "Yotarō" is a name no parent would give a son.

Along with Yotarō's name, the introduction at the beginning of the narration cues us that the interaction is going to be about a fool. With the characters' opening lines we are given other clues as to the nature of this performance in the dialect of the speech of Magobei and Yotarō, that is, Shitamachi speech. I have described the connotations or associations this has for Japanese audiences in the introductory pages of this paper: it alone is considered reason for laughter.

These two features, dialect and names, in addition, of course, to the whole physical context of the theater, "sets up" the audience for the kind of speech event they can expect to hear.

As the narration progresses, the narrator frames each of the events within the story. In other words, he provides a context for each of the incidents of misunderstanding which occur. Thus, the context of leave-taking serves as an opportunity to have Yotarō break a closing-discourse rule. The context of interaction opening, calling for an introduction,

---

[8] This may occur because the narrator wants to insure that the audience "gets" the joke and is not sure whether in fact they know the meanings of these somewhat archaic slang forms.

provides a frame within which to violate rules of self and other reference.

In order to account for what the narrator is communicating about to the audience we must recognize that the following constitute elements in the metacode shared by the narrator and the audience:

sender	code	message
receiver	topic	

The narrator is by mention communicating about messages — messages that are not completed. The reason that the messages do not get completed is due to the characterization of one of the characters, the receiver of most of the incomplete messages. The narrator's examples tell the audience that this is because the receiver's code is deficient. Without considering these concepts, we could not account for what is being thought about the meta-communication that is taking place in the theater. Possibly more importantly, we must acknowledge that the audience has these concepts, else nothing in the monologue would be humorous to them.

The narrator communicates with the audience in yet another way — by successfully manipulating the interaction of the two related events taking place. This is pointed out at the end of the monologue by a special device I have already presented although not explained.

Up until this point, the narrator has presented his narrative straight. That is, he has communicated his messages on the meta-level indirectly by characterizing language and cultural rules through examples of their violation. He has never referred to any meta-language unit directly. As the last sequence ends, he breaks this pattern. When the third customer asks: *ne ja No, no, the price* and Yotarō, thinking *ne → ne'oto sound,* replies, *zudon,* the two levels, i.e., the "pseudo-level" of communication with its referential use of language between the characters within the narration and the "real" level of communication with its use of language as mention between the narrator and the audience, are brought together and the distinction between them is neutralized. This, in turn, serves as another kind of message: a comment on the speech event itself.

Zudon$_1$ bang, the sound of a gun going off is a perfectly appropriate response by Yotarō, given his inappropriate reading of *ne → ne'oto sound.* But at the same time *zudon$_2$ the sound of something falling* refers to the performance itself in the following way: The label of this particular genre, *rakugo* "punning word play monologue," might better be glossed on the basis of its derivational meaning. That is:

rakugo → raku-	'to fall, Sino-Japanese morph shape'	$\Big\}$ = *falling words*
plus *-go*	'language, speech'	

Similarly, the individual "puns", *ochiba,* would seem to be better glossed as "falling words" on the basis of:

ochiba → *ochi* 'to fall, indigenous Japanese morph shape'
plus *-ha* 'place', point

These meanings are recognized by Japanese speakers, and the functional implication of the "falling words," that is, puns for the narrative, is that with the occurrence of an *ochiba,* interaction "falls" from the line one would normally expect to be its course. That is, each time a pun appears, the expected line of interaction is interrupted and "dropped" in a direction from that in which it appeared to be going.[9] Thus at all those points in the narration where the fool can not properly match semantic representations and responds with a different meaning for a lexeme than the one intended by the sender, the interaction "falls" away from the direction in which it was supposed to have been going. This is especially true in those instances where the puns are elaborated. By way of signaling the end of the event, the narrator cleverly brings to the audience's consciousness the two levels of communication and comments on this characteristic definition of *rakugo* in one meta-pun: *zudon.*

The use of *zudon* to serve as mention referring to the total speech event *rakugo,* and within the speech event the individual points at which cultural rules are violated, does something else: By association it connotes all of the characteristics of this event as opposed to other kinds of speech events, and, by extension, cultural behaviors. By calling attention to the characteristics of the genre, the narrator brings it into focus as typifying a set of behavioral attributes and evaluations about this category of verbal (and associated cultural) behaviors as opposed to the category with which they contrast.

As I outlined in the introductory section of this paper, the general category of cultural behavior in which *rakugo* takes place is *asobi,* "play," found within the physical context of the *kanrakugai* "entertainment district." The evaluations which characterize this *rakugo* performance, and by extension, the rest of the *kanrakugai* behavioral world are:

bakabakashii 'ludicrous, silly, ridiculous'
bakageta 'foolish, stupid, absurd'
tsumaranai 'useless, profitless, meaningless'
joshiki no nai 'senseless'
yawarakai 'soft, loose'
zokupoi 'cheap, vulgar, crude'
okashii 'funny, strange, having the unexpected happen'

---

[9] Another expression for this type of verbal activity is *otoshi banashi,* "dropped story, speech, talking".

Although these characteristics are implied by the narrator's closing
/*zudon*/, the whole narration from beginning to end, from "top" to
"bottom" — in the sense of the mechanisms and elements it involves — contributes to the sense of "absurdity". In the "top"-most
sense there is the story line: A first old man gives a basket of junk — and
that this is the case is communicated and acknowledged by the audience's laughter when Yotarō is looking through the basket of merchandise and mentions that the head is loose and the nose is off the doll he
discovers — to an incompetent. The fool is then sent to the place of a second old man, ostensibly to set up shop in the "antique business." The
"shop" consists of nothing more than a reed mat in the street — not a
shop at all, and this is communicated to the audience by Yotarō's *Huh?*
of disbelief in response to Jimbei's telling him *This is the place.*
Although under "normal" circumstances, we would expect interaction to
produce sales with customers, all of Yotarō's subsequent interactions
end in complete cognitive disarray. Within the framework of the story
line, from the highest level down to the smallest unit identifiable in the
rakugo event, nothing is as one would "normally" expect. Each successive utterance is an absurdity. No business is transacted, no messages
get communicated, the main character is the opposite of everything considered to be characteristic of an ideal man, and even the event itself is
not closed, ending, literally, "falling," in mid-air.

However, in the context of *asobi* "play," within which the event
occurs, these characterizations of it are not negative evaluations. "Absurd" is what play is supposed to be. A negative evaluation of a *rakugo*
performance would be to say that it was *jittomo okashikunai* 'not even a
little bit strange, funny, that is, nothing unexpected'.

The characterizations of the category of *asobi* "play," contrast
directly with everything that typifies the world of *shigoto* "work":

> *majime* 'serious, straight'
> *kachi no aru* 'profitable, having value, having meaning'
> *jōshiki no aru* 'making sense'
> *katai* 'hard, tight'
> *kōshō* 'noble, refined'
> *okashikunai* 'not funny, strange, unexpected'

It follows that speech events in this domain of behavior must observe
all those rules which, in their violation, are mentioned in *rakugo* monologues. Thus, by commenting on the "absurdity" of the play world, the
narrator implies the "realness" of the world of work.[10]

This dichotomy of the behavioral universe into the worlds of *asobi*

---

[10] For discussion of contextualized appropriateness in another society, see Abrahams &
Bauman, 1971.

"play" and *shigoto* "work" parallels a distinction which has been described as lying behind most traditional conflict in Japanese society (e.g., Benedict, 1946): that between *giri* 'duty' and *ninjo* 'one's personal inclination, human feelings'. Thus, what one does in the world of *shigoto* "work" is *giri* "obligations, duty," while the activities which take place within the domain of *asobi* "play," especially in the physical setting of the *kanrakugai* "entertainment quarter," is linked with *ninjo* "individual inclinations." One of the messages communicated in this narration is: Within the framework of the *kanrakugai, ninjo*-type behaviors and their implied "absurdity" are quite appropriate. But the absurd must occur in context. The unframed performance of *ninjo* "personal inclination"-type behavior is quite inappropriate. We might conceptualize the conflict between *giri* and *ninjo* which forms the plot of so much traditional Japanese literature as due to the fact that the individual wants to take his *ninjo*-determined personal relations out of the domain of *asobi* and place them in the context of the *shigoto* world. Another way of looking at the same thing would be to say that he wants to neutralize the distinctions between the two categories of behaviors. The classic example is the case in which the boy from a good family wants to marry the girl from the bar. In traditional Japanese stories of such conflict, such a situation can only be resolved in suicide.

I would now like to attempt to formalize somewhat a statement of the features I have abstracted as necessary criteria for a theory of this particular event.

1. There must be two simultaneously-occurring communication events and they must exist in conjunction with two kinds of language usage. The one event occurs as narration. It is that of the characters who only have their existence within the story. On this level, language is used to talk about things in the world, that is, for reference. In the "real" communication event, language is used in its function as mention, that is, as a meta-communication about language and culture.

2. The messages sent on the real level of communication, that is, the meta-communication about the cultural system or any of its subsets, must be indirect. That is, the narrator can not communicate about the cultural rules by directly talking about them and create humor. He can only communicate about them by referring to elements through which they are implied. This is usually accomplished in one of two ways: (a) by reversals, that is, referring to rules by breaking them, and (b) by association.

3. The event must be framed in such a way that it is defined as "extranormal," outside the bounds of, or in a category other than usual, everyday behavior. This framing can be done in any number of ways: by having the event occur in a special physical location; by the use of

dialect, intonation or paralinguistic features. What is interesting here is that each of the meta-messages that communicates about a linguistic rule by breaking it is "framed" within the context of the next higher unit of the event.

4. The distinction between the two levels of communication, and thus, of the two functions of language must be neutralized at the end of the event. This can only be done by the use of a form that has meanings on both levels.

It would be interesting to see if any or all of this set of features has any applicability beyond this immediate, Japanese culture-bound genre. That is, how well could it serve to predict the occurrence of a type of speech event in other languages. Could it be used as a definition, or the start of a definition, for a specific class of verbal behaviors identifiable cross-culturally?

Bibliography

Abrahams, Roger & Richard Bauman
 1971 Sense and nonsense in St. Vincent: Speech behavior and decorum in a Caribbean community. *American Anthropologist* **73**, 762.
Bateson, Gregory
 1955 A theory of play and fantasy, *Psychiatric Research Reports* **2**, American Psychiatric Association, 39.
Benedict, Ruth
 1946 *The chrysanthemum and the sword: Patterns of Japanese culture.* Boston: Houghton Mifflin.
Brower, Robert H. & Earl Miner
 1961 *Japanese court poetry.* Stanford, California: Stanford Univ. Press.
Fischer, J. L.
 1964 Words for self and others in some Japanese families, *American Anthropologist* **66**, 115.
Frake, Charles
 1966 How to ask for a drink in Subanun, *AA.* **66**, 127.
Hrdličkova, V.
 1969 Japanese professional storytellers, *Genre* **3**:179–210.
Hymes, Dell
 1962 The ethnography of speaking. In *Anthropology and human behavior.* P. B. Washington, D.C.: Anthropological Society of Washington.
Labov, William & Joshua Waletsky
 1967 Narrative analysis. In Essays in the verbal and visual arts. *Proceedings of the 1966 annual spring meeting of the American Ethnological Society.* Seattle: University of Washington Press.
Martin, Samuel
 1964 Speech Levels in Japan and Korea. In *Language in culture and society,* edited by D. Hymes. P. 407.

Children's Insults: America and Samoa

CLAUDIA MITCHELL-KERNAN
KEITH T. KERNAN

It has become increasingly clear in the past few years that communicative competence depends on a knowledge of more than the rules of lexicon, grammar, and phonology of the language or languages spoken in one's speech community. Hymes, in a number of articles (cf. 1962), and others (Slobin, 1967; Ervin-Tripp, 1964) have pointed out that such factors as topic, interlocutors, cultural setting, etc., may determine not only what is talked about but the way it is talked about. A number of empirical studies have demonstrated that relative status of interlocutors may influence such seemingly diverse linguistic activity as choice of pronoun (Brown and Gilman, 1960), choice of term of address (Brown and Ford, 1961; Ervin-Tripp, 1969), choice of language (Rubin, 1968), and even the display or concealment of linguistic virtuosity (Albert, 1972). In such instances, and others, it is necessary for a competent speaker of the speech community to know not only the structural rules of his language but also the cultural rules of speaking that dictate the choice of one linguistic variant rather than another in situations in which status of interlocutors is considered relevant. Moreover, the competent speaker must have the knowledge that enables him to identify the relevant situations and to assign the situationally appropriate status to each of the participating interlocutors.

Cultural and social structural knowledge beyond that implied in traditional linguistic analyses is, of course, necessary for appropriate speech performance in other speech situations than those in which relative status is important. A black American teenager must know exactly how close he can come to speaking the truth when engaged in "sounding" with his peers (Labov, Cohen, Robins, and Lewis, 1968). A Belizian Creole speaker must know which variety in his verbal repertoire is likely to arouse feelings of cultural pride and which variety is not (Kernan, Sodergren, French, 1973). A verbal performer, to be successful, must know what his culture considers humorous, tragic, ironic, and so on. It is probably true that all speech acts in all speech communities involve

some cultural or social structural knowledge for their adequate performance and appropriate realization. A speaker whose linguistic competence
consisted only of the rules described in a typical linguistic analysis
would be anomaly and, as Hymes (1972) has pointed out, would spew
out utterances that were grammatically correct but situationally inappropriate in both content and form in a machinelike manner.

Since competent speech both depends on and displays cultural and
social knowledge, it follows that an examination of the speech of individuals will reveal something of their knowledge of social and cultural rules
and their application. A French speaker's use of either *tu* or *vous* as the
second-person singular pronoun of address to specific interlocutors in
particular speech situations, for example, should indicate his interpretation of the status relationships between himself and various others (cf.
Brown and Gilman, 1960). As a child acquires the sociolinguistic skills
that will enable him to become a competent member of his community,
he is, at the same time, acquiring the underlying social and cultural
knowledge that will allow him to correctly apply those skills to his
speech behavior. The study of a child's acquisition of sociolinguistic
skills, then, is also a study of his acquisition of at least some aspects of
the culture and social structure of his speech community. The acquisition of linguistic and cultural knowledge is, of course, not a matter of
separate and mutually exclusive processes. The child does not acquire
his knowledge of his culture in a linguistic vacuum and then apply his
newly discovered knowledge to his speech behavior. Rather, the processes are interacting, and the knowledge of his culture is both applied
to and derived from the verbal interaction in which the child engages.

In this study we will examine some instances of the speech behavior
of children in American Samoa and in an urban black community in the
United States for evidence of the knowledge and acquisition of certain
cultural values. Specifically, we will deal with the use of insult by the
children in the two speech communities in terms of the knowledge of
cultural values the insults exhibit and the linguistic interaction that may
have produced that knowledge. The examples of insult behavior used by
the children were collected during the course of research on the acquisition of linguistic structure, and their analysis is intended to be illustrative
of the possibility of using such data in studies of enculturation, rather
than descriptive of the acquisition of cultural values in the two communities.

Children do, of course, talk about their beliefs and values just as
adults do, and much can be learned from such data that is of potential
value for understanding their socialization and enculturation. Concerning morality and immorality, for example, the following conversa-

tion between two four-year-old girls in our black American sample took place:

SUZY: *If you bad, he [Jesus] don't like little girls to be bad.*

PAT: *Little boys either.*

SUZY: *He don't love you if you be bad.*

PAT: *The devil put fire on your back too, Suzy.*

SUZY: *And if you be bad it gonna get put on your back.*

PAT: *I know it, that's why I not gonna be bad.*

SUZY: *I'm not either.*

These views do not exactly match the adult views, but with respect to supernatural punishment and reward according to one's deeds, they do reflect the rather fundamentalist views of the parents. It is of interest that all are equal in the eyes of Jesus, who favors neither boys nor girls, and that the devil metes out punishment in a similarly egalitarian fashion. Later, Suzy was asked if the devil had ever put fire on her back. She replied, "I don't think so." Further questioning led to admissions that she had been bad but had never been really bad. She had done nothing, we suppose, that would merit the devil's attention.

If one is interested in values, however, searching for these kinds of statements can be rather unproductive in that one must go through a tremendous amount of data to find them. We have discovered, however, that in speech acts that can be labeled *insults* a value statement is almost always made. In fact, a comment on a cultural value is one of the defining features of the utterance. In both our American and Samoan samples, we have numerous instances of such speech acts. Moreover, we have some instances of insult *speech events* that are composed of a number of separate insult speech acts and are governed by their own rules of internal structuring.

Although in the Samoan case one such speech event was initiated by our assistant, who suggested to a group of four-year-olds that they quarrel, in both Samoa and America children did not need to be prompted to engage in such behavior. They found in their play numerous occasions to practice this art.

We will define insult here in terms of its function and the nature of its content. Functionally, insult behavior is designed to have some negative effect on the addressee. That is, at least part of the intended function of an insult is to in some way injure the feelings or lower the self-esteem of the addressee. It may also have functions such as the elicitation of some sort of behavior from the addressee, but the defining function here is the intended malice.

The central point of our definition, the point that makes the study of insult behavior particularly productive, however, is that insults are predicated on some shared cultural value. That is, for an insult to perform its malicious function it must make a comment that in some way links the addressee and a cultural value. The structural features of children's insults include, on the stylistic dimension, a hostile and aggressive delivery and, on the content dimension, some statement about the addressee's deviation from a culturally defined value. Insults in both America and Samoa accuse the addressee of deviance from some cultural value. Insult is formulaic in the sense that any number of cultural values can be utilized as content. The formula can, therefore, be used productively, and the content will always include a value statement.

The statements of cultural values that can be heard in children's insults do not, of course, exhaust the values they have acquired. Since some insults consist of standard phrases of verbal abuse that are heard in the culture by adults and other children, they may be unanalyzed by the child, that is, learned simply by rote. Such insults are not very revealing. In both America and Samoa, the child will initially draw upon these standard abusive terms and phrases and, in some cases, use them in culturally aberrant ways. For example, in Samoa a rather standard insult is *mata Saina* 'Chinese eyes'. A Samoan two-year-old will hurl this phrase not only at people who exhibit epicanthic folds but at anyone whom he is attempting to insult. The insults to be examined for the cultural values they exhibit, therefore, are not instances of some kind of standardized name calling.

One type of Samoan insult that illustrates that the child has internalized certain cultural values relates to the hearer's own individual deviance. These are negative comments about his looks, his intelligence, his hygienic habits, sores on his body, etc. For example, a 4-year-old girl insulted a 4-year-old boy by telling him the following kinds of things: "You have sores on your legs." "Your nose is running." "Your lavalava is dirty." "You are stupid." "You urinated and defecated inside your house." The little boy countered with similar insults: "You have lice." "You are stupid." "You have Chinese eyes." They have learned the cultural values of intelligence, cleanliness, and particular physical features.

These particular insults occurred in a setting in which insults were being traded back and forth. This was the speech event mentioned earlier, and it had an internal structure created by the fact that there were sequencing rules. The most general kind of sequencing rule in both

Samoa and America is that an insult calls for some kind of response. It is almost as if it were a game in which one of the rules is that failure to respond appropriately brings about a loss in points. One of the stylistic features that demonstrates this powerful rule to respond is the rapidity with which responses are made. In addition, the stuttering and false starts that take place when a child is searching for a suitable response, but is unwilling to wait until he has one framed for fear of being one-upped, are not ordinary features of his speech. There are also a number of pause fillers in Samoa, including *mala* 'shame on you for saying that'.

A simple response to an insult is not the only type of sequencing rule. Certain kinds of insults appear to elicit certain responses. The kind of insult mentioned previously, having to do with a person's personal appearance, hygiene, etc., elicits responses in kind. That is to say, the response also comments on the personal cleanliness, etc., of the individual. Another broad class of insults exhibited by the Samoan children in this particular insult event relates to the children's parents' deviation from cultural values: "Your father beats your mother." "Your father dove into the sea." "Your father does not have this or that possession." These examples of insults illustrate the child's acquisition of a social structural fact; that is, they represent the child's recognition of certain equivalence classes. It is possible to insult an individual by mentioning his father's deviance because it is recognized that the child is a member of a social unit and that the nature of this social unit is such that an insult directed at any member is also an insult to the other members. The sequencing rule for this is denial; that is, the children deny the truth of the acquisition and then respond with any other kind of insult. A third kind of insult, of which we have only two instances, is the accusation that the addressee is stingy. The reaction in both cases was tears.

If we examine the responses that particular insults elicit, it appears that some insults are more serious than others. Insults about self elicit responses in kind, except when the insult is directed toward the highest of cultural values, generosity. Such insults elicit tears. Of intermediate seriousness are insults that have to do with one's family, which are responded to with anger and denials.

We have been able to ascertain that children have acquired certain cultural values by examining their insults. Moreover, we have been able to rank the strength of the insult and, therefore, the potency of the value that underlies it by examining the nature of the response to that insult. In these cases it appears not only that the values children express match adult values but also that their ordering of the potency of these values matches adult ordering.

Black American children also make comments about the appearance and beauty of the addressee as well as his intellectual capacity. They get major mileage out of accusing others of being babies. The latter was not characteristic of Samoan peer–peer insults. In addition, black 4-year-olds do not make comments about the addressee's parents as do Samoan 4-year-olds. This does occur among older black children in ritualized insults, in which the comments are maximally removed from reality, such as "Your mother eats Chinese roaches." In this ritualized context a statement too close to reality can serve to destroy the ritual. The black children also have a metalinguistic filler that they use in the insult context, *u–u–u–u*. We do not have enough instances of black children's insults occurring in insult speech events to establish sequencing rules. Comments about beauty seem to evoke stronger responses than others. Black adults also seem to place higher value on physical beauty than do Samoan adults. While it is true that beauty is measured along different dimensions in America and Samoa, it still seems to be the case that black American children place a higher value on the abstract quality "beauty." Black children, particularly girls, insult others by accusing them of being conceited about their physical beauty, expressing another kind of value. That is, one should not be overly concerned with one's own beauty, even though beauty is valued. We do not get like comments from Samoan children.

The examples we have listed are instances in which the children had clearly acquired cultural values, and such instances are easily recognized as insults. Equally interesting, however, are insults that do not seem to be based on any value that exists in the culture. The problem then becomes how they are recognized as insults. One way of recognizing them as insults is that they are given in the same style as the insults that clearly state cultural values. Another way of recognizing them is that they are generated by a sequencing rule in response to another insult. Thus, if something occurs in a speech event of insult behavior and has the linguistic markers of an insult, it will be interpreted as an insult by the child.

We, as ethnographers, can interpret similarly, that they are intended as insults and that they are based on something that the child believes to be a shared cultural value. Mistakes of this kind are particularly interesting. When a child insults appropriately, he indicates that he has internalized a cultural value. When his insults are not appropriate, we should not assume that they are not based on what he believes to be a cultural value. When a child insults correctly, he indicates the cultural value he has internalized; how he acquired the value is not revealed. His mistakes, however, are informative because they indicate something about the process by which the child acquires cultural values.

One 3-year-old black American girl said of her sister, in an obviously censuring way, that she had a baby. She later said of a married woman, in an equally censuring way, "She got a baby." Samoan children insult each other by saying "You sleep with so and so." A Samoan child once attempted to insult another child by saying "Your father sleeps with your mother." Another child insulted a peer by saying "Your father dove into the sea." In the last example, the preceding circumstances involved an American government official who had capsized his boat on the reef outside of the village and lost his outboard motor. It required a considerable amount of effort on the part of a chief to dive repeatedly in deep water and inch the motor to shore in order to accomplish its retrieval. A number of Samoans were heard to remark of this event that the chief had gone too far in attempting to curry favor with the government and that this ingratiating behavior made him look like a fool.

In all three cases the antecedent circumstances under which the child has been misled about a value are easy to envision. He has obviously heard some behavior spoken of in a censuring style. That is to say, he knows that behavior is being censured because of the linguistic and paralinguistic features of the comments about it. However, because of the shared understandings of adults and older children, it is not necessary for them to state explicitly all of the attributes of the situation that make it objectionable. The defining features that make the behavior subject to censure have been either implicit or, if stated, not recognized as such by the child. He appears to have taken the most visible attributes of the situation and assumed that they and they alone are what define the behavior as deviant. In each case, the child has yet to learn which parameters of the situation are defining of the cultural value and which are not. They have not yet learned that having children and sleeping with a member of the opposite sex are negatively valued only if the individuals involved are not married. Similarly, the evaluation of behavior that involves diving into the sea is evaluated according to the supposed motivation of the diver.

These examples are interesting for two reasons. The fact that in each case the child was mistaken about his culture's attitude concerning a particular behavior helps explicate both a process and a mechanism for the acquisition of cultural values. The children have learned that the culture disapproves of certain behavior but have yet to learn that such disapproval is contingent on factors such as marriage and motivation. They have, in a sense, overgeneralized and do not yet realize that there are finer distinctions to be made. That is, the children fail to recognize that there are contextual factors that define instances of a particular form as members of a certain class. They will, presumably, progress toward a more complete knowledge of their culture by learning to make those finer distinctions and to differentiate cases according to culturally relevant contextual factors. This type of overgeneralization and later differentiation is not unlike that which occurs in the child's acquisition of lexical items and grammatical structure (cf. Kernan, 1970).

Though in each case the children have overgeneralized, they have learned that at least some aspect of the behavior in question is disapproved of by their culture. The mechanism that produced this knowledge was the disapproving manner in which that behavior or similar instances of behavior were spoken of by other members of their speech communities. It is particularly clear in the case of the man who dove into the sea that it was not what was said by the adults but the way it was said that indicated to the child that the behavior was disapproved of.

We have found, then, that by examining insults produced by children one can discover something of the internalization of cultural values and the process of that internalization. Similarly, information about the child's internalization of his culture can be gained by examining the form, function, and content of other kinds of speech acts. For example, in the speech act "joke telling" we find that the child acquires the joke-telling style and the notion of the function of a joke before he understands that jokes also imply certain content. He can, thus, be seen to imitate joke-telling styles and to laugh at the end of a joke when the content of his jokes makes no sense at all. An examination of a child's jokes as he grows older can undoubtedly tell us something about his acquisition of his culture's sense of humor.

An examination of the child's acquisition of sociolinguistic skills, then, can tell us something of the child's acquisition of the cultural and social knowledge that underlies such skills. The use of naturally occurring speech behavior as the data on which such studies might be based has the advantage of not being structured by the preconceived notions of the investigator in a way that interviews, questionnaires, and testing procedures too often are.

References

Albert, Ethel M.
　　1972　Culture Patterning of Speech Behavior in Burundi. In *Directions in sociolinguistics: The ethnography of communication,* edited by J. J. Gumperz and D. Hymes. New York: Holt.
Brown, Roger W. and Marguerite Ford
　　1961　Address in American English, *Journal of Abnormal and Social Psychology* **62,** 375–385.

Brown, Roger W. and A. Gilman
  1960   The pronouns of power and solidarity. In *Style in language,* edited by T. Sebeok. Cambridge, Massachusetts: M.I.T. Press.
Ervin-Tripp, Susan M.
  1964   An analysis of the interaction of language, topic, and listener. In *The ethnography of communication,* edited by J. J. Gumperz and D. Hymes. *American Anthropologist* **66,** 6, 86–102.
  1969   Sociolinguistics. In *Advances in experimental social psychology,* edited by L. Berkowitz. Vol. 4, pp. 91–165. New York: Academic Press.
Hymes, Dell
  1962   The ethnography of speaking. In *Anthropology and human behavior,* edited by T. Gladwin and W. C. Sturtevant. Washington, D.C.: Anthropological Society of Washington.
  1972   *Towards communicative competence.* Philadelphia: Univ. of Pennsylvania Press.
Kernan, Keith T.
  1970   Semantic Relationships and the Child's Acquisition of Language, *Anthropological Linguistics* **12,** 171–187.
Kernan, Keith T., John A. Sodergren, and Robert French
  1973   *Speech and social prestige in the Belizian speech community.* To appear in second volume of this collection of papers.
Labov, William, Paul Cohen, Clarence Robins, and John Lewis
  1968   *A study of the non-standard English of Negro and Puerto Rican speakers in New York City.* Vol. II. New York: Columbia Univ., Dept. of Linguistics.
Rubin, Joan
  1968   *National bilingualism in Paraguay.* The Hague: Mouton.
Slobin, Dan I.
  1967   *A field manual for cross-cultural study of the acquisition of communicative competence.* Univ. of California, Berkeley (ASUC Bookstore).

Linguistic Creativity in Song[1]

BRIAN STROSS

Introduction

Linguistic and sociolinguistic analysis has, for the most part, been concentrated on the task of finding patterns or regularities in speech in order to specify the underlying language structure from which speech is generated. In contrast with our growing knowledge about the constraints implied by structure, little attention has been paid to the other side of the coin: freedom for creative expression that is allowed within limits imposed by the structural framework necessary for comprehension and production of speech. True, it is often pointed out that one of the marvels of language is the fact that, with a quite finite number of elements and rules for their interrelation, an infinite number of interpretable messages can be constructed (due largely to embedding and recursive rules). This tells us very little, however, about the bounds for creativity in the use of any particular language.

Because structure implies constraints on the form that a message may take, it might seem reasonable to assume that the more highly structured a system is, the less freedom there is for creative expression. On the contrary, however, constraints are not inimical to creativity. It is, rather, by means of constraints that creativity may be judged. This is so for language and its use just as well as in any other human activity, as I hope to show in this study. Creative expression, a cornerstone of linguistic change, can presumably be found on all levels of integration in all societies. The focus here will be on one particular expressive genre in a single society. Specifically, I want to outline some of the formal and substantive constraints imposed in the culturally appropriate production of

[1] Research relevant to this paper was conducted during the months of January–May of 1971. Supporting funds were made available by a National Science Foundation USDP Grant GU-1598.

Tzeltal songs, and to point out the ways in which creativity has been manifested in three sample song texts.[2]

Setting

The Tzeltal are a highland Maya group numbering some 100,000 people who live in central Chiapas, the southernmost state in Mexico. The people occupy 12 *municipios,* among which are distributed 17 corporate Indian communities. Each of these communities has its own native civil–religious hierarchy. One such community is Tenejapa, which comprises the *municipio* of Tenejapa and from which the data for this study were drawn.

The *municipio* of Tenejapa, with an Indian population of 9000, consists of 21 *parajes,* or hamlets (of 200–900 inhabitants each), corresponding to approximately the same number of dispersed patrilineal settlements. These *parajes* are integrated politically and religiously through a ceremonial center, Teklum, which is the seat of municipal government. Teklum is occupied by about 100 Ladino (i.e., non-Indian) families and by a very small permanent Indian population. Some Indian political officials live in the ceremonial center during their tenure in office. Others remain in the outlying *parajes* throughout the year, making regular visits to Teklum for the purpose of carrying out their duties. Municipal religious ceremonies, sponsored and organized by appointed cargo holders, also take place primarily in Teklum.

On the *paraje* level, political and religious authority and responsibilities lie primarily with the *principales,* each *paraje* having from one to three of these men, respected elders who have already held high positions in the cargo hierarchy and are appointed by previous *principales,* and their younger assistants. Curers, current cargo holders, local teachers, and household heads also wield authority in varying degrees and influence community affairs on both the local and municipal levels.

The household, which normally consists of a man, his one or more wives, and their children, is the basic unit of Tzeltal production and con-

---

[2] Text A was recorded from a performance by Nicolas Guzman Lopez that took place on a Sunday in a drinking context in Tenejapa center with an audience of friends and relatives of both sexes. Texts B and C were recorded from a performance by Antonio Giron Luna that took place in the evening at home upon my request, the audience including the singer's wives and children as well as two neighboring male relatives. The performance was taped and, at the request of the singer, was played back the following Saturday morning in the Indian regional market plaza, called *yočib,* for all to hear. Every one of the 500 or more people present appeared to enjoy the songs tremendously.

sumption. As slash-and-burn subsistance farmers, Tenejapans rely on maize, beans, and squash as dietary staples, which are supplemented by turkeys, chickens, fruits, and wild greens. Money enters the economic system when individuals sell small crop surpluses, limited specialty crops (e.g., coffee, peanuts, oranges, or bananas), or firewood and charcoal. In addition, in times of need a male will leave the *municipio* to contract wage labor on Ladino-owned coffee plantations located as far away as the Chiapas–Guatemala border. Cash outlays are made for clothing, machetes, radios, shotguns, tools, flashlights, and other necessities, in addition to such important ceremonial items as candles, cigarettes, rum, *chicha,* and Pepsi-Cola.

Social interaction outside of the household and kinship network centers on weekend activities and a yearly cycle of ceremonial occasions. There are two nearby regional market plazas on Saturdays, and one on Sundays in Teklum. Municipal ceremonies include the change of office for political cargos, Carnaval, Semana Santa, Todos Santos, Navidad, and the saints' days of San Alonso (the patron saint of Tenejapa) and San Diego, among others. Earth and crop renewal ceremonies and Carnaval also find expression on the local level within the *parajes.*

Singing

Singing has an important place in Tzeltal society, yet the casual outside observer could easily come away convinced that no native singing is done at all. For the most part, song performances are private or semiprivate, reserved for whiling away lonely hours in the home or fields. On occasion, though, an old man, drunk, may be seen by the side of the footpath singing, or an old woman might be heard crooning softly at a noisy fiesta. Native songs, more important and more frequently performed, are less conspicuous than Mexican songs, which some of the Tzeltal have picked up. Nowadays, some simple Mexican songs are taught to children attending the native schools in order to facilitate their introduction to the Spanish language; and some young unmarried men will walk home drunk together in groups, harmonizing in bad Spanish to the tune of some popular ranchero song heard on the radio and laboriously, if inaccurately, memorized.

Singing is not restricted to any particular segment of the Tzeltal community. Children, adolescents, and adults, males and females, all know some songs and are potential singers. Children and older people are more often heard singing native songs before a nonintimate audience, however. During early socialization the child is usually first exposed to its mother's singing. Singing is believed to lull a restless child to sleep, although I have heard no songs uniquely serving this purpose. A woman will also sing when she is lonely or unhappy, and this the child hears also. Children pick up the tunes that they hear very early, beginning around the age of two or two-and-a-half. By the age of ten, a boy has usually begun to accompany his father to the *milpa* and other places where he hears men's songs. By listening, but with no explicit instruction, children acquire knowledge of song structure and content. Learning how to sing is useful for the child being socialized, for many songs affirm sex role distinctions and reinforce ideal sex role behavior as well as beliefs about cross-sex role relationships.

A preliminary grouping of native songs distinguishes three separate categories: (1) standards, (2) women's improvised songs, and (3) men's improvised songs. Further distinctions could easily be made within each category on the basis of such criteria as tune, content, performance location, supposed function, etc., but that will not be necessary for the purposes of this work.

Standards are songs that have titles, go with specific (albeit not unique) melodies, contain some obligatory invariant phrases, and are more or less familiar to most of the members of the speech community. Some are more appropriate to male singers (e.g., *poka ʔaʔk'ab* 'Wash Your Hands'), others to female singers (e.g., *muc'a ʔaʔsit* 'Wink Your Eyes'); still others are appropriate to either sex (e.g., *hkanan čih* 'Shepherd'). Standards function variously for humor, insult, courtship, expressive pleasure, creative expression, and assorted combinations of these. On occasion, a portion of a standard will be hummed only, so as to produce the desired effect on an audience, for the audience knows the significance of the song and is left to guess at only the specific improvisable but unstated phrases. A majority of standards allow for and even demand considerable improvisation from the singer, and the topical content of the various standard songs is too diverse to allow for any general thematic description.

One interesting standard, *poka ʔaʔk'ab,* urges the addressee, understood to be a girl, to leave her family and go away with the singer. Everyone in the community knows the significance of the song, even though the words employed never overtly state the singer's intentions. Because this standard is sung in noncourting contexts as well, and because the words are allusive rather than direct, a young man may feel free to hum or sing a few measures of it while visiting the home of a young woman even though her parents are present. Any direct proposition by the boy in such a situation, however, would immediately provoke the girl's father to violent anger.

Women's improvised songs have no titles, contain no obligatory invariant phrases, are not familiar to most members of the speech community because they are highly individual (and, for that matter, in all probability, could never be duplicated exactly even by the singer herself), can select from at least six different melodic patterns, and have lyrics that are almost completely improvised within the phrasing and metrics appropriate to the melody chosen. These songs most often voice complaints and/or praise the womanly attributes of the singer herself. Complaints are usually about the treatment the woman singer is suffering from her husband, parents, children, in-laws, or other relatives; or the singer may complain that she is an orphan (if she has lost one or both parents) and has no one to protect and care for her. Complaints are often followed up by or interspersed with declarations of the singer's worth to a man in terms of socially valued feminine characteristics. These declarations themselves are sometimes followed up by or interspersed with mentions of the singer's stereotypically female desires in life (e.g., a rich, truthful, respectable, generous husband who can give her good clothing, ornaments, and money). Finally, with or without the intervening steps, the singer describes what she is thinking about doing to change her present unfortunate situation (e.g., drinking *chicha,* running away to her parents' house, running off with a lover, etc.). Women sing their improvised songs most often at home while doing their chores during the day, when nobody except perhaps children or close female relatives are present.

Men's improvised songs have no titles, contain no obligatory invariant phrases, are not familiar to most members of the speech community, can select from at least four different melodic patterns, and have lyrics that are almost completely improvised within the phrasing and metrics appropriate to the chosen melody. These songs sometimes voice complaints about the singer's wives or in-laws, frequently mock disvalued physical and social characteristics attributed by the singer to other specified males, usually praise the singer's own valued physical and social attributes, and often suggest in metaphoric or direct scatological terms what the singer does or intends to do with his women. Men sing their improvised songs either while working in the fields (with or without male company), when drinking at a fiesta or walking on the trail, or during a house visit.

Text A — Standard

The following text and glosses are of a humorous standard song, *hkanan čih* 'Shepherd', consisting of 57 four-measure verses, each of which is composed of paired lines (a couplet) of 2 measures that are supposed to be of parallel syntactic construction.

1. *luk luk ʔaʔwakan hkanan čih;*
     šot šot ʔaʔwakan hkanan čih.
   What twisted (bowed) legs you have, shepherd;
       What bent (bowed) legs you have, shepherd.

2. *bec' bec' ʔaʔwakan hkanan čih;*
     bic' bic' ʔaʔwakan hkanan čih.
   What twisted (pigeon-toed) legs you have, shepherd;
       What scrawny legs you have, shepherd.

3. *het het ʔaʔwiti hkanan čih;*
     pac pac ʔaʔholi hkanan čih.
   What a wide crotch you have, shepherd;
       What thickly matted, unkempt hair you have, shepherd.

4. *šap' šap' ʔaʔholi hkanan čih;*
     bot bot ʔaʔsiti hkanan čih.
   What disheveled, bushy hair you have, shepherd;
       What pop-eyes you have, shepherd.

5. *č'e č'e ʔaʔsiti hkanan čih;*
     cun cun ʔaʔsiti hkanan čih.
   What drooping lower eyelids at the corners you have, shepherd;
       What thick eyebrows you have, shepherd.

6. *čaw čaw ʔaʔholi hkanan čih;*
     sep sep ʔaʔholi hkanan čih.
   What a very large head (in proportion to your body) you have, shepherd;
       What a flat-topped head you have, shepherd.

7. *puš puš ʔaʔčikin hkanan čih;*
     tek' tek' ʔaʔčikin hkanan čih.
   What forward-folded ears you have, shepherd;
       What pointy-topped ears you have, shepherd.

8. *kul kul ʔaʔčikin hkanan čih;*
     bec' bec' ʔaʔniʔi hkanan čih.
   What cut-off (i.e., no ears) ears you have, shepherd;
       What a twisted nose you have, shepherd.

9. *k'uh k'uh ʔaʔniʔi hkanan čih;*
     peč' peč' ʔaʔniʔi hkanan čih.

What a long, thin nose you have, shepherd;
What a small, thin, flat nose you have, shepherd.

10. *leš leš ʔaʔniʔi hkanan čih;*
    pum pum ʔaʔčoi hkanan čih.
    What very large nostrils you have, shepherd;
    What puffed-out cheeks you have, shepherd.

11. *lib lib ʔaʔčoi hkanan čih;*
    cun cun ʔaʔwisim hkanan čih.
    What fat cheeks you have, shepherd;
    What a bushy goatee you have, shepherd.

12. *barbontik ʔaʔwelaw hkanan čih;*
    barač'tik ʔaʔwelaw hkanan čih.
    What a bearded face you have, shepherd;
    What a bushy-bearded face you have, shepherd.

13. *c'oy c'oy ʔaʔwei hkanan čih;*
    šuy šuy ʔaʔwei hkanan čih.
    What a mouth twisted to one side of your face you have, shepherd;
    What a mouth turned to one side of your face with teeth showing, shepherd.

14. *lew lew ʔaʔwei hkanan čih;*
    leš leš ʔaʔwei hkanan čih.
    What a wide mouth stuck in a grin you have, shepherd;
    What a wide mouth with large sides (back teeth showing) you have, shepherd.

15. *luš luš ʔaʔwei hkanan čih;*
    wel wel ʔaʔwei hkanan čih.
    What protruding lips you have, shepherd;
    What a protruding and everted lower lip you have, shepherd.

16. *bot' bot' ʔaʔtiʔi hkanan čih;*
    lek' lek' ʔaʔsiti hkanan čih.
    What an everted upper lip you have, shepherd;
    What crusty, watery eyes you have, shepherd.

17. *hoč'oben ʔaʔsiti hkanan čih;*
    buyemtikleh scocil ʔaʔsiti hkanan čih.
    What diseased skin around your eyes you have, shepherd;
    What an absence of eyelashes (from disease) you have, shepherd.

18. *haʔ haʔ ʔaʔsiti hkanan čih;*
    č'uš č'uš ʔaʔnuk'i hkanan čih.
    What constantly watering eyes you have, shepherd;
    What a spindly neck you have, shepherd.

19. *tuč' tuč' ʔaʔnuk'i hkanan čih;*
    tub tub ʔaʔhalaw hkanan čih.
    What a long, stringy neck you have, shepherd;
    What a prominent adam's apple you have, shepherd.

20. *wol wol ʔaʔmancana hkanan čih;*
    tom tom ʔaʔnuk'i hkanan čih.

What a large, round adam's apple you have, shepherd;
What a thick neck you have, shepherd.

21. *not not ʔaʔnuk'i hkanan čih;*
    t'as t'as ʔaʔwoʔtan hkanan čih.
    What a short neck you have, shepherd;
    How pigeon-chested you are, shepherd.

22. *čah čah ʔaʔmoči hkanan čih;*
    hic' hic' ʔaʔbakel hkanan čih.
    What bony ribs you have, shepherd;
    How scrawny you are, shepherd.

23. *c'ar c'ar ʔaʔmoči hkanan čih;*
    k'ahk'etik ʔaʔmoči hkanan čih.
    How very bony your ribs are, shepherd;
    How charred your sides look (from dirt), shepherd.

24. *totoltik ʔaʔmoči hkanan čih;*
    c'irintik ʔaʔwelaw hkanan čih.
    What dirty ribs you have (from not bathing), shepherd;
    Your sides are striped with dirt, shepherd.

25. *totoltik ʔaʔwelaw hkanan čih;*
    c'irintik ʔaʔwelaw hkanan čih.
    What a dirty face you have, shepherd;
    Your face is striped with dirt, shepherd.

26. *ik'muhč'tik ʔaʔwelaw hkanan čih;*
    t'aš t'aš ʔaʔhak'am hkanan čih.
    What a dirt-spotted face you have, shepherd;
    What a receding hairline (on the sides) you have, shepherd.

27. *leb leb ʔaʔholi hkanan čih;*
    t'aš t'aš ʔaʔholi hkanan čih.
    What a bald pate you have, shepherd;
    What a bald head you have, shepherd.

28. *sasamtik ʔaʔholi hkanan čih;*
    c'al c'al ʔaʔtiʔba hkanan čih.
    What a nearly bald head you have, shepherd;
    What a wrinkled forehead you have, shepherd.

29. *pum pum ʔaʔcaʔi hkanan čih;*
    lib lib ʔaʔč'uhti hkanan čih.
    What a swollen belly you have, shepherd;
    What a roll of fat you have on your hips, shepherd.

30. *t'en t'en ʔaʔč'uhti hkanan čih;*
    k'ayobtikleh ʔaʔč'uhti hkanan čih.
    What a puffed-out abdomen you have, shepherd;
    What a large, drumlike paunch you have, shepherd.

31. *bur bur ʔaʔč'uhti hkanan čih;*
    kot kot ʔaʔniʔi hkanan čih.

What a fat, pendulous belly you have, shepherd;
What a hook nose you have, shepherd.

32. *č'oč'omtik ʔaʔniʔi hkanan čih;*
   wol wol sba ʔaʔniʔi hkanan čih.
   What a pockmarked nose you have, shepherd;
   What a bulbous-tipped nose you have, shepherd.

33. *lak lak ʔaʔk'ak'uʔ hkanan čih;*
   pak'antik ʔaʔk'ak'uʔ hkanan čih.
   How shredded and tattered your old *chamarra* is, shepherd;
   How full of patches your old *chamarra* is, shepherd.

34. *wocwunel ʔaʔwit hkanan čih;*
   tub tub ʔaʔmušuk' hkanan čih.
   What free-swinging, frayed strands on the seat of your *chamarra*, shepherd;
   What a long, protruding bellybutton you have, shepherd.

35. *peš peš ʔaʔmušuk' hkanan čih;*
   luš luš ye ʔaʔmušuk' hkanan čih.
   What a large, deep bellybutton you have, shepherd;
   What a corrugated opening your bellybutton has, shepherd.

36. *nač'ohtikleh ʔaʔholi hkanan čih;*
   tespatikleh ʔaʔk'ak'uʔ hkanan čih.
   What a rat's nest your hair is, shepherd;
   Your old *chamarra* is like a leather backrest, shepherd.

37. *sak wek' wek' ʔaʔk'ak'uʔ hkanan čih;*
   sak p'at p'at ʔaʔk'ak'uʔ hkanan čih.
   What a dirty faded color your old *chamarra* is, shepherd;
   How clearly the white stripes show on your old *chamarra*, shepherd.

38. *k'an tem tem ʔaʔweši hkanan čih;*
   t'ohobtikleh ʔaʔluʔi hkanan čih.
   What a dirty burnt yellow your *calzones* are, shepherd;
   What a yellow-stained crotch area on your *calzones*, shepherd.

39. *lom bayel st'ohobila ʔaʔkahči hkanan čih;*
   šot šot ʔaʔwaʔi hkanan čih.
   How very yellow-stained your *calzones* are, shepherd;
   What a misshapen thigh you have, shepherd.

40. *t'on t'on ʔaʔwaʔi hkanan čih;*
   nač'ohtikleh ʔaʔconi hkanan čih.
   What fleshy thighs you have, shepherd;
   What a rat's nest your pubic hair is, shepherd.

41. *woc woc ʔaʔconi hkanan čih;*
   tuc tuc ʔaʔconi hkanan čih.
   What bushy, unkempt pubic hair you have, shepherd;
   What tufted pubic hair you have, shepherd.

42. *šap' šap' ʔaʔconi hkanan čih;*
   mormoštikleh ʔaʔholi hkanan čih.

What tattered and frayed pubic hair you have, shepherd;
What kinky hair you have, shepherd.

43. *šay šay ʔaʔnei hkanan čih;*
    tay tay ʔaʔnei hkanan čih.
    What folded ends of the tail of your *chamarra* has, shepherd;
    What a long back your *chamarra* has (relative to the front), shepherd.

44. *kʼet kʼet ʔaʔnei hkanan čih;*
    lotʼ lotʼ ʔaʔwiti hkanan čih.
    What rumpled tails your *chamarra* has, shepherd;
    What scraping upper thighs you have (from knockknees), shepherd.

45. *litʼ litʼ ʔaʔwakan hkanan čih;*
    koh koh ʔaʔwiti hkanan čih.
    How trippingly you walk (heel off the ground, semitiptoes), shepherd;
    How limpingly you walk (from bad legs and hips), shepherd.

46. *tač tač ʔaʔwiti hkanan čih;*
    tʼon tʼon ʔaʔwiti hkanan čih.
    What a protruding ass you have, shepherd;
    What large, rounded buttocks you have, shepherd.

47. *tʼaš tʼaš ʔaʔwiti hkanan čih;*
    sep sep ʔaʔmaši hkanan čih.
    What a large, bare ass you have, shepherd;
    What a large, circular hipbone you have sticking out, shepherd.

48. *sep sep ʔaʔkʼošoš hkanan čih;*
    ʔikʼ pil pil ʔaʔmaši hkanan čih.
    What a large, circular hipbone you have sticking out, shepherd;
    What a black (bruised) hipbone you have, shepherd.

49. *ʔikʼ sep sep ʔaʔmaši hkanan čih;*
    tub tub ʔaʔmaši hkanan čih.
    What a black, circular hipbone you have, shepherd;
    What a protruding, bulbous hipbone you have, shepherd.

50. *cʼu cʼu ʔaʔniʔi hkanan čih;*
    law law ʔaʔniʔi hkanan čih.
    What a long, thin, pendulous nose tip you have, shepherd;
    What a long, thin, beaklike nose you have, shepherd.

51. *čʼakultikleh ʔaʔwiti hkanan čih;*
    snaʔučʼtikleh ʔaʔholi hkanan čih.
    How full of fleas your ass is, shepherd;
    What a louse nest your hair is, shepherd.

52. *ston ʔučʼtikleh ʔaʔholi hkanan čih;*
    ston čʼaktikleh ʔaʔwiti hkanan čih.
    How full of louse eggs your hair is, shepherd;
    How full of flea eggs your ass is, shepherd.

53. *cel cel ʔaʔniʔi hkanan čih;*
    pocemtikleh ʔaʔholi hkanan čih.

What a sharp, thin nasal bridge you have, shepherd;
How wrapped up (in cloth) your head is, shepherd.

54. *woh woh ʔaʔluʔi hkanan čih;*
     say say ʔaʔluʔi hkanan čih.
     Your genitals look like a cluster of grapes (through *calzones*), shepherd;
     What a limp penis you have, shepherd.

55. *wel wel shol ʔaʔluʔi hkanan čih;*
     čun čun ʔaʔwati hkanan čih.
     What an exposed-glans penis you have (with foreskin retracted), shepherd;
     What a thick penis you have, shepherd.

56. *bot' bot' ʔaʔluʔi hkanan čih;*
     bic' bic' ʔaʔluʔi hkanan čih.
     Your penis is erecting, shepherd;
     What a thin, stringy penis you have, shepherd.

57. *šberontikleh ye ʔaʔluʔi hkanan čih;*
     cub cub ʔaʔluʔi hkanan čih.
     How like a tadpole('s mouth) your urinary meatus is, shepherd;
     How covered your penis is with pleats of foreskin, shepherd.

Analysis of Text A

In order to indicate loci of creativity appropriate to the performance of this song, we must first consider constraints on form and substance that direct its construction and provide the traditional boundaries within which individual expression can be operative. The following constraints, or guidelines for the construction of the song *hkanan čih,* are enumerated here.

1. Each line of the song constitutes a complete, grammatically well-formed sentence in Tzeltal.

2. Each sentence consists of elements filling the following categorical slots in the following order:

VERB + POSSESSED NOUN + ADDRESSEE

The VERB category represents a stative predicate, and this is followed by POSSESSED NOUN, being the subject of the sentence, and, in turn, by ADDRESSEE (the named social role "shepherd").

3. The VERB slot is filled by a reduplicated one-syllable root (e.g., *luk luk*).

4. The POSSESSED NOUN slot is filled by a noun that is inflected by the prefixed second-person singular pronoun.

5. Each line (or sentence) is composed of eight syllables, each syllable falling on one note in the two-measure line.

6. The possessed noun in each line refers either to an anatomical segment or to an article of clothing.

7. The sentence that constitutes each line is a direct and insulting description of the addressee's (i.e., shepherd's) physical appearance. This description is in accord with shepherd's being a male.

8. Lines (sentences) are paired to form couplets, each couplet corresponding to the four measures completing the melodic pattern (which begins anew as each new couplet commences).

9. No two lines in the song can be lexically identical (although duplication of the semantic content of lines in couplets occurs and is desirable).

10. There are as many couplets (nonduplicating) as the singer's repertoire, inventiveness, and stamina will allow.

While the constraints just outlined constitute a system of rules, they are also a generalized description of a Tzeltal song standard, a description that cannot capture the particular details of the song performance represented by and unique to Text A. But these details are where the creativity lies and should, therefore, be generalized as well if we are to point out the ways in which an individual can create a unique product while using a traditional system of rules. If Text A is really an individual and unique product, then it is novel, and novelty is, then, the essence of creativity. Novelty is easily separated analytically into two different types, one static in that it does not tend to change the established system, and the other dynamic in that it does tend to change the established system. Static novelty, in other words, violates none of the rules of the system. Dynamic novelty, on the other hand, violates some or all of the rules of the system. More will be said about this later: The distinction is made here only so that the two aspects of individual creativity exemplified in Text A can be discussed separately.

Static novelty, perhaps better labeled here as creative conformity, shows up in three essential ways in the song text, all of them a matter of choice on the part of the individual singer.

1. Given the set of all possible Tzeltal insulting descriptions of personal appearance involving reduplicated monosyllables, the singer has chosen a particular subset to use in his song. Part of his creativity, then, is embodied in the particular subset that he chooses (whether it exhausts his own personal repertoire being irrelevant), and in the size of the subset. It should be mentioned here, also, that song performances of "Shepherd" usually represent to the Tzeltal an informal display of

verbal skill and do not imply a contest. A skillful singer will frequently tailor his subset of insulting descriptions so that they allude, by virtue of their applicability, to a particular individual in the community, not infrequently someone in the audience. The descriptive subset can also be tailored by the singer to include varying quantities and degrees of vulgarity.

2. The singer has also chosen a particular order of presentation for the subset of insults that he employs. His skill at ordering is evaluated by an audience, especially in terms of the images that are juxtaposed within couplets. It is good for a couplet to contain two different descriptions of the same body part, or to describe body parts related in some way. It is also desirable to have all descriptions of a specific body part appear in one area of the song rather than having them appear and reappear at various points. Furthermore, it is desirable that the descriptions follow some consistent ordering of body parts such that the genital descriptions come last and are led up to in some logical manner.

3. In reference to several of the body parts, the singer has made lexical selections from among alternative possibilities. For example, *k'ošoš* (literally, "tortilla tostada") and *maš* (literally, "monkey") are both standard metaphorical images referring to the hipbone (*sbakel kubil*). Creative conformity appears in the singer's decision to use one of the terms with one stative predicate and another with another stative predicate. This example exhibits another interesting feature. Whereas most Tzeltal body part terms have either one or two syllables and can be employed without difficulty in the eight-syllable line, *sbakel kubil* has four syllables and therefore cannot be used in the song. Moreover, the locative determiner *-i* is suffixed to *maš* in the song (as it is to other monosyllabic anatomical terms) so as to add a necessary syllable, whereas *k'ošoš* can be used as is. Tzeltal lends itself rather well to lexical selection and couplet formation because of (a) the large number of referents that have standardized metaphorical expressions, (b) the large number of terms that have synonyms, and (c) the large number of terms that have multiple meanings.

Dynamic novelty (or creative nonconformity) involves a violation of some or all of the rules of the system. The singer who produced Text A did not adhere completely to two of the constraints enumerated earlier. In this way he created a slightly more open framework for the performance of "Shepherd," a framework with a larger number of alternatives, and yet rule violation was not extensive enough to distort the original system beyond instant recognizability and complete comprehensibility.

1. In several lines, although by no means the majority, the singer replaced reduplicated roots in the VERB slot with stative predicates bearing the derivational suffixes (and combinations thereof) *-tik* (e.g., *totoltik,* couplet 24), *-tikleh* (e.g., *k'ayobtikleh,* couplet 30), *-V₁mik* (e.g., *č'oč'omtik,* couplet 32), *-V₁mtikleh* (e.g., *buyemtikleh,* couplet 17), or *-ben* (e.g., *hoč'oben,* couplet 17). This violation of constraint number 3 immediately increases the singer's capacity to enumerate insulting descriptions of bodily appearance. It also puts either one or two extra syllables in lines where constraint 3 is violated, a fact leading to violation of constraint 5, which limits the number of syllables per line to eight. The singer deals with this new violation in two ways. First, he reduces some words by one syllable by slurring over the second vowel in these words (e.g., *barbontik* becomes *barmtik, totoltik* becomes *totltik*). Where this fails to reduce the number of syllables per line to eight, the singer divides the first quarter note into eighths, sixteenths, or whatever is appropriate so that each syllable corresponds to one note and so that the last seven syllables in every line always receive the normal note values.

2. In a few cases the singer chose POSSESSED NOUNS of more than three syllables (e.g., *ʔaʔmancana,* couplet 20). Here the extra syllables were dealt with in the manner described previously, by dividing the first quarter note. The longest line in the song has twelve syllables (couplet 17) owing to innovations in both the VERB and POSSESSED NOUN slots. Informants, including the singer, state that the line is clumsy and detracts from the song because it could not be adequately shortened or accommodated by division of the first quarter note.

To summarize the analysis, individual freedom of expression has two aspects relevant to the performance recorded in text A. Creative conformity, novelty within the system of rules, is reflected in the singer's repertoire or choice of insults, his ordering of the insults, and his particular lexical selections where alternatives were possible. Creative nonconformity, novelty by breaking rules (and adjustments made necessary by such rule breakage), is reflected in the singer's violation of constraints 3 and 5, and in the characteristically patterned ways in which he adjusts the modified output that results.

Text B — Woman's Improvised Song

The following text and glosses are of a woman's improvised song, with no title, consisting of 20 twelve-measure verses, each of which comprises three paired lines of two measures.

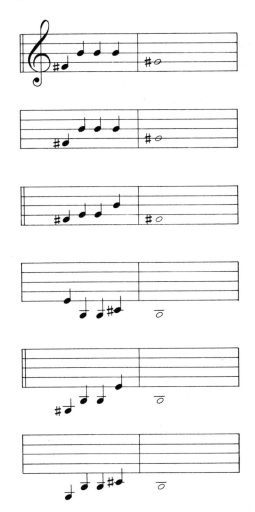

1. *mančuki taton*
        mančuki me?on
    ya šbaon ta sna htat
        ya šbaon ta sna hme?
    ?ala hbalambohč
        ?ala ht'ont'on we?el
    No matter father
        No matter mother
    I'm going (home) to my father's house
        I'm going (home) to my mother's house
    Little "bald head" [nickname of a man in *paraje* of *cahal č'en*]
        Little "meal of calf muscle" [nickname of son of *hbalambohč*]

2. *sok ta sna hši?lel*
        kala li cunkin
    kala li kerem
        hcunkinil winik
    hcunkinil kerem
        ha? tatil stukel
    And to my elder brother's house
        My little "hairy one" [referring to *ht'ont'on we?el,* her elder brother]
    This boy of mine
        "Hairy one" the boy
    "Hairy one" the man
        He is a father himself

3. *ma me ša?mahon*
        ma me ša?wuton
    ya me kalbe hmam
        ya me kalbe htat
    ya kalbe hši?lel
        ya kalbe kahwal
    Don't hit me
        Don't scold me
    I'll tell my grandfather (if you do)
        I'll tell my father
    I'll tell my elder brother
        I'll tell my master

4. *ha? htat hč'akul?it*
        ha? htat hč'akultop
    melel ča?kah yit
        melel ?oškah stop
    melel čankah yit
        melel ho?kah stop
    My father is "flea ass" [nickname]
        My father is "flea anus" [same man's nickname, and of his son]
    Truly he has two asses
        Truly he has three anuses
    Truly he has four asses
        Truly he has five anuses

5. *melel ha? hši?lel*
        melel ha? kahwal
    hč'akul ?itetik
        hč'akul topetik
    ha? me hwinikil
        ha? me hkeremal
    Truly he is my elder brother
        Truly he is my master
    "Flea asses" [familial nickname]
        "Flea anuses" [alternate nickname for same family]
    It is the man
        It is the boy

6. *ma ša²wuc'inon*
    ma ša²labanon
ya me kalbe htat
    mamali koral
mamali winik
    lučul ta koral
Don't molest me
    Don't make fun of me
I'll tell my father
    Old man "corral" [nickname for brother of "flea ass"]
The old man
    Squatting on the corral fence (to defecate) [nickname alternant]

7. *ha² k'ahk'al winik*
    ha² k'ahk'al kerem
mamali čirin
    mamali stenle
sok htat mamal no
    sok hluna mentes
He is a vigorous man
    He is a vigorous boy
Old man "screech" [nickname]
    Old man "plain" [nickname]
And my father, old man "no" [nickname]
    And my Luna Mentes [surname]

8. *bayuk ²a baokon*
    bayuk me k'ookon
ta sna kala tat
    ta sna kala ²ahwal
č'iš č'iš ši martin
    č'iš č'iš ši winik
Wherever I may have gone
    Wherever I might have arrived
To my dear father's house
    To my dear master's house
"It's spiny, he says" Martin [nickname + first name]
    "It's spiny, he says" the man

9. *čikan ba² solon*
    čikan ba² k'ašon
ta sna kala me²
    ta sna kala tat
hpoketil winik
    hč'akul top kerem
Wherever I pass by
    Wherever I go by
To my dear mother's house
    To my dear father's house
"Wide-mouth jar" the man [nickname]
    "Flea anus" the boy [nickname]

10. *mač'a swentaon*
    mač'a yočelon
    ʔay kala meʔ c'i
    ʔay hkašail č'i
    šun kawayu ʔanc
    šun kawayu hmeʔ
Whoever cares about me
    Whoever I matter to [literally, "whoever his-entrance-I-am"]
There is my dear mother for sure
    There is my mother [literally, "mother-earth"] for certain
"Joan horse" is a woman [nickname]
    "Joan horse" is my mother

11. *ʔay sk'ahk'al hmam č'i*
    k'ahk'al winik htat
    mamal htespatil
    mamal hsempatil
    hweʔ kašlan wah č'i
    mamal šʔamač'il
My grandfather really has vigor
    My father is a vigorous man
Old man "cushion back" [nickname]
    Old man "padded back" [nickname alternant for "cushion back"]
I eat bread [literally, "Ladino tortillas"]
    Old man "lace bug" [nickname]

12. *sk'an bal šaʔwalbe*
    sk'an bal šaʔkuybe
    kalali šikuč
    kala šikunerol
    hšikučil winik
    hšikučil kerem
You don't talk much
    You don't believe much
My dear "says I'll bear it" [nickname, son of "cushion back"]
    My dear "says President" [nickname, alternant for above]
"Says I'll bear it" the man
    "Says I'll bear it" the boy

13. *ma me šaʔmahon*
    ma me šaʔwuton
    kalali taton
    kalali meʔon
    kalali šiʔlel
    kalali muetik
Don't hit me
    Don't scold me
I have my dear father (to protect me)
    I have my dear mother
I have my dear elder brother
    I have my dear brothers-in-law

14. *k'ahk'al winik hmam*
         p'ihil kerem htat
     ya sna? slikel moč
         mamal hč'ultatik
     mamal hlimpeču
         hlimpeču mamal
     My grandfather is a vigorous man
         My father is a smart boy
     He knows his basket raising [i.e., he can divine with basket and scissors]
         Old man "sun" [nickname]
     Old man "thick chest"
         "Thick chest" the old man

15. *bayel ta htul hmam*
         cobol ta hčahp htat
     h?isimil winik
         hcocil čo kerem
     h?opašil tatil
         hčimbakil mamal
     My grandfathers are many
         I have many fathers
     "Whiskers" the man [nickname]
         "Furry cheek" the boy [nickname alternant for "whiskers"]
     "Hairy" the father [nickname alternant for "whiskers"]
         "Marrow" the old man [nickname alternant for "whiskers"]

16. *ma?bal ?ayuk hmam*
         ma?bal ?ayuk htat
     k'ušon ta yo?tan
         halon ta yo?tan
     ?ay kala ši?lel
         ?ay kala ?ihc'in
     Don't I have a grandfather indeed
         Don't I have a father indeed
     He needs me [literally, "I rest his heart"]
         He is fond of me [literally, "I pass time in his heart"]
     There is (also) my dear elder brother
         There is (also) my dear younger brother

17. *kalali me?on*
         kalali wišon
     kalali muetik
         kalali ši?lel
     kalali ?ihc'in
         kalali tatoni
     I have a dear mother
         I have a dear elder sister
     I have my dear brothers-in-law
         I have my dear elder brother
     I have my dear younger brother
         I have my dear father

18. *bayuk ?abaokon*
          ta sna kala tat
     sna kati hši?lel
          hkaranca k'a?k'u?
     hnač'ohol winik
          hkaranca kerem
     Wherever I may go
          To my dear father's house
     Perhaps my elder brother's house
          "Rat old *chamarra*" [nickname]
     "House rat" the man [nickname alternant]
          "Rat" the boy [nickname alternant]

19. *ha? čikan ko?tan*
          ba k'alal ya šban
     ta sna kala tat
          mamal hšemperin
     hšemperin winik
          hšemperin tatilon
     I (will always) know
          Wherever I may go
     To my dear father's house
          Old man "bald top" [nickname]
     "Bald top" the man
          "Bald top" my father

20. *yu?un bal mayuk hwiš*
          kalali me?on
     kalali wišon
          ?ala hšemperin
     hšemperin ?a?č'iš
          hšemperin k'inalon
     Don't I have an elder sister [rhetorical]
          (There is) my dear mother
     (There is) my dear elder sister
          Dear "bald top"
     "Bald top" the girl
          "Bald top" my lands

Analysis of Text B

The framework of rules defining Text B appears to comprise the following constraints.

1. Each line in the song constitutes a complete sentence or phrase in Tzeltal.

2. Each line in the song is grammatically well-formed and, with one striking exception, correctly interpretable in terms of Tzeltal grammatical rules.

3. Each line in the song contains five pronounced syllables, one for each note in the two measures corresponding to a line.

4. Lines in the song are grouped into couplets (a pair of adjacent and semantically related lines), which, in turn, are grouped into verses (three adjacent and related couplets).

5. Each verse corresponds to the twelve measures in which the full melodic pattern is completed.

6. No two lines in a verse are lexically identical. It happens in this song that no two lines in the whole song are identical, but such is rarely the case in women's improvised songs, so it seems better to generalize the constraint.

7. The song is sung by a female.

Given these few constraints, almost all of the song is uniquely individual, much of the originality remaining within the context of what I have called creative conformity. In this context, two aspects of the song command attention, for they epitomize the creative skill of the singer according to Tzeltal evaluations. First, there is the humorous and allusive use of nicknames. Second, there is the resourceful utilization of synonymy in several of the couplets.

Every Tenejapan has a nickname, usually pertaining to some feature or fact that seems characteristic of the person. Nicknames are used, in general, only for people who are not present. They are never used for address. This may be so partly because many nicknames are derogatory or vulgar or describe some weakness about which the person nicknamed is sensitive. It is, therefore, somewhat risqué and very humorous to have a song in which nicknames play a major role. Every nickname in Text B represents a real person living in the Tenejapa *paraje* of *cahal č'en* at the time the song was recorded. Many, but not all, of the people are geneologically related, and each nickname has a derivational history known to most members of the *paraje,* as well as guessable to many members of the *municipio.* For example, *t'ont'on we?el* 'meal of calf muscle' has legs so fat that they would make a good meal, *mamal koral* 'old man corral' was once seen squatting on top of a corral fence to defecate, *mamal no* 'old man "no"' says only "no" when he gets drunk so that he will appear to speak Spanish (of which the only word he knows is *no*), and *htespatil* 'cushion back' was so nicknamed because he never takes off the cushion that he uses to protect his back while carrying heavy loads (even in town). The singer who produced Text B cleverly introduces, plays with, and produces alternants for well-known nicknames, all within a framework that necessitates five-syllable lines.

The reader will notice from the glosses for Text B that many of the couplets involve the reiteration of an idea through the use of synonyms (e.g., "Wherever I may have gone"–"Wherever I might have arrived," verse 7). With some, the synonymy is not so readily apparent, however, for it is produced through metaphorical extension. Such is the case, for example, in the third couplet of verse 5 (i.e., "It is the man"–"It is the boy"). In this case "boy" (the literal interpretation of *kerem*) is a metaphoric image referring to "man," a metaphor routinely used in this context. Similarly, in the third couplet of verse 20 "lands" is a standard metaphoric image referring to "woman." Here the one metaphor is coupled with another, for "girl" is a standard metaphoric image also referring to "woman." Additional metaphors participating in synonymy can be found in verses 8, 9, 12, 15, and 18.

Creative nonconformity is present in this song also. The song was sung by a man, clearly a violation of constraint 7. This very interesting and rare innovation caused much comment in Tenejapa. The man was plainly imitating the voice, style, and general content of a woman's improvised song, as well as using kinship terminology appropriate to a female ego. But the singer was a man, and to the listeners the song was twice as funny as it would have been if the singer were a woman.

Another feature of the song warrants mention here: the relaxation of a grammatical constraint, allowing for easier attainment of a five-syllable line. In Tzeltal a noun is inflected for possession with subject person prefixes identical to the set of subject person prefixes that inflect a transitive verb. Intransitive verbs, on the other hand, are inflected for person of subject with a different set of morphemes, and these are suffixes. The person suffixes inflecting intransitive verbs, when attached to a noun (adjective, numeral, or particle) stem, transform it into a stative verb inflected for person, stative verbs being a subclass of intransitive verbs. Possessed nouns *taton, me?on, wison,* and *k'inalon,* appearing in verses 1, 13, 17, and 20, however, do not conform to these rules. Instead of the prefix *h-* that should appear with *tat, me?, wis,* and *k'inal,* the person suffix for stative intransitive verbs *-on* is attached. In any other context *taton,* for example, would be correctly interpreted as "I am a father." In the song, however, this form is correctly interpreted as "my father." It is apparent that this grammatical deviation results from the need for an extra syllable in the lines where it is found (to complete the necessary five). The grammatically correct prefix does not add a syllable, while the grammatically anomolous suffix does, so the latter is substituted. If this violation of a normal grammatical constraint were attributable to this song and singer in terms of priority, then it would constitute an example of creative nonconformity. In fact, it is a device employed by many singers to add a syllable to a line, and, thus, its strategic use here exemplifies creative conformity. This means that the device must be incorporated as a specific exception in constraint 2. It is conventionally employed relaxation of a Tzeltal rule of grammar, occurring only in Tzeltal song.

Text C—Man's Improvised Song

The following text and glosses are of a man's improvised song, with no title, consisting of 17 twelve-measure verses, each of which comprises three paired lines of two measures.

1. *htiniente winikon*
   htiniente keremon
   hkoronel winikon
   hkoronel keremon
   ši k'alal la yalben
   ši k'alal la skuyben

    I am the "lieutenant man"
       I am the "lieutenant boy"
    I am the "colonel man"
       I am the "colonel boy"
    They said it when they talked to me [i.e., other women]
       They said it when they listened to me

2.   *melel hič la yalben*
      k'alal la hta hbah sok
   ʔaltik ma šaʔk'anon
      ʔaltik ma šaʔč'unon
   lom ya hnaʔ lek 'a'tel
      lom ya hnaʔ lek moc'aw
   Truly thus they called me
      When I found myself with them
   Too bad you don't love me
      Too bad you won't accept me
   I know how to work very well
      I know how to make love very well

3.   *hoʔon ya hnitula*
      hoʔon ya hočila
   hoʔon ya hkilula
      hoʔon ya htahsula
   hoʔon ya hbohc'ila
      hoʔon ya hlehk'ula
   Me, I pull it along repeatedly (as an object attached to a rope)
      Me, I drag it repeatedly (as hauling along the ground)
   Me, I pull it repeatedly (as a rope pulled across a surface)
      Me, I pull on it repeatedly (as pulling a machete from its scabbard)
   Me, I jab it in and out (as a stick into wet ground)
      Me, I slide it back and forth (as with tongue licking lips)

4. *hoʔon ya hlowila*
      hoʔon ya hc'apula
   hoʔon ya hulila
      hoʔon ya hkoc'ila
   hoʔon ya hpihc'ula
      hoʔon ya ht'ašula
   Me, I insert it (like a knife in flesh)
      Me, I insert it (like a post in the ground)
   Me, I insert it (like a needle through cloth)
      Me, I insert it (like the tip of a machete through a banana stalk)
   Me, I insert it (like a foot stepping in mud)
      Me, I slap it on (like slapping a face with an open hand)

5.   *hoʔon to me ya hta ši*
      hoʔon to me ya kil ši
   hoʔon to me ya hac ši
      hoʔon to me ya hčiʔ ši
   hoʔon to me ya hk'ep ši
      hoʔon to me ya hliw ši

It's still me who will encounter her (first)
It's still me who will see her (first)
It's still me who will tear her (first) (as in tearing cloth in two)
It's still me who'll rip her (first) (as making a tear in paper)
It's still me who'll part it (as pulling hair off forehead) (first)
It's still me who'll open it up (first) (as widening a hole)

6. *ho?on me ya hpikula*
ho?on me ya hašula
ya me hpikbe yelaw
ya me ka?ybe sti?ba
ya me hpikbe ščo ši
ya me ka?ybe sni? ši
Me, I'll touch (her/it) (with my fingers) repeatedly
Me, I'll rub (her/it) gently (with the palm of my hand) repeatedly
I'll touch her face [metaphor for vulva] for her
I'll feel her forehead [metaphor for mons veneris] for her
I'll touch her cheeks (of her buttocks) for her, I say
I'll feel her nose [metaphor for clitoris] for her, I say

7. *?altik bal la hman ši*
?altik bal la htoh ši
melel manbil ku?un
melel tohbil ku?un
bayel la kak' htak'in
bayel la kak' hmeru
It wasn't for nothing that I bought her
It wasn't for naught that I paid for her
Truly she was bought by me
Truly she was paid for by me
I gave many coins (for her)
I gave much money (for her)

8. *la htuhki htak'in ši*
la htuhki hmeru ši
hašbil ta pulatu
melel manbil ku?un
melel tohbil ku?un
manbilat ku?un ši
I scattered my coins (as with broadcast sowing of seeds), I say
I scattered my money, I say
A plate of it, full to the brim
Truly bought by me
Truly paid for by me
You have been bought (and paid for) by me, I say

9. *te me ya ?a?cak yan ši*
te me ya ?a?k'an yan ši
hk'ašel ya hmilat ši
ya me htuhk'ayat ši
ya bal ?a?toy ?a?ba
ya bal ?a?se? ?a?ba

If you take another (man), I say
  If you want another (man), I say
I will surely kill you, I say
  I will shoot you, I say
Would you (dare to) be conceited (and walk with your nose in the air)
  Would you be uppity (and wiggle your hips while walking)

10. *ya šč'ayat ta k'inal*
  ya šway ʔaʔbak'etal
melel hʔištahelat
  melel htoybahelat
melel hseʻbahelat
  melel hkotkowilat
You will (die and) get lost in the countryside
  Your body will sleep
Truly you are a brazen one (with other men)
  Truly you are an insolent one
Truly you are one who walks flirtatiously
  Truly you are an unfaithful one (going from man to man)

11. *bi to kati ya ʔaʔk'an*
  bi to kati ya ʔaʔč'un
hnahtil ʔat winikon
  hčunčun ʔat keremon
hk'ečk'eč ʔat tatilon
  hyeʔyeʔ ʔat mamalon
What more do you want
  Who [literally, "what"] else would you obey
I am a long-penised man
  I am a thick-penised boy
I am a wiggling-penised father
  I am a waggling-penised old man

12. *k'alal ta ʔaʔsehk'ub ši*
  k'alal ta ʔaʔbikil ši
k'alal ta ʔaʔcukum ši
  k'alal ta ʔaʔsot'ot' ši
k'alal ta ʔaʔwoʔtan ši
  k'alal me ta ʔaʔpuc ši
Up to your liver, I say (that my penis will reach)
  Up to your intestines, I say
Up to your pancreas, I say
  Up to your lungs, I say
Up to your heart, I say
  Up to your lungs, I say

13. *ʔaltik bal ya kal ši*
  ʔaltik bal ya hkuy ši
melel winikon ši
  melel keremon ši
melel tatilon ši
  melel mamalon ši

It's not for nothing that I say it, I say
    It's not for nothing that I believe it, I say
Truly I'm a man, I say
    Truly I'm a boy, I say
Truly I'm a father, I say
    Truly I'm an old man, I say

14. *ya me hkohtanat ši*
    ya me hawanat ši
 ya me hlewanat ši
    ya me hc'eanat ši
 ya me hbuhtanat ši
    hk'ečbet ʔaʔwakan ši
I'll put you on all fours, I say
    I'll put you on your back, I say
I'll open you up, I say
    I'll lay you on your side, I say
I'll turn you over, I say
    I'll raise up your leg for you, I say

15. *mančuk me ta sab ši*
    ta k'aleltikuk ši
 ta ʔoliluk k'al ši
    ta smaleluk k'al ši
 ta ʔihk'uk k'inal ši
    htoybet ʔaʔwakan ši
No matter if it's early in the morning, I say
    (Or) indeed in the daytime, I say
(Or) indeed at midday, I say
    (Or) indeed in the afternoon, I say
(Or) indeed in the evening, I say
    I'll lift up your leg for you, I say

16. *čikan ba la kak'be*
    čikan ba la hmulan
 mančuk me ta k'inal
    mančuk me ta ti ʔbe
 mančuk me ta patna
    mančuk me ta ʔamak'
Wherever, I'd give it to you (anywhere)
    Wherever, I'd make love (anywhere)
No matter whether it's in the woods
    No matter whether it's on the side of the trail
No matter whether it's behind the house
    No matter whether it's in the patio

17. *yuʔun niš winikon ʔa*
    yuʔun niš keremon ʔa
 yuʔun niš tatilon ʔa
    yuʔun niš mamalon ʔa
 htiniente winikon
    htiniente keremon

It's just because I'm a man then
    It's just because I'm a boy then
It's just because I'm a father then
    It's just because I'm an old man then
I'm the "lieutenant man"
    I'm the "lieutenant boy"

Analysis of Text C

The framework of rules applicable to Text C appears to comprise the following constraints, which are quite similar to those of Text B.

1. Each line in the song constitutes a complete sentence or phrase in Tzeltal.
2. Each line in the song is grammatically well-formed and, with one exception, correctly interpretable in terms of Tzeltal grammatical rules.
3. Each line in the song contains six pronounced syllables, one for each note in the two measures corresponding to a line.
4. Lines in the song are grouped into couplets (a pair of adjacent and semantically related lines), which are, in turn, grouped into verses (three adjacent couplets).
5. Each verse corresponds to the twelve measures in which the full melodic pattern is completed.
6. No two lines in a verse are lexically identical.
7. The song is sung by a male.

Within the framework of these few rules, almost all of the song is uniquely individual. All of the originality here falls into the category of creative conformity; none of the defining formal and substantive rules are violated. In this context, one aspect of the song commands particular attention because it demonstrates so well the creative skill of the singer by Tzeltal evaluations: the use of metaphoric description for alluding to copulation. Metaphoric description of copulation and attendant sex play occurs throughout verses 3, 4, 5, 6, 12, 14, and 16, as well as in portions of verses 2 and 17.

Couplet formation through synonymy (verse 7, couplets 1, 2, and 3), antonymy (verse 15, couplet 1), and metaphor (verse 2, couplet 3), a characteristically Mayan pattern of construction in formal speech genres (cf., Bricker, 1975; Edmonson, 1973), is also expressed in this song.

One final note: The exception referred to in constraint 2 has to do with a lexicosemantic interpretation rule for the quotative. The quotative form *si* literally means "he/she/it says/said" in other contexts. In Text C it is glossed as "I say/said" because the speaker is referring to himself even though using the form inflected for third person rather than the form inflected for first person (which would be *šon*). The reader may prefer to view this as a metaphorical usage rather than a relaxation of a grammatical rule. In either case, this use of the quotative is not uncommon in Tzeltal song.

Discussion

A distinction has been made in this study between two basic kinds of creativity (or novelty), both kinds being exemplified in Tzeltal song performances. The distinction applies, moreover, to creativity in any artistic endeavor; in fact, in any communicative event.

The first kind of creativity, creative conformity, is more common than the second in performances, and more appreciated by the audience majority in general; it includes the stimulation of some novelty and the safety of the status quo. Creative conformity, or static novelty, is tentatively defined here as (the results of) individual selection and arrangement of details within restrictions imposed by formal and substantive rules that constitute the generic framework applying to a particular communicative event. In an absolute sense, if no rules are imposed or followed, then the quantity of creativity may be infinite in a given performance. The creativity would then, however, be quite random and, therefore, meaningless. Where there are many restrictions on form and content, then the amount of creativity in absolute terms might be quite low. However, any individual and unique performance could necessitate skill and be very meaningful and, thus, interesting and highly valued. Selection and arrangement within a framework of rules can be done either well or poorly as judged by an audience of individuals, whether they judge through familiarity with the rules, an on-the-spot-induced reconstruction of the rules, a purely intuitive aesthetic sense, or any combination of the three. Creativity seen as novelty has, of course, no necessary correlation with skill or beauty (which are what is usually evaluated).

The second kind of creativity, creative nonconformity, is less common than the first in performances, and less appreciated by the audience majority in general; it forsakes the safety of convention (the establishment, the status quo) for the stimulation of even more novelty. Creative nonconformity, or dynamic novelty, is the essence of change and is tentatively defined here as (the results of) individual nonadherence to some or even all the formal and substantive constraints that constitute the generic framework applying to a particular communicative event. This nonadherence can be viewed as the addition (to the system) of new rules saying that certain old rules do not apply, a change in status for old rules (from applicable to nonapplicable), or simply a violation of old rules; the result is the same, novelty from outside the system because a different system is applied. The resulting change in performance can be either evolutionary (if few rules are violated) or revolutionary (if many rules are violated).

The reader may well wonder how, if a performer violates many or all of the rules that are stylistic markers of the genre being performed, the result can be termed creative, or how the genre can even be identified from the performance. Consider, for example, a Tzeltal performer purporting to sing a man's improvised song who simply spews forth an ungrammatical string of gibberish with no couplet, verse, or syllable structure and, thus, communicates very little to his audience aside from his lack of desire and/or ability to sing a man's improvised song. Is this creative? According to the etic definition that I have proposed, it is creative. Theoretically, in fact, it could constitute the introduction of a new genre, provided that it gained acceptance and currency in the society. This certainly does not mean that the performance is good, structured, appropriate, or even believed by the Tzeltal to be creative, however. The Tzeltal themselves, who evaluate performances in terms of good and bad, have no words denoting anything like "creative" or "creativity," making it difficult to get at an emic definition of the concept. It may be desirable, nevertheless, in some circumstances to add an intelligibility criterion to the definition of creative nonconformity so that gibberish and other extreme degrees of rule violation cannot be considered creativity. This alternative definition could be phrased in the following way: (the results of) individual nonadherence to some of the formal and substantive constraints that constitute the generic framework applying to a particular communicative event, but only insofar as the results retain enough stylistic marking to identify the performance as pertaining to the expected genre (and insofar as the performance is intelligible to an audience). Where these limits lie must necessarily vary with the genre and with the culture.

In cultures and/or genres in which novelty is appreciated, eventually much, most, or everything that can be said within the old framework will have been said. Artistically, performances will become boring because of their predictable form and content; scientifically, the point of diminishing returns will be reached, necessitating a new paradigm (cf. Kuhn, 1962). In our society music and painting are areas of aesthetic expression in which creativity is deeply appreciated, but radical changes wrought through dynamic novelty take some time to become appreciated, even when they are highly structured (witness Thelonius Monk), and attempts to disregard many or all rules to the point where structure is lacking are even less appreciated (witness Ornette Coleman or Max Ernst's "drippings").

Richmond Browne, a jazz pianist, has written penetratingly on memory and prediction in listener evaluation and appreciation of a jazz solo. He says that the listener is constantly making infinitesimal predictions about what will come next.

> The player is constantly either confirming or denying these predictions in the listener's mind. As nearly as we can tell (Kraehenbuehl at Yale and I), the listener must come out right about 50% of the time—if he is too successful in predicting, he will become bored; if he is too unsuccessful, he will give up and call the music "disorganized" [Coker, 1964:15].

If this concept of predictability can be generalized, then appreciated creativity would appear to lie in a marginal area somewhere between too much predictability and too little. Perhaps the old homilies are applicable to art if "familiarity breeds contempt" while "total strangers are consummate dangers." Variety, then, is the spice of life, but not too much nor too little.

On the basis of informant interviews concerning song performance evaluations, the Tzeltal seem to appreciate structured creativity within an established generic system much the same way we do. They become bored with too much repetition as well as with too much unfamiliar variation. They appreciate complexity, but only when it is a complexity with which they are partially familiar. Where the Tzeltal differ from us is in the constraints that guide the production of their performances.

Conclusion

Formal and substantive constraints guiding the construction of Tzeltal song performances comprise systems that can be described as grammatical rules plus additional generic rules. The additional rules generate, among other things, lines of specified syllable length, couplets (paired semantically related lines), and verses (composed of three adjacent couplets). In general, repetition of form is eschewed and repetition of content desirable. Particularly important loci of creativity in the song texts were specified as insults, metaphors, synonymy, and nicknames, all of which are well provided for in the Tzeltal lexical larder. Tzeltal morphology was also shown to be quite adaptable to the production of lines with a specified number of syllables (as are the phonetic realization rules). An interesting relaxation of a grammatical (morphological) rule occurred in one song, the exchange of a transitive verb prefix with an intransitive verb suffix denoting subject and person.

Analysis of the texts warranted a distinction between creative conformity and creative nonconformity, and examples were given of each. Creative conformity was identified with tradition, while creative nonconformity was identified with change.

References

Bricker, Victoria
  1975   The ethnographic context of some traditional Mayan speech genres. In *Explorations in the ethnography of speaking,* edited by R. Bauman and J. Sherzer. New York: Cambridge Univ. Press.
Coker, Jerry
  1964   *Improvising jazz.* Englewood Cliffs, New Jersey: Prentice-Hall.
Edmonson, Munro S.
  1973   Semantic universals and particulars in Quiche. In *Meaning in Mayan languages,* edited by M. S. Edmonson. Pp. 235–246. The Hague: Mouton.
Kuhn, Thomas
  1962   *The structure of scientific revolutions.* Chicago: Univ. of Chicago Press.

An Ethnoscience View of Schizophrenic Speech[1]

OSWALD WERNER
GLADYS LEVIS-MATICHEK
WITH MARTHA EVENS AND
BONNIE LITOWITZ

What is verbally not odd is devoid of disclosure power.

—I. Ramsey

Introduction

Possible referents of the word schizophrenia cover a wide range of phenomena. Lacking reasonably unambiguous criteria, it is much less a theoretical term than a useful "handle" for speaking about a vast range of an otherwise poorly lexicalized domain.[2]

The breadth of the term *schizophrenia* transfers inevitably to any attempt to characterize "schizophrenic speech." Consequently, this study will deal with *some* aspects of *some* schizophrenic speech. In no instance is the term *schizophrenic* ours. In this work we look at the speech of people labeled "schizophrenic" by the authors of the studies we used as our sources. That is, this study uses only published sources. We consider the investigation of "live" samples a subsequent step.

We were led to this investigation through the problems of the control

[1] This research was supported by a grant from the National Institute of Mental Health MH-10940. Numerous people have participated in several seminars, which started during the winter quarter of 1972 and dealt with the general model of an "ethnoscience machine" and, concurrently, with such problems as "schizophrenic speech," and "context," and many others. Although the participants changed, major contributors of many ideas are John Farella, Mark Schoepfle, Martin Topper, Ed Maxwell, Professor Raoul Smith, Allan Darrah, and Ricardo Melo.

[2] This is not unlike terminology in other fields: In linguistics proper, the nineteenth-century language typology of isolating, agglutinating, inflecting, and (Sapir's) polysynthetic languages represents a useful way of speaking about languages. Similarly, in ethnoscience the etic–emic dichotomy is low in theoretical import but useful for speaking. Recent attempts to extend the range of these terms (e.g., Harris, 1968) has resulted in a broadening that threatens total desemanticization (Weinreich 1963). Such "sloganization" of technical terms undermines even their heuristic use.

of speech—its flow—in a simulation model of human question–
answering behavior. Some samples of speech labeled schizophrenic
seem to exhibit problems of proper sequencing. Our procedure was simply to look at a large variety of samples of speech from the literature and
to typologize these samples on the basis of their "fit" into our model.
Since both our model and the label "schizophrenic speech" are problematic, this undertaking is exploratory rather than definitive.

The plan of this study is as follows: First we discuss briefly our model
of human question answering. Then we discuss some hypotheses
regarding schizophrenic speech from the literature. This is followed by a
discussion of metaphor. Subsequently, we deal with the related problem
of the control of the "flow" of speech. Based on the nature of our model,
we call this "path control." Next, we discuss a set of phenomena that
appear to be "inversions" of speech, and finally, we present some general conclusions.

Model and Problem

This brief description of a model of human question-answering behavior is an abstract of a more detailed proposal by Werner in several recent
publications (e.g., Werner, 1972a). This model is the theoretical basis of
our approach. The following section deals with some difficulties associated with the present model. These, in turn, lead to our investigation
of schizophrenic speech.

SKETCH OF THE MODEL

The basic assumptions of the model are as follows:

1.   All semantic relations (following Casagrande and Hale, 1967) are
radically binarized. In other words, complex sentences do not consist
only of simple sentences but, ultimately, of binary semantic relations.[3]

2.   The semantic relations of Casagrande and Hale (1967) are reduced to a fundamental set: taxonomic relation (T), or asymmetrical,
transitive, partial synonymy; the limiting case of the taxonomic relation,
or "true" synonymy (S); and the relation of modification (or attribution)
(M). A further fundamental relation is queuing (Q) representing any
serial order. It contains possible subtypes—at least an intransitive distal
queuing (QD). Additional fundamental relations overlap with symbolic

---

[3] There are a few exceptions to binary relations: Negation N is unary; some spatial relations (e.g., between) relate three arguments.

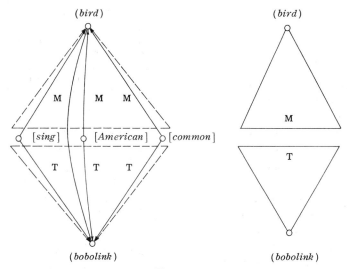

Figure 1.

logic: unary negation (N), binary conjunction (C), disjunction (D), implication (F) (conceivably modified by "possibility" and "necessity" from modal logic and "sometimes" and "always" from temporal logic, and possibly others), and double implication, or identity (X).

3. These basic relations form lexical–semantic fields. The fields are multilayered (see Figure 2, p. 352), but the basic organization is around taxonomies (T) and modification (M) (see Figure 1). Arrows with a "downward" component represent the relation of taxonomy (T); arrows with an "upward" component represent the relation of modification (M); thus, each link on each level of a taxonomy may be represented by two triangles: the "upper" modification triangle and the "lower" taxonomic one (see dotted lines in Figure 1). Looping through the taxonomy in Figure 1 once will return the answer *All bobolinks are birds that sing* (or *songbirds*); looping through three times, *All bobolinks are common American songbirds* (Thorndike Barnhart Junior Dictionary, 1959:70). Note that [*sing*], [*American*], and [*common*] are all attributes of (bird) (linked to it by M).

If it is accepted that a semantic paradigm is the lexical–semantic structure that patterns every level of a taxonomy (Werner and Fenton, 1970), then the union of modification triangles on one level of a taxonomy is isomorphic with a componential paradigm. However, the "components" are here unambiguously (see Lyons' critique, 1968) tokens (in square brackets) of types (in parentheses). (This is somewhat

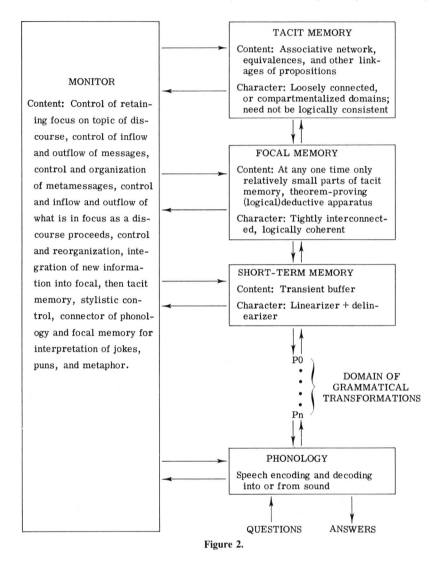

Figure 2.

analogous to Quillian's (1969) use of type and token). Thus, token [*sing*] is internally linked to the taxonomy of verbs and the occurrence of type (*sing*), [*America*] to the taxonomy of continents and (*America*), and [*common*] to (*common*). Changes of modifier [*sing*] and [*America*] to *song* and *American*, respectively, are left to late rules near the surface structure.

4. The multilayered organization of the model may be schematized as in Figure 2.[4]

5. Perhaps the most significant feature of the model is that all of human cultural knowledge does not need to be logically coherent. Large areas of knowledge can coexist without danger of contradiction. Discrepancies will show up only under traumatic conditions, at which time it may precipitate a "world view" change and/or a fresh reintegration.

SOME PROBLEMS OF THE MODEL

In the present model, movement of associated information is synchronized to the movement of the discourse. Such synchronization is achieved by a largely unknown mechanism of the MONITOR (see Figure 1). Schizophrenic speech is marked by the fact that it is often unintelligible to the listener. It is important to emphasize that this opacity creates difficulties of comprehension not only for "normals" but also for other schizophrenic patients.

A cursory examination of samples of schizophrenic speech from the literature reveals that they represent at least (1) problems in the sequencing of speech because ideas seem to intrude upon ideas (interfering association, Bleuler, 1950), but that the interference may also be due in part to (2) problems of retrieval or, finally, to (3) a combination of both. No doubt the area is sufficiently underexplored that the likelihood of other factors should not be excluded.

The difficulties encountered in the interpretation of schizophrenic speech appear to be difficulties of control in the component we call MONITOR. Since the MONITOR is also the least understood aspect of the model, any light that can be shed on its operation is valuable. The possibility of learning more about the role and function of the monitor is the major justification for this preliminary undertaking. The task we set for ourselves is not so much to find out why a schizophrenic does what he does, that is, what makes his speech look unrecognizable, opaque, obscure, or at least different from the speech of normals, as to explore

---

[4] The schema, though greatly abbreviated, is within its limitations self-explanatory. Greater detail will be given as the need arises. Previous versions of this model are discussed in Werner (1972a, 1972b, and 1972c). These do not contain the MONITOR, which represents at least one level of control or, facetiously, "consciousness." It is by far the least understood component of the model. Interest in "pathological" forms of speech seems to throw light on the nature of some of the controls.

Subsequent versions based on a review of the literature on memory and human inference making complicate the device (Werner, 1973, 1974) without substantially altering the general schema.

possible mechanisms that could account for it. In this pursuit we agree
with Fromkin that all forms of unusual speech (errors) ". . . provide important evidence as to the storage of vocabulary and the generation [we
prefer *production* or *flow*] of speech [Fromkin, 1971:46]."

Some Hypotheses Concerning Schizophrenic Speech

There are several hypotheses that try to explain schizophrenic speech.
A summary of some proposed hypotheses is given by Maher (1968),
Adinolfi and Barocas (1970), Wolcott (1970), and others.

The first of these is the *cipher hypothesis,* which claims that the patient is disguising what he wants to say in some potentially predictable
ways. Second is the *avoidance hypothesis,* namely, that the patient's intentions are to avoid communication altogether.

Third, the *hypothesis of interfering associations* is most popular with
psychologists. It maintains that attention is disrupted, that there is vul-
nerability in the associative "stream" at various points of the sentences
but especially near the end, that there are unsuccessful sequential inhibi-
tions, that intrusions may occur where attention is lowest, that so-called
weaker associations are more vulnerable than strong ones, and that the
norms for strength of association have semantic (cultural) origins that
may override subjective preferences.

Maher (1968) does not consider the possibility that the three hypotheses are not mutually exclusive. Laffal's (1965) material seems to suggest
that his much-quoted patient, whose speech was somewhat reminiscent
of Ken Hale's (1971) Walbiri "upside down speech,"[5] was both
disguising (ciphering) his speech (note Laffal's exasperation with the patient's responses) and, thus, also successfully avoiding ordinary communication. Ciphering and secrecy of speech are also the aim of the
Walbiri initiates.

Fourth, a hypothesis closely related to interfering associations is the
overinclusion (underinclusion?) hypothesis. It states that the patient has
a tendency to include irrelevant and extraneous aspects in responding to
stimuli (Buss and Lang, 1965). With underinclusion one argues that,
even with all the added irrelevant material, the patient's response still
shows a certain amount of poverty in comparison to normals. In general,
the comparison to normals is rarely conclusive. It seems that all normals
have schizophrenic aspects to their speech, especially under extreme

---

[5] Replacement of every word by its antonym, which in many cases was determined by
cultural convention rather than any a priori universal language structure — though that possibly is not excluded. See also discussion of inversion.

conditions, for example, fatigue. [There seems to be little or no evidence for loss of abstractness, which has been claimed for the speech of schizophrenics, nor does there seem to be any value in comparing schizophrenic regression to children's speech (Buss and Lang, 1965)].

Most of the psychological literature we have reviewed seems to be content with measuring various rates or frequencies based on poor theoretical foundations. There is a general tendency to assume the label "schizophrenia" as given and to attempt to design tests that differentiate those diagnosed by other means as "schizoid" from normals, aphasics, alcoholics, children, and others. Since there is such a tremendous variation in samples of unrestricted (by experimental conditions) schizophrenic speech, it seems that the opposite strategy may be more productive: to investigate variations of speech and to see if these fall into categories that could be used for diagnosis of schizophrenic subtypes.

Amazingly little experimental work has been done on Bateson's "double bind" hypothesis. However, Bateson's version needs to be correctly identified as the *metacommunicational* double bind. Some authors discuss the double bind theory simply as the discrepancy between two messages. It is crucial that the double bind (or even multiple bind) be perceived as metacommunicational. In the etiology of schizophrenia, says Bateson, what is attacked is ". . . the use of what [he has] called the [meta-] 'message identifying signals' — those signals without which 'ego' dare not discriminate fact from fantasy or the literal from the metaphoric [1972:199]" and "the ability to communicate about communication, to comment upon the meaningful actions of oneself and others, is essential for successful social intercourse [ibid., p. 215]." For example, it is the loss of metacommunicational control that makes the schizophrenic's metaphors bizarre. Poetical metaphors are no less strange, but the metacommunicational context is well defined. We perceive the richness of poetry by letting multiple readings evoke new associations. In this context Laffal's (1965) content analysis of pathological speech and Ellen Spolsky's (1970) semantic analysis of poetry are akin. The metaphor of the schizophrenic is unlabeled; that is, he systematically distorts his metacommunicational signals. Thus, one patient remarked on Bateson's departure, "That plane flies awfully slow." This seems like a comment on planes but is in fact a metaphor for expressing regrets about the length of the therapist's absence (Bateson, 1972).

According to Bateson, and fortunately for the study of schizophrenic speech, the metamessage can never completely obliterate the message. "The context (or metamessage) classifies the message, but can never meet it on equal terms [ibid., p. 247]." It is for this reason that repeated readings of schizophrenic messages, even word salad, may lead to the discovery of the appropriate context. This discovery can be executed by mechanical aids (e.g., concordances in the case of Laffal, 1965), by experimentation with models of speech (e.g., the ultimate goal of this work), or by intuitive searching of the content of schizophrenic speech samples (e.g., in the work of H. S. Sullivan and much of the interpretation that follows here).

Our goal is to isolate in what way some schizophrenic speech differs from the speech that we usually accept as the norm. To this end, we will start with a heuristic typology.

Heuristic Typology of Samples of Schizophrenic Speech from the Literature[6]

We will start our typology with an initial contrast of the speech of diagnosed schizophrenics with that of normals. We are fully aware of the fact that this dichotomy is more artifact than what "really" goes on in the world.

"Schizophrenic speech," as we shall call it for the sake of brevity, consists of samples of the speech of diagnosed schizophrenics and falls, in our investigation, into two categories: samples that we were able to interpret within the framework of our model and samples that we were unable to account for. The first category will be discussed in some detail. The second needs some explanation. Some samples we find perfectly normal, even though the authors tell us that it is not. For example, we offer the following as a partial substantiation of this claim (Forrest, Hay, and Kushner, 1969:34):

Q: *What is this?* (shows cigarette)

A: *A cigarette.*

Q: *What does one do with a cigarette?*

A: *One puts it in the mouth, lights it up, and smokes it . . .*

---

[6] We have quite consciously avoided using "live" samples of speech of people diagnosed as schizophrenic. That could become a second (or third, etc.) aspect of this line of research. Most long, recorded interviews are, at this point, of limited use because they are too rich. Before turning to very rich data, it seems useful to look at what has been done in the past. Our "cooked" examples may often be a bit artificial, contrived, and too simple (many psychological studies do not give even illustrative examples, but those given are often very simple). The simplicity is often based on more or less "intuitive" knowledge of the investigator. Such knowledge, though surely questionable, often contains valuable leads.

We consider the above response normal and, therefore, uninteresting in the context of this study. However, after a brief pause this patient added:

A: *. . . and it gets in key with thought.*

This is abnormal and, therefore, interesting. Other samples are either excessively vague and/or very complex in their structure, especially as reflected by the length of sentences. We are unable to analyze them successfully at this point. The following example (Laffal, 1965) is of this nature of sentential complexity coupled with "vagueness" of reference:

I personally don't believe these, these different circumstances should come to that . . . arousing different ideas and everything like that. I don't necessarily know that stories are — I believe, I see you had some brief ideas about different circumstances that did arise at certain times, different procedures or approaches, anything like that. Is that right? I generally don't realize the circumstances but . . . [patient is interrupted by doctor] [p. 80].

Other examples have such strange associations, which may extend all the way to the so-called word salad, that our wildest speculations are incapable of solving even a part of the problem.

Q: *When the cat's away the mice will play.*

A: *That means feline absence and rodential job, which has its sources in the nature of the Savior; divine forgiveness, Heaven and Hell, inscrutability.*

We must assume that these examples may be cases of underinclusion. It is reflected in some proverb interpretations. For example (Woods, 1938:302):

Q: *Barking dogs never bite.*
A: *Bluff.*

and the projection of such condensations (see Freud, 1915:199) on the entire train of thought. However, for the preceding cases we will be able to suggest some explanations. The following example we do not explain. It is the summary of a Western the patient has seen earlier.

Capture and captured, tied to a rope and shootin'.

The associations are reasonably clear. Although it may be possible to interpret even word salad, it surely requires more detailed knowledge of the patients and their speech patterns than we have available for most samples from the literature.

We will, therefore, restrict our purview to a class of samples that we are able to interpret by following our model closely or by simple extensions of it. This, we hope, will contribute to the improvement of our model, which in turn, we hope, will then enable us to interpret still more of the samples judged as abnormalities of speech.

Our discussion focuses on three problems of schizophrenic speech. These are the problem of metaphor and syllogisms, the problem of path control, and the problem of inversion. We will discuss each in turn.

METAPHOR

Metaphor interpretation is located in what we call FOCAL MEMORY in conjunction with the MONITOR. The key to the understanding of metaphor seems to lie in what we term the "syllogism of metaphor." We will discuss this aspect first.

Syllogisms. Several investigators have noted the unusual nature of the syllogisms of patients labeled schizophrenics. Bateson (1972:205) gives the following striking example:

> Men die.
> Grass dies.
> Men are grass.

Any argumentation between three classes is a syllogism. There are only four possible arrangements of three terms such as *men, die,* and *grass.* These are the four *figures* of the syllogism. Each figure ". . . admits of $4 \times 4 = 16$ forms of the premise; therefore we have 64 forms in all. A valid form thus constructed is called a mood. Of these, only a few lead to a conclusion [Reichenbach, 1947:201, slightly rearranged]." The most common form of a syllogism that rests on the transivity of the relation of implication (or the relation of taxonomy) is *modus Barbara.* This modus is in the first figure. If the letter *A* is interpreted as the relation *all,* it is traditionally symbolized as follows:

> MAP
> SAM
> SAP

For example (men = M, are mortal = P):

> Men are mortal.
> Socrates is a man
> Socrates is mortal.

Two transpositions are necessary to get from the usual mood Barbara to the syllogism exemplified by Bateson's at the beginning of this section. First, the first line is inverted from MAP to PAM; second, lines one and two are inverted. The latter is significant, though, as far as we know, of no concern in traditional logic (to be discussed). These inversions transform the syllogism into the following:

SAM

PAM

SAP

It is not particularly surprising to find that this form is not a valid argument. However, we claim, it is a (the?) major argument of metaphoric extension. The following illustration shows this with a metaphor that is well accepted (e.g., *Webster's Seventh New Collegiate Dictionary,* 1967:383, exactly: "The heart . . . acts as a force pump . . ."):

Hearts move liquid, have valves, etc.

Pumps move liquid, have valves, etc.

Hearts are pumps.

As mentioned before, the order of the first two lines is crucial for the proper formation of a metaphor: The converse *Pumps are hearts* is not acceptable. Similarly, it is compelling in Bateson's example that *Men are grass* and not the other way around.

A fair number of examples from the literature of schizophrenic speech that lists equational sentences rather than syllogisms can be explained by an underlying metaphoric syllogism. Freeman, Cameron, and McGhie (1958:77) provide the following example:

Men are socks.

Analysis:

Men are x $(x =$ dirty, smelly, warm, etc.)

Socks are x (and as long as $x = x$)

Men are socks.

Similarly:

The therapist is a bus with a big bumper.

Analysis:

The therapist has a big bumper.

The bus has a big bumper.

The therapist is a bus . . .

Indirect evidence for the metaphorical mood comes from Pittenger, Hockett, and Danehy (1960:167a), where the analysts are puzzled by the occurrence of *another* in the only unusual statement of the first five minutes of their interview. If we set up a metaphoric syllogism, the referent of the patient's unusual choice of the word *another* in "Divorce is another emotional death" becomes clearer:

Analysis:

> Marriage is emotional death.
> Divorce is emotional death.
> ‾‾‾‾‾‾‾‾‾‾‾‾‾‾‾‾‾‾‾‾‾‾‾
> Marriage is divorce.

Pittenger *et al.* (1960) guessed that *another* refers to *marriage*, but without exploring the nature of the metaphoric syllogism that supports their conjecture.

There are a large number of examples available that illustrate this type of reasoning. It is entirely appropriate and "logical." It is certainly a method of reasoning and/or explanation that is frequently applied by normal human beings. What is often bizarre in schizophrenic speech is the content or the source of the metaphor.

Proverbs. In this section we take for granted the strangeness of metaphor. Our emphasis, however, is the nature of proverb interpretation. Two syllogisms of metaphor seem to be involved:

If a proverb is of the schematic form:

$$F \ IMPLIES \ L$$

and X and Y are, respectively, attributes of F and L, while G and M are new terms, then it follows from:

FAX		LAY
GAX	and	MAY
FAG		LAM

that	G IMPLIES M

For example, if F stands for *rolling stone* and L for *gathers no moss,* then in the proverb *A rolling stone gathers no moss,* F IMPLIES L. Furthermore, if *a rolling stone moves* and *an active person moves,* then *a rolling stone is an active person.* And further, if *not gathering moss is not being inactive,* then *not gathering moss is staying fit.* Still further, therefore, *Being an active person implies staying fit,* which is one possible interpretation of the proverb.

The flexibility of proverb interpretation is contained in the flexibility of metaphor. Alternate interpretations of the preceding proverb are *A rolling stone moves, A shiftless person moves,* therefore, *A rolling stone is a shiftless person;* and *Not gathering moss is not achieving anything,* and *Lack of possessions and friends is not achieving anything,"* therefore, *Gathering moss is lack of possessions and friends.* Therefore, still further, *A shiftless person lacks possessions and friends,* another interpretation of the same proverb.

Thus, proverbs underscore Niels Bohr's dictum (as quoted by Heissenberg, 1971) that "the opposite of a scientific truth is a falsehood, the opposite of wisdom is often another wisdom." Proverbs are, thus, notorious examples of human wisdom par excellence. The same statement can be interpreted in two or more different ways because of the flexibility of the metaphoric syllogism. Either version may express a different human wisdom.

With this preparation we are ready to look at proverb interpretation by schizophrenic patients.

The first example is a proverb from Harrow, Tucker, and Adler (1972:434)

Q: *Interpret "A rolling stone gathers no moss."*

A: *You can't still on life. You must go on to one and ask another or you'll become decent.*

Dispensing with the syllogism of metaphor, the first equation is *A rolling stone is 'You can't still on life'* and *You must go on* (to ask another). We have placed "to ask another" in parentheses because it appears as an aside. Though we have "interpreted" this phrase in various ways, it seems farfetched.

Possibly, on the basis of the second sentence, the first should read *You can't* [stand] *still* [in] *life.* We will return to this point. The second equation is *Not gathering moss is you'll not become decent.* Or, together, *If you can't* (stand) *still* (in) *life and you must go on* (to ask another) *then you'll not become decent.* Although the interpretation of the strange metaphor may not be easy, since either not all is expressed or too much is said, the gist of the message appears to be *If you can't stand still and you must go on, then you'll not become decent.* However, the material that was added and deleted is still controversial. Nevertheless, we quibble about the interpretation of the patient's metaphor, not his use of the metaphoric syllogism (Forrest *et al.,* 1969:834).

Other examples are considerably more unusual:

Q: *Interpret "A rolling stone gathers no moss."*

A: *A rolling stone is the new moon, it is the other side and it is blue.*
      It is the far side where the Russians are.

Let us break down the answer into simple sentences:

A rolling stone is the new moon.
  The new moon is the other side.
                    is blue.
                    is the far side.
            The far side is where the Russians are.

There is always more than one interpretation of the syllogism, but
here is one:

A rolling stone rotates.
The new moon rotates.
A rolling stone is the new moon.

Dispensing with the syllogisms of metaphor, we obtain the further
equations:

The new moon is the other side.
The other side is blue.
The blue [side] is the far side.
The far side is where the Russians are.

The formula for this kind of interpretation is

FAG
GAH
HAJ
JAK
· · · · ·

We find here a definite breakdown of "normal" proverb interpretation.
The first term of the proverb is interpreted, but instead of the interpretation of the second term, the second term of the first interpretation is
reinterpreted, and so on.

Thus, comment on the proverb never reaches closure. One has the
feeling that the process could go on and on as long as the respondent
continues his chain of associations. This feeling is enhanced by the fact
that all comment departs from the first term, as if the second term
. . . *gathers no moss* had never been uttered. Examples of this kind of
loss of language context abound. Often there is a great deal of abbreviation. The following example is from Woods (1938:309):

Q: [Interpret] *You can't touch pitch without being tarred.*

A: *Music.*

> Pitch has something to do with tone, melody, etc.
> Music has something to do with tone, melody, etc.
> Pitch is music.

or:

$$
\begin{array}{l}
\text{F IMPLIES L} \\
\text{FAX} \\
\underline{\text{GAX}} \\
\text{(FAG IMPLIES) G}
\end{array}
$$

The right side of the proverb is again ignored.

The striking brevity of the following proverb (Woods, 1938:302) can now be clarified:

Q: *Barking dogs never bite.*

A: *Bluff.*

This requires perhaps a new twist in the interpretation of the syllogism of metaphor. There is a symmetry of the two underlying syllogisms:

> Barking dogs fake
> Bluff is fake
> Barking dogs (are) bluff.

> Never biting is fake
> Bluff is fake
> Never biting is bluff.

Therefore: *Bluff* Or, in formula form:

$$
\begin{array}{ll}
\multicolumn{2}{c}{\text{F IMPLIES L}} \\
\text{FAX} & \text{LAY} \\
\underline{\text{GAX}} & \underline{\text{EAY}} \\
\text{FAG} & \text{LAG} \\
\hline
\multicolumn{2}{c}{\text{G}}
\end{array}
$$

Barking dogs bluff implies *Never biting is bluff,* and the answer *bluff* summarizes it all, i.e., *Bluff is bluff.* The succinctly brilliant response appears to be the result of the symmetry of the metaphoric syllogism.

Similar interpretable and nearly interpretable examples are fairly numerous in the literature.

Path Control

The deflections of thought could be viewed as problems of input, but we do not think so. It appears that it is in the output that the train of thought loses its way. This is not unusual in itself. The anomaly lies in the fact that closure is not reached. The retrieval control function never returns to its original focus. This seems to be—if memory is viewed as a huge associative network or lattice—a failure of path control. If speech events are linearized subgraphs of the lattice, then the proper (normal) selection of subgraphs is what we mean by path control. Until we demonstrate our conclusions, we will disregard the strangeness of schizophrenic metaphor and take it for granted.

Folk Definitions

Eliciting folk definitions is often the most expeditious method for getting at folk knowledge. The question "What does _____ mean?" is simple, straightforward, and in most cultures appropriate in many cultural contexts.

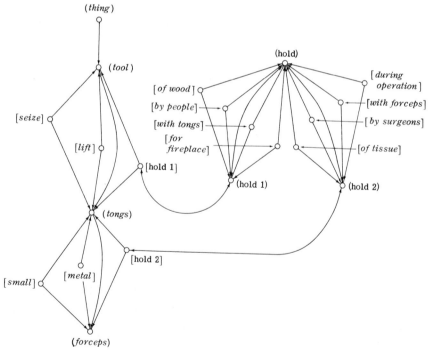

Figure 3.

There are at least two major types of folk definitions: (1) the method of genus and differentiae and (2) a "less educated" method usually found in the speech of children and with (some?) people who have very little education. The first step we would like to undertake is to show that these two types are not very dissimilar and may, perhaps, represent styles of speaking rather than distinct cognitive styles (distinct retrieval strategies). Figure 3 illustrates this point.

Whereas the "schooled" informant may respond to the requested definition of *forceps* with '. . . small, metal tongs,' a child or an "unschooled" informant may say ". . . something used by surgeons" or, perhaps, ". . . something used for holding tissue," including many more possibilities, some of which can be "read off" our diagram.

The defining behavior of normal subjects can be schematized as in Figure 4.

Upon request for a definition of *forceps,* the network of associations

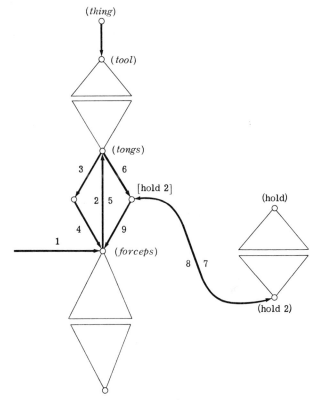

Figure 4.

is entered at the appropriate level (1). (In our schematic diagram we have raised the levels in order to be able to show better some aspects of schizophrenic speech later.) By reversing the relation of taxonomy (T), the definer arrives at (tongs) (2), and cycles downward following one path through the attribute "triangle" (3) and (4). If "necessary," several such cycles may follow (5, 6, 7, 8, and 9), which may or may not include "detours" to representations of verbs (see diamonds) especially path (7, 8). The number of cycles to be included in a definition depends on meta-messages perceived by the definer that tell him how extensive a definition is appropriate.

In schizophrenic speech we find several types of folk definitions. We discuss each type in turn.

Type 1. Some schizophrenic definitions found in the literature immediately become problematic. For example, Bleuler (1950:20) quotes a patient who defined *hay* as "means of sustenance of cows." Although the wording is odd and perhaps stilted, all of us know normals who tend to speak in this "unusual" manner. The definition (other than the unusual choice of words) follows the normal procedure: "Go to the next (or some)-higher node and cycle down through the attribute space — if necessary, several times." In this example *hay* is a kind of *means, a means of maintenance* where *maintenance* is a modifier of *means;* and, more specifically, is further modified by the next cycle, *of cows.* Thus, this definition is a semantic (near) paraphrase of . . . *that which cows eat* or . . . *that by means of which cows are kept alive* and . . . *that by means of which cows are maintained* or, more shortly, *feed for cows.* We are, at this point, unable to account for the selection of unusual words; however, we will attempt a tentative explanation later.

The rule for Type 1 folk definitions can be stated as follows: Go to the most closely associated superordinate term, find the subordinate field of attributes (M triangle), pick one, and, if necessary, repeat the cycle. In the example just given, the superordinate term is *means,* first attribute is *of maintenance,* second *of cows* (see Figures 1, 3, and 4).

Summarizing, a Type 1 folk definition is normal except for the "strange" choice of words. Some schizophrenic definitional behavior is undistinguishable from that of normals.

Type 2. Arieti (1955:211) gives the following examples, both of which are definitions of the same type, though the second seems "odder" than the first:

Q: [Define] *table.*

A: *What kind of table?*

A wooden table, a porcelain table, a surgical table, or a table you want to have a meal on.

The schema in Figure 5 represents our retrieval procedure in definitions of this type:

The diagram is entered at the appropriate level of *table* (1). Instead of cycling up and down through the attribute space, the definer tries exemplifications by cycling downward, repeating the pattern several times. The inversion of the direction presents the definer with alternatives. He answers by asking a question. He hopes this will resolve the perceived ambiguity of the question.

In the next example (Arieti, 1955:211), the ambiguity is stated but not questioned explicitly:

Q: [Define] *house.*

A: *There are all kinds of houses, nice houses, nice private houses.*

Here, instead of trying different types of houses, the patient states his awareness of different types first, then he retrieves a second attribute in the same attribute space on the second cycle. At that point he terminates his response (see Figure 6).

Thus, the sample definition of *house* is a subtype of the sample definition of *table.*

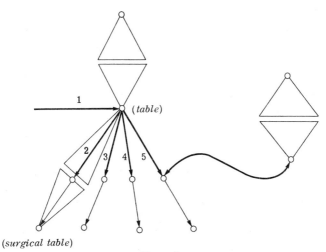

(*surgical table*)

Figure 5.

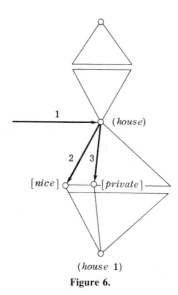

(*house* 1)

Figure 6.

Rule: Do not go to a superordinate node. Instead, explore the field of subordinate terms or the attributive field of subordinate terms (see Figures 5 and 6).

Summarizing, in Type 2 definitions the respondent cycles downward toward greater specificity rather than upward. He may retrieve either alternative subtypes of the word to be defined or a sequence of lower-level attributes.

Type 3. Before we deal with examples, the model needs some amplification.

It is a well-documented fact that high-frequency or "significant" items are more accessible than items of less importance. Taxonomies are usually unordered (except in unusually important cultural domains, e.g., Navajo body parts). Folk taxonomies may often have levels of quite extensive membership (e.g., the Navajo weed (*ch'il*) taxonomy may have as many as several hundred items on one level). However, there appears to be considerable "intercultural agreement" on what examples are to be given if (contextually or explicitly) the investigator asks for a short list. For example, in the case of animals in English such a short list usually contains most or all of the most salient animals: *horse, cow, dog, cat,* and *sheep* (*American Heritage Word Frequency Book,* 1971). Unusual retrievals are regularly accompanied by increased retrieval time: One of us responded to this unrehearsed listing task with "horse, cow, dog, cat, . . . (pause) . . . platypus." Since at present we lack a reasonable

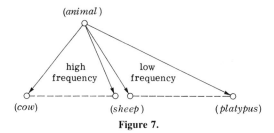

Figure 7.

measure of "salience," we replace it (temporarily) with frequency. Thus, we order taxonomies, including attributive spaces, by frequency: The most-used items occupy positions on the extreme left. All other items follow in decreasing order from left to right, with very low-frequency items on the far right. It is conceivable and compatible with our model that, depending on the topic of a potential discourse, the "accessibility distribution" changes dynamically and according to the demands of the context. However, we cannot here pursue that idea further.

Thus, the representation of a taxonomy is ordered as in Figure 7.

We envision a similar ordering by frequency for our attribute spaces (see Figure 8). With this preparation, let us look at examples.

Goodstein quotes the following (1951:95):

Q: *What is a mammal?*

A: *It is a cow, for example, a wet nurse.*

Goodstein attributes this example to Stransky, although the reference has no year of publication in Goodstein's bibliography. The title of the article implies that it was written in German. Possibly, therefore, the

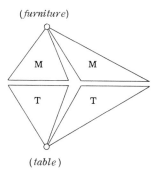

Figure 8.

sample is a translation from the German. *Die (Saeug)Amme* is the German word for 'wet nurse' (Heath's German–English Dictionary, 1906:504). The German word for 'mammal' is *das Saeugetier,* phonologically similar to *die Saeugamme. Die Hebamme* is 'midwife,' and *die Amme* is also translatable as 'nurse'; *die Amme* is short for both. The translation 'midwife' used in Goodstein's original text is, thus, very probably faulty. As an example of a "far out" member of the mammalian taxonomy, and concurrent dynamic regrouping, this possible error makes a difference only insofar as this is, at present, our only example of this kind of definition.

Two not necessarily exclusive explanations are possible: (1) "Wet nurse" was retrieved as a far out member of the mammalian taxonomy. No doubt, wet nurses are mammals. (2) The mammalian attribute field was dynamically restructured around the attributes of large mammaries, especially since apparently cows and females with ample breasts are frequently so associated: *I like coffee, cream, cows, and Elizabeth Taylor* was a similar response of another patient (Maher, 1968:33). The definition of "mammal" is further noteworthy because it proceeds exactly like our Type 2 definition: from the term to be defined downward to either specific attributes or specific subordinate taxons. In the "wet nurse" example the dynamic restructuring of the mammalian field was probably accomplished by sorting on (large) mammaries. The procedure can be diagramed as shown in Figure 9.

Rule: Either (1) pull in a far out association ("wet nurse"), as this happens when we try to be funny in "normal" speech, e.g.,:

Q: *Animals?*

A: *Horse, cow, dog, cat, . . . platypus*

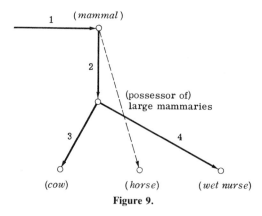

Figure 9.

or, more likely, (2) "sort" the retrieval on an unusual (exaggerated?) attribute, in this case "large mammaries" (see Figures 7, 8, and 9).

Summarizing, Type 3 definitions are like those in Type 2. The definer sorts, however, on some "unusual" attribute, and the retrieval is in terms of that attribute.

Type 4. This type is not unlike the "far out" retrieval in Type 3. Here is an example (Storms and Broen, 1969:129):

Q: *Who is the President of the United States?*

A: *White House.*

Let us assume that the attributes *Gerald R. Ford* and *White House* are "strongly associated." (The nature of "strong association" will be made clearer.) The definer enters his memory network at the appropriate level (1) of *President(s) of the United States* (see Figure 10).

He moves along paths 2, 3, and 4. He does not return to [live 1] but responds with the label of the terminal node of his retrieval.

It is obviously possible that the question was "misunderstood," i.e., as a search for "where" (place), rather than "who" (person). All of us

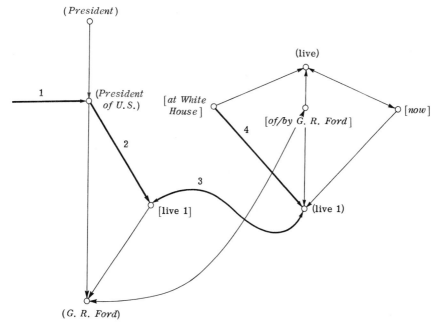

Figure 10.

frequently answer questions in this manner. However, if we assume that the question was understood properly, then something went "out of control" in the [live 1] loop. Control does not return to (*G. R. Ford*) but exits at [White House].

Rule: Respond to the question with a strong association to the first term and exit (see Figure 10).

Type 5. This example of an unusual definition is not a perfect type but appears to be logically possible:

Q: *What is summer?*

A: *Summer is boiling hot harsh (days), dry (days), perspiring skin, damp, burning blinding, providing hot amoebic conditions for the disapparelment* [at this point the patient seems to shift into another mode of definition which goes beyond our present ability] " . . . or what is thought to be observed and musical symbols of trees and that becoming depleted with em hot outstanding reasonatogen tones [Forrest *et al.,* 1969:835]."

The definition as it stands raises the question of the role of the word *days,* which we inserted. It is reasonably clear that *summer* belongs with a taxonomy of "seasons," but not equally clear whether it also belongs with a taxonomy of "days," The patient seems to believe so. Possibly *days* and *seasons* may be lumped together as "time." The striking aspect of the definition is the long string of attributes. In this context we may interpret the word *days* as representative of one of the possible superordinate nodes of *summer.* According to our convention of definition, the attributes belong to "summer time" (however "strange" these may be).

This leaves two possible interpretations: (1) to interpret the definition as conventional but with an unusual entry into the associative network at token [*summer*] (as an attribute of time) rather than the more usual entry at type (*summer*). Whether the entry is of this type we are unable to determine with certainty at this time. Other than that, the definition is normal, except perhaps for the rich attributive space and the unusual or extraordinary nature of this space (metaphor). (2) It may be possible to disregard "time" and consider the definition as a mere list of attributes of *season* in the sense shown in Figure 11.

The definer enters his "associative memory" at (1). Instead of cycling up to the proper superordinate term, he begins to list a series of attributes. Although these belong to the superordinate level, they do not explicitly refer to it.

Conceivably, because we do not have a pure example of this kind of definition in our sample, the preceding example leaves several more interpretations open:

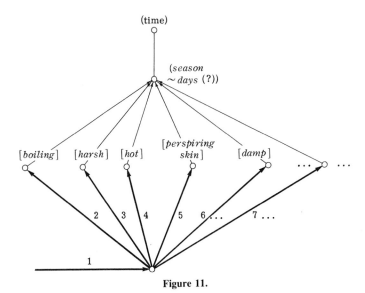

Figure 11.

1.   The definition is simply a variant of the normal definition of genus and differentiae in which the species is suppressed or elided. It seems perhaps arbitrary to claim a significant difference, for example, between *A table is something to eat on, a kind of something or thing,* and *A table is to eat on.*

2.   On the other hand, the striking difference of children's so-called functional definitions seems to be that they are more like *A table is to eat on* than *A table is something to eat on.*

Rule: Do not go to a superordinate node; instead, list the most highly associated attributes of the superordinate node (see Figure 11).

Summarizing, Type 5 definitions appear to list attributes of a superordinate node without explicitly referring to it. In this sense it is the mirror image of Type 2. However, until further clearer examples are found, this type of definition remains not much more than merely a logical possibility.

Type 6. Needless to say, not all definitions found in the literature are interpretable. The following example (Woods, 1938:303) is, at present, beyond our model.

Q: *Can you tell me what love is?*

A: *Love? Gians . . . vitrous of the vein and rhenebal of the wherein.*

Q: *What does that mean?*

A: *Vaigs.*

If problems of "path control" as seen in the preceding types and in some proverb interpretations are on the lexical/semantic/syntactic level, then neologisms found abundantly in "schizophrenic" speech (see Forrest, 1969 for an interesting example) appear to be analogous failures of "path control" on the morpho/phonological level.

INVERSION

In both "normal" and schizophrenic speech there are examples of inversion. Laffal's most extensively quoted patient drove him to exasperation because he used common antonyms instead of the appropriate words. This often happens accidentally in everyday speech (Fromkin, 1971:46). People will accidentally say *up* when they mean *down, left* when they mean *right,* etc. In Navajo, some inversion is codified by prefixes like *dah,* which may mean 'up' or 'down,' depending on the grammatical construction, although generally the prefix derives from 'down' (*dego*); similarly, *yah* may stand for "up" or "down," though it may derive from 'up' (*yaago*).

Laffal's patient was generally consistent. He faltered, apparently, only when confused by the psychiatrist.

The phenomenon of inversion is not unlike other forms of conventionalized "upside-down" speech. Ken Hale (1971) has reported on the speech of Walbiri initiates who use common, culturally standardized, and possibly language universal antonyms as a cipher (*antonyms* is used here in the widest possible sense). Similarly, the analogous phenomenon, extending to forms of behavior as well, is found among the contraries of the American Indian cultures of the Great Plains.

One area in schizophrenic speech in which inversion is striking are sentence completion "tests" that imply causation. Cameron (1947) administered a large number of these. Many of the ones he cites in detail (but by no means all) become interpretable by assuming their inversion.

Cameron's best example of inversion comes from his Case 17 (1947):

Q: *The wind blows . . .*

A: *. . . because it howls.*

Here our reinverted sentence *The wind howls because it blows* is perfectly normal. Similarly, Case 22:

Q: *The sun comes up in the morning . . .*

A: *. . . because it's windy.*

is clearly the inversion of *It is windy because the sun comes up in the morning.* With the exception of a few examples that contain sentence fragments or bizarre metaphors, many elicited forms appear to be normal. That it, our reinversion appears to be even more bizarre than the originally elicited sentence.

The following is such an example. It is Cameron's (1947) Case 23:

> Q: *A man fell down in the street . . .*
>
> A: *. . . because of the World War.*

Our inversion [There was] *a World War because a man fell down in the street* is odd. (However, the sentence could refer, e.g., to a newsreel of the World War.) The same patient, after what Cameron calls "partial recovery," completed the same sentence "normally":

> Q: *A man fell down in the street . . .*
>
> A: *. . . because he slipped.*

Other examples of Cameron's are still more difficult to interpret; Case 22 is an example:

> Q: *The wind is blowing . . .*
>
> A: *. . . because something about the clouds move it.*

Something about the clouds move it because the wind is blowing appears perhaps more "normal" but is still far from acceptable.

Several further inversions are possible: The *it* possibly refers to *wind* because if it referred to *clouds,* the other possibility, it ought to be in the plural. *Something* is questionable. The remainder of the sentence also appears to be completely inverted (except for the article); the end is its beginning: *Wind(s) move the clouds about because the wind is blowing.* Superficially, at least, if some of this is correct, some inversions appear to be unusual grammatical transformations.

Inversion is perhaps one pervasive aspect of schizophrenic speech. The implications of the observation are explored in the conclusion.

Conclusion

We have observed three types of processes. All occur in normal speech but are strikingly highlighted in schizophrenic speech. They are

(1) unusual metaphors, (2) problems of "path selection," and (3) inversion. We will conclude with each in turn:

METAPHOR

Every good metaphor should both come as a surprise and be obvious after we have accepted it.

Bateson points out that poetry abounds with strange metaphors. However, poetry is labeled metacommunicationally as discourse that need not be necessarily understood fully on first reading. In fact, every new reading of a poem opens new associations that let us appreciate the meaning of the poem more deeply. It is only in ordinary everyday speech that we hope to understand another person's message on first "reading." It is in this need to understand another person *right away* that some schizophrenic patients fail us. That mental patients transmit their ideas in strange but potentially comprehensible metaphors was illustrated by Laffal (1965). The investigations of poets and their works by Ellen Spolsky (1970) are, in spirit, similar to Laffal's.

It seems that any device imitating human verbal behavior needs to have a metaphor-creating component. But parallel to the creation of metaphor there must be an evaluation function that is capable of judging the acceptability of a metaphor. In ordinary discourse and, therefore, in all largely ephemeral communication, the metaphors must remain close to the literal. Only in written poetry can we afford extremely obscure metaphors that may take a protracted effort to unlock. Schizophrenic metaphor is of this kind. The claim of some therapists that they are able to learn schizophrenic speech (Sullivan, 1964) rests on recurrent metaphorical themes, e.g., Laffal's (1965) concordances. As in the case of poetry interpretation, it is too much to expect that *any* therapist can learn to understand *any* schizophrenic. Some poetry remains impalatable to some readers forever. The schizophrenic patient needs the right therapist, who can empathize with his metaphors.

Ordinary creative speech can perhaps never go to the extremes of written poetry. Nevertheless, it is constantly torn between the intelligible, overly literal, or banal and the overtly metaphorical and unintelligible.

The fate of our model appears clear through an analogy to computer music: It is relatively easy to construct a program that can write Mozart-like music. But it is remarkably undistinguished Mozart. Surprises are lacking. So, too, in speech it is the unusual but apt phrase that makes one person's speech more pleasurable than another's.

A metaphor-evaluating function belongs in our model with the MONITOR and the level of metacommunicative control. We can only conjecture at this point about the nature of this function. It is certain that the attribute fields of the first term (to be explained) and the second term (which does the explaining) must overlap in some manner. But the relationship is not simple. The acceptability of a metaphor may depend on at least the following criteria: The attribute overlap is in the token rather than the type field, and there are some contextual indicators of the metacommunicational channel. That is, the nature of a metaphor and context are closely linked. To find out why a metaphor is more bizarre in some contexts than in others will require a lot more work. However, such understanding is a necessary corollary for any simulation of human cognitive behavior.

PATH CONTROL

Our representation of associative memory as a graph is rich in detail. We assume that the graphs are nonlinear, vast, and redundant. One of the functions of the control of speech events is linearization, the reduction of the richness and of redundancy. Unusual types of definitions, deflection of associations (in folk definitions and proverb interpretation) without apparent goal, are seen by us as breakdowns of the MONITOR's control over the flow of speech. We see analogies to path control on the semantic/lexical/syntactic level in the neologisms of schizophrenic speech. These may be failures of path control on the morpho/phonological level. Path selection and inversion are closely related. Which one should be subsumed under the other remains to be worked out. Whether "path control" is a deep aspect of speech or a disorder of the short-term or linearizing memory has to await more understanding of the phenomena.

INVERSION

Viewing inversion as a generalized condition of schizophrenic speech is seductive because it seems to encompass many of the observed phenomena that we have grouped under "path control." We have shown that in definitions some schizophrenic patients do not search up to one of the more general nodes and down through the most frequent part of the attribute field. Instead, these patients cycle down and are prevented from defining by the apparent indeterminacy of the choices.

The metaphoric syllogism is a twice inverted form of *modus Barbara*. Though a large number of proverb interpretations show the "normal" application of the metaphoric syllogism to proverbs, some respondents do not stay with the stimulus proverb and trail off on idiosyncratic paths into new associations. The use of reinversion for the interpretation of sentences linked by *because* is also striking. Unfortunately, however, the apparent pervasiveness of inversion may be less than real. It may most simply be an artifact of our ignorance.

Epilog

Neologisms seem to be strangely reminiscent of the problems of "path control," perhaps on the morpho/phonological level. If, indeed, some sequencing control is uniformly distributed through semanto/syntax and through morpho/phonology, it appears likely that the condition may have biophysiological roots. Unusual metaphors, on the other hand, appear to be much less likely to have such biophysical corollaries because they appear on a high level of mental organization and seem to have little or no connection with problems on the lower levels. Analogous difficulties on several levels of organization are more likely to be organic than difficulties associated with a very high level exclusively.

Explanation of causation was not our aim. Our interest centered on the identification of problem areas for lexical/semantic investigations and the *nature* of the breakdown. It is by means of such limitation that we hope to isolate evidence for the structural properties of the MONITOR in our model (see Figure 2.).

This study is, obviously, not conclusive. We hope it marks a beginning in semantic investigations that some day may shed more light on both "normal" and "abnormal" forms of speech.

References

Adinolfi, A. A. and R. Barocas
    1970   Conceptual performance in schizophrenia, *Journal of Clinical Psychology* **26**, (2), 167–170.
Arieti, S.
    1955   *Interpretation of schizophrenia.* New York: Robert Brunner.
Bateson, G.
    1972   *Steps to an ecology of mind.* New York: Ballantine Books.
Bleuler, E.
    1950   *Dementia praecox or the group of schizophrenia.* New York: International Univ. Press.
Buss, A. H. and P. J. Lang
    1965   Psychological deficit in schizophrenia. I. Affect, reinforcement, and concept attainment, *Journal of Abnormal Psychology* **70**, (1) 2–24.
Cameron, N. A.
    1947   *The psychology of behavior disorders.* Boston: Houghton Mifflin.
Casagrande, J. B. and K. L. Hale
    1967   Semantic relationships in Papago folk definitions. In *Studies in Southwestern ethnolinguistics*, edited by D. Hymes and W. E. Bittle. The Hague: Mouton.

Forrest, A. D., A. J. Hay, and A. W. Kushner
1969   Studies in speech disorder in schizophrenia, *British Journal of Psychiatry* **115**, 833–841.
Forrest, D. V.
1969   New Words and neologisms. With a thesaurus of coinages by a schizophrenic patient, *Psychiatry* **32** (1), 44–73.
Freeman, T., J. L. Cameron, and A. McGhie
1958   *Chronic schizophrenia.* New York: International Univ. Press.
Freud, S.
1957   The unconscious, 1915. In *The Standard Edition,* edited by J. Strachey. *Vol. XIV.* Hogarth Press: London.
Fromkin, V.
1971   The nonanomalous nature of anamalous utterances, *Language* **47**, (1).
Goodstein, L. D.
1951   The language of schizophrenia, *Journal of General Psychology* **45**, 95–104.
Hale, K.
1971   A note on Walbiri tradition of antonymy. In *Interdisciplinary reader in philosophy, linguistics and psychology,* edited by D. D. Steinberg and L. A. Jakobovitz. Cambridge: Cambridge Univ. Press.
Harris, M.
1968   *The Rise of Anthropological Theory.* New York: Thomas Crowell.
Harrow, M., G. J. Tucker, and D. Adler
1972   Concrete and idiosyncratic thinking in acute schizophrenic patients, *Archives of General Psychiatry* **26**, 433–439.
Heissenberg, W.
1971   *Physics and beyond: The part and the total.* New York: Harper Torchbooks.
Laffal, J.
1965   *Pathological and normal language.* New York: Atherton Press.
Lyons, J.
1968   *Introduction to theoretical linguistics.* Cambridge: Cambridge Univ. Press.
Maher, B. A.
1968   The shattered language of schizophrenia, *Psychology Today* **2**, (6), 30–33, 60.
Pittenger, R. E., C. F. Hockett, and J. J. Danehy
1960   *The first five minutes: A sample microscopic interview analysis.* Ithaca, New York: P. Martineau.
Quillian, M. R.
1969   The teachable language comprehender: A simulation program and theory of language, *Communications of the Association for Computing Machinery* **12**, 459–476.
Spolsky, Ellen.
1970   Computer assisted semantic analysis of poetry, *Computer Studies in the Humanities and Verbal Behavior* **3**, (2), 163–168.
Storms, L. H. and W. E. Broen, Jr.
1969   A theory of schizophrenic behavioral disorganization, *Archives of General Psychiatry* **20**, 129–143.
Sullivan, H. S.
1964   The language of schizophrenia. In *Language and thought in schizophrenia,* edited by J. S. Kasanin. Pp. 4–16. New York: Norton.
Weinreich, U.
1963   On the semantic structure of language. In *Universals of language,* edited by J. H. Greenberg. Boston: MIT Univ. Press.

Werner, O. and Joann Fenton
  1970   Method and theory in ethnoscience or ethnoepistemology. In *A handbook of method in cultural anthropology,* edited by R. Naroll and R. Cohen. New York: The Natural History Press.
Werner, O.
  1972a Ethnoscience 1972. In *Annual Review of Anthropology,* edited by B. Siegel. Pp. 271–308. Annual Reviews.
  1972b *The structure of ethnoscience.* The Hague: Mouton (to appear)
  1972c The synthetic informant. Paper read at the Central States Anthropological Association Meetings, Cleveland, 1972, and at the Theory on the Fringes Meetings, Oswego, New York, 1972.
Werner, O.
  1973   The synthetic informant model, Proceedings of the 9th International Congress of Anthropological and Ethnological Sciences, Chicago, The Hague: Mouton, (to appear).
Werner, O.
  1974   Intermediate memory: A central explanatory concept for ethnoscience. In *Communication and Cognition,* edited by R. Pinxten. The Hague: Mouton.
Wolcott, R. H.
  1970   Schizophrenese: A private language, *Journal of Health and Social Behavior.* **11,** (2), 126–134.
Woods, W. L.
  1938   Language study in schizophrenia, *Journal of Nervous and Mental Disease* **87,** 290–316.

Subject Index

A

Aaronson, Elliot, 12–13
Abstraction, in schizophrenic speech, 355
Absurdity, in *rakugo,* 304
Achievement, of rules, 148
Action-schema, in similes (Ilongots),
    188–189, 193
Acts, metacommunicative, 163–176
Addict
    argot, 42–43
    cognition and events in study of, 41–55
    cognitive structure of, 49–51
    decision-making, 45
    emic studies of, 49
    ethnography of, 44
    events
        cognitive anthropological study,
            47–49
        concepts of, 49–52
        outcomes of, 44–45, 46–47, 53
        prerequisites of, 44–45, 46–47, 53
        structure, 43–47
    frame elicitation results
        for events, 50–51
        for prerequisites, 51–52
    lexemes of, 44
    psychological reality of, 49–52
    sentence completion tests for, 50–52
    subculture of, 7
    types of, 43
Address
    choice of, 307
    generation of, 85
Addressee, in songs (Tzeltal), 327
Affliction ritual (Ga: *daimɔ*), *See* Ga ritual
    (*daimɔ*)

Agar, Michael, 7, 41–55
Age, in genealogy (Luo), 119–120
Agriculture, spells (Ilongots), 198
Albert, Ethel, 71
Algebraic notation, in performance
    analysis, 213–214
Alice in Wonderland, 137–138, 142, 152
Ambiguity, in schizophrenic speech, 367
America, *See* Black America
American Samoa, *See* Samoa
Analysis
    conversational, *See* Conversational
        analysis
    of *rakugo* performance, 269–306, *See*
        also Rakugo
Annual rites (Ga), 207
Answers, alternative, in greetings, 75–76
Anthropologist, social, 81
Anthropology
    cognitive, 4, 6, 47–49
    creativity in linguistic, 2–3, 6
    decomposition in, 41, 42, 54
    ethnography and linguistic, 5
    ethnomethodology and linguistic, 5–6
    ethnoscience and linguistic, 3–4, 6
    generative grammar and linguistic, 2–3,
        6
    grammatical theory and linguistic, 1–2, 6
    linguistic, 1–9, 163
    segmentation in, 41, 42, 54
    social psychology and, 11–12
    sociolinguistics and linguistic, 4–5, 6
    transformational grammar and linguistic,
        1–2
Antonyms
    in schizophrenic speech, 374
    in songs (Tzeltal), 344

381